Praise for

The Food, Folklore, and Art of Lowcountry Cooking

"Joe Dabney is a treasure to be around, but I like him even better when he is writing about food. His first cookbook is a James Beard Cookbook of the Year award-winning classic. His new cookbook is just as spellbinding and definitive. It would make me move to the Lowcountry if I did not live here already. Southern food has staged such a bold comeback in American culinary circles and Joe Dabney's new cookbook is just another layer of scrumptious icing on the cake. Its recipes are hymns of praise to the South."

—Pat Conroy, *New York Times* bestselling author of *South of Broad*

"Through delightful interviews and stories, Joe Dabney takes readers beyond the kitchen and into the heart of Lowcountry culture and cuisine."

—Nathalie Dupree, cookbook writer and TV host

"Dabney...captures the true Lowcountry spirit like a man who was weaned on sweetgrass, swamp hollerin', and hush puppies."

—James Villas, author of *Dancing in the Lowcountry*
and *The Glory of Southern Cooking*

"It would be hard to imagine anything edible being served in the sea-breeze sweep of South Carolina and Georgia that Dabney has not eaten and documented for the benefit and pleasure of all the rest of us."

—John Egerton, author of *Southern Food* and *Cornbread Nation*

"Joe takes you on a wild ride from one adventure to another...And the recipes—an incredible treasure...A massive amount of research went into this book—not just library research, but people research—finding the right living people with real stories and real recipes of the past. Thank you, Joe, for such a treasure!"

—Shirley O. Corriher, author of *CookWise* and *BakeWise*

Praise for James Beard Cookbook of the Year Award Winner

Smokehouse Ham, Spoon Bread & Scuppernong Wine

"Joe's book makes my mouth water for Southern food and my heart hunger for Southern stories. Not since the Foxfire series has something out of the Appalachian experience thrilled me as much."
— Pat Conroy, *New York Times* bestselling author of *South of Broad*

"Joseph E. Dabney knows as much about the South as just about anyone…Don't read this heady amalgam of folklore, history, and literature on an empty stomach."
— Willie Morris, author of *My Dog Skip*, *North Toward Home*, and *New York Days*

"Joe Dabney's prize-winning book humanizes Southern food with its charming stories and interviews."
— Nathalie Dupree, cookbook writer and TV host

"It's the first 'cookbook' I've actually read from the top like a novel. It's a helluva book, and I haven't even taken it to the kitchen yet."
— Paul Hemphill, author of *Lovesick Blues: The Life of Hank Williams*

"This book is like a treasure uncovered in Grandmother's attic. Recipes and histories of their origin reminisce of the old days with such longing that even a Yankee will hanker for more."
— *Today's Librarian*

"This thang's so good it'll make you want to marry your cousin."
— Sam Venable, *Knoxville Sentinel*

THE FOOD, FOLKLORE, AND ART OF LOWCOUNTRY COOKING

A Celebration of
THE FOODS, HISTORY, AND ROMANCE HANDED DOWN FROM ENGLAND, AFRICA, THE CARIBBEAN, FRANCE, GERMANY, AND SCOTLAND

JOSEPH E. DABNEY
FOREWORD BY MATT LEE AND TED LEE

CUMBERLAND HOUSE

Published by Cumberland House, an imprint of Sourcebooks, Inc.
P.O. Box 4410, Naperville, Illinois 60567-4410
(630) 961-3900
Fax: (630) 961-2168
www.sourcebooks.com

Library of Congress Cataloging-in-Publication Data

Dabney, Joseph E.
  The food, folklore, and art of lowcountry cooking : a celebration of the foods, history, and romance handed down from England, Africa, the Caribbean, France, Germany, and Scotland / Joseph Dabney.
     p. cm.
  Includes bibliographical references and index.
    1. Cookery, American—Southern style. 2. Cookery—South Carolina 3. Cookery—South Carolina—History. 4. South Carolina—Social life and customs. I. Title.

TX715.2.S68D42 2010
641.5975—dc22

2009039343

Printed and bound in the United States of America.
SB 10 9 8 7 6 5 4 3 2 1

This book is dedicated to Geneva, Earl,
Mark, Scott, and Chris, who grew up eating
their share of Susanne's Chicken Purloo.

Contents

———◆———

Foreword

W̲e knew of Joe Dabney long before we'd met the guy. Heck, every aspiring food historian knows *Mountain Spirits*, Dabney's groundbreaking, definitive book on moonshine and its culture, and his first gift to the library of culinary study. For that contribution alone, Dabney ranks among M. F. K. Fisher, Laurie Colwin, and Calvin Trillin in the food writer's pantheon. But in his own way, Dabney is a far more brave and illuminating author. While it may take talent to write lyrically about what you do in your kitchen, or about how you hunt down the best barbecue or Peking duck joint, it takes an altogether different skill set to immerse oneself in a food and beverage community hell-bent on secrecy, with a predilection for firearms and volatile liquids, and to get folks to sit down and tell their stories. Reading *Mountain Spirits*, you get the sense that Dabney is truly as fearless as they come: who else would poke around the hollers, get up in moonshiners' faces with pad and pencil, and then ask hard questions?

When we finally met Dabney at the Southern Foodways Symposium in 2000, we found he was an altogether different presence than the lion we had imagined—easy to laugh, an adept storyteller with eyes that crackled with enthusiasm. It wasn't difficult to imagine him walking up an Appalachian dirt road, a tote bag slung over his shoulder, and charming his way into a kitchen conversation about—and perhaps with a slice of—dried apple pie. Which is exactly what he'd done for *Smokehouse Ham, Spoon Bread & Scuppernong Wine: The Folklore and Art of Southern Appalachian Cooking*. When we met Dabney, the book had just won the James Beard Foundation Cookbook of the Year award. So when we heard that Joe planned to bring his intellect, curiosity, and wit to the subject of Lowcountry cooking, we were thrilled beyond belief. Dabney's books are elbows-deep affairs—yes they're journeys in themselves, and yes they're feasts, but those metaphors don't accurately portray the way a Joe Dabney book unfurls, his own travelogue threaded with the narratives he excavates from rare sourcebooks and with the voices of the people he meets. Joe Dabney's books get us fired up to travel, to cook, and to eat.

With his lowcountry cookbook, Dabney has done it again. He's unearthed recipes we haven't seen, and has us itching to get in the kitchen to develop new directions for fire-roasted conch, a stew called ribbles, rice-flour puddings, and persimmon beer. And we're excited to explore the Dutch Fork and Saxe Gotha areas, German settlements in South Carolina that seem new to us, with baking and meat-curing traditions all their own. Dabney's talked to all the right people—here are Glenn Roberts, Nathalie Dupree, Damon Lee Fowler, Martha Nesbit, Sallie Ann Robinson—and close readers of *Saveur* and *Food & Wine* will smile and nod their heads. But Dabney's also found the sages locals try to keep to themselves, like Ben Moise, the former game warden and sometime Charleston caterer. This book is worth its cover price alone for the number of Moise family recipes Dabney's cajoled out of him! As always, Dabney's ear for the voices that best animate a place, that give it meaning, is keen. We meet the Rev. James E. Rich, who tells the story of a Brunswick Stew dinner his father made for a crew of convicts who'd helped pave a road in Tattnall County, Georgia. And we have the testimony of long-time Murrells Inlet oyster-picker Franklin Smalls, whose passion for the marsh is as searing and indelible as poetry. We hear the stern voice of the father of Ervena Faulkner, a retired educator and food writer for the *Beaufort Gazette*, admonishing her, "Everything cannot be wrapped up in a meal—how you treat people means more than what you chew." It's a statement that seems to speak directly to the marvel and the triumph of Dabney's book, which, after all, is an exploration of the meaning of "what we chew." Dabney's attentive, uncommonly humane treatment of his subjects kindles their conversations and primes them to give generously of themselves and their traditions and stories. In doing so, Dabney's new book not only explains how people eat here; it says so much about the personality, language, and customs of this place. Quite simply, it portrays the Lowcountry way of life.

—*Matt Lee and Ted Lee*
winners of the 2007 James Beard Foundation Cookbook of the Year
Charleston, South Carolina, October 2009

Acknowledgments

It gives me great pleasure to express my heartfelt thanks to a host of wonderful individuals who gave me crucial help during the three years when I was researching and writing this book. Without their valuable assistance and guidance, I would have been unable to take on such a daunting task.

In contrast to my earlier cultural cookbook on the Southeastern hill country, in which I was writing about a region and a people with whom I was intimately familiar, this book deals with a territory, culture, and history about which my knowledge was somewhat limited. So I am deeply grateful to the many friends, old and new, who gave me a three-year education and a learning experience that I will never forget.

I would like to cite especially the marvelous and unfailing support from Washington resident and supreme Lowcountry historian and author John Martin "Hoppin' John" Taylor. In the earliest days of my research, John Martin suggested that I get in touch with Charlestonian Ben McCutchen Moise. That proved providential. Moise (pronounce that mo-ease), a retired state game warden who resides in historic Charleston with his wife, Anne, and who owns his own island in the Charleston area, graciously shared with me his encyclopedic knowledge of all facets of Lowcountry culture and foodways. Ben's quick response to each and every email question, however seemingly insignificant, was essential to my work.

I also received early and continuing help from longtime friend and Atlantan W. F. (Dub) Taft, a talented writer and cook who was instrumental in helping me obtain a lot of interesting food lore from the Georgia Lowcountry interior as well as recipes from his mother, Mrs. Doris Taft, one of Southeast Georgia's truly great food treasures.

Other Atlanta friends with Lowcountry connections who gave valuable historical suggestions and support were Gordon Sherman, Allison Creagh, Charles Seabrook, Professor John Burrison, Margaret Lee, Chef Scott Peacock, Tommy Irwin, Arty Schronce, Grayson Daughters, Bennett Brown III, Fred Brown, Shirley Corriher, Krista Reece, Pam and Mike Smith, Arnold Sego, Robert Coram, Christina Bledsoe, and Walter Weeks.

I wish to express a deep debt of gratitude to author and *Savannah* magazine food columnist Martha Nesbit for her unstinted and valuable assistance, including driving me on a grand tour of the Hostess City, and giving me at the same time an amazingly informative running interview. I'm grateful also for her continuing suggestions and responses to my questions.

Other Savannahians who provided extensive help and guidance were Dr. Richard Schulze, who, with his wife, Patricia, was responsible for restoring Carolina Gold rice to the Lowcountry; Sallie Ann Robinson, a native of Daufuskie Island, who graciously gave me a lengthy interview at her home in Savannah; food historian and author Damon Lee Fowler; cookbook author Margaret W. DeBolt; the management team at the Wilkes Dining Room, Marcia, Ryon, and Ronnie Thompson; and restaurateurs Aileen and Andrew Trice.

Supreme cook, author, and former television personality Nathalie Dupree of Charleston gave me important and continuing help, as did her husband, Professor Jack Bass, for which I am deeply grateful. Other South Carolinians I wish to thank are Lake High of Columbia and John Bruce of Cayce.

A host of dedicated librarians provided valuable help in locating books via the interlibrary loan system. In this connection I would like to thank most sincerely the Atlanta metro area's great DeKalb County Library System, headed by Darro Willey, and in particular Susan Williams in its interlibrary loan department. Also many thanks go to librarians George Ford and Leslie Barber in the Dunwoody branch library, and Kitty Wilson and Mei-yun Lee in the Chamblee branch library.

Valuable assistance came from the South Caroliniana Library in Columbia, the Georgia Historical Society Library in Savannah, the South Carolina Historical Society, Charleston, and the Charleston County Library, whose Nick Butler confirmed for me the dumping of taxed British Tea in Charleston's Cooper River in the years leading up to the Revolutionary War. I also received special help from James E. Fitch, director of the Rice Museum in Georgetown, South Carolina; Saddler Taylor at the McKissick Museum at the University of South Carolina; and librarians at the Charleston Museum.

Along the Georgia and South Carolina seacoast and barrier islands, I wish to thank a number of people. I received special help from Mrs. Nettye Evans, then acting director of the Sapelo Island Cultural and Revitalization Society (SICARS), who arranged and facilitated my visit to the island. Others whose help was vital include author Vertamae Grosvenor of Palm Key, Ridgeland, South Carolina; writer Ford Walpole of Johns Island; Elaine Freeman of Edisto Island; historian Buddy Sullivan of Darien, Georgia; Alix Kenegay of Jekyll Island; Kate Buchanan of Brunswick; Maude Russell, editor of the *Darien News*; Ann Irvin of Wadmalaw Island; Mildred Seabrook of Johns Island; Dew James of Myrtle Beach; columnist David Lauderdale of *The Hilton Head Island Packet*; and Stephanie Barna of the Charleston *City Paper*.

I would like to express my great appreciation to a number of friends around the country, including Richard Gay of Broken Arrow, Oklahoma (a Lowcountry native); Dr. Dan Carter of Brevard, North Carolina; Donna Florio of *Southern Living* magazine in Birmingham; Elizabeth Terry, former owner of Elizabeth's at 37 Street in Savannah; and South Carolinians Dan Huntley of Fort Mill, and Stan Woodward of Greenville.

I wish to thank Bill Chandler, operator of an oyster plantation at Murrells Inlet, his sister, author Genevieve Chandler Peterkin, and Bill Chandler's colorful oysterman, Franklin Smalls.

My profound thanks go to Charlestonians Bob and Jenelle Grooms, who on my first Lowcountry research tour not only provided me a room for three nights at their beautiful home on James Island but also provided valuable tours of Charleston and took me on a scrumptious "eating tour" of the legendary Bowens Island Seafood Restaurant at Folly Beach. What an experience, including steamed oysters and Frogmore Stew (i.e., Lowcountry Boil) fit for a king.

Valuable assistance came from Charlestonians Henry Lowndes, attorney Robert Rosen, Robert Manning, Matt Lee and Ted Lee, restaurateur Dana Berlin Strange, Everett Presson Jr., Meta Carter, Pierre Manigault and Heidi Herrington of the *Charleston Post and Courier*, and Sara Wattercutter of the venerable *Charleston Receipts* cookbook.

A number of chefs provided interviews and valuable help. In particular I wish to express heartfelt thanks to Chef Louis Osteen and his wife, Marlene, formerly of Charleston and Pawley's Island, who are now based at Lake Rabun Hotel in Northeast Georgia and who generously shared a number of outstanding Lowcountry recipes. Thanks go also to other chefs who provided help—Charlestonians Robert Carter, Fred Scott, Robert Stehling, Jimmy Hagood, and Robert Barber; Chef Joe Randall of Savannah; and Chef Marvin Woods, Mableton, Georgia.

I am very grateful for the help of a number of wonderful recipe testers. Among these were Diane Kennedy, Molly Curlee, Kathy Sadler, and Dottie Cowen of Dunwoody,

Georgia; Brenda Jarman of Atlanta; Beryl Wallen, Cartersville, Georgia; and Linda Waugh of Daytona, Florida.

Old friends Jack and Lib Beach, my wife's cousins, of Charleston's James Island, gave me a warm welcome (and a grand interview), as did Professor Richard Porcher of Mount Pleasant, South Carolina, who provided valuable information about the history of Carolina Gold rice as did Huguenot descendant Jack Bonieu.

In the Beaufort area, I very much appreciated the help extended to me by restaurateurs Harry Chakides and Bill Green, as well as William Gay, Hilda Gay Upton, novelist Pat Conroy, Cindi Collins, Martha Hoke, and Ervena Faulkner. In nearby Bluffton, help came from the Larry Toomer family, operators of the Bluffton Oyster Factory.

I would like to thank most sincerely University of Georgia Professor James E. Kibler, who gave me permission to quote from the informative cookbook *Dutch Fork Cookery*, written by his late mother, Mrs. Juanita Kibler.

Other Georgians giving assistance were Lee Davis of Claxton; Bob Addison of Abbeville; Wendy Brannen of Vidalia; Eleanor Beasley Akins, Myrtis Akin, Betty Lane, Libba Smith, Dr. Del Presley, Joe Anderson, and Ken Meinhardt, all of Statesboro; Sally Tonsmeire and Liz Hood, Cartersville; Rev. James E. Rich and Mrs. Nettye Evans, Brunswick; Mary Nichols and Jessie Hart Conner, Reidsville; Frank Pressley, Lakeland; Phil Whitley and Grace and Owen Riley of Pine Mountain Valley; and Juanita Hudson of Dunwoody, GA.

At the University of South Carolina's McKissick Museum in Columbia, I was educated about South Carolina barbecue hash by the museum's Saddler Taylor, who also put me in touch with Conway banjo player, mandolin maker, and fisherman supreme Jennings Chestnut. He, in turn, took me to lunch at Donzelle's Restaurant in Conway, where I interviewed chef Larry Dickerson, who told me all about cooking a whole pig on a grill, and also enlightened me about chicken bog. This man really knows how to cook a bog. Back in Conway, I also interviewed Jennings about his freshwater fishing experiences. His wife, Willi, told me about the art of pulling the chicken wishbone. Thanks also go to Professor Charles Joyner of Myrtle Beach.

In the Florence-Darlington-Hartsville area of South Carolina, my old stomping grounds, I received assistance from former Congressman Ed Young; Campbell Coxe, one of the region's leading Carolina Gold rice planters, and his key assistant, Harold Kelly; as well as Clemson Extension Service county agent Trish DeHond, whose help included taking me in her pickup truck out to Coxe's Darlington County Plumfield Plantation. I'm also grateful to others in the same area: Pressly Coker, Extension Agent Jody Martin, and cookbook publisher Kathy Boyd.

I would like to express my profound appreciation for the confidence shown by Ron Pitkin, president of Cumberland House, who had earlier published my first "cultural cookbook," *Smokehouse Ham, Spoon Bread & Scuppernong Wine*, that went on to win (a great surprise to me) the James Beard Cookbook of the Year medal, and to my new publisher at Sourcebooks Inc., Dominique Raccah, and her great team including editor Sara Kase.

And last but certainly not least, I would like to thank my wife, Susanne, for her ever-present and dedicated help in so many ways, particularly in obtaining photographs via the internet.

Joseph Earl Dabney

June 1, 2009

The Lowcountry: A Different World

We found out the next day that Charleston was not the dead city we had imagined it to be; in fact, we would call it one of the most charming, most visually exciting, of American cities.

—*Dale Brown*
American Cookery *(1968)*

It was in the late 1950s when I saw Charleston, South Carolina, for the first time. I had been called to jury duty at the grand old 1896 Federal Courthouse—a Renaissance revival style building at the corner of Meeting and Broad streets in the heart of the city's downtown historic district.

Arriving from Florence, an hour and a half drive to the north, I underwent something of what today we would call "culture shock." Charleston was certainly a different world. For centuries it had dominated the (much wealthier) coastal half of South Carolina, as well as the entire Southern region.

I was bedazzled, indeed overwhelmed, by the city's visual delights on that first visit, particularly the garden-filled peninsula between the Ashley and Cooper rivers. Downtown Charleston had an "another world" look to it, and the homes were much more elegant, the gardens more lush than anything I'd ever seen.

The friendly people I met in Charleston even spoke with a wonderfully new-to-my-ear accent, quite lyrical in fact, and much different from the upcountry Southern twang I was accustomed to mostly spoken north of the state's "fall line." Then and there, I fell in love with the unusual "Charlestonese" spoken by the natives. It was a dialect that I would later hear numerous times in the booming baritone voice of Charlestonian Ernest "Fritz" Hollings. Fritz came through Florence in the late 1950s running for lieutenant governor. He later became the state's governor and after that was elected to the U.S. Senate. (I feel sure his flamboyant, eloquent speeches on the Senate floor left many C-SPAN television viewers looking on in awe, although sometimes they likely didn't understand exactly what he was saying!)

In my research, I learned the unique Charleston dialect was flavored not only by the Carolina colony's original English settlers but also by the West Indian Englishmen known as the Barbadians. They also immigrated to Charleston shortly after the colony's establishment, coming up from the Lesser Antilles islands in the Caribbean. They left behind sugarcane plantations to open new plantations in the Carolina Lowcountry.

Experts explained to me that the other major influences on the Charleston speech patterns (and its cuisine) were the French Huguenot Protestants who swarmed into Charleston in big numbers the 1680s. That was about the same time as the beginning of the greatest emigrant stream of them all—the "Gullah" blacks who arrived in shackles on the infamous slave ships that brought them from the coastal regions of West Africa. They would work the vast plantations of rice, indigo, and cotton being built up and down the coast and alongside interior waterways. In time the Negroes would outnumber whites two to one in Charleston and across the Lowcountry.

From that first visit to Charleston, I became fascinated by the coastal land called "Chicora" by the Indians and that later became known as "the Lowcountry" by one and all.

With all this as background, I decided that this would be a great subject for another cultural cookbook!

REBUILDING CHARLES TOWN AFTER THE 1740 FIRE

The Charles Town oligarchs not only rebuilt their town after a sweeping fire in 1740 but also tried to bear out its pretension as the British Empire's second city.

In the next quarter century, they graced it with most of the public and private buildings that survive to manifest its currently antique and profitable Georgian demeanor. Wrought iron, stucco, and tiered piazzas suggest a Franco-Spanish origin, but basically the old quarter, nestling between the convergent Ashley and Cooper Rivers, takes its line from the London Sir Christopher Wren reconstructed after the Great Fire of 1606. Both dwellings and public structures were…adapted from London models.

—WILLIAM FRANCIS GUESS
SOUTH CAROLINA: ANNALS OF PRIDE AND PROTEST

~

The Lowcountry's boundaries are often debated, but the consensus is that the coastal plain begins at the top of the Waccamaw Neck at Pawley's Island, South Carolina, and runs southwestward around two hundred miles to the mouth of the Altamaha River at Darien, Georgia, the colonial-era seaport southwest of Savannah.

As to depth, the coastal plain (including the tidewater Lowcountry and the interior) runs eighty miles from the Atlantic coastline to the mysterious Fall Line, the ancient sugary sandhills seacoast of eons ago. It is crowned on the northeast by Sugarloaf Mountain, which today is encompassed in a state park. (General Sherman's Civil War Union troops viewed the sandy mountain in 1854 on their trek north after destroying Columbia, South Carolina's capital city.)

Within the Lowcountry's tidewater coastline can be found an amazing network of marshes, grassy savannas, serpentine rivers, creeks, and estuaries teeming with shellfish—shrimp, oysters, crabs, and clams. These, along with finfish, have enabled residents from the earliest years to walk out to marshes and creeks and quickly take home seafood feasts. The abundant seafood has provided the basis for the Lowcountry's world-renowned cuisine, a Lowcountry icon, about which I will have much more to say in chapter 9.

The Lowcountry's two other historic and romantic cities are Savannah and Beaufort. Both, like Charleston, boast colorful downtowns, deep water bays, natural harbors, and eight-foot tides, the strongest in North America. And both have their own colorful histories and beautiful downtowns due to outstanding preservation efforts.

On my first visit to Savannah in the 1960s, I promptly fell in love with the city and its people just like in Charleston. I immediately came to appreciate the seaport city's international air and its gorgeous historic district embracing a series of twenty-plus parks.

Savannah was established by British General James Oglethorpe in 1733, who laid out the parks after bringing in a band of hardy settlers from London. Today, Savannah is known as "the hostess city" due to the unusual friendliness of its people. This is particularly true on St. Patrick's Day, when the city salutes its Irish population and plays host to tens of thousands of visitors. Like Charleston, Savannah early on became a major center for rice, indigo, and cotton plantations.

~

My preliminary research gave me an exciting glimpse of the Lowcountry's amazing past and present, so I made a number of research trips in 2008, covering the entire southeastern coastal plain from Murrells Inlet and Conway on South Carolina's northern seacoast to

Savannah and Darien, Georgia, on the south. The visits—including many interviews—proved to be an eye-opening educational experience, giving me a deep appreciation for the Lowcountry's tumultuous history, folklore, and exciting foodways. With this book, I am delighted to share the results of my Lowcountry travels, plus a lot of library research.

Of particular interest to me, of course, was the area's unique cuisine, based first and foremost on the abundant seafood found up and down the coast, including the Lowcountry's tidal creeks and estuaries numbering in the thousands. I was fortunate to obtain several authentic recipes for the humble but glorious Lowcountry icon breakfast dish—Shrimp and Grits. Typically, hosts serve well cooked grits, plus gobs of butter and lightly sautéed creek shrimp. Some garnish the dish with slices of fresh-from-the-vine tomatoes.

As far as the recipes you'll find herein, I was fortunate that I was able to call on friends old and new. In particular, I am grateful to Louis and Marlene Osteen, who emailed me a number of great recipes starting off with Oyster Stew with Benne Seeds. I also was able to obtain recipes from chefs in Charleston and Savannah, as well as a number of friends in the Lowcountry interior.

Part of my culinary research involved the fascinating story about the restoration of "Carolina Gold" rice that had been thought lost forever following the War Between the States. That is, until Savannah opthamologist Dr. Richard Schulze tracked down the last surviving seeds stored in a USDA seed bank in Idaho!

As you will hopefully read in the Carolina Gold chapter, Dick Schulze—after a number of plantings on his Turnbridge plantation near Savannah—was able to offer seeds to several Lowcountry

---

THE GEORGIA PROVINCE EXPERIENCES
ITS OWN RICE BOOM

During [Sir James] Wright's term as governor [1760–1782], Savannah would continue to establish herself as the social, political, and intellectual center of the province...

The prominent factor in Savannah's first boom was the rice trade. The industry—like the rice center next door, in South Carolina—required massive amounts of manual labor—namely, slaves.

A prosperous plantation society arose on elegant estates with romantic names like Silk Hope (James Habersham), Wormsloe (Noble Jones), Mulberry Grove (Patrick Graham), Fair Lawn (James Wright), Brampton (Jonathan Bryan), Isle of Hope, and Wild Heron.

—PRESTON RUSSELL & BARBARA HINES
SAVANNAH: A HISTORY OF HER PEOPLE SINCE 1733

growers. Now Carolina Gold is back on the market and is being distributed—and relished—worldwide.

Thanks to Dr. Schulze's effort, people in the Lowcountry in particular can now enjoy eating the succulent Carolina Gold rice in popular dishes such as purloo (called pilaf in the rest of the country), red rice, and Hoppin' John, a New Year's Day favorite.

One of the important things I learned on my Lowcountry research tour is that some Charlestonians still maintain the city's time-honored tradition of serving midday meals at two o'clock, sometimes followed by a siesta afterward. What a way of life!

My fond hope is that you will find the contents of this book—like a scrumptious Lowcountry meal—to be tasty and satisfying.

Joseph Earl Dabney
Atlanta, August 27, 2009

The Lowcountry Mystique

———⬦———

Speak O Ye Charlestown Gentry, who go in Scarlet and fine Linen and fare sumptuously ev'ry day. Speak O Ye overgrown Planters, who wallow in Luxury, Ease and Plenty.

—*Reverend Charles Woodmason*
1760, Charleston-based Anglican missionary

The Lowcountry's mystical aura over the centuries—its glamour and glory, triumphs and tragedies—have intrigued outsiders since the beginning of its economic "golden era" in 1740.

Doubtless the continuing worldwide curiosity came about by the coastal colony's amazing accumulation of riches in its first two centuries of existence. The wealth derived from vast plantations of rice, indigo, and cotton and, of course, the greatly profitable slave trade.

As author Robert Rosen wrote in his *Short History of Charleston*, early Charlestonians "came to the New World on their own 'errand into the wilderness' to recreate the luxurious, cosmopolitan, pleasure-filled world of Restoration England." This reflected the hedonistic King Charles the Second. Rosen added, "The aristocratic city that developed in the 18th and 19th centuries reflected Restoration England just as 18th and 19th century Boston reflected Puritan England."

The Charlestonians' success in accomplishing their "errand" came within a century after the colony's founding. By the mid-1700s, some had dubbed Charleston "America's London of the

Southeastern coast." Harvard-educated Josiah Quincy Jr. (1744–1775), one of Boston's outstanding lawyers and patriots, was astounded at the glittering opulence he found in Charleston in 1773. "In grandeur, splendor of buildings, decorations, equipages, numbers, commerce, shipping, indeed in almost everything," Quincy wrote, "it far surpasses all I ever saw, or expected to see, in America."

But the pursuit of pleasure among the colony's upper crust drew severe criticisms from some of the colony's Protestant preachers. "I now leave Charleston, the seat of Satan, dissipation, and folly," proclaimed itinerant minister Francis Asbury (1745–1816). This was after four frustrating years. Asbury later became a Methodist bishop and America's leading Methodist.

The colony's bent toward luxury began with its founders. Sandlapper-born satirist William Francis Guess noted that South Carolina was "the only state in the Union (except her stepsister state to the north) that looks back to a native order of hereditary nobles."

In his 1957 book *South Carolina: Annals of Pride and Protest*, Guess noted, "For half a century, from 1670 to the royal eviction of the Lords Proprietors, men of title…owned vast baronies along the coastal rivers and creeks," being a state that "grew up in scorn of its democratic cousins [in North Carolina]."

Historian George C. Rogers Jr. described Charleston as "a Greek city-state, independent and proud," ruled by its wealthy oligarchy of merchants, traders, and planters. Ironically, the Lowcountry capital city would in time become known as "The Holy City" due to the magnificent houses of worship erected in the lush Eden-like peninsula between the Ashley and Cooper Rivers.

Even in the decades following the disastrous War Between the States that virtually destroyed the Lowcountry's planter and merchant aristocracy, members of Charleston society continued to hold their heads high.

Famed British actress Fanny Kemble—on a visit in 1880—found Charleston surprisingly devoid "of the smug mercantile primness of the Northern cities." She described the postwar city as having "a look of state, as of quondam wealth and importance, a little gone down in the world, yet remembering still its former dignity." Kemble described the city as "highly picturesque, a word which can apply to none other of the American towns and although the place is certainly pervaded with an air of decay, it is a genteel infirmity…"

> A proper Charlestonian lady once was asked why she didn't travel to the far corners of the world, as others of her social level did.
>
> "Why should I go anywhere?" she retorted. "I'm already here."
>
> —COLIN BESSONETTE
> BACK ROADS & CITY STREETS

(Fanny Kemble later married wealthy Pierce Butler and resided with him on his Georgia sea island plantation for a number of years. While there she wrote a controversial diary describing the shameful conditions experienced by plantation slaves. The couple later separated, and she returned to her home in England.)

Most plantations became so profitable, they led to the New World's first leisure society, as described by German Johann David Schoep. In his 1783–84 travel journals, he wrote that the rice and indigo plantations "are abundant sources of wealth for many considerable families who therefore give themselves to the enjoyment of every pleasure and confidence…."

He went on, "There prevails here a finer manner of life and on the whole there are more evidences of courtesy than in the northern cities…There is courtesy here without punctiliousness, stiffness, or formality."

This lifestyle carried over to succeeding generations, as many wealthy Lowcountry families were able to send their children to England, France, and Switzerland for college and graduate schooling.

At the same time, there emerged a cadre of brilliant young planters—well-read, highly educated—who helped create Charleston as the region's cultural and political capital, and from which came four young signers of America's 1776 Declaration of Independence.

The Lowcountry's amazing cultural diversity was another major reason for its being the subject of the world's curiosity. More than any other American colony, South Carolina attracted new emigrants not only from Great Britain but also enthusiastic newcomers from Europe, the British West Indies, and, less enthusiastic, slaves from West Africa's Windward coast. All of these population streams brought to the burgeoning colony their unique voices and mores.

FRANCIS MARION, THE REVOLUTIONARY WAR "SWAMP FOX" HERO

Among the Carolina colony's French Protestant immigrants were Gabriel and Esther Cordes Marion, who settled at a plantation near the Santee River in St. John's Parish (Berkeley County). Their son, Francis Marion, would become America's acclaimed "Swamp Fox" hero in the Revolutionary War.

Francis Marion learned Indian guerilla tactics while serving first as a lieutenant in Charleston's mid-1700s war against the Cherokee Indians in South Carolina's Appalachian foothills. In one of the episodes, he took pity on Cherokee families when his commander ordered the burning of every cabin in a Cherokee "Middle Towns" village and the slashing to the ground every stalk of corn.

"Poor creatures, thought I," he wrote in his essay "Sowing Tares of Hate." "We surely need not grudge you such miserable habitations. But when we came, according to orders, to cut down the fields of corn I could scarcely refrain from tears...."

During the Revolutionary War, Marion led an amazingly effective band of guerilla-type fighters in eastern South Carolina that demoralized the British and helped turn defeat into victory in 1780 after Charleston and Camden had fallen. The late Professor Robert D. Bass wrote that Marion was a haunting nemesis to the British and Tory forces, "terrorizing them from White Marsh to Black Mingo...Hiding in his lair on Snow's Island or Peyre's Plantation by day and emerging stealthily after sunset; he usually struck at midnight...throwing his enemies into a panic. Before day he vanished again behind the morasses of the Peedee or the Santee River.

Relatively soon after the colony's founding, settlement came to the surrounding Lowcountry whose "highways" at the time were inland waterways.

In his magisterial book, *South Carolina, A History,* Walter Edgar noted settlers' diverse origins: "The English [newcomers] were from Old and New England and the West Indies, the Scots from their homeland and the north of Ireland, the Germans from Baden, Wurttemberg, the Palatinate, and the German-speaking cantons of Switzerland; the French from France, the French-speaking cantons of Switzerland or Canada, and the Jews from Spain, Portugal and central Europe."

From this cosmopolitan melting pot—encouraged by cheap land and freedom of worship after early attempts for a state religion failed—the colony flourished.

In particular, French Huguenot Protestants came by the shipload in the colony's early years. Retired Citadel botany professor Richard Porcher (pronounce that pohr-SHAY), a prominent Charleston Huguenot descendant, told me the big Huguenot influx occurred in 1685, about the time of the French King's revocation of the Edict of Nantes. For more than eighty years, the Edict had given the French Protestants freedom of conscience and public worship in the predominantly Catholic country. All that ended with the Revocation, and to America they flocked, mostly to Charles Town.

"I've traced my family all the way back to France," Professor Porcher said. "Most of the refugees during that period fled first to England and Holland, then to America." In addition to the Porchers, arriving Huguenots included families whose names soon became prominent in the Lowcountry—the Ravenels, Manigaults, Gaillards, Legares, Laniers, Prioleaus, Hugers, and Laurens families. Henry Laurens, one of Charleston's wealthiest landowners and slave traders, became one of the Lowcountry's four signers of the Declaration of Independence.

Professor Porcher, whom I interviewed at his hometown of Mount Pleasant, across the Cooper River from Charleston, told me that, "Many of the French newcomers were skilled artisans, merchants, artists, and intellectuals." They very quickly came to dominate the culture way out of proportion to their numbers. "In one generation," Professor Porcher said, "they became a land-granted family. The whole Lowcountry was in time full of Huguenot plantations."

Among the arrivals in 1685 was Mademoiselle Judith Giton, who worked eight months in Charleston to pay for her passage across the Atlantic.

"We have seen ourselves, since our departure from France, in every sort of affliction: sickness, pestilence, famine, poverty, very hard work," she remembered. "I was in this country a full six months without tasting bread… whilst I worked on the ground like a slave…"

Mademoiselle Giton subsequently married Pierre Manigault, and their descendants became quite wealthy, one of whom became North America's wealthiest individual.

"Carolina, and especially its Southern Bounds, is the most amiable Country in the Universe: that Nature has not bless'd the World with any Tract, which can be preferable to it…Vines, naturally flourishing… bear Grapes in most luxuriant Plenty."

"They have every Growth which we possess in England, and almost every Thing that England wants besides including pears, plums, peaches, apricots and nectarines that bear from stones within three years."
PAMPHLET PUBLISHED IN LONDON IN 1717 PROMOTING EMIGRANTS TO THE CAROLINA COLONY

Traveler Carlton H. Rogers gave a revealing view of French Huguenot Charlestonians. He described them in 1865 as "proud and imperious in their bearings, yet courteous and graceful in their hospitalities, retaining in an eminent degree many of the peculiarities of the French Huguenots, from whom they are descended."

But the tone of the fledgling colony was set early on by wealthy English sugarcane planters who moved up from the Caribbean Antilles looking for plantation land. Called the Barbadians, among them were people such as the Lucases from Antigua, the Meylers from Jamaica, the Middletons from Barbados, and the Lowndes and Rawlins from St. Kitts.

Many of these brought with them their own African servants and slaves. According to historian Edgar, the West Indian economic model produced a society in which, by 1720, "blacks outnumbered whites two to one."

An elite group of the wealthy Barbadians emerged—the "Goose Creek Men." As historian Guess would record, they brought with them "a fervid addiction to slavery." He added that the "brash and shrewd" Barbadians "wasted no more time in staking out choice lands than they did in voting each other to elective office. Bestriding the province, they made it seem an outpost of Caribbean empire."

A century after its founding, Charleston had become not only the capital of the booming Carolina province but also its seaport and town of trade, the heart and soul of the pioneer settlement of all the Southeast. This according to the late Lowcountry bard Samuel Gaillard (pronounced Gilly-ard).

> CHARLESTON: AMERICA'S MAJOR SLAVEPORT
> *Here was a thin neck in the hourglass of the Afro-American past, a place where individual grains from all along the West African coast had been funneled together, only to be fanned out across the American landscape with the passage of time.*
> —PETER H. WOOD, *BLACK MAJORITY*

Also, I might add, a province possessing a booming economy built almost entirely on the backs of African slave labor. The blacks came in the mid-1700s in the holds of infamous slave ships, purchased by planters for the Lowcountry's rice, indigo, and cotton plantations. Much of the slave trade avalanche followed Eli Whitney's invention of the cotton gin.

Meanwhile, Britain's Georgia province, which in its early years attracted emigrants from Ireland, Scotland, Germany, Spain, and Portugal, found itself also becoming a slave state. It occurred when the London trustees buckled under to planter pressure in 1749, squelching the antislavery sentiments of founder James Edward Oglethorpe.

In short order, the slaves were dispatched to Georgia province plantations springing up alongside rivers such as the Savannah, Altamaha, and Ogeechee and also on the barrier islands.

Numerous Charleston merchants such as Miles Brewton, Henry Laurens, and Samuel and Joseph Wrang became even wealthier in the slave trade, working with British brokers in London and Liverpool who controlled the transatlantic African slave trade market.

Similar to Charleston, Savannah's magnificent downtown historic district (saved by dedicated preservationists) is a living museum of its historic past. James Oglethorpe would be proud to see what has happened to his 1733 venture where he laid out the twenty-plus squares that have become the city's "precious jewels."

Beaufort, located between Charleston and Savannah, and founded in 1711 by indigo and rice planters, is often considered to be a smaller-scale Charleston. It boasts lovely historic homes and stunning views of the vast Port Royal Sound. During the golden era of rice, indigo, and cotton, Beaufort became popular with planters as a forested and cool summertime haven.

GENERAL OGLETHORPE'S VICTORY OVER THE SPANISH

Savannah, established in 1733 by James Edward Oglethorpe and a boatload of London colonists, was viewed by Charleston colonists to be a great Godsend; they would serve as a potential bulwark against the Spaniards based at Saint Augustine to the south.

In 1742 General Oglethorpe gave the Charlestonians great pleasure when his troops soundly squelched the Spanish Army in the decisive St. Simons Island "Battle of Bloody Marsh." As a consequence, the Spaniards withdrew from Georgia with their dead and wounded, never to return.

The lands are laden with large tall oaks, walnut and bayes, excepting facing the sea, it is most pines tall and good. Good Soyl...we think may produce any thing as well as most part of the Indies...Plenty of corn, pompions, water-mellons, musk-mellons...

The countrey abounds with grapes, large figs and peaches; the woods with deer, conies, turkeys, quails, curlues, plovers, teile, herons...and innumerable of other water-fowls... which lie in the rivers, marshes, and on the sands; oysters in abundance, with a great store of muscles; a sort of fair crabs and a round shellfish called horse-feet. The rivers are stored plentifully with fish that we saw fly and leap.

Captain William Hilton after Claiming Hilton Head Island for the British Crown in 1664

As far as this book is concerned, the Lowcountry was blessed early on with a growing cadre of African cooks who became the incubator and catalyst for a wondrous new cuisine, skillfully blending food traditions from West Africa, England, France, and the Caribbean.

The plantation kitchens in Carolina and later Georgia were particularly noted for their sumptuous servings, such as this Georgia plantation menu as described by W. E. Woodward, a historian of the early 1800s:

> *Turtle soup followed by trout fried in butter, then baked sweet potatoes and roast ham, wild turkey stuffed with walnuts and cornmeal, accompanied by dishes of rice, asparagus and green beans, with cooling orange sherbet to give the guests a breather before they tackled the cold venison, stewed corn and cheese, and the dessert of corn fritters with syrup and sweet potato pie, Madeira wine, beer and milk were the beverages.*

Similar splendorous spreads were commonplace at dinner parties in the stately town homes in Charleston, Savannah, and Beaufort, with emphasis on the readily available seafood. Cooks also commonly served at least one or two meals a day featuring an amazing rice called Carolina Gold, which would come to be called "the grandfather of long grain rice in America."

Today's Charleston and Savannah have become two of America's top tourist destinations, mainly due to their historic preservation efforts that showcase their splendid homes, gardens, and parks. Charleston's historic beauty is showcased every spring in the annual Spoleto Arts and Music Festival, which draws huge crowds. And Savannah's St. Patrick's Day celebration every March draws huge crowds from all over the country, at which the Hostess City shows off its splendors to an awed audience.

As for the Lowcountry as a whole, I could give no better description than to quote the late Archibald Rutledge, South Carolina's former poet laureate, who declared that the area's people "were enamored with the art of living. They enthroned honor; and as Edmund Burke says of them, they felt a stain like a wound."

CONROY'S LOVE OF THE LOWCOUNTRY

The great salt marsh spreading all around as far as my eye could see has remained the central image that runs throughout my work. I cannot look at a salt marsh, veined with salt creeks swollen with the moonstruck tides, without believing in God.

The marsh is feminine, voluptuous when the creeks fill up with the billion-footed swarm of shrimp and blue crabs and oysters in the great rush to creation in the spring...The people in the Low Country measure the passing of the seasons not by the changing colors of the leaves of its deciduous trees but by the brightening and withering of its grand and swashbuckling salt marshes, the shining glory of the Low Country and the central metaphor of my writing life...

PAT CONROY, *THE PAT CONROY COOKBOOK*

PORGY AND BESS: "THE GREAT AMERICAN OPERA"

One of the enduring portraits of Charleston has been the long-running Porgy and Bess, *a Broadway play based on the black characters along the renamed "Catfish Row," whom Charlestonian DuBose Heyward came to know in writing with his wife the 1925 novel* Porgy. *The book's main character was a crippled African-American beggar. The New York Times praised Porgy for demonstrating "an intimate and authentic sense of the dignity, the pathos... the very essence of his chosen community."*

Heyward later teamed up with Ira and George Gershwin to create the 1935 Porgy and Bess *musical, which was called by some "The Great American Opera" and reviled by others as "the most degrading act...perpetrated against colored Americans of modern times."*

THE CHARLESTON PORT: SHIPPING DEERSKINS TO LONDON

Charles Town—with a superb natural deepwater port—quickly took on the role as the region's trading center, especially when deerskins and other pelts began pouring into the port from Creek and Cherokee Indians. They first arrived on the backs of the Native Americans. But soon horses took over the task. Long strings of fifteen or more of the beasts of burden could be seen arriving in the port city, each horse carrying on his back a hundred and fifty pounds of pelts. Over several decades, Charleston traders bought upward of a million Indian deerskins, which they shipped to London to satisfy Englishmen's "insatiable desire for buckskin breeches."

THE ARCHITECTURE OF ROBERT MILLS

In the 1800s, Charleston-born Robert Mills became America's first truly professional architect, designing many of the outstanding public buildings and churches in Charleston and the Lowcountry, and who later would design the Washington Monument in the nation's capital among other outstanding national structures.

He, along with Charleston-born architect Gabriel Manigault, were responsible for much of Charleston's outstanding architecture. In this connection, Samuel Gaillard Stoney declared that, "Charleston has more [earlier era] architecture now than Williamsburg ever had even when it was truly new."

CHAPTER 1

Carolina Gold!

You can smell this [Carolina Gold] rice when it's growing. Smells like it's going to be an extremely good year.

—Rice planter Campbell Coxe
Darlington, South Carolina

Even if you have no leaning towards the doctrine of predestination, the story of the Low Country can almost persuade you that this coastal region of South Carolina was foreordained to plantations... The lay of the land, its climate, even the way its tidal rivers run, fitted it for them peculiarly.

—Samuel Gaillard Stoney
Plantations of the Carolina Low Country

Campbell Coxe. (Photo by the author.)

In the decades leading to the dawning of the eighteenth century, the merchants in Britain's burgeoning Carolina colony sensed that an Oriental-West African long-grain rice grown near Charles Town might prove to be a gainful enterprise, possibly more profitable than growing indigo.

Their optimism was understandable; the rice was found well-suited to the coastal region's fertile soils and subtropical climate. And as experts would later find, the resulting rice was amazingly easy to cook, had a sweet buttery taste and aroma, "plus a creamy texture." Carolina Gold Rice soon came to define the Carolina Rice Kitchen, which will be covered fully in chapter 10.

Sometime in the mid-1700s, enthusiastic Lowcountry planters proudly viewed the head-high rows of golden-hued grain swaying in the autumn breezes. Charleston warehouses soon were flooded with rice orders from customers in the West Indies, England, and Europe. Someone called the rice Carolina Gold, and indeed, it was gold in more ways than one. The super strain soon spawned a plantation frenzy that in a few decades would help make Charleston the preeminent economic and cultural capital of the Lowcountry—from 1720 up to the Civil War, Charleston would be celebrated as the wealthiest city in North America.

Richard Porcher, a retired botany professor at The Citadel, has studied the history of Carolina Gold, the Lowcountry's super strain of rice that flourished prior to the Civil War and has been restored in recent years. (Photo by the author.)

The late Karen Hess, eminent food historian, expressed amazement at Carolina Gold's eighteenth-century ascendancy, calling it "a rice so esteemed that its very name early became a generic term in much of the world for the finest long-grain rice obtainable." In her 1992 book, *The Carolina Rice Kitchen*, Hess noted that even the Chinese emperors were said to have favored Carolina Gold as their chosen rice.

While early accounts credit an English sea captain for bringing the initial Carolina Gold seed stock from Madagascar, knowledgeable experts are not so sure. Among them is previously mentioned former Citadel botany professor Richard Porcher, who has studied the Carolina Gold history for years, including travel to West Africa's rice coast region.

"The fact is that we don't know where those first seeds came from," he said during a 2008 interview at his hometown of Mount Pleasant, across the Cooper River from Charleston.

One theory is that the seeds with a likely West African pedigree may have reached the Carolina colony on a slave ship from Africa's windward coast, often called the rice coast, whose people had been engaged in rice farming for centuries. Or perhaps they came via one of the Caribbean islands in the British West Indies.

While indigo and long and short staple cotton would come along as major Lowcountry cash crops, it was the strongly marketable Carolina Gold super rice that became North America's most profitable enterprise, much more so than tobacco in Virginia, although with a requirement for many, many more slaves per plantation.

By the time Confederates fired on Fort Sumter in 1861, more than a hundred thousand acres of Lowcountry land were devoted to Carolina Gold on sixteen hundred plantations and farms. Annual production yields at the time incredibly topped more than a hundred and eighty million pounds of rice. Most was exported through the ports of Charleston and Savannah to eager customers in the West Indies, England, and the European continent.

The rice affected everything in Charleston living. As historian Samuel Gaillard Stoney noted, "For two hundred years, it…moulded Lowcountry life as did nothing else." With a few bags of the super rice, one could make purchases or even pay rent.

WILLIAM BARTRAM VISITS A GEORGIA RICE PLANTATION

In the evening, I arrived at the seat of the Hon. B. Andrews, esq. [near Sunbury, Georgia] who received and entertained me in every respect…I viewed with pleasure this gentleman's exemplary improvements in agriculture; particularly in the growth of rice, and in his machines for shelling that valuable grain, which stands in the water almost from the time it is sown, until within a few days before it is reaped, when they draw off the water by sluices, which ripens it all at once, and when the heads or panicles are dry ripe, it is reaped [by hand] and left standing in the field, in small ricks, until all the straw is quite dry.

The machines for cleaning the rice are worked by the force of water. They stand on the great reservoir [that] flood the rice-fields below.

THE TRAVELS OF WILLIAM BARTRAM (1700s)

Charleston's astute merchants and traders had already become independently wealthy. They exported Indian furs and deerskins, as well as lumber, turpentine, tar, and pitch emanating from the colony's endless forests of long leaf and loblolly pines and hardwoods such as oaks, cypress, and tupelo gums. These enterprises provided the wherewithal for many to buy up vast tracts of Lowcountry land for rice plantations. Wealthy Barbados sugarcane planters started migrating into the new colony and bringing along their slaves, ready to go to work clearing swamps and creating plantations on which to plant rice and indigo and, later, cotton.

The Rice Plantations

The Lowcountry's subtropical climate and swampy geography proved ideal for growing rice, especially those near the vast network of rivers and creeks. Planters established their initial rice fields—called "inland plantations"—on interior dry land, with the crops watered from reservoirs, artesian wells, springs, and rainwater.

By the mid-eighteenth century, planters began converting to more efficient tidal technology. Powerful eight-foot-high ocean tides, heavy with salt, were used to push the rivers' lighter fresh water up through plantation sluice gates into the Lowcountry rice fields.

The aforementioned Professor Porcher told me, "I'm led to believe that the black Africans had a lot to do with the establishment of the rice industry [in the Lowcountry]." After all, he added, "they'd been cultivating rice over there in the Niger River delta hundreds of years before arriving in the Lowcountry [in slave ships]. And way before the Europeans got to Africa in the fourteen hundreds."

Swamps were cleared of cypress trees such as this to make way for rice plantations in the Carolina and Georgia Lowcountry. (Photo courtesy Del Presley, Statesboro, Georgia.)

An early reference to the use of the tidewater technique was contained in a 1738 Georgetown County land sale notice. The owner, William Swinton, proclaimed that, "Each [field] contains as much River Swamp, as will make two Fields for 20 Negroes, which is overflow'd with fresh Water, every high Tide, and of Consequence is not subject to the Droughts."

With the tidal technology, which Rice Museum Director James A. Fitch described as "a huge hydraulic machine," workmen controlled the strong tide-waters with a unique system of sluices, locks, and wooden floodgates, which they called trunks.

Fitch described the floodgates as two facing dike doors that opened and closed automatically from the pressure of the tide waters. The planters and their slaves also constructed canals between the fields that provided workers access to the rice fields using barge-type flats. Trained African "trunk minders" kept the tidal river floodgates under constant surveillance.

Tidal rice-growing called for the flooding of the rice fields from May to November. About that time of year, plan-

Rice Museum dioramas depict eighteenth-century Carolina rice being harvested and transported from plantation rice fields. The Rice Museum is located in Georgetown, South Carolina. (Photos by the author.)

tation owners and their families would head to second homes situated on the cool Atlantic coast "to escape the miasmic fumes" and mosquito-borne malaria, according to Archibald Rutledge, leaving their fields under the care of their white overseers and the Negro slave "drivers." (Most blacks, natives of Africa, were immune to the "sickly season" illnesses.)

Elizabeth W. Alston Pringle told about her family's summertime exodus in her *Chronicles of Chicora Wood*:

"At the end of May, my father's entire household migrated to the sea, which was only four miles to the east of Chicora…but only to be reached by going seven miles in a rowboat and four miles by land. The vehicles, cows, furniture, bedding, trunks, provisions were all put into great flats…at first dawn and sent ahead. Then the family got into the rowboat and were rowed down the Pee Dee, then through Squirrel Creek, with vines tangled above them and waterlilies and flags and wild roses and scarlet lobelia all along the banks, and every now and then the hands would stop their song a moment to call out: 'Missy, a alligator!…' There were six splendid oarsmen, who sang from the moment the boat got under way."

Many other Lowcountry planter and merchant families would spend their summers at Beaufort, Bluffton and Edisto Island, and other cool sites while still others (several hundred altogether) would sail to New England, their favorite destination being Newport, Rhode Island.

The tidal plantation technology was demonstrated successfully by planter McKewn Johnstone at his Winyah Bay plantation and Gideon Dupont at Goose Greek in St. James Parish in the early 1700s.

"Once the West African strategy of [tidal] rice growing was discovered," noted James Fitch, in his book *Pass the Pilau, Please*, "the Huguenots and the British [planters] began to settle north of Charles Town into the Georgetown region," some sixty odd miles to the northeast. They, along with other European planters to follow, selected plantation sites along the Waccamaw, the Great Pee Dee, the Little Pee Dee, the Black River, and the Sampit. In time, the "Waccamaw Neck" became the Carolina colony's primary rice growing territory. These were in addition to rice grown along other Lowcountry rivers such as the Ashepoo, Santee, Combahee, Stono, Edisto, Ashley, and Cooper, among others, and including Georgia's Savannah, Ogeechee, and Altamaha Rivers, as well as on some barrier island locations.

Of course the essential element in the Charlestonians' grand visions was the importation of African slaves. Boatloads of African slaves came first from the British West Indies and later directly from the coastal areas of West Africa. It was the African blacks who would provide the essential manpower—and at times the technical know-how—to convert Lowcountry jungles into profitable rice domains.

In 1751 Carolina Governor James Glen wrote that on the larger plantations, planters considered thirty slaves to be the correct number for a rice plantation with one white overseer. Glen calculated that a plantation would produce 2,250 pounds of rice "for each good working hand."

By the mid-1700s the Lowcountry's slave population had zoomed to around seventy thousand Africans, a distinct Lowcountry majority, according to George Milligen Johnston. In his 1763 pamphlet, "A Short Description of the Province of South Carolina," he said, "They with a few exceptions do all the labour, or hard work in the country, and are a considerable part of the riches of the province…They are in this climate necessary…their number so much exceeding the whites."

Rice planter Nathaniel Heyward, arguably the Lowcountry's largest and most productive planter, was said by the 1850s to have owned more than two thousand slaves on his various plantations.

The planters' initial task was using slave labor to clear the floodplain swamps. They cut the deep-rooted cypress trees just above the ground level. Stumps can still be seen today at low tide on many abandoned plantation sites.

Plantation rice farming was labor intensive. The annual cycle began in March with the plowing of fields using mules and oxen wearing snowshoe-looking boots to keep them from sinking into the soft soil. A month later, slave women began planting the seeds that they had soaked and dried in clay to prevent them from floating to the surface.

During the summer, between floodings of fields, slaves hoed the rows of rice periodically. This was followed by harvesting in the fall, using hand sickles, and threshing, first with flailing sticks, later by threshers powered by mules and steam. Similarly, milling the rice to remove hulls and bran also evolved from mortar-and-pestle techniques to devices

RICE GRITS, OR MIDDLINS

In Colonial Lowcountry, African slave women were tasked to hand-pound Carolina Gold rice: to hull it to brown rice, then winnow it, then pound it again, winnow it again and screen it for brokens (middlins), then hand-pick it to produce grain for white rice. The resultant rice was considered the finest quality, exclusively for the tables of the elite.

However, the grains fractured like mad in the field and the mill as well. The best colonial hand pounders (slaves who hulled and polished rice grains) managed to come up with only about 70 percent whole grains.

These were saved for export. The remaining middlins grew in preference across the local population, because middlins, round and rolling on the tongue, accepted flavors with more enthusiasm than whole grains. Many Charlestonians and Lowcountry people remain loyal to broken rice and the dishes associated with it. Today, middlins are called rice grits.

—KAY RENTSCHLER
ANSON MILLS, COLUMBIA, SOUTH CAROLINA

powered by animal, water, and steam. Remnants of steam-powered mills have been found on former plantation sites.

The aforementioned Archibald Rutledge (1883–1973) told about returning in the twentieth century to his own two-thousand-acre historic Hampton Plantation, located near the Santee River, that he had inherited long past the Lowcountry's two-hundred-year rice-growing era. In his 1941 book, *Home by the River*, the poet told of finding evidence of Hampton fields that had been closely cultivated for rice, featuring ancient canals surrounding former rice fields. At the head of the canals, Rutledge noticed heavy wooden floodgates. Regarding other plantations nearby, he said:

"Sixteen miles from its mouth, the Santee divides; and these two streams flow independently into the ocean. Between them is the lonely delta of the Santee, formerly one of the greatest rice-growing areas of North America…On the South Santee, I remember Waterhorn, Wambaw, my own Hampton, Romney, Montgomery, Peafield, Peachtree, Fairfield, Palo Alto, the Wedge, Harrietta, Woodville, Egremont, Mazyck's and Washoe…Ormond Hall was near by. Of all these great plantations, Hampton alone is occupied by its owners; Fairfield is still owned by the Pinckneys, but it is not occupied."

Professor Charles Joyner of Myrtle Beach detailed the history of the Waccamaw Neck slave plantations with wonderfully nostalgic images in his highly regarded history of that era, *Down by the Riverside*. Included was this scene drawn from a Waccamaw River cruise he took on the *Island Queen*:

"As we gaze beyond the broken trunks of the rice fields now reclaimed by river

Former slave Ben Horry is pictured at his home at Murrells Inlet, South Carolina, in the late 1930s. He recalled for WPA Federal Writers Project interviewer Genevieve Willcox Chandler his earlier days working on a Waccamaw River rice plantation in Eastern South Carolina with his father. (Photo by Bayard Wooten. North Carolina Collection, University of North Carolina Library at Chapel Hill.)

and swamp, we can almost see the workers keeping pace with one another as they move across the fields. We can almost hear their singing as their hoes rise and fall on the beat. Here, at the edge of the river, there is an eerie feeling that we can almost reach out and touch these [Gullah slave] people."

A Carolina Gold Revival

Lowcountry rice plantations went into a steady decline after the Civil War, and Carolina Gold became virtually extinct following a disastrous 1911 hurricane.

But in the 1980s, something of a miracle occurred as far as the long-lost Carolina Gold rice was concerned. Savannah eye surgeon Dr. Richard Schulze, who had been growing rice to attract ducks to his Turnbridge Plantation across the Savannah River in South Carolina, ran across two important pieces of information.

The first, he told me in a telephone interview to his office in Savannah, was "a wonderfully comprehensive article" he read in the *New Yorker* magazine, written by E. J. Kahn. "It mentioned that scientists studying the genetics of rice had accessioned some sixty-five thousand varieties of rice that had been stored for future studies."

About the same time, Dr. Schulze read a label that accompanied his modern hybrid rice and discovered that Carolina Gold was in its pedigree!

A NEW STRAIN COMING: CHARLESTON GOLD

A brand-new Carolina Gold super strain, to be called Charleston Gold, is scheduled to go on the market in 2010. The Carolina Gold Foundation called it "an exceptional rice with an elegant aromatic long grain Japonica dwarf of pure Carolina Gold with a very promising future."

This followed more than a decade of research and development led by Dr. Merle Shepard of the Charleston-based Clemson University Coastal Research Center, who partnered with Dr. Gurdev Khush, a professor from the University of California at Davis. Intensive testing was conducted under the supervision of Dr. Anna McClung, leader of the U.S. Department of Agriculture's Beaumont, Texas, rice research project.

"It didn't take much imagination," he related in his book, *Carolina Gold Rice*, "to assume that somewhere, someone must have the original seed," the equivalent of what had reached the Lowcountry in the 1680s, three hundred years earlier. Dr. Schulze launched something of a detective seed hunt. The Rice Foundation put him in touch with the U.S. Department of Agriculture Research Service in Beaumont, Texas. There, Dr. Charles Bolich, a USDA rice research scientist, informed him that the USDA had, indeed, kept a small sampling of Carolina Gold seeds in its Idaho gene bank seed collection. Bingo!

"Dr. Bolich very generously grew some Carolina Gold rice for me," Dr. Schulze said, "and in 1985 sent me two small bags of seed rice totaling fourteen pounds."

The following spring of 1986, throwing all caution to the wind, he planted the entire fourteen pounds in one of his Turnbridge plantation catfish ponds, carefully prepared as to grade and drainage. As the plants grew and matured, he said, "I raised the water level to act as a natural weed control and also to support the long stems."

The first harvest that fall yielded sixty-five pounds of Carolina Gold, "none of which made its way to the table!" It was all used for a second planting the following spring, "but in two former catfish farms!" That fall the harvest totaled four hundred and seventy pounds.

By 1988, "we were well on our way," Dr. Schulze said. Moving the springtime planting to a full field, the harvest that fall totaled about five thousand pounds.

"At long last," he related in his book, "the fabled rice could be tasted." That Christmas season, Dr. Schulze's wife, Tricia, his co-worker in the Carolina Gold reintroduction saga, arranged a banquet at Savannah's Oglethorpe Club where they shared their success story with forty-eight friends. The rice did indeed live up to its reputation, and everyone there enthusiastically partook of a series of sumptuous rice dishes including a rice pudding dessert.

Glenn Roberts, president of the Carolina Gold Foundation, praised the Schulzes for "repatriating pure heirloom Carolina Gold

Campbell Coxe checks his Carolina Gold rice fields at his Plumfield Plantation near the Pee Dee River in Darlington County, South Carolina. (Photo courtesy of Robert Manning.)

to its former home" in the Lowcountry. For the first time, lowcountry descendants were able to savor the supreme taste of the long rice as their ancestors did.

Rice planters Campbell Coxe of Darlington County, South Carolina, and Glenn Roberts and his Anson Mills, headquartered in Columbia, have become major producers of Carolina Gold rice, shipping their product worldwide.

"We have thirty sustainable acres of Carolina Gold rice at our Prospect Hill field on the Edisto River near Charleston," Roberts told me. "This field is located on one of the oldest tidal trunk and dike rice fields in the Americas." He has also funded Carolina Gold rice fields on Charleston's Cooper River and has supported Carolina Gold Rice research fields in Arkansas and Texas.

Meanwhile, Coxe, with an initial grant of fourteen hundred precious pounds of Carolina Gold seeds from the Carolina Gold Rice Foundation, quickly became a major producer of the super rice using his Carolina Plantation brand, planting and harvesting the fabled rice on fields formerly devoted to cotton.

Brooke Byrd holds a bag of Carolina Gold rice ready for the market at Campbell Coxe's Plumfield Plantation in Darlington County, South Carolina. (Photo by the author.)

In the spring of 2008, with the help of Clemson University Agriculture Extension agent Trish DeHond, I visited with Campbell Coxe at his family's Plumfield Plantation, which straddles the Great Pee Dee River in Darlington and Marlboro Counties, South Carolina.

"All the water we use comes from the Pee Dee," Coxe told me during the interview. "In the spring and summer, we pump it onto these flat clay-based alluvial fields," from four to six inches deep. "We plant different rice varieties usually in late April and we harvest in September, usually around Labor Day." In jest, he calls it "Pee Dee tidal rice."

Initially, Coxe had been planting Della, an aromatic long grain basmati rice. "Five years ago," he

RICE-CORN FISH FRY MIX: A BIG SELLER

Campbell Coxe's family-owned Plumfield Plantation near Darlington, South Carolina, operates a gristmill. One of his big sellers is a fish fry mix using 50 percent rice flour and 50 percent cornmeal.

"We take broken rice and grind it and make a very fine textured flour," Coxe says. "What makes this fish fry so unique, when you dip fish into it, it doesn't have that 'caked-up' look. It has a very, very thin coating and provides the aromatic taste of the rice. It's going to be a big product for us, and it's based on by-products from our regular milling process."

Coxe's gristmill also grinds yellow and white grits, plus cornmeal. "We thought the grits business was oversold," he said, "but we can't keep up with the orders."

told me, "we started growing Carolina Gold. Now we're one of the largest suppliers in the United States. It's been fun. It's a pretty crop to watch grow."

Coxe—who duck hunts with Dick Schulze and his wife, Tricia—called the Savannah eye surgeon "a true patron of the rice culture; he's taught me a lot about the history of rice. He's semiretired from that project now," he said. In the meantime, Schulze has turned his Turnbridge plantation over to his son, Richard Jr., also a Savannah ophthalmologist.

Carolina Gold rice can be obtained from Anson Mills at ansonmills.com and Plantation Rice at carolinaplantationrice.com.

Classic Carolina Gold Rice

- 1 cup Carolina Gold rice
- 2 teaspoons unsalted butter, cut into pieces
- ½ teaspoon fine sea salt
- ¼ teaspoon freshly ground black pepper

How to Cook Carolina Gold, or "Charleston Ice Cream"

Carolina Gold is prized by rice growers the world over for its sweet flavor and superior mouthfeel. Some people call it "Charleston Ice Cream."

It differs from other long grain rice in its chameleon starch quality, which will produce classic fluffy long grain, creamy risotto, or sticky Asian-style rice depending on how it is cooked.

Here is a Carolina Gold Rice Foundation recipe for cooking "new crop" separate grain rice. In contrast to shelf-stable rice, says Glenn Roberts, "This type of rice is highly perishable and must be stored in the freezer to preserve its subtle almond and green tea aroma and flavor." It will yield three cups of rice. Cooking time is 25 minutes plus an hour of soaking.

Turn the rice into a medium bowl and cover with cold water. Soak 1 hour. Drain through a fine-mesh colander and rinse. Set aside.

Heat the oven to 200°F. Fill a large bowl halfway with water and ice cubes and set aside.

Bring 4 cups water to a boil in a heavy-bottomed 2-quart saucepan. Add the rice, stir once, cover, and return to a boil. As soon as the water boils, uncover the pot and reduce heat. Simmer gently, stirring occasionally, until rice is just tender, about 5 minutes. Drain through a colander. Turn the rice immediately into the ice water and swirl with your fingers to chill. Drain well.

Spread the rice evenly over a rimmed sheetpan. Dry in the oven, turning gently from time to time, for 10 minutes. Dot with butter and season with salt and pepper. Return to the oven until the butter has melted and the rice is hot, about 5 minutes more. Serve immediately.

CHAPTER 2

The West Africa Connection

Ef you hol' you mad, e would kill eby glad.
If you hold your anger, it will kill all your happiness.

—African proverb in the Gullah language

The early history of the rice kitchen in South Carolina is inextricably bound up with slavery. It was the black hands of African slaves who cultivated the rice and cooked it…

—Karen Hess
The Carolina Rice Kitchen

Gullah All the Way

I'm as Gullah as you can get," Bill Green laughed as we sat down on a beautiful April afternoon in his office near his Gullah Grub Restaurant. It's located on the scenic Sea Island Parkway that runs from Beaufort, South Carolina, down through the salt marshes of Port Royal onto St. Helena Island. I had just finished a tasty meal at Bill's eatery: shrimp gumbo and she-crab soup, topped off with a big helping of sweet potato pie. Also on hand were friends Ervena Faulkner and Martha Hoke, who told me a lot about the legendary Frogmore community nearby, namesake for Frogmore Stew, which many now call Lowcountry Boil.

Bill Green grew up on James Island, near Charleston—a descendant of Gullah slaves. He is pictured in his office near his Gullah Grub Restaurant on St. Helena Island near Beaufort, South Carolina. (Photo by the author.)

A man of many hats, Bill Green first came to my attention in a letter I received from Charleston's Meta Carter, the aunt of Atlanta friend Grayson Daughters.

"He is one of the last of the great deer drivers [at the Middleton Hunt Club]," Ms. Carter wrote, "and he would be someone you should go see." So I made it one of my primary stops on my 2008 tour of the Carolina-Georgia Lowcountry (more on Bill's hunting is in chapter 19).

Speaking proudly in a deep baritone voice as a true Gullah gentleman, Mr. Green, now past sixty years old, said that his ancestors were brought into the Lowcountry as slaves from West Africa, going first to South Carolina's Bull Island as log cutters and then to James Island, a modern-day Charleston suburb.

"James Island was where I was raised up," he said. "All my people who came over from Africa and their descendants were hardworking men, and my grandfather—the late great Bill Green—carried on our family tradition. He had a great love for people, a love for the land, and a love for animals. I think I picked that up 'hind him."

His ancestral background is similar to that of the hundreds of thousands of West Africans brought by slave ships to Lowcountry ports such as Charleston and Savannah and put to work on the plantations producing rice, indigo, and cotton, as well as forest products.

"The main thing about Gullah people is loving kindness," Bill said. "That and the spirits and of course hard work."

When he first started working at the Bay View Farm on James Island, Bill made $13.86 a week, working all day long for six days. "Growing up there," he said, "I learned to drive a mule and a cart wagon harvesting collards from the field, among other things."

He went fishing every chance he got, particularly for mullet, "an important fish in our diet along the coastline. We sold the big ones and kept the little finger mullet to eat ourselves." When Bill bought home an unusually big catch, he would share his surplus with neighbors.

He remembered the song of the street vendors: "MULLET MAN, TWENTY FIVE CENTS…MULLET MAN!"

"Late in the afternoon, starting to walk home, I could smell the mullet from a mile away…everybody cooking mullet!"

After attending a Jobs Corps school in Colorado, Bill Green returned to Charleston in the early 1970s and began work at the Middleton Place Restaurant, part of the historic Middleton Plantation. "It was there that I was privileged to meet a lot of great cooks," he said, "such as Misses Edna Lewis, Anna Perry, and Mary Sheppard. That's where I started developing my cooking skills, working in the kitchen and out in the garden.

"They were so very kind to me, those ladies were, and when they smiled it would make your hair rise. So much kindness and love. They taught me all about cooking. They had lovin' in their cooking, and everything they fixed tasted so good! I learned how to cook so that a dish would smell good and taste good. If you had that, you knew you were on the right track."

Bill had special praise for Miss Lewis, the late grand dame of Southern cooking who authored such classic cookbooks as *The Taste of Country Cooking*, *In Pursuit of Flavor*, and *The Gift of Southern Cooking* with prize-winning Atlanta chef Scott Peacock. "She really helped me get into cooking," Bill said. "I'm probably the only one around who could follow her way of freehand cooking."

In recent years, in addition to his ongoing work as a deer driver every fall at the Middleton Hunt Club, Bill Green set up shop at St. Helena, one of the Lowcountry's largest barrier islands with a strong African Gullah presence. In centuries past, the island's slave plantations produced rice, indigo, cotton, and truck crops (vegetables). Today he encourages African Americans there to start planting gardens again and to become more self-sufficient.

"We Gullahs were great farmers [in the past], but we let that slide under us. Now we're working to bring it back, we're coming back to that. I hope to fix up the shed here where we can buy local produce, bring it in here [to the big kitchen behind his restaurant] where we'll process it and cook it and sell it back to the store and to the public as fresh or frozen food. We already sell many of our own products—barbecue sauce, fresh chowder, collard greens, crabs, gumbo, and so forth."

He recalls how earlier generations ate off the land. "From now on through the summer and the fall, there is food out there for the picking. Right now, for instance, there are berries and herbs coming on.

"You look out there in the springtime and see something reddish in the fields. Looks like grass with red tops; we call that 'rabbit's sauce.' We used to eat that all spring long. Behind the rabbit's sauce come the blackberries.

"Also in the spring," he continued, "we would dig up turnips and eat the turnip greens. And that's when I made what I call the 'Cadillac of the brunch.' I'd slice up turnips and cook them, and with a little salt I would put them over a plate of grits. Man, that's somethin' good! And lima beans, they're top-notch when you serve them over grits. I've been eatin' that from childhood. Man, that's a beautiful dish."

"Lord, bless this house and keep the soul." That was the expression Hagar Brown used when entering a house. Born into slavery prior to the Civil War, she lived in her later years at Murrells Inlet, on the South Carolina coast. (Photo by Bayard Wooten. North Carolina Collection, University of North Carolina at Chapel Hill.)

Bill Green hailed the tastiness of okra—the seeds of which came to the Lowcountry on the slave ships in the seventeenth century. "I love to serve okra over grits along with tomatoes and chopped sausage," he said. "And of course I can't get along without getting my fill of okra soup when fresh okra is in season."

Green recalled that his mother would serve shrimp and gravy on Thursdays. "Then on Friday and Saturday came the seafoods, particularly the mullet," he said, "along with rice and beans cooked together, plus macaroni and cheese. That was some good eatin'." And Sunday was the special day of the week when his mother served fried chicken.

"Now for desserts, my mother was big at doin' a bread puddin', and sweet potato pone and pie. Ah, man, you'd be in heaven then. You know there's a difference between sweet potato pone and sweet potato pie. The pie you have to whip it up more and you leave some chunks of the sweet potato in the pie. I loved those little chunks… they're so sweet." Pies are generally baked with a crust, whereas pones are not, and include eggs and milk in the mix.

Bill Green also had positive words for slow-cooking. "If you cook meat or vegetables at high temperatures," he said, "you lose the taste; the seasoning doesn't get to set in with the food."

Looking to the future, he wants to put together "programs for our young people, to teach them the freehand way of cooking, and how to get the best out of a dollar [in food purchases]. We want to teach them how to shop carefully, particularly in the purchase of meat, and how to choose healthy foods."

He also hopes to set up classes to teach youth about foods that can be grown in gardens at their homes as in earlier generations. "Beans, tomatoes, okra, and so forth," he said. "We want to teach them how to grow those vegetables, and how to cook our Gullah type foods."

Sallie Ann Robinson Remembers Daufuskie Island

About twenty-five miles south of St. Helena Island as the crow flies is Daufuskie, another

barrier island. There, enslaved Africans and Native Americans labored in the fields and the kitchens during the centuries leading up to the Civil War. Among those were the ancestors of Sallie Ann Robinson, who in 2003 wrote *Gullah Home Cooking the Daufuskie Way*, a beautiful and insightful cookbook published by the University of North Carolina Press.

Decades earlier, Sallie had become famous as one of the students taught by novelist Pat Conroy as chronicled in his nonfiction bestseller, *The Water Is Wide*. In his foreword to Sallie's cookbook, Pat wrote, "My year on Daufuskie was one of the best-fed years of my overfed life." He praised Islanders' deviled crabs and deviled eggs and noted that when Sallie Ann was only eleven years old, she baked very teacher-friendly, "light and fluffy" biscuits.

Sallie Ann Robinson prepares to bake corn bread at her home in Savannah, Georgia. She was born and grew up on Daufuskie Island, South Carolina. (Photo by the author.)

For her part, Sallie Ann remembers Pat Conroy as "a great teacher. He was so smart, a man ahead of his time. He was a wise young man with an old heart. When he came to the island, he loved us because we kind'a intertwined with each other. We would tell him about the snakes and the spirits, and he'd listen to us very respectfully, and then, all of a sudden, he'd come up with a wild story of his own! He made learning fun. He was a challenging person. He wanted us to challenge our minds. For us, Daufuskie was our world, and he wanted to help us explore the world outside."

I was privileged to visit Sallie Ann Robinson in 2008 at her home in nearby Savannah, where she works as an in-home nurse. That Sunday she was busy in her kitchen, cooking up a deliciously fragrant lunch starting with corn bread to take to her mother at Hilton Head, another of the barrier islands that had a large African slave population.

"Daufuskie has changed a lot from the old country days when I was growing up there," Sallie Ann told me. "Back then, it was our Garden of Eden; we had big gardens and we raised our own hogs and chickens and cows. We grew most everything we ate except seafood—corn, beans, greens, cucumbers, okras, and onions. And peanuts grew well on the island's virgin soil. We didn't hoard food we didn't need," she said. "Families shared their bounty with their neighbors."

Her love for Daufuskie was more than just living there. "I felt connected to it a whole lot. I'm the sixth generation of my family to have been born there. I just love the old life."

Her ancestors were Gullah blacks and Native Americans, particularly on her grandmother's side. "My grandmother, who was born in 1889," Sallie Ann said, "was a firm woman. Like E. F. Hutton, when she spoke everyone listened."

When Sallie Ann was growing up in the 1960s, about two hundred people resided on Daufuskie, folks whose families had lived there for many generations. "Years back," she said, "the population topped a thousand. Now only fifteen head still reside there."

That reflects the trend at commercialized Lowcountry barrier islands (except for Edisto Island, South Carolina); black natives often find themselves rooted out. Many natives departed Daufuskie for cities, and others sold their land to outside developers. Members of Sallie's family still own twelve acres on Daufuskie, but the ocean side of the island is pretty much commercialized with the usual swank developments that cater to the wealthy.

Daufuskie's near neighbor, the gorgeous Hilton Head resort, was also the scene of major cotton and rice plantations that depended on enslaved blacks during the near two centuries of slavery.

Most of inland Daufuskie is still very remote and self-contained, accessible only by boat. When Sallie Ann was a young woman, her father had a job for a time with the county and had to go to work by boat.

Her family killed a hog or two when the weather turned cold in the winter. But according to superstitions at the time, Daufuskie women were told to refrain from eating fresh pork if they'd just had a baby. "And trust me," she said, "people still believe it."

Sallie Ann told me what happened when she violated the ancient rule. "I'd just had my second child and I suddenly had a terrible cravin' for pigs' feet. Three days after the delivery, I wanted pigs' feet like I'd never wanted pigs' feet before. I went in and cooked a pot of pigs' feet, boiled 'em until they were tender, along with some onions and seasoning, and sat down and ate a good mess. A day or two later, I was in the hospital."

She told me about the unusual foods she and her siblings grew up on, such as chitterlings and chicken feet, "that people today frown up their noses at. I love chicken feet and chitlins. They are so flavorful. It's the bones that add flavor to dishes. We weren't afraid to use those things as seasoning in our dishes." For more of Sallie Ann's comments on chitterlings, see chapter 14.

In years past, Sallie Ann's mother would go to the market in Savannah where butchers would almost give the bones to customers free of charge. "Now they're very expensive," she said.

The Fate of Daufuskie Island

Daufuskie is an apt symbol for the fate of the South Carolina Sea Islands in our time. Not too many years back, Daufuskie was a truly isolated island, a place of deep mystery...Though only four miles from booming Hilton Head and less than twenty miles from downtown Savannah, Georgia, Daufuskie seemed to belong to another age...

The giant of development that was stalking down the coast, squashing sea island after sea island, had stepped over Daufuskie...

But, as it turned out, Daufuskie was not immune—it was just on hold. Its number was called in 1980. In that year, developers moved in and began buying up land for what they termed a "low density" resort. By 1984, the developers owned all the waterfront land on the island resort. And they were ready to build. Today, Daufuskie's star shines brightly on the resort map.

—David Laskin, *Eastern Islands*

"We didn't need to spend a lot of money to live good," Sallie Ann recalled. "We got up early in the morning to plant and work those fields. Nowadays everything is high tech. I think in a way we've gotten spoiled, depending on the things that are easy to buy and without our having to perform hard work that once made us proud of what we had done."

Seafood, Sallie said, was a major component of her family's diet. "We ate a lot of shrimp and crab stew. Everything was fresh."

Her family also ate fresh tomatoes and peas straight from the garden during summers. "And we loved sweet potatoes. We roasted them on an outdoor fire. They were so sweet; we ate them without adding butter or a sauce." She remembered her mother baking sweet potato pies on her wood-burning stove. As for French fries, her family ate them plain, minus ketchup and salt.

She told me of the survival skills that came from her father: "He taught me how to cook as early as I could see over the top of the stove," she said. "And he taught us all how to fish. He'd send us to the mullet hole in the creek and have us to stand there. When the tide came in, bringing in the fish, he'd have us stop the fish so they'd go into his net."

For extra income her parents sold crabs and shrimp, scuppernong grapes, plums, and pecans. Their best sales came when "Captain Sam" brought his sightseer excursion boat to the island. These days, Sallie Ann Robinson likes living in Savannah. "I like to say it's my third home. My second home is Hilton Head," where family members own property and where she has a lot of friends.

Nettye Evans, then acting director of the Sapelo Island Cultural and Revitalization Society (SICARS), prepares to board the State of Georgia's Sapelo Queen ferry boat at the Meridian dock near Darien, Georgia, for the morning run to Sapelo Island, where she grew up. (Photo by the author.)

Nettye Evans Recalls Life on Sapelo Island

Farther down the coast south of Savannah, I visited Sapelo, another big barrier island, which was claimed by the British in 1757 and was the site of vast sugarcane and cotton plantations that operated during the nineteenth century prior to the Civil War. Their slaves, of course, worked the fields and ran the huge kitchen at the "big house"—across the South, this general term is used to describe the plantation owner's residence.

I drove from Darien, Georgia, a booming seaport in the colonial era, down to the Meridian Dock, where I was greeted by Mrs. Nettye Evans, then acting director of the Sapelo Island Cultural and Revitalization Society (SICARS). She arranged for me to accompany her on an 8:30 a.m. ride to the island on the State of Georgia's ferry boat, *Sapelo Queen*. After we arrived at the Marsh Landing dock, her son, Chuck, drove us to the society's office in the heart of the Hog Hammock community. Father north, near Raccoon Bluff, stands Blackbeard Island, the haunt of pirates led by Blackbeard himself, the notorious Edward Teach, who preyed on ships up and down the Carolina-Georgia coastline.

Some seventy-seven native African Americans still live on Sapelo Island. They are descendants of slaves from West Africa and the Caribbean, brought to Charleston and Savannah on slave ships in the 1800s. As mentioned, they worked Sapelo's cotton, rice, and sugarcane fields, beginning with its first major private owner during the Georgia colony's era of slavery, Thomas Spalding, a wealthy young Scot planter.

Nettye said that, "Our Sapelo people are considered to have more of a Geechee culture than Gullah," although they are considered much the same. "Only a few people at Sapelo still speak the Geechee dialect," she said. One such person is George Walker, whom I met, who has lived on the island all of his life. Along with his wife, Lula, he runs Lula's Kitchen, a cafe noted for its Geechee-Gullah foods: gumbos, smoked mullet, lowcountry boil, collard greens, and sweet potato pies.

Mrs. Evans grew up at the aforementioned Raccoon Bluff, about four miles from Hog Hammock. "It was a beautiful place, right on the water, and our church was the center of our life there, the First African Baptist Church of Raccoon Bluff." Built in 1866, a year after the end of the Civil War, the church is on the National Register of Historic Buildings and was lovingly restored in recent years by students at the Savannah College of Art and Design.

Mrs. Evans spoke with pride about her family's ties to the old church. "My mother and grandmother were very religious people, God-fearing people," she said. "My mother, the late Nettie Handy McClendon, was a dedicated worker at the church there, the First African Baptist Church of Raccoon Bluff, just as my grandmother years earlier, the late Nettie Handy." Both were Sapelo Island natives.

Unfortunately, the site of the old Raccoon Bluff community for many decades now has been something of a ghost town—except for the historic church—after the people living there were forced to leave. Their old homes were torn down at the behest of the island's last private owner, tobacco tycoon Richard Reynolds, who wanted to create a hunting

"A Sweet Potato a Day Will Keep the Doctor Away"

"Our family has a great tradition as lovers of baked sweet potatoes!" Mrs. Nettye Evans told me on my visit to Sapelo Island in 2008.

"My mother, the late Nettie Handy McClendon, who was born here on Sapelo and lived here for many years before moving to a job as a nurse's aide in Savannah, baked sweet potatoes each and every morning, and she kept them on a TV table next to her stove." These were for members of her family.

"Miz Nettye's" brothers dropped by every day around noontime to get their daily sweet potato fix. "I love sweet potatoes also," Mrs. Evans said, "and I try to eat at least one every day. And did you know sweet potatoes have more potassium than bananas?"

Her mother was known as a superb cook. In addition to baking sweet potatoes, she "always cooked up a pot of rice every day," Mrs. Evans said. "So you could always count on getting rice if you came to have dinner with her. She also made excellent potato salad and macaroni and cheese. But no matter what starch that she had on the table, she absolutely had to have rice along with all the other side dishes."

Her mother cooked grits for breakfast each and every day along with homemade biscuits. "They were oooooh so good," Mrs. Evans recalled. "Everything she cooked was from scratch and delicious. She was a great one for making pies and pound cakes on weekends, along with fried chicken, especially to take to church dinners."

preserve on that part of the island. And the church on the bluff today is difficult to reach for the surviving natives, due to the high tidewater erosion of the only access road.

The native families, after being moved to new homes at Hog Hammock, in the island's southeast section, built replacement churches. The first one was called the First African Baptist Church in memory of the original church at Raccoon Bluff.

Devotion to their church at both sites continues unabated. "Our church was, and still is, one big family," Mrs. Evans said. As before, the womenfolk lovingly make meat dishes, casseroles, cakes, and pies for "dinners in the churches and dinners on the ground."

The first major outsider to purchase "Sapeloe" in the slavery era (1802) was the aforementioned Thomas Spalding, of Darien, son of Loyalist Scot planter James Spalding of St. Simons Island who had fled to the Bahamas during the Revolution. The younger Spalding, twenty-eight, acquired a big part of Sapelo's 10,000 high-ground acres. He turned it into a successful plantation, pioneering the production of long-staple "sea island" cotton and sugarcane. Spalding used oyster shell, or "tabby," to build his residence and the homes of his slaves.

According to Darien author Buddy Sullivan, Spalding "was greatly adverse to the concept of slavery," but nevertheless realized that slaves were necessary for a profitable plantation. He imported slaves from West Africa and from the Caribbean. One of the latter, a dedicated Muslim whose name was Bilali, became Spalding's key "driver" among the plantation slaves and who daily bowed down to the ground to worship "Mahomet." A native of Guinea, West Africa, Bilali—knowledgeable in long-staple cotton—was brought to the island from the Bahamas along with his daughters, whom Spalding purchased to keep the family intact.

Spalding died in 1851. A decade later, at the start of the Civil War, the era of Lowcountry slave plantations came to an end. With the Union Navy moving in to take control of the Sea Islands, many owners fled, leaving their slaves to shift for themselves. However, to protect everyone from war harm, the Spalding decendents took the Sapelo black families along with their own families to a rented plantation almost two hundred miles deep into the Georgia interior, according to William S. McFeely in *Sapelo's People*.

Unfortunately, Sapelo's exodus throng, whites and blacks, ended up directly in the path of the Union Army's destructive 1864 March to the Sea. Afterward, some of them, along with thousands of other emancipated blacks, followed the Union troops on their slash-and-burn trail down to Savannah. After the war, a good number of the Sapelo natives managed to straggle back to the island.

General Sherman, reaching the coast, issued his so-called Forty Acres (but no mule) order that the Sea Islands were "reserved and set apart for the settlement of the negroes," and that "on the islands, no white person, unless military…will be permitted to reside." He later expanded his order to include a strip of the Lowcountry.

Unfortunately, after the Army departed, Sherman's edict turned out to be a short-lived occasion of joy for the freed slaves. Sapelo eventually fell back into the hands of the Spalding heirs, similar to the fate experienced by former slaves across most of the Lowcountry and Sea Islands. Andrew Johnson, Abraham Lincoln's successor as president, put the nail into the repatriation coffin when he revoked most of the Army's orders benefitting the former slaves.

In 1912 Spalding's descendants sold Sapelo to Howard Coffin, vice president of Detroit's Hudson Motorcar Company, who put the island plantation back on track as an ongoing farming enterprise. He employed the slave descendants on his cattle ranch, timber forests, and sawmill and hired black women to work in his new oyster and shrimp cannery.

But Coffin was most remembered for entertaining luminaries at his oceanfront Sapelo mansion and cruises on his 124-foot yacht. Among them were Presidents Calvin Coolidge and Herbert Hoover and aviator Charles A. Lindbergh, who landed his plane in one of

Coffin's cow pastures. Then the stock market crash in October 1929 took Coffin and his associate Bill Jones down with it, and they had to sell Sapelo.

Onto the scene in 1934 came the aforementioned Richard J. Reynolds, the North Carolina tobacco heir, who provided jobs at his Sapelo dairy and financed construction of school and recreational facilities for blacks and whites alike. In the 1950s Reynolds operated a free summer camp for underprivileged children. He also provided facilities on the island that led to the creation of the University of Georgia's Marine Biology Center, which today carries out important research and hosts scientists and students from Georgia and other states year-round.

With all the best intentions, R.J. Reynolds put into motion a strong drive to create a wildlife preserve. However, this meant the potential destruction of a number of the African-American communities except for one, where all of the blacks were to be herded.

After Reynolds's death in 1964, his widow, Annemarie Reynolds, sold most of the island to the State of Georgia. She sold the first part in 1969. The second she sold in 1976, with the designation of the current Sapelo Island National Estuarine Research Reserve put under the jurisdiction of the Georgia Department of Natural Resources.

"Today," Nettye told me, "our primary objective here at SICARS is to preserve the land

A SAPELO ISLAND TRANSACTION

At the end of the Civil War, General Sherman named Major General Rufus Saxton as commander in charge of Union Forces on the South Carolina and Georgia Sea Islands. He had responsibility for carrying out Sherman's order to turn over the island plantations to the former slaves.

Here is one of the warrants he issued relating to Sapelo Island:

To Whom It May Concern
Savannah, Ga April 16, 1865

Fergus Wilson having selected for settlement forty Acres of Land on Sapelo Island Spaulding plant'n Ga pursuant to Special Field Order No. 15, Headquarters Military District of Mississippi [Sherman's command], Jan. 16, 1865; he has permission to hold and occupy the said tract, subject to such regulations as may be established by proper authority; and all persons are prohibited from interfering with him or his possession of the same.

By command of R. Saxton
Brev't Maj. General
A.P. Ketchum Lt A[ide] D C[amp]

and the ownership of this part of the island by the slave descendants. We're trying to discourage any more selling of the remaining land."

As part of this effort, the society sponsors a Cultural Day every October to celebrate the Geechee heritage, to display the island's foods and handicrafts, and to bring back former residents and visitors from across the country.

Cornelia Walker Bailey, a Sapelo Island native and storyteller, tells a great deal about Sapelo's people and history in her revealing book, *God, Dr. Buzzard, and the Bolito Man: A Saltwater Geechee Talks about Life on Sapelo Island, Georgia*.

One of the poignant passages tells of how the black communities on the island, except for Hog Hammock, were forcibly closed down one by one due to the wishes of the last owner in the Big House. The first to go was Belle Marsh in 1950, followed by Lumber Landing in 1956 and Shell Hammock in 1960. By 1964, other than Hog Hammock, only Raccoon Bluff, the largest of the communities, was left. "The Bluff" had been created right after the Civil War, in 1871, when three newly freed African Americans had bought land there under the short-lived government policy of Sea Island land ownership reversal as enunciated by General Sherman.

By 1964, after almost a century as an ongoing native black community, the island's Gullah-Geechee survivors knew that the signs of the Bluff's survival were not good. Later that year, under strong "persuasion pressure," the Bluff was closed down permanently, its homes destroyed, and its people moved into Hog Hammock.

"We had lost the Bluff," Cornelia Walker Bailey wrote, "and nothing would ever be the same." Later that year, Richard J. Reynolds died of emphysema while living in Switzerland with his fourth wife.

Hunting Sapelo Island Squirrels, Rabbits, and Raccoons, Plus Netting Mullet on Sapelo Beach

Sixty-five-year old Cephus Walker describes his experiences hunting and fishing as a youth on Sapelo Island south of Savannah. This is based on my 2008 interview with Mr. Walker:

Growing up here on Sapelo Island, I loved going fishing and hunting. Yes sir. We cast nets right off the beach. Mostly caught mullet back in those days, plus whiting, red bass, and sea trout. When we'd get home with the mullet, Mother liked to feed us mullet and grits. They were delicious that way.

And huntin' oysters, that was one of our favorite things to do as kids. We'd go to the creek banks and dig oysters. That would be our meal for the day. Our mother fried 'em, and made a gravy with bacon and flour. It was mighty good eating.

I loved going squirrel hunting out in the woods— also rabbits and raccoons. Raccoon is delicious meat. Yes sir. On all the wild game

Cephus Walker, sixty-five, is pictured during a break from his job as a carpenter on Sapelo Island, Georgia, where he was born and grew up. (Photo by the author.)

like that, though, Mother would parboil it first, and after that, she would put it in the oven for the final cooking.

Now there was something else I loved to eat—squirrels and rice. To go with that we always had plenty of biscuits and corn bread. Oh yeah.

Another of my favorite amusements these days is playing the Georgia lottery, like Fantasy Five, which has taken the place of the old Bolito numbers games that were popular on the island in earlier years.

—*Cephus Walker*

CHAPTER 3

Historic Charleston

People had told me of spring in the Carolinas. They had tried to describe the voluptuous abandon of it, the wanton beauty that draped the trees and garmented the earth...

—English-born artist Claire Leighton
Southern Harvest

The time to visit Charleston is in the spring when the "Holy City" is "bathed in the intoxicating beauty" of its jasmine, azaleas, camellias, and magnolias. Its lovely gardens, such as Middleton Plantation and Magnolia Gardens, are often called the most beautiful in the world.

From late April into early June, the capital of the Lowcountry—flanked by the lazy, slow-moving Ashley and

This scene spotlights Charleston's beautiful residential architecture along the Battery facing the Charleston Harbor. (Photo courtesy of the Charleston Convention and Visitors Bureau.)

Cooper Rivers—shows off its many-splendored beauty to the ultimate. Jasmine fragrances ride every gentle breeze, enveloping lucky strollers with their heady perfumes. As historian George C. Rogers Jr. stated in *Charleston in the Age of the Pinckneys*, "When the spring came, the fragrance of the flowers hovered sweetly in the air."

It must have been such a springtime when the late Gian Carlo Menotti first visited Charleston. I can envision the Italian-born composer and impresario walking around the palmetto-lined historic district and visiting the city's splendorous gardens. He doubtless realized that Charleston, with its old-world architectural ambiance and its romantic yet stormy history, would be the perfect city to host his Spoleto Arts Festival. This would be the American counterpoint to the festival Menotti launched earlier in his hometown of Spoleto, Italy. As the saying goes, the rest is history.

For more than thirty years since the first festival in 1977, Spoleto—with the entire city of Charleston hosting—has drawn upwards of eighty thousand eager fans every spring for three inspiring weeks of music, drama, and art.

Theatrical arts played a central role in Charleston from the opening of the famed Dock Street Theatre in 1736. The theater is still going strong: It serves today as a key venue for Spoleto, along with Charleston's churches, auditoriums, and outdoor gardens and parks. In fact, Charleston is universally admired for achievements in preserving, restoring, and protecting its unique architecture.

A fairly new and exciting event is Charleston's five-year-old Food and Wine Festival. Held every March, it's a weekend celebration encompassing dine-arounds in restaurants and homes as well as large-scale events and tastings. According to Nathalie Dupree, a founder and the first president of the festival, it attracts some of the country's top chefs, authors, and wine professionals.

To understand Charleston, according to Professor Jack Bass (Nathalie Dupree's husband) is to know that history is everything.

Indeed. Consider that Charlestonians staged their own version of the Boston tea party in November of 1774, dumping a shipment of highly taxed British tea into the Cooper River. Later the Lowcountry sent four signers of the 1776 Declaration of Independence to Philadelphia. Incredibly, they were young, three under thirty years old: Edward Rutledge, twenty-six; Thomas Heyward Jr., twenty-nine; Thomas Lynch, twenty-six; and Arthur Middleton, thirty-four.

Consider also that by the first half of the eighteenth century, some six or seven decades after the British colony's birth, Charleston was fast becoming the capital of the Lowcountry's rice, indigo, and soon-to-be cotton plantation systems, helping turn Charleston into one of the wealthiest cities on the North American continent. And practically all was carried out on the backs of slaves imported by the thousands.

At the same time, Charleston also became a "booming and boisterous seaport city," the fourth largest in North America. Hundreds of sailing vessels daily awaited their turn in the busiest seasons to dock at the Charleston wharves to deliver cargo to and pick cargo up from England, the Caribbean, and Europe. Many of the arriving ships carried human cargo—Africans destined for the city's auction blocks and Lowcountry enslavement.

And consider that Charlestonians fired the first shot of the Civil War at Union-occupied Fort Sumter on April 12, 1861. A century later, conservative Charleston and environs were one of America's strongest hotbeds of resistance to racial desegregation (but later, in the twentieth century under progressive Mayor Joseph Riley, Charleston provided much needed accommodations for African Americans).

Most importantly, as far as this book is concerned, with the valued help of enslaved Africans in the kitchens, Charleston created an exciting new cuisine embracing English, African, Caribbean, and French foodways. Ranging from distinctive rice purloos to

scrumptious seafood dishes such as she-crab soup and beyond, this new fare tickled the taste buds of the New World's gourmets.

Despite a tumultuous history plagued with pirates, malaria, hurricanes, and fires—plus British and Union bombardments—Charleston emerged from it all as one of America's most charming cities.

On March 15, 1670, the English Colony's first ninety-three settlers debarked from their three-masted, two-hun-

> ### THREE O'CLOCK DINNER
> *In the days of King George, before the Revolution, elegant people served dinner at three o'clock and Charleston does not like change…*
>
> *As you wake up in the golden mornings in your high ceilinged, paneled room on the Battery overlooking the sea, you…hear a soft negro voice intoning on the streets a song about "she-crab;" he also sells "he" crab, but few buy.*
>
> *The crabman charges ten cents a dozen extra for "she" crabs with the eggs in. The crab eggs are picked and put with the crab meat and give a delicious glutinous quality to the [she] crab soup…*
> —HELEN WOODWARD, *TWO HUNDRED YEARS OF CHARLESTON COOKING* (1930)

dred-ton frigate, the *Carolina*, and an unnamed sloop. The ships had eased up the Ashley River into Town Creek off the river's west side. The place was Albemarle Point, known today as Charles Towne Landing.

For the newcomers the sight was spectacular—a lush jungle of giant long-limbed oaks decorated with Spanish moss, lofty palmetto and pine trees, and strange and exotic shrubs and vines unknown in England.

Having set sail in three ships from England in August 1669, the settlers—carrying a few incidentals such as fifteen tons of beer, thirty gallons of brandy, and a hundred thousand four-penny nails—experienced an exhausting seven-month odyssey. They stopped off first in Kinsale, Ireland (where many Englishmen attempted to jump ship and no Irishmen could be found to join the journey to the New World), then proceeded to Barbados in the British West Indies. They spent several months there. Captain Joseph West picked up some Barbadians, as well as indigo and cotton seeds, sugarcane cuttings, ginger roots, and sets of olive trees, before proceeding through stormy seas to the North American continent.

Only the *Carolina* got to Charleston on schedule. Among the first settlers were twenty-nine men of property and sixty-three indentured white servants. Each of the free male settlers received a hundred and fifty acres of land and one hundred additional acres for each able-bodied manservant they brought along. Stephen Bull, a "lesser gentry master" according to Walter J. Fraser Jr., accompanied by nine servants, was granted a thousand and fifty acres of land.

In 1679 the colonists decided to move Charles Town to a permanent site on the peninsula's southern tip at the confluence of the Ashley and Cooper Rivers. It was called Oyster Point, where huge native American oyster shell "middens" had accumulated over centuries. To protect themselves against the Spanish and against pirates, the colonists encircled their town with a high brick wall fortification. It was located near what would become today's Battery (Bot'try in Charlestonese).

Charleston was founded by lords and ladies as the home of the only American nobility…a reflection of the English Restoration across the sea. Only here can barons, landgraves, and caciques live on, minus their titles and perhaps their land holdings, but secure in their lineage.
—CHARLES KURALT
CHARLES KURALT'S AMERICA

Early arrivals in 1680 included a boatload of French Huguenots, followed by hundreds more in 1685. They were fleeing religious oppression in France where the new king, Louis XIV, in 1684 revoked the Edict of Nantes that had given the Huguenot Protestants eighty-seven years of official religious tolerance.

Most of the French refugees fled first to England and Holland before heading to Charleston. Included were Huguenots destined to become some of the Lowcountry's most distinguished family names: the Ravenels, Manigaults, Marions, Duprees, Hugers, and Porchers, among others. By the time of the colony's economic golden era between the 1730s and 1820, Huguenot merchant and planter Peter Manigault was hailed as the wealthiest individual in British North America.

A "speedy peopling" took place in Charleston, including the early arrival of the first black slaves from Bermuda and the British West Indies. In time, the slave trade would bring thousands of Africans through the Charleston port. Robert Rosen wrote that the institution of slavery "shaped and defined Charleston as much as, if not more than, any other force in its history," since the colony's entire economy rested on slave labor.

Charleston's Sullivan's Island soon became the site of what some historians called "the Ellis Island of Black Americans." It was there that the West African newcomers went through a ten-day "pest house" quarantine and "cleansing" before being cleared and put up for sale to eager Lowcountry planters.

By the mid-1700s Charleston had welcomed hundreds of Europeans led by French Huguenot Protestants and Sephardic Jews from Portugal and Spain, followed by Germans, Irish, Scots, and Welsh, all seeking land and religious liberty as expected under the colony's constitution, which had been written mostly by philosopher John Locke.

In 1708 Gideon Johnston was quoted as saying, "The people here…are a perfect Medley or Hotch potch…who have transported themselves hither from Bermuda, Jamaica [and British West Indies islands of] Barbados, Montserat, Antego, Nevio, New England, Pennsylvania &c." Among the newcomers were affluent Barbados sugarcane planters, bringing with them what historian Walter Edgar described as the "Barbadian cultural model," seeking fame and fortune in Lowcountry slave plantations.

Thanks to the wealth brought by plantations, the slave trade, shipping, Indian trading, and naval stores, Charleston's social life became grandiose, but not for everyone. A social structure evolved based on class, race, and family. This was reflected in the social clubs that sprang up—the St. Cecelia Society, the Huguenot Society, the Charleston Club, the St. Andrews Society, and the Carolina Yacht Club.

Here the rich people have handsome equipages; the merchants are opulent and well-bred; the people are thriving and extensive, in dress and life; so that everything conspires to make this town the politest, as it is one of the richest in America.
—London Magazine (1762)

Extravagant parties took place not only in social clubs but also in private homes, such as one given by Emma Pringle Alston, who, in February of 1851, threw "the most splendid ball the city ever knew." It took place at the Alstons' three-piazza mansion on East Battery. She had the wherewithal to do it, being the wife of wealthy Georgetown County rice planter Charles Alston.

As starters for the dinner party, Mrs. Alston's cookbook listed four wild turkeys, four hams, sixty partridges, twelve pheasants, twelve canvasback ducks, five pair "of our wild ducks," ten quarts of oysters, eight Charlotte Russes, four pyramids of crystallized fruit and coconut, four orange baskets, four Italian creams, seven dozen kiss cakes (possibly meringues), seven dozen macaroons, four molds of jelly, four cakes of chocolate, four small black cakes, and "immense quantities" of bonbons.

Charleston's wealth also brought about distinctive, pastel-hued "single houses" and "double houses" that remain today—dutifully restored and many flush to the street—in the downtown historic district. Numerous homes were graced with East Indian silk curtains, dining tables covered with Dutch linens, and sideboards glittering with silver teapots, bowls and goblets, and impressive imported China.

> ## "CHARLESTON IS DIFFERENT"
> Charleston is "different."...You will find whole sections of the city which...will hardly seem American: where street after street will have a look of having been brought over like very practical stage settings...When you start guessing at the possible country, you will realize that that the town is something of a special creation. There are churches that might have come from the England of Christopher Wren, but neither they nor the town are exactly English...Along the harbor end of Queen Street, you will find rows of close-set, narrow old houses that might have come from some French seaport...The more you feel the atmosphere of the place, the more you are going to sense its West Indian flavor, but...you will comb the Antilles vainly to find its counterpart...
> —SAMUEL GAILLARD STONEY
> CHARLESTON: AZALEAS AND OLD BRICKS (1937)

The three-story piazza structures, also called "the Charleston House," were positioned with their sides to the street to take advantage of what Samuel Gaillard Stoney called "the sacred Charleston wind that every hot afternoon blows up from the southwest across Ashley River and cools off the town for the evening."

One of the best examples of the Double House (also called Charleston House) was that of Thomas Heyward, a signer of the Declaration of Independence, whose brick home built by his father in 1772 was used by President George Washington during his 1791 visit to Charleston. It contained twelve rooms with a fireplace in each, a separate kitchen, a cellar and loft, and a carriage house and stables, "all of brick surrounded by brick walls."

New England's distinguished statesman Josiah Quincy, later to become president of Harvard, was astounded at the grandeur of Miles Brewton's King Street mansion when he came for dinner in 1773, calling it "the grandest hall I ever beheld, azure blue satin window curtains, rich blue paper, with gilt, mashee borders, most elegant pictures, excessive grand and costly looking glasses."

All told, modern-day Charleston preservationists are reported to have saved and restored 73 pre-Revolutionary War buildings, 136 from the late 1700s, and more than 600 erected before 1840.

It was to the beautiful town homes that plantation gentry flocked during the glittering January social seasons. And they came back to the cooling breezes of Charleston and Beaufort during the hot summers or sailed to summer retreats in New England, their favorite being Newport, Rhode Island, which they reached by boarding Captain Joseph's sloop *Charlestown* for the two-week voyage.

Fine detail is evident in this close-up of a Charleston mansion. (Photo courtesy of the Charleston Convention and Visitors Bureau.)

Along with the magnificent homes of the 1720–1800 golden age, Charleston's cuisine also soared to greatness. J. Hector St. John Crevecoeur, the French-born historian, noted that Europeans visiting Charleston for the first time would be greatly surprised "when they see the elegance of their houses, their sumptuous furniture as well as the magnificence of their tables."

John Martin Taylor, the modern-day bard of Lowcountry foodways, wrote of the region's cooking supremacy, declaring in *The New Encyclopedia of Southern Culture* that "an exotic cuisine" evolved based on "the advanced hunting, fishing, and cooking skills of the Africans, the superior meat curing techniques of the Germans, the worldly pretentions of the aristocratic English, and the country French traditions of the Huguenot craftsmen…"

Great food traditions have carried on to this day, with scores of outstanding restaurants found in Charleston and its environs. The influence of the late Edna Lewis, renowned Southern chef, still is remembered at Middleton Place Restaurant. Its kitchen turns out authentic Lowcountry dishes Lewis developed such as okra gumbo, she-crab soup, pan-fried quail, and a Charleston favorite, shrimp and grits. For more recipe details, see chapter 6, the Art of Lowcountry cooking.

For more recipe details, see chapter 6, the Art of Lowcountry cooking.

America's Holy City

People began to refer to Charleston as "the Holy City" in recognition of the increasing construction of houses of worship, whose imposing spires rose to grace the peninsula's skyline. Today, 188 religious houses embracing 36 denominations call Charleston home. These range from the historic St. Phillip and St. Michael Episcopal Churches to the First (Scots) Presbyterian Church, the First Baptist Church, the French Protestant (Huguenot) Church, the St. Mary's Roman Catholic Church, the Old Bethel Methodist Church, the Congregation Beth Elohim (Jewish synagogue), the Mother Emanuel A.M.E. Church, and the St. Johns Lutheran Church.

Fred Scott's The Wreck—A Destination Eatery

One of Charleston's celebrated modern-day eateries is The Wreck of the Richard & Charlene. It's located at Mount Pleasant, across the Cooper River from the peninsula.

A bit of background: In 1989, when Hurricane Hugo struck Charleston and the South Carolina coast, "a derelict North Atlantic-style trawler" broke loose from Wando Seafood on Mount Pleasant's Shem

Fred Scott, owner of The Wreck of the Richard & Charlene Restaurant, stands on his dock facing Shem Creek at Mount Pleasant, a suburb of Charleston, South Carolina. (Photo by Ford Walpole.)

Creek. It crashed into respected Broad Street attorney Fred Scott's fishhouse property.

His dock, as well as his tenant shrimpers' business, were wiped out. The trawler ended up impaled on his dock's bare pilings.

Afterward, Scott decided to pursue his dream of opening a restaurant in the old fishhouse. His wife, Patricia, agreed on the condition that it be named in memory of the awesome hurricane. Scott opened his restaurant early in 1992 as a breakfast diner, later adding lunch and dinner.

He credits the *Charleston News and Post*'s Jane Kronsberg for putting The Wreck on the map. Along with her rave review, she urged Scott to prepare for a customer avalanche. Almost overnight, the place became a popular Charleston destination. Mirroring its oft-received high praise, *New York Times* contributors Matt Lee and Ted Lee would soon call The Wreck one of their hometown favorites.

Today, Scott's pièce de résistance is his deviled crab cake recipe that came from the Hesselmeyer family, owners of Henry's, one of Old Charleston's famous downtown restaurants.

In fact, seventy-nine-year-old Henry Shaffer, Henry Hesselmeyer's grandson, urged Scott to adopt the deviled crabs and clam chowder recipes from the old Henry's. Scott wisely accepted the suggestion. Today, according to writer Ford Walpole, Shaffer comes in to do the prep work on the crab cakes using his Grandmother Hesselmeyer's recipe and cooks them on a part-time basis.

"Here at the Wreck," Scott told Walpole, "we just do fried seafood and we keep a very limited menu. Our mantra has always been fresh seafood; we don't quibble about price."

As for the cooking, Scott taught his cooks early on to zero in on several fundamentals, especially timing consistency. "If the timing is right and the oil is hot and the seafood is fresh," Scott said, "it's just a matter of physics to get it right."

Scott attributes much of his success to his early suppliers along Shem Creek. Among them was Cuban-born fisherman Raul Morales who, until his death, supplied The Wreck with fresh blue crabs.

Due to the disappearance of all but one of South Carolina's oyster shucking houses, Scott now sources oysters from the Gulf Coast. The same supplier also provides The Wreck with the finest of scallops from Virginia and Nantucket. "People who like scallops really like our scallops," Scott said. "But we had to learn to do scallops; they can turn to rubber just like that" if overcooked, gesturing with a snap of his fingers.

The epitome of a distinguished Southern gentleman with a distinctive Charleston brogue and the eloquence of a scholar, Fred Scott seeks to honor tradition and to provide good food in a warm and friendly atmosphere. Some Charlestonians compare The Wreck's charm and character to the long-gone Andre's near Folly Beach on James Island. As for Scott, he believes patrons appreciate the "primitive all-around facility."

In 2008 acclaimed North Carolina artist-architect Woody Middleton visited The Wreck. On looking out over Shem Creek's imperfectly perfect wooden pilings, welcoming fowl, weathered shrimp boats, and magnificent marsh, he said, "This is the most splendid representation of the Lowcountry, and I hope it stays like this forever."

Southern Food with Lots of Soul

On a chilly, windy April day in 2008, I decided to check out Jestine's Kitchen, a small but popular downtown Charleston restaurant boasting "Southern Food with Lots of Soul." My Atlanta retina specialist, Dr. Paul Kaufman, told me about the eatery. He said Jestine's was owned and operated by his cousin, Dana Berlin Strange. So I joined the long yet happy lunchtime line of people that led up to 251 Meeting Street in the heart of Historic Charleston.

After finishing off a plate of crab cakes and fried okra, I felt fortunate when Dana walked over and gave me a stand-up interview at my table right in the middle of her crowded eatery. She told me she named the restaurant in honor of Jestine Matthews, a Lowcountry native who died on December 18, 1997, at the age of 112. Jestine had been a valued caretaker in Dana's family home for many decades.

Jestine Matthews. (Photo courtesy of Dana Berlin Strange.)

Jestine Matthews, Dana said, was the daughter of a Native American mother and an African Gullah father, the son of a freed slave who farmed land at Wadmalaw Island's Rosebank Plantation.

"I don't know if I was born there," Mrs. Matthews told Dana later, "but when I first know myself, that's where I was living."

Jestine moved to Charleston shortly after the turn of the twentieth century, finding work as a laundress and later as a housekeeper. In 1928 she began work for Dana's grandparents, Mr. and Mrs. Aleck Ellison, who were expecting a baby. It was the beginning of a lifelong relationship between Mrs. Matthews and the Ellisons.

REBECCA MAYZCK'S RABBIT TOBACCO CURE

When Anne and I were living on Church Street in downtown Charleston back in the early 1970s, there was an old black woman named Rebecca Mayzck who pushed a vegetable cart made out of an old steamer trunk with iron wheels. She called all her female clients "Miss Lady," and all the male ones "Mr. Billy."

It was through her that we were introduced to "Chainey Briar," available in the late spring. Chainey briar is the tender emergent shoots of the smilax vine and was boiled and steamed just like asparagus with the same texture and taste. She would bring by small bundles of them wrapped in a twisted Spanish moss rope.

If we were not at home when she came by, she would leave a squash or carrot stuck in the door knocker to remind us of her visit.

One day when she came by she found that Anne was sick in bed with a bad cold. The next day she arrived with a wad of rabbit tobacco (called "life everlasting") and insisted on coming in and "biling" it to make a sort of vile tea, which Anne gamely swigged. Rebecca's instructions were, "You tek um and biles she in de pot."

It must have worked because in seven days Anne's cold was gone.

—BEN MOISE, RETIRED GAME WARDEN
CHARLESTON, SOUTH CAROLINA

Dana Berlin was the daughter of the Ellisons' only child, Shera Lee Berlin. "And this restaurant," Dana said, "is my way of sharing Jestine's wonderful style of home cooking and the warm atmosphere she provided for generations of our family and friends."

Dana asked me to extend to readers an invitation to Charleston visitors to drop in and share a meal that could have come from Jestine's kitchen—traditional vegetables, seafood, and fried chicken—"and raise a glass of Jestine's Table Wine in a toast to her memory."

Recalling Charleston "Swimp Sellers" of the 1930s, the Banana Boats, and Picking Oysters and Tomatoes on Edisto Island

In 2008 I visited my friend Jack Beach, a ninety-year-old Charleston native, at his home on James Island where he resides with his second wife, Lib Poston. His daughter, Jenelle Grooms, also added to the conversation. Here's how Jack described in his own words the sights, sounds, and tastes of Charleston in the 1930s and since:

Jack Beach. (Photo by the author.)

"SWIMP…SWIMP…TWENTY FIVE CENTS A POUND!" That's what the street venders shouted when they walked by our house in Charleston first on Spring Street and later on State Street. That was a long time ago, back in the 1930s on up to the '40s. I remember it well.

Vegetables were cheap then. Tomatoes, squash, cucumbers. We had plenty of food. I lived with my parents in Charleston, and at times I would go out to live out in the country with my grandparents, Mr. and Mrs. Bill Perry. They had a big kitchen [in a building] behind the house. Grandpa was with the county for many years, the head man taking care of the county roads. Road superintendent. Dirt roads ran all over Charleston County back then. Grandpa made $135 a month and everybody thought he was rich. But people lived good back then.

This whole country was full of farms back then. I remember coming into Charleston on Highway 17 from Savannah; they used to be fields of cabbage on both sides of the road; big fields with cabbages growing. Now they're covered with houses. Ain't no farmland now along there.

I remember when they put in the first paved road from Charleston to Savannah, Highway 17, the King's Highway, and it went right by our front door at Adams Run. That was a wonderful thing, gettin' that road paved. Everybody loved it and it meant that we kids could skate on it.

Every time the banana boat came in, my father, Arthur Brown Beach, would buy two stalks of bananas there at the Charleston docks, one that was green, he'd take home to hang up [to ripen], and the other, a ripe one, that he'd keep in his car, to eat when he was at work, on the road, and so forth.

I came to love bananas. Boy, back then, I ate more bananas than the law allowed. I'd go ridin' with someone and they'd say, "Jack, you always seem to be carryin' around a hand of bananas." A hand, you know, was a bunch you would cut off the stalk. I'd say, "Ay golly, I was raised on bananas."

And my mama always loved to make banana cake. We had a downstairs closet and my father would hang a stalk of bananas in there. So every Sunday, Mama would cook a banana cake, especially for the grandchildren.

(Jenelle added: "We used to eat her banana cake every Sunday, didn't we, Daddy? We'd sit around the table and eat banana cake and play penny bingo. That was about the time when I'd just learned my numbers.")

Yeah, and another thing: One of my favorite foods back then was tripe. Grandma Perry used to cook tripe [the stomach of an ox] and I loved it. We'd have tripe for supper, OOOO-EEEE, was it good! And boy, I loved to eat sweet potatoes any way Grandma wanted to fix 'em—sweet potato pie, sweet potato pone, sweet potato casserole, just a plain baked sweet potato, I loved those sweet potatoes.

I was born in our home on Spring Street on October 15, 1917. Later we lived on State Street, one block from Broad in downtown Charleston; nice residential section.

The man that owned the building told Daddy one year that we might have to move, that he planned to sell the place. My brother said, "How much does he want for it?" Told that the owner was asking $8,000, my brother bought it, a fine two-story house. My brother told Mama and them, "Y'all just keep on staying here and I'll live here too, free of board."

I got in the car business and later I became a salesman for Thomas and Howard, wholesale grocers. Worked for them over forty years, covering several counties in the Lowcountry around Charleston.

"Tell him about picking tomatoes on Edisto Island," Jenelle urged her father.

I had a good friend, Bunt Fisk, who had a fifty-five-acre field of tomatoes on Edisto Island. He told me, "Jack, any time you want tomatoes, you just go down there and get 'em." So we'd drive down and pick all we wanted. When we'd go to the mountains [in the summer to Hendersonville], we'd take along a bushel or two of those tomatoes with us in the back of the car.

"Tell him about the oyster factory out on Edisto Island, Daddy," his daughter said.

Yeah, it was run by old man Steve Flowers, the Flowers Brothers. They'd hire black women to come in and shuck the oysters. Big operation. He'd sell a gallon of [shucked] oysters for two and a half dollars but he'd let me have a gallon for a dollar. I'd take 'em home for Mama and them.

I loved to eat oysters raw; put 'em in your mouth and they would go down so slick and smooth. If you'd find oysters on a [tidal] creek bank near your home, you could raise your family on that bank, dig those oysters from the mud. I've eaten oysters raw right from the bank and spit the mud out.

"I remember the old oyster roasts," Jenelle said. "We'd get some cement blocks and make a fire pit, and put a tin on top, spread the oysters on the tin, and cover them with a burlap bag. Then we'd sprinkle some water on top and steam 'em. Then we'd take a shovel and shovel them out onto the table. Had any left over, we'd take our oysters home in that croaker sack."

Now they put old oyster shells back out on the banks, they call it cultivatin'. Those shells give young oysters something hard to attach to when they start growin'.

Back then watermelons were plentiful, too. A friend of mine was ridin' down the road in his wagon with a load of unsold watermelons. I said, "How much do you want for those watermelons?" He said, "Cap'n Jack, you can have them for free." I gave him a dollar and a half for that wagonload of watermelons.

When I was working as a salesman for Thomas and Howard, Lib [his wife] dearly loved boiled peanuts, particularly those from my friend Donny Jones. Donny always called Lib "my girl."

One time Donny said, "You in a hurry, Jack?" I told him no. He said, "Let's go down to the farm and get some peanuts for my girlfriend." He didn't pick just a few peanuts, he just pulled up several bunches, filled up the trunk of my car, and we brought them home to Lib. Lib boiled them up good with a lot of salt, then I had to go out and vacuum all that dirt out of the trunk. It was a job. We had so many boiled peanuts left over, Lib packed them into empty milk cartons and froze 'em. We had boiled peanuts for a long time after that.

Charleston street vendor rolls his cart along in the heart of historic Charleston. (Photo courtesy of the Charleston Museum, Charleston, South Carolina.)

But you know what? I told my wife that if I died tomorrow, I know I've lived a good life. Always had a job. Good parents and grandparents. And always had a dollar or two in my pocket. You know what I mean?

A Special Tongue

As Samuel Gaillard Stoney has written, *"Pronunciations, intonations, the sense of words… have taken on a Charlestonian twist."* Native Charlestonians speak with a special tongue, personified by Charleston-born ex-U.S. Senator Ernest "Fritz" Hollings' speeches. The speech patterns and patois of the residents, black and white, have a lyrical quality to them based on French Huguenot, Gullah, and West Indies influences.

There was the story about the unfortunate European who was at a loss attempting to find a Mr. Huger who lived on Legare Street. He finally found a kind native who translated it for him: YOU-gee and Luh-GREE!

A Dictionary of Charlestonese

In the 1960s, the venerable Charleston News and Courier, *the morning voice of Lowcountry conservatism, put out a sprightly* Dictionary of Charlestonese *compiled by popular columnist* "Lord Ashley Cooper," *the nom de plume of staffer Frank Gilbreth.*

Here's a selection of the Charleston Gullah dialect from the pamphlet that I purchased back then, with thanks for permission to reprint from the chairman of today's Charleston Post & Courier, Pierre Manigault.

—A—

A BOOT—Approximately.

AIN'T—Sister of one of your parents.

AIR—What you hear with: "Friends, Romans, countrymen, lend me your airs."

—B—

BALL—To heat a liquid until it bubbles.

BARE—A beverage made from malt and hops.

BARTER—Something to spread on bread.

BONE—A very blessed event, as in "I was bone a Charlestonian."

BO-AT—Something you sail in, off to the Bot'try.

BOY—To purchase.

—C—

CANADA—A politician running for office.

CANE CHEW—Aren't you able to: "Cane chew talk like a good Charlestonian?"

CHALK-LET—A flavor.

CHAIR—"Let me hair you chair and hawler for The Citadel."

COAT—"Stannup for hizzoner, coat's in session."

COINED—Humane: "He was always coined to animals."

—D—

DEARTH—The world we live in.

DES MOINES—They belong to me.

DOLLAR—Less sharp: "My knife was dollar than his."

—F—

FAN-ELLA—The flavor of white ice cream.

FARE—To be a'scairt: "I fare it may rene, snow, and heel."

FLOW—What you stand on in a house.

FORKS—Bushy-tailed animal hunted by red-coated riders.

—G—

GAY-YET—A fence opening.

GO-IT—A smelly animal that eats tin cans.

GRANITE—Given: "He was granite a pardon by the guv-ner."

GROAN—Increasing in size.

—H—

HAIL—The abode of some damyankees and other evil spirits.

HAIR—At this place.

HARMONY—Cooked grits.

HAWSERS—Hay-eating quadrupeds.

HERRING—The auditory function: "Pappa's hard of herring."

HONE—Something on the auto that you blow.

—J—

JELL—Confinement place for criminals.

—K—

KIN—Something usually made of tin that food is packed in.

—L—

LACK—Enjoy: "I lack fried chicken."

LAYMAN—The fruit from which layman-ade is made.

LEAN—A little road: "Lovers' Lean."

LOIN—Not telling the trut'.

LOSS—To mislay: "He loss his match balks."

—M—

MARE—Hizzoner.

MINE EYES—Salad dressing.

MINUET—You and I have dined.

MOW—An additional quantity.

—N—

NEW SAND KOREA—Ashley Cooper's paper. (See Pay-upper)

NOISE—Pleasant: "Noise weather we're having."

—O—

OIL-AND—Body of land surrounded by water.

—P—

PACKING—- Maneuvering an auto to the curb.

PAIN—A writing instrument mightier than the sword.

PAT—Portion, but not all.

PAUNCH—Blow struck with the fist.

PAY-UPPER—What sells for a ne-y-cal and prints news.

PIE-SUN—What you put out to kill roaches.

PLAY-IT—Something you eat grits off of.

POET—To transfer a liquid: "Poet from the pitcher."

POKE—Hog meat.

—R—

RAH-CHAIR—Where you're at.

SANE—Speaking: "I can hardly hair what he's sane."

SEND-WICHES—Food spread on bread, handy for a picnic.

SEX—Two less than eh-et, three less than noine, foe less than tin.

SHOT—Not long.

SNOW—To breathe loudly while sleeping.

—T—

TARRED—Weary.

TIN CIN STOW—The foive and doyme.

TOE—Preposition meaning toward: "I went toe the Oil of Pams.

TOY—Cravat.

TOYED—Something that ebbs and flows in the ocean off the Bottry.

TRUE—Hurled: "He true the ball."

Spoke Gullah as a Kid, Learned "English" in College

My good friend Charles Seabrook, a Lowcountry native, told me about his own experiences with the "Gullah" language after leaving Johns Island, a Charleston suburb, to go to college. We conducted this interview at Chef Scott Peacock's famed Watershed Restaurant in Decatur, Georgia.

Johns Island is my old stomping ground. I grew up on that island. I tell people that I spent half of my boyhood trying to get off the island, and now I spend half of my adulthood trying to figure out how to get back.

Shrimp boats docked at Shem Creek, across the Cooper River from the City of Charleston. (Photo courtesy of the Charleston Convention and Visitors Bureau.)

Growing up there, like everyone else, I spoke the Gullah dialect. I thought everyone spoke that way. When I left Johns Island to go to the University of South Carolina, I had to learn to speak English just to communicate; nobody in the outside world could understand me otherwise.

Everyone loved to fish on Johns Island. Most every morning early, my daddy was down there on the dock just down from our house. He had what we called a drop net, a round thing like a hula hoop, with a net on it. You put some sinkers in it and attached a herring or chicken heads, on a string, and lower 'em into the water. Let 'em sit there for a minute or two. It'd fill up quick. You'd get all kind of shrimp, crabs, mullet. And what we called those little sweet creek shrimp that made popcorn shrimp. My mama made delicious shrimp gravy. I asked her how she made it; she said, "I just make it."

As a boy, one of the first things I'd want to do every day at the island was to go crabbin'. Then I'd go down to Mister John Limehouse's big old country store. He used to sell everything. It was redolent of bananas, smoked herring in a barrel, and cookies kept in big jars on the counter. I loved to open his drink box and feel around in that cold water for a Coca-Cola or a Pepsi.

Later I worked at the other general store run by Mr. John Glover. He'd go off and leave me there to run the place and I'd sit on a hundred-pound sack of rice all day between selling gas and running the cash register.

Speaking of rice, there was seldom a meal, outside of breakfast, that we did not have rice to eat. My mama used to tell about how when I was little, when we went to a lady's house to eat, that I pushed away my plate. My mother would say, "Why aren't you eating, son?"

"There's no dinner here, Mama."

"What do you mean there's no dinner here?"

As it turned out, I was equating rice as dinner! The lady had no rice on my plate!

And my mama loved to cook crab cakes; I don't think she ever thought of using bread [crumbs] in making crab cakes. I remember she'd be in the kitchen many a night, picking the meat off the crabs that Daddy caught that day.

She loved to fix shrimp and mix them up with grits. They were soooo good. And my mother cooked the best cabbage; I can't get my wife to cook 'em like that. Of course a lot of the vegetables down there were cooked with fatback that gave them a superb flavor. A lot of the older folks at Johns Island, like my mother, loved to use fatback in a variety of their foods and yet they lived to ripe old ages. Of course she worked out in the garden a *lot, wearing her big Mexican sombrero. Back then, people on the island like my mother didn't have written recipes. They knew the ingredients to use, and how much salt to add. They did it every day. Today, my sister-in-law, Mildred Seabrook, comes closest to anybody I know in cooking food like my mother did, particularly making that shrimp gravy.*

Johns Island: "The Stronghold of the Gullah Culture"

Dad was postmaster at Johns Island and had several other jobs—farming, working as a bookkeeper in Charleston, and working with his brother in a tugboat business. Only about a thousand people lived there on the island at the time. Many were blacks. Johns Island was said to be the stronghold of the Gullah culture, the voodoo. They call it Cunjuh. Comes from the word conjure. This was said to be the biggest stronghold of voodoo culture outside of Haiti, and Haiti was the biggest stronghold outside of Africa. So the Gullah culture was quite prevalent at Johns Island. Lot of people came down to study the Gullah culture, including Guy and Candi Caraway [famed folklorists] who spent a couple of years there.

I was next to the youngest of ten children and I was pretty low on the pecking order [when the property was divvied up], but the fifteen-acre piece I did get is very nice. It's part of our old family land and my part backs up to the salt marsh. When I was growing up on Johns Island in the '50s and '60s, you couldn't give away land like that, next to an old smelly salt marsh. Now hardly a week goes by that I don't get an inquiry from someone who wants to buy my property.

A SEAMAN'S VIEW OF CHARLESTON
*Black and white all mixed together
Inconstant, strange, unhealthful weather
Burning heat and chilling cold
Dangerous to both young and old
Boisterous winds and heavy rains
Fevers and rheumatic pains
Auges plenty without doubt,
Sores, boils, the prickly heat and gout…
Houses built on barren land
No lamps or lights, but streets of sand
Pleasant walks, if you can find 'em…
Many a widow not unwilling
Many a beau not worth a shilling
Many a bargain if you can strike it
This is Charlestowne, How do you like it?*
—CAPTAIN MARTIN
AN ENGLISH SEA CAPTAIN (1769)

Of course, the problem is that taxes are eatin' me alive. It's prime development property but I'm trying to put it in a conservation easement. The land has been in the family for two hundred years, probably longer. But I feel that I can't give up my heritage so long as I can pay the taxes on it.

Come with me. Below Carolina, we shall create an ideal colony. No one will go hungry, and everyone will have work. It is the opportunity of your lifetime.

—James Oglethorpe in London in 1732

CHAPTER 4

Savannah: The Hostess City

There cannot be, in the whole world, a more beautiful city than Savannah!
—*Fredericka Bremer (1853)*

Everybody has the right to think whose food is the most gorgeous, and I nominate Georgia's.

—*Ogden Nash*
The Savannah Cook Book

*M*idnight in the Garden of Good and Evil, John Berendt's dramatically revealing book that came out in 1994, put Savannah on the map. Not that it wasn't already there. Paris's *LeMonde* years earlier had called Savannah "the most beautiful city in North America." And Conrad Aiken, native-born poet of renown, had described Savannah as "That most magical of cities… that earthly paradise."

The Savannah skyline as seen from the Savannah River. (Photo courtesy of the Savannah Convention and Visitors Bureau.)

But it was far from a paradise in 1733 when its founder, James Edward Oglethorpe, arrived from London with 114 "sober, moral, and industrious" English settlers—thirty-five families. Their vessel *Anne*, "a stout little ship of 200 tons," dropped anchor first at Charleston and then proceeded down the coast to Beaufort.

James Oglethorpe, founder of the Georgia Colony, is depicted in this sketch from the 1700s. (Courtesy of the Georgia Historical Society.)

During the stop near what was to become Port Royal, Oglethorpe declared a day of thanksgiving for their safe arrival. From his own pocket, Oglethorpe paid for a sumptuous feast, including "four fat hogs, eight turkeys, many fowl, English beef and other provisions, and a hogs' head each of punch and beer, and a large quantity of wine." According to the written report of the day's event, "Everything was conducted in the most agreeable manner; no one got drunk, neither was there the least disorder among the crowd."

Theologian John Wesley had described Oglethorpe as "big almost to hugeness, with a wig flowing down his shoulders, heavy jowls, brusque manner—a military man," yet with "a voice mellow in sympathy and understanding."

From Beaufort, Oglethorpe made an advance reconnaissance trip by boat to the site of the new colony. With the help of friendly Creeks, he picked the exact spot for the settlement: a level forest of pines and oaks atop the forty-foot high Yamacraw Bluff. It overlooked the Savannah River "so high it put a man out of breath before he can reach the top."

A few years later, William Bartram would call the new colony, "A wilderness still in the cradle of nature." But the thirty-six-year-old Oglethorpe, a wealthy English aristocrat with a big heart, had a grand vision for what the site could become. His concept would evolve into the first (and one of the best) planned cities in North America. And of course it would become the foundation for England's new colony Georgia, named for Britain's King George the Second.

In his first report to the British trustees, Oglethorpe wrote:

"The [Savannah] River has formed a half moon, around the side of which the banks are about forty feet high, and on top of a flat which they call a bluff…Upon the river-side, in the center of the plain, I have laid out the town, opposite to which is an island of very rich pasturage. The river is pretty wide, the water fresh, and from the quay of the town you can see its whole course to the sea [16 miles away]."

The newcomers arrived January 30, 1733, in a sloop and five periaguas. As they neared the Yamacraw bluff, an armed British contingent fired a welcoming salute. An hour later, eighty-year-old Tomo-chi-chi, mico of the Lower Creek Yamacraws, welcomed the settlers, "his bare chest marked by sweeping black tattoos of bear claws," and accompanied by his wife, Senawky.

According to University of Georgia professor Phinzy Spalding in his authoritative *Oglethorpe in America*, the chief was preceded by

an Indian singing, dancing, and carrying a giant feather fan and rattles. He waved his fan over Oglethorpe, stroking him on every side. Oglethorpe then invited the natives into his tent for a formal ceremony.

The arrival went smoothly, thanks to an attractive interpreter, half-breed Creek Indian Princess Mary Musgrove (born Coosaponakeesa), who with her husband, white trader John Musgrove, operated a nearby trading post. Afterward, the Indians served the newcomers "roast, boiled pork, buffalo, beef, fowl, pancakes, and tea."

On another occasion, the Native Americans served the new arrivals deer and wild boar barbecued over large open pits, plus platters of oysters, clams, shrimp, turkey, roasted corn, wild berries, honey, nuts, and seeds. After all this, the Indians performed tribal dances for the settlers, who in turn treated the Indians to several English Country dances accompanied by instruments strange to the natives' ears.

During the ensuing weeks, Oglethorpe and Charleston's Colonel William Bull laid out the new settlement with the help of black slaves from South Carolina. Some accounts said Oglethorpe's inspiration for the Savannah-to-be came from a sketch in the book *Villas of the Ancients* by Oglethorpe's good friend Robert Castell. It was said that when Castell died of smallpox in Fleet Jail, one of the infamous English debtor gaols, Oglethorpe was stirred to chair a commission to clean up such prisons, and secondly, to persuade King George to open a colony in America to offer a second chance to people such as Castell whom he described as "gentlemen of decayed circumstances…some undone by guardians, some by lawsuits, some by accidents in commerce…" But none of Savannah's first settlers came from British prisons.

Oglethorpe was generous to his new Savannahians, each of whom received a sixty-by-ninety-foot in-town lot, a five-acre garden in the town common, and forty-five acres for farming outside the town. Each head of household was also given a musket and bayonet, a hammer, a hatchet, a handsaw, a gimlet, an iron pot and frying pan, and a watch coat, plus forty-four gallons of "strong beer."

On the ten-acre Trustees Garden, the newcomers planted mulberry trees and grape vines that were envisioned as the beginning of a silk and wine industry (both of which failed), plus oranges, olives, figs, peaches, "and many curious herbs."

> *In Atlanta, the first question people ask when they meet you is, "What business are you in?" In Augusta, it's "What was your grandmother's maiden name?" In Macon, it's "What's your religion?" In Savannah, it's "What would you like to drink?"*
> —Colin Bessonette
> Back Roads of Georgia

A year and a half later, in December 1734, with quite a few houses completed and occupied, settler Robert Parker sent a letter to the trustees in London:

"Being Christmas Eve, my people desired leave to go out this morning to provide themselves a dinner, tho we have good Beeff, Porke, Cheese Flower ec. They are now come home and have brought 3 ½ Couple of Ducks 1 pair of Doves one Turkey and a fine Buck together with a fine young pig."

Parker and others drank "best beer" with their Christmas dinners (rum was prohibited), and Parker himself ordered twenty hogsheads of beer to be shipped from London by "freight cheepe."

In 1736, the first five-hundred-acre plantation in the new colony, Wormsloe, was established on the Isle of Hope south of Savannah. The London trustees awarded it to Noble Jones, the town's constable and surveyor. It is today a state historic site, featuring a long entrance road flanked by live oaks and described as "the most beautiful avenue in America."

From the start, Oglethorpe welcomed all from Europe, mainly Protestants. Some of the earliest settlers, in addition to the English, included Scotch-Irish and Irish Catholics from Ulster, German Salzbergers, and European Jews. One commentator noted that "there was a babble of languages spoken among the five hundred residents who trod Savannah's sandy paths, including English, German, French, Spanish, and various African and Native American dialects." By the mid-1800s, the Irish and the Europeans made up more than half of the city's population.

Years later, a joke made the rounds: "The Jews own Savannah, the Irish run it, and the Crackers enjoy it." And two centuries after its founding, Savannah would trumpet its well-earned title of being Georgia's "Hostess City."

At Oglethorpe's urging, among the early visitors who came from England in 1736 were two energetic young Anglican brothers, John and Charles Wesley. In less than two years, however, Charles departed the colony, leaving a pastorate at St. Simons Island where his Fredericka congregation had dwindled to two Presbyterians and one Baptist. He returned to London, where he gained fame for writing more than six thousand hymns, including "Christ the Lord Is Risen Today" and "Hark, the Herald Angels Sing."

His brother John was disappointed at his inability to convert Tomo-chi-chi to the Christian faith. The Indian chief told Wesley, "Christians drunk! Christians beat men! Christians tell lies. Me no Christian!"

Although John Wesley was credited with starting in Savannah the world's first Sunday school class with separate instruction for children (at Christ Episcopal Church), he also left the Georgia colony shortly after his brother.

"I shook off the [Georgia] dust of my feet," John Wesley later recalled, "after having preached the gospel there not as I ought, but as I was able." Back in London he became the key founder of the Methodist Church.

In July 1743, James Oglethorpe himself, at age forty-seven—after a decade dedicated to the newly founded colony including a decisive St. Simons Island defeat of the Spanish in the Battle of Bloody Marsh—also left Savannah.

As he prepared to leave, a lightning strike demolished the colony's flagstaff. The following week, two of the five oaks left standing on the Savannah bluff were destroyed by another bolt of lightning.

Finally, Oglethorpe departed on July 22, 1743, without incident, never to return. Back in London, he was reelected to a seat in the British Parliament. His statue stands today among the oaks of Savannah's Chippewa Park.

During the following century, Savannah went through many ups and downs, including pirate attacks, hurricanes, fires, and the Revolutionary War, made notable by the city's "Liberty Boys" movement, followed by the Civil War eight decades later.

Although the Georgia colony's trustees prohibited slavery for seventeen years, the British Parliament relented under planters' pressures and legalized the practice in 1750. Carolina and West Indies planters began moving into Georgia to carve out rice plantations in the bottomlands of the Altamaha, Ogeechee, and Savannah Rivers. They created cotton plantations on the barrier islands like Sapelo and St. Simons, as well as deeper inland where short-staple cotton was beginning to flourish.

Soon, with the ensuing slave trade boom, cotton became king, propelling the Savannah port into a major player, shipping thousands of bales to mills in Britain and New England. The 1793 invention of the cotton gin by a Yale-trained tutor, Eli Whitney, at nearby Mulberry Plantation only boosted the stimulus. By the onset of the Civil War, the state's cotton production had zoomed to an amazing seven hundred thousand

Statue of James Oglethorpe, which stands today in Savannah's Chippewa Park. (Photo courtesy of the Savannah Convention and Visitors Bureau.)

bales year, with each compressed bale weighing five hundred pounds.

The grand finale of Savannah's role in the Civil War—called "the War of Northern Aggression" by many Southerners—came when, miracle of miracles, General William Tecumseh Sherman's Union Army, having spared little in its destructive march from Atlanta to the coast—gave Savannah a pass. This was thanks to the diplomatic intervention by the mayor and other leaders who met up with General Sherman before he reached the city limits. Sherman soon took over one of Savannah's beautiful mansions, the Green-Meldrim House. It was from there that he sent to President Lincoln the following note, one of the great pieces of correspondence to come out of the War Between the States:

Savannah, GA. Dec. 22, 1864
To his Excellency, President Lincoln

Dear Sir,
   I beg to present you as a Christmas Gift, the City of Savannah with 150 heavy guns
and plenty of ammunition; and also about 25,000 bales of cotton.

W. T. Sherman
Maj. Genl.

President Lincoln's Reply:

Many, many thanks for your Christmas gift—the capture of Savannah…but what next?
I suppose it will be safe if I leave General Grant and yourself to decide.

Meanwhile, historic downtown Savannah, built into an elegant checkerboard series of twenty-four parks as envisioned by Oglethorpe, blossomed into a city of beauty, grace, and charm. In 1820 Englishman James Silk Buckingham asserted, "Philadelphia itself is not more perfect in its symmetry than Savannah."

In her haunting *Lost Legacy of the Golden Isles,* Betsy Fancher wrote that Savannah had become not so much a city as a region of the heart, with a quality of grace and leisure that had nearly vanished from urban life in industrialized America.

The city Lady Astor once called "a beautiful woman with a dirty face" is now, according to Ms. Fancher's writings, "a seductive and overpowering beauty." She cited azalea-splashed squares, grill-fretted row houses, walled gardens patterned with camellias and boxwood, the waterfront's torch-lit restaurants, and its "moss-shrouded cemeteries with their immutable stone angels…"

Many of the squares, considered the city's "precious jewels," are named for people with historic links to Savannah over the years, beginning, of course, with Oglethorpe, and including the Marquis de Lafayette, James Madison, Benjamin Franklin, and George Washington.

In the early 1940s, Hal Steed, a Georgia newspaperman, expressed delight in downtown Savannah: "European in appearance, with a festive, cosmopolitan air as befits a seaport with international contacts. Easy-going, yet alive with trading activity…" And Savannahians, it was said, favor large verandas, small gardens, "and any courtyard or patio where they can take advantage of the gentle climate…"

One of Savannah's favorite sons, songwriter and singer Johnny Mercer (1909–1976), arguably America's greatest lyricist and author of such classics as "That Old Black Magic," "Blues in the Night," "Fools Rush In," and "Moon River," grew up in Savannah and spent summers at the Mercer country home, riding out in the family's T-model Ford on a crushed oyster shell road flanked on either side by live oaks splashed with Spanish moss.

"It was a sweet indolent background for a boy to grow up in," he wrote. "Savannah was smaller then and sleepy, full of trees and azaleas that filled the parks…."

In 1951, Mercer's "In the Cool, Cool, Cool of the Evening" (his lyrics with Hoagy Carmichael's music) spotlighted some of the foods that he likely remembered from his Savannah years: barbecue, bouillabaisse stew, ham, steaks, and layer cakes. And in his "Lazy Bones," he wrote that, "Long as there is chicken gravy on your rice, Everything is nice."

But in the 1950s, some of the beautiful old buildings in the heart of Historic Savannah began deteriorating and bulldozers began making destructive inroads. All, of course, in the name of progress, and in some cases just to salvage Savannah's celebrated gray bricks. One of the big shockers came in 1954, when the grand old City Market on Ellis Square was demolished to make room for a parking garage. That set off a rallying cry by a small group of furious and determined women, headed by Mrs. Anna Hunter. They in turn aroused a larger cadre of Savannah's finest movers and shakers. Standing down the developers, they created the Historic Savannah Foundation. In time, most of the older buildings identified as being in danger of bulldozing were subsequently restored.

Savannah today, with its two-and-a-half-square-mile historic district, is a living museum of earlier centuries. In particular, Savannah showcases the architecture of the 1700s and 1800s, with homes ranging from Greek Revival to Georgian Colonial, Classical Revival, and Victorian. Many were built of the previously mentioned, highly prized gray Savannah brick.

Savannah's most infamous mansion in the historic district today is the Mercer-Williams house on Monterey Square. It was completed at the end of the Civil War by General Hugh Mercer, Johnny Mercer's great-grandfather. During the height of the 1990s' *Midnight in the Garden of Good and Evil* publicity bubble, the Mercer House was the heart of John Berendt's novelistic bestseller that detailed the shooting there and the subsequent trials of its owner, antique collector Jim Williams. After Williams's death (before the publication of Berendt's book), his house went to his sister, Dorothy Kingery, and quickly became a prime stop for tour buses. Though the house was closed to visitors, some fans would climb up on the gate for better views. Ms. Kingery fought back as best she could to discourage such tourist exploitation, but in 2004 she quietly opened the mansion's first floor to paying guests.

One of Savannah's unique architectural trademarks is its cast-iron raised stoops. Conrad Aiken wrote of "That wonderful stoop…which led to the second story, with its iron railing and brownstone stops…"

The late Charles Kuralt also fell in love with Savannah, particularly its springtimes. In his *A Life on the Road,* he praised the city's beauty, "when the yellow forsythia gives way to the dogwood, dazzling white. Then the citizens feel the urge to inhale April while strolling the cobblestones of the waterfront…"

And as the Savannah Symphony Orchestra noted in its classic cookbook, *Savannah la Carte,* "To walk through the squares of the Historic District with their moss-decked oaks and blazing azaleas, is to return to a past when cotton was king and square-riggers lined the wharves on the river."

THE WAVING GIRL OF SAVANNAH

In 1972 the City of Savannah erected a bronze statue on River Street honoring "The Waving Girl of Savannah," Florence Martus (1869–1943).

Florence, sister of the Elba Island lighthouse keeper, was well known to seamen as she waved a greeting to ships entering Savannah Harbor. At night, Florence used a lantern to flash her greeting.

The Savannah Waving Girl, Savannah's symbol of hospitality (Photo courtesy of the Savannah Convention and Visitors Bureau.)

The story goes that Florence's waving was related to a sailor who stole her heart but who had left Savannah and never returned. Even after her death, stories were told of seeing her waving, such as the Savannahian who had come back to Savannah after a twenty-year absence and reported seeing the waving girl. He was told that she had been dead for seven years.

—Colin Bessonette, Back Roads of Georgia

Remembering the Good Life in Savannah

My friend, Savannah native Sally Bond (Mrs. Louis) Tonsmeire, grew up in the Hostess City, the daughter of the Rev. and Mrs. James Sullivan Bond.

Her father attended the Episcopal Virginia Seminary at Alexandria, Virginia. He served his first post as rector of Christ Church Fredericka on St. Simons Island. He also served twice a month as rector of the Jekyll Island Chapel. When Sally was a little girl, her parents bought "a wonderful cottage" at Tybee, Savannah's long beachfront suburb. "So every summer I spent three months there at the beach," she said. The old Tybrisa pier-pavillion at Tybee was another Savannah landmark where her parents and grandparents would join Savannah's elite in dancing to big-name dance bands. Her maternal grand-parents, the Pierponts, also had a summer home at Tybee Island. Her grandfather had a manufacturing business in Savannah, so he would take the train into the city to work.

Savannah native Sally Tonsmeire holds her paternal grandmother Elise Bond's recipe book. Lower photo shows the former home of her grandparents, James and Elise Bond, on Washington Avenue in historic Savannah. (Upper photo by the author; lower photo courtesy of Sally Tonsmeire.)

Sally spoke of equally enjoyable times visiting her paternal grandparents, Elise Guerard and James Sullivan Bond, who lived at 35 Washington Avenue not far from Victory Drive. There was an alleyway behind their house, Sally said, "and the black folks would come by with big baskets on their heads, selling seafoods and vegetables and singing some wonderful rhymes."

The Bonds had servants, including a cook, a nurse, and a chauffeur, "and meals were served very formally by the servants in the dining room. We were not allowed to eat in the kitchen with the servants, even though we loved to." She remembered the time her grandfather caught her brother in the kitchen eating.

"Young man," she recalled her grandfather saying, "you will either come to the dining room table to eat like a gentleman or you will leave this house."

"So my brother chose to eat in the dining room."

After her grandmother Bond was in a car wreck, her grandfather arranged for their chauffeur to drive Sally's grandmother around town. "It was so much like the movie, *Driving Miss Daisy*," Sally said.

A favorite eating spot for her parents and grandparents was the Johnny Harris Restaurant on Victory Drive. "That was the most popular restaurant in Savannah at the time," she said. It's still going strong as a popular dining destination.

Sally Tonsmeire also spent summers with her Pierpont great-grandparents, Wallace Joshua and Sarah Perkins Pierpont, at their home at the Isle of Hope. "I used to ride the open-air street car to get out there and I always had a wonderful time," she recalled. (One of her Pierpont ancestors, James Lord Pierpont, became famous for writing "Jingle Bells" in 1857. Still another ancestor founded Yale University.)

Sally told me that her great-grandparents, the McKees, had

> ### ISLE OF HOPE'S BEAUTIFUL BLUFF DRIVE
> *One of the most scenic streets in all of scenic Savannah is Isle of Hope's Bluff Drive, with beautiful old estate-type homes (some dating to pre–Civil War) on one side and the wide Skidaway River, dotted with private docks and numerous boats, on the other…*
>
> *Majestic live oak trees draped with Spanish moss line both sides of the street, with arching limbs reaching out, creating a tunnel for those passing by…*
>
> *Many of the early African Americans in Savannah were baptized in the Skidaway River at the oyster shell beach…*
>
> *Some of the original docks on the Skidaway River were double decker, built when ladies did not swim in public. While men swam in the river, the women sat in the closely slatted bottom story and swam in the enclosed pool underneath…*
>
> *A number of films have been shot here including* Cape Fear *with Robert Mitchum and* Gator *with Burt Reynolds. For the move* Glory, *the street was covered with dirt to simulate the time period.*
>
> —MOSS, MARSHES & MEMORABLE MEALS
> ISLE OF HOPE UNITED METHODIST WOMEN

a home in Beaufort before the Civil War and are buried at Beaufort's St. Helena Episcopal Church. She was told that when the Union troops came through on their way to Columbia, South Carolina, Sherman gave the McKee home to their black overseer, George Smalls.

"After the war, my great-grandmother went back to Beaufort, and George Smalls and his wife, then residing in the old McKee Home, took care of her there until she died. I thought that was awfully kind of them. The Smalls must have loved my great-grandmother very much."

When Sally was younger, she went out to the Savannah Yacht Club with her friends. "The only way we could get out there was to have Grandfather's chauffeur take us. We were so embarrassed when riding up in a chauffeur-driven car; we would hide on the floor in the backseat so our other friends wouldn't see us."

As a young lady Mrs. Tonsmeire also attended Savannah's debutante balls. "They always served that potent Artillery Punch," she laughed. "You had to be very careful not to drink too much of it!"

Crabbing and Fishing off Tybee Island

Tybee Island Lighthouse. (Photo courtesy of the Savannah Convention and Visitors Bureau.)

Although her parents and brother Jim were big into fishing, Sally Tonsmeire opted to go crabbing instead.

"I'd put those chicken necks out in the sun so they would be good and smelly," she recalled, "and I'd take them out to the north end of Tybee where the rocks were, and let that line down. After a little while," she said, "I'd feel that crab nibble and I'd pull it up ever so slowly and then I'd take my crab net and scoop him up."

Placing the crabs in a bushel basket, she would take her day's catch home where her mother would cook them. "She'd spread newspapers all around the dining room table, and we'd pick the meat out. To tell the truth I ate as much as I picked!" Sally remembered cooking crab stew from a recipe that her mother had inherited from her grandmother. "It was soooo good. But Daddy had to translate the recipe for me where it called for a 'jill' of sherry."

In cooking shrimp, her mother mostly boiled them "and we ate them with cocktail sauce. Sometimes my mother would fry them just a few minutes until they turned pink."

Sally's brother Jim started fishing and shrimping when he was ten or twelve years old. He'd take his boat on the Savannah River Tybee Inlet "and he would spend hours and hours out there by himself. He'd cast his net and catch all the shrimp we could eat. Our parents never gave it a thought that he stayed

> ## SAVANNAH'S SAINT PATRICK'S DAY PARADE
> One of Savannah's nationally recognized events comes every March 17 with the annual Saint Patrick's Day Parade. The city's population doubles as visitors pack the downtown streets and the waterfront. The first parade occurred on March 17, 1813, organized by the Hibernian Society. With occasional lapses, the event has taken place ever since. The public rituals are perpetuated by the Hibernians and Irish Catholics, many of whose ancestors came to Savannah during the great potato famine of the 1840s. The modern-day celebration "is something akin to Mardi Gras"—part civic, part religious, and mostly fun when everything to eat or drink takes on the color green, including beer and grits.

out there alone so long." Today, Sally's brother is "Captain Jim," taking Savannah bar pilots out to board incoming ships to guide them up the Savannah River docks.

She recalled going with her parents to the great Williams Seafood Restaurant, which later burned. It was on the road to Tybee. "We children considered it a great treat to go out there. They had the most wonderful seafood. It was a large, one-story building, very plain." Her mother also took her and her siblings to the old Triple X eatery on Victoria Drive. "That's where we drank a type of root beer milk shake. We all loved it, very much."

Newsman Ben Green Cooper's Remembrances

A *Savannah Morning News* and *Evening Press* police reporter at the turn of the twentieth century, the late Ben Green Cooper had nostalgic memories of his native city. I got to know Ben briefly when he worked later at newspapers in Rome and Marietta, Georgia. He packed many Savannah memories into his delightful privately published 1967 book, *Savannah's Cookin': Well-Remembered by a Somewhat Prodigal Son Who Loves Crab, Shrimp, Fish, Oysters and the Traditional Fatted Lamb.*

It was in Savannah's Yamacraw community, he wrote, that he "first heard the pleasant, slurring dialects of Gullah and Geechee, differing, yet similar, both being adaptations of English as diluted with African words."

Cooper was born on Savannah's Jones Street not far from where the late Mrs. Sema Wilkes started her boardinghouse restaurant. Later he moved with his family to the Collinsville and Cattle Park neighborhoods.

He remembered traveling the seven-mile trip to downtown Savannah by horse and buggy or by taking the Montgomery-Isle of Hope trolley line. "The horse plodded a familiar route along dirt streets of Yamacraw," he wrote, "stopping by habit at key points where Dad would collect rents, swap pleasantries with tenants, and at noon we detoured to the B&B Cafe, where hard-crusted rolls dotted with seeds were wonderful. The cuisine was Grecian-American as interpreted by Negro cooks." Cooper wrote of his family's buying shrimp, fish, and vegetables from peddler carts.

He recalled that at Cattle Park, his mother buried Spanish moss in marsh muds

> ## YOU MAY BE A GEECHEE IF...
>
> *If you were born in Savannah or Chatham County, Georgia, you can rightly be called a "Geechee," according to esteemed Georgia historian and author Dr. Del Presley. A retired English and history professor at Georgia Southern University in Statesboro, Presley says the phrase comes from the Ogeechee River that runs two hundred and thirty miles from Greene County in middle Georgia, down through southeastern Georgia to the coast.*
>
> *In an interview at his home in Statesboro, Georgia, I asked Dr. Presley if he thought that the river was the namesake for the "Geechee" phrase.*
>
> *"Absolutely," he replied, "and we can document it."*
>
> *"The Ogeechee River," Presley said, "ends just south of Savannah, and you had all these plantations along the river upstream. From the early days, the black people who worked the plantation fields were called 'Geechee blacks' or just 'Geechees.'"*
>
> *While the term "Geechee" referred originally to blacks, it later came to embrace whites as well. Today, Professor Presley said, "We think Geechee can refer to anyone, black or white, who grew up as a native-born person in Chatham County."*

for months, then used the hairlike fibers to stuff mattresses. "In the overflow of the ram pumping artesian water," he wrote, "she grew watercress for salads. Nearby [at a creek] a trap kept our larder supplied with blue crabs."

He remembered "Old Albert," a strong half-breed Indian woman who strode miles from and to her shack on Montgomery Cross Road near Waters Avenue, and planted and hoed [the] garden at our home, "doing more in a day than three men do today. Albert became irked when a small boy mocked her and she chased him towards the house, brandishing a grubbing hoe. Mother halted the chase and applied a peach twig to young legs for a well-remembered lesson, not to sass."

Cooper wrote that Albert had ended up in Savannah after eating pineapples up North, and afterward walking south looking for the land where it grew. "She got as far as Chatham County, Savannah, found an old shack and lived there until she was a hundred years old."

"In her later years," Cooper wrote, neighbors tore down her battered shack and built her a nice new home and gave it to her. "But Albert wouldn't live in it." She felt the house was too nice for her dog to occupy, so Albert slept under the house with her old dog.

Cooper remembered his family's days living in Savannah's Collinsville neighborhood, where backyard oyster roasts were a frequent enjoyment.

"Unshucked oysters were washed clean of mud," he wrote, "laid on a steel sheet under which a fire had turned into hot coals, and wet crocus sacking was placed over the oysters. After a few minutes, the Pop! Pop! Pop! of the oysters said they were done and ready to be opened with steel oyster knives, then consumed with catsup or chili sauce and crackers."

He recalled the hilarious "Bill Biffen" columns written for Savannah's *Evening Press* by William Greenleaf Sutlive. "Occasionally 'Bill Biffen' whetted the appetites of Savannahians by referring to the wonderful crab stew he had just eaten at Allen Broome's cafe a few blocks south on Whitaker Street."

THE PIRATES HOUSE LEGENDS

"Fifteen men on a dead man's chest…and the devil take the rest." So it is told, said Flint, the most treacherous of all pirates, as he lay dying in an upstairs room of what is now Savannah's Pirates' House Restaurant. Built in 1753, it is legendary for strange happenings.

As a tavern and inn, The Pirates' House welcomed the buccaneer brothers Jean and Pierre Lafitte. It also saw the likes of "Billy Bones," "Black Dog," and "Blackbeard." (In Treasure Island, Robert Louis Stevenson says, "Blackbeard was a child of Flint.")

Most believe it is Flint's murderous voice heard on moonless nights, along with the cursing of his crew and the cries of those they killed. A veil of sadness hangs over parts of the Pirates' House. It may be those who were shanghaied. Drunk or unconscious, they were often dragged through secret tunnels that led to the Savannah River. They awoke to find themselves enslaved on an outward-going ship. Some may have preferred the quick death that followed any failure to swear to the pirates' oath.

—First Come, First Served, in Savannah

On the New Tybee Road at Bull River, Mrs. T. W. Williams discovered a secret of crab meat cookery, Cooper wrote, and sold motorists hundreds of deviled crabs daily. "Mrs. Williams started off selling fresh fish in a small shack," and later, about 1940, moved to the west side of the highway, enlisting the help of her husband and their son, Hubert, eventually seating several hundred customers in a much bigger restaurant.

"Mother loved the place and would stop on the way home from Tybee to Savannah, picking up some of the stuffed deviled crabs for supper."

CHAPTER 5

Beautiful Beaufort by the Sea

Beaufort, for all its turbulent history of wars and hurricanes, preserves its Old-World charm and tranquility. Almost inaccessible until the advent of good roads…the march of progress has touched it lightly and in appearance it is today very much as it was a century and a half ago.

—South Carolina WPA Guide (1936)

Nestled in among live oaks…at the head of a system of creeks and estuaries called Beaufort River, the once sleepy Southern town is one of the loveliest on the East Coast.

—John Martin Taylor

Beaufort is *"a place where fresh water meets salt and where creeks, marshes, and rivers meld with sunshine, tides, and sea breezes."*

—Southern Living

Palmetto trees line Beaufort's Port Royal Sound Waterfont. (Photo courtesy of Beaufort-Port Royal Convention and Visitors Bureau.)

I've had an ongoing love affair with beautiful Beaufort since the spring of 1945, when our upstate high school basketball champion team from Lancaster County drove down to Beaufort for the state title game.

Although I was serving only as the team's manager (i.e., the go-fer, mostly looking after the bandages, basketballs, and score books), I'll never forget the ever-so-cordial reception we received on our first visit to the Lowcountry. The Beaufort townspeople warmly welcomed our team with open arms and put us up in some of their fabulous historic homes up the incline from Bay Street.

Coming from the poorer section of the state (and having no gymnasium!), we were overwhelmed, indeed stunned, by Beaufort's gracious people and their magnificent mansions (to our young eyes) filled with antique period furniture unknown to us, along with dinner tables that glittered with silver and china.

We lost the game by one point, but I'll never forget Beaufort's charming Southern hospitality, plus the ever-so-wonderful food!

It was also my first time viewing the coastal area's magnificent countryside. As we drove down through Dorchester and Colleton Counties, we were dazzled by row after row of lush springtime vegetables that flashed by our car windows. We were amazed at such a flat yet beautiful country and commented among ourselves that the fields of

Photo depicts an oyster company that operated in Beaufort in the 1940s. Workers are pictured "shucking" oysters from their shells. The firm also distributed canned oysters in the earlier era. (Photo courtesy Harry Chakides.)

tender young plants of cabbages, beans, onions, okra, and the like were weeks ahead of our upstate crops.

Beaufort County, located in the heart of the Lowcountry about halfway between Charleston and Savannah, is made up of sixty-four islands surrounded by a seafood treasure. From Beaufort, shrimp boats can be seen at work in the distant horizon. And with the daily rise of huge tides, the sound's tributaries, marshes, and creeks are flush with shrimp, crabs, and fish. Oysters abound on the banks of creeks and estuaries, and nearby Bluffton is the home of South Carolina's last remaining oyster shucking operation. The area is also blessed with abundant truck crops growing in the county, including islands such as St. Helena. At one time, Beaufort County led the nation in the harvesting of tomatoes followed closely by melons, corn, okra, and corn, among other vegetables.

Beaufort and the Port Royal Sound have an intriguing history that goes back to the 1500s. France, Spain, and England all cast envious eyes at the big bay. Spain and France established some of their earliest colonies there, both of which failed.

In 1562 French seaman and explorer Jean Ribaut, writing to Gaspard II de Coligny in Paris, called the Beaufort Sound "one of the greatest and fairest havens in the world, where without danger all ships in the world might be harbored." He named the place Port Royal Sound, noted later for its deep waters and powerful eight- to nine-foot tides.

In 1670 South Carolina's first English colonists came close to settling in Beaufort rather than Charleston. But taking the advice of a local Indian chief, the newcomers from London voted instead to go on up the coast to what they named Albemarle Point. In time, Albemarle Point became Charles Towne, and later moved farther down to Oyster Point on the peninsula's tip.

Actually, Britain had laid claim to the Port Royal Sound area in the 1600s. The first English settlers—mainly planters and traders seeking to make their fortune in indigo—founded Beaufort in 1711, making it South Carolina's second oldest city. It was named for Englishman Henry Somerset, the second Duke of Beaufort.

Indigo, and later rice, provided the primary crops for local plantations prior to the 1776 Declaration of Independence. After the war, long-staple Sea Island cotton, "the finest grown in America," became the big moneymaker for planters on nearby barrier islands such as St. Helena, Hilton Head, and Daufuskie. Meanwhile, cotton plantations farther inland prospered with the use of Eli Whitney's newly invented cotton gin on its short-staple cotton. Thousands of five-hundred-pound bales were shipped weekly to mills in New England and England.

It's no wonder that from the start, seemingly everyone loved Beaufort, particularly the inland planters who descended on Beaufort during the summers in the years prior to the Civil War. The aforementioned 1940 South Carolina WPA Guide noted, "Seldom is the day that the sun does not shine on Beaufort, and flowers are always in bloom. Scarlet poinsettias are framed against tabby walls; an avenue of palmettos lines Boundary Street. Great spreading live oaks, festooned with Spanish moss, weave shifting patterns on the narrow, crooked streets…Beneath the trees, a carpet of lush grass slopes down to ancient sea walls, and through green vistas gleams the gray-green tidal river, with little fleets of sailboats in the bay beyond."

And the admiration extended to wealthy Europeans, who also fell in love with Beaufort and its environs. After all it is a natural seaside paradise, boasting a smaller-scale ambiance rivaling that of Charleston and Savannah. In more recent times, the old *LIFE* magazine named Beaufort the "Most Romantic City on the East Coast." For five years running, *Southern Living* magazine's readers have picked Beaufort as the "Best Small Town" in the South.

Beaufort is noted for its twelve square blocks of elegant mansions, many of which were built in the 1700s and 1800s. The homes range from Classical Revival to adapted small plantation houses. Spotted here and there are homes with an air of semitropical Spanish influence and others with the more formal Georgian architecture.

The houses were designed primarily for coolness. The South Carolina Guide noted that with high basements and spacious verandas, "they are set in old-fashioned gardens where yellow jessamine, moss, and wisteria intermingle; where oleanders, camellias, and evergreens grow riotously."

Beaufort and its great homes were saved from Civil War destruction, since from the early months of the war,

> *Henry Bernard, visiting in Beaufort, South Carolina [in the 1800s], was served strawberries with rich cream and white sugar in the evening.*
>
> *Harriett Martineau observed that planters' families sometimes sat around the table in the evening, but that more commonly a tray was handed around and the guests took plates, which they held on their laps. Tea or coffee was drunk with waffles, ham, beef, and cake.*
>
> *Somewhat later, just before going to bed, guests were offered cake and wine.*
>
> —JOE GRAY TAYLOR
> EATING, DRINKING, AND VISITING IN THE SOUTH

Union troops occupied and used Port Royal and Beaufort as their Southeastern seacoast blockading base against Confederate maritime movements. Indeed the Northern naval forces had occupied the Sea Islands up and down the South Atlantic Coast, including nearby St. Helena Island.

One of the Beaufort area's historic landmarks is the famous Penn Center, located on St. Helena Island. The school was created prior to the Civil War to educate slaves as part of the Port Royal Experiment supported by Northern abolitionists. After the war began, plantation owners, hearing of Union naval forces moving in, fled the Sea Islands by the droves, leaving the freed slaves to fend for themselves. The earliest Penn Center classes were started in a single room of Oaks Plantation. Due to the blacks' eagerness to learn to read and write and become self-sufficient, the school soon outgrew the room and moved into the Brick Baptist Church and later into a prefab building sent there by Philadelphia abolitionists.

By the 1960s, Penn Center had become a major African-American institution. Martin Luther King Jr. used the college-like center as a retreat where he did much of his writing. He was said to have planned his 1963 March on Washington while staying at the center's Grant Cottage.

In Beaufort many people "entertain" on their docks overlooking tranquil tidal creeks with names such as Rock Springs, Combahee and Whale Branch. A simple appetizer such as French Bread Pesto comes in handy, as you may have unexpected guests come by boat!

—Full Moon, High Tide: Tastes & Traditions of the Lowcountry
(Beaufort Academy Parents Association)

Ervena Faulkner on Lowcountry Food, with a Bit of Guidance

While in Beaufort and environs during a research trip in May of 2008, I had the privilege of visiting with one of the area's interesting characters, retired educator Ervena Faulkner. A native South Carolinian who for many years taught school along with her husband Willie ("T.O.") Faulkner, Ervena writes a sprightly food column for the *Beaufort Gazette*.

We met at Bill Green's Gullah Grub restaurant a few miles out of Beaufort on St. Helena Island. (See other stories on Bill Green in chapter 2 and chapter 19.)

I asked Mrs. Faulkner about her favorite foods.

"All seafoods are my favorites," she said. "I like shrimp and crabs (particularly crab cakes), and I love flounder and croaker, mussels, and mullet."

Ervena Faulkner. (Photo by the author.)

Even though she resides in the heart of Lowcountry seafood country, her true favorite is peanuts. "I loooovve peanuts," she said. "I mostly roast them in the oven. Set it on 350°F for ten minutes. Turn the oven off and let them stay in the oven until they cool, and eat them in the shell with no salt. I do put a put a little oil on them."

And then she loves collards. "I chop my collards, cut the stems about an eighth of an inch before putting them in the pot with a piece of fatback."

She told me that the easy availability of food "has placed our people at risk of obesity, high blood pressure, heart disease, and diabetes."

As a retired African-American female who has reached "the age of creativity," she feels vulnerable to health problems, and although she has good genes, she rejects some of her parents' food preferences.

"Mama was a lover of meat more than I am. But I inherited her sweet tooth, her love of salads, and her desire to prepare wholesome meals." Her mother lived to the age of eighty-nine, surviving for nine years after experiencing a heart attack and stroke.

"Now my father loved his pork; he favored every part of the hog," she recalled. "He ate six meals a day, the last one at 10 p.m." before going to bed, "and he was a great lover of coffee." He stopped smoking at age seventy, she said, and lived to age ninety, dying of kidney failure.

Her parents counseled her about lifestyle and eating habits. "Everything cannot be wrapped up in a meal," her father told her. "How you treat people means more than what you chew."

And her mother urged her to zero in on good and noble thoughts. "If you treat people right," her mother often told Ervena, "you'll have a good life."

"So as I make resolutions every New Year's Eve," she said. "I try to follow up during the year to model after my parents and to be a good role model for my children and the grands."

In her columns she preaches the need to eat healthy, low-fat foods, a variety of fruits, vegetables, fish, skinless poultry, and lean meats. And she stresses regular physical exercise.

Speaking of good foods, here is her recipe for crab cakes, with thanks to the *Beaufort Gazette,* in which it was published. This recipe will yield fifteen servings.

Beaufort-Style Crab Cakes

- 2 tablespoons margarine
- 1 green bell pepper, diced fine
- 1 red bell pepper, diced fine
- 1 stalk celery, diced fine
- ½ onion, diced fine
- ½ cup mushrooms, diced fine
- 1 lb. crab (claw meat), well picked
- ½ cup water or fish stock
- Dash each ground red, white, and black pepper
- Dash of salt
- 2 slices white bread, cut into small pieces

Using a sauté pan, sauté the margarine, bell peppers, celery, onion, and mushrooms until tender. Add the crab meat, gradually add the fish stock, and continue to sauté 1 to 2 minutes. As the crab meat cooks, any shells that were missed will turn white and can be removed. Remove pan from heat.

Add the pepper, salt, and bread pieces to the crab meat mixture. Form into 15 patties. Place cakes on a hot grill or nonstick skillet to brown on both sides. Serve hot with salsa or picante sauce.

Where Frogmore Stew (a.k.a. Lowcountry Boil) Got Its Start

Frogmore Stew, one of the most popular seafood dishes along the Carolina coastal country and beyond, has its beginnings in Beaufort in the early 1960s.

John Gay, owner of the widely known Gay Seafood Company, presented his son Richard with a high school graduation present in 1958, a nice fishing boat. Richard immediately became an accomplished shrimper in the vast Port Royal Sound and beyond. About that time, Richard also joined Beaufort's National Guard unit, where he served for twenty-one years.

At the unit's weekend drills, he would cook up supper for the outfit at the Beaufort Armory. At one such weekend in the 1960s, Richard dumped some of the chow hall leftovers

Richard Gay, inventor of shrimp-based Frogmore Stew, later to be known as "Lowcountry Boil," displays a platter of the Lowcountry delicacy. (Photo courtesy of Richard Gay.)

into a very large pot, beginning with potatoes and adding onions, sausage, and corn on the cob. The key ingredient that he put in last for a short cooking time was shrimp that he obtained from his father's seafood company on the Port Royal dock.

From start to finish, in less than an hour Richard had a meal ready, and he spread it out on the tables, without dishes. It was an instant hit. At first, it was called Beaufort Stew, and his Guard companions asked him to keep it up.

At the time, the Gay family lived at Frogmore on St. Helena Island, an area dominated by the old Frogmore Plantation (named for an ancestral English country estate). Frogmore was also noted for its diamondback terrapin and caviar trade. Richard's National Guard buddies often teased him about his home community's name and laughingly told him the dish should be called Frogmore Stew. The name stuck.

Steamer Restaurant on Beaufort's Lady's Island was one of the first eateries to begin serving Gay's creation, and the owners made up recipe cards that they handed out to tourists going to Fripp Island, he recalled.

From that humble beginning, Richard Gay's invention spread far and wide. He and his stew subsequently received publicity all over the country, plus press attention from British journalists.

I recently interviewed Richard on the phone to his current home in Broken Arrow, Oklahoma, where he resides with his wife. He told me that before he left South Carolina, he petitioned the South Carolina General Assembly to name his stew the state's official seafood dish. Unfortunately, nothing came of it.

Another sad note to the Frogmore Stew saga: The town of Frogmore, South Carolina, lost its identity in 1988 when its post office was removed by the Postal Service. The area is now known simply as St. Helena Island. Another regret: Many people in the Lowcountry and throughout the country have started calling Richard Gay's creation Lowcountry Boil, which for many people has become the generic term for the tasty dish.

Even so, for purists Frogmore Stew is the real name that will remain forever. For folks in the know, such as caterer Ben Moise of Charleston, "we'll never call it Lowcountry Boil."

"I sat down to eat some time ago at a restaurant in Branson, Missouri," Richard Gay told me in the phone interview, "and I was delighted to see that they had Frogmore Stew on their menu! So the original name is still out there."

Here's Richard Gay's recipe for Frogmore Stew. As an optional ingredient, he suggests the addition of blue crabs. This recipe will serve five or six people.

The Original Frogmore Stew

- ¼ pound butter
- 4 tablespoons salt
- 2 pounds Hillshire Sausage, cut in small slices
- 1 large onion, diced in large pieces
- 4 tablespoons Old Bay seasoning or 1 bag Crab Boil
- 5 ears fresh corn, cut in half
- 2 pounds small new red potatoes, diced
- 3 pounds medium shrimp
- 6 blue crabs, cleaned and broken in half (optional)

Fill a 6- to 8-quart (or larger) pot half full of water. Add the butter, salt, sausage, onion, and Old Bay or Crab Boil seasoning. Bring to a boil and begin stirring, using a large slotted spoon long enough to reach the bottom of the pot.

Add the corn and potatoes, boil for 4 minutes, and keep stirring.

While continuing to stir from the bottom of the pot, add the shrimp and crab meat, if using, and continue boiling for 3 to 6 minutes or until the shrimp start floating to the top. Be careful to avoid overcooking the shrimp.

Turn off the heat and let the ingredients set for 4 minutes.

Drain all liquid and place the Frogmore Stew in a large bowl or spread out on a table covered with butcher paper. Serve with hot butter, dip, or seafood sauce.

Note: Today, Richard Gay and most Frogmore Stew cooks use a removable drain pot with holes that fits inside a larger pot. This facilitates easy draining when removed. Other Frogmore Stew recipes can be found in the Seafood chapter on page 132.

Beaufort Restaurant Closings: The Passing of an Era

Harry Chakides ran two restaurants on Beaufort's Bay Street for almost five decades prior to retiring. He followed in the footsteps of his father, who was a Beaufort restaurateur at the same site for twenty-five years before Harry Jr. launched his own eateries. (Photos courtesy of Harry Chakides).

The conclusion of an American success story was celebrated on February 22, 2007, when Harry Chakides Jr., son of Greek immigrants, retired after closing John Cross Tavern, the second of his two restaurants on Beaufort's historic Bay Street. The *Beaufort Gazette* described it as the passing of an era.

The Chakides family story began in 1907 when Harry's father, Harry John Chakides Sr., immigrated to America from Greece. His wife, Katherine, emigrated from Greece in 1922. The senior Chakides first ran an eatery in Savannah and then in 1935 moved to Beaufort, where he opened the Ritz Cafe, operating it until his death in 1960.

When his father died, Harry Chakides Jr., then twenty-two and a June graduate of the Citadel, decided to return to Beaufort to open his own restaurant. In September of 1960, after gutting the building, he opened Harry's Restaurant, serving breakfast and lunch. Thirteen years later, in 1973, he opened his second restaurant, remodeling the second floor and calling it John Cross Tavern, open evenings.

Over forty-seven years, the two restaurants were favorites of locals, who relished Harry's traditional Lowcountry dishes such as shrimp and grits, along with Greek favorites that he learned to cook from his parents.

Evan Thompson, executive director of the Historic Beaufort Foundation, said the restaurant's structure had been built around 1800, during the era of Captain Francis Saltus, a Beaufort shipbuilder and merchant, who owned a nearby storefront.

Among Beaufort County people saddened by the restaurant closings was novelist Pat Conroy, who lives on a nearby island and who first visited Harry's eatery when he was fifteen years old. "Everything in my childhood is disappearing," Conroy was quoted as saying, "and it makes me sad."

CHAPTER 6

The Art of Lowcountry Cooking: The Eateries, Recipes, Cooks, and Traditions

When sitting down to a meal [in Charleston], be it grand or humble, always be prepared to have a culinary epiphany.

—Jessica Harris
Beyond Gumbo

Shortly after the Revolution, John F. D. Smyth, an English traveler, wrote of the wealthy widows on Edisto Island and suggested that the demise of their husbands was due partially to the rich food and drink in which they indulged.

—*South Carolina WPA Guide* (1940)

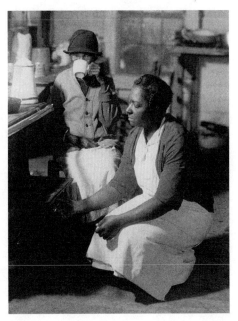

I t was in Charleston in the eighteenth and nineteenth centuries that the four major elements of the Lowcountry's distinctive cuisine evolved—a mix of English, West Indian, French, and West African cooking, along with New World staples—to create a food fit for a king, or more to the point, for the Lowcountry era's wealthy merchants and planters.

Taking a break in the Chandler family's kitchen at Murrells Inlet, South Carolina, in the 1930s are Hagar Brown (left) and Lillie Knox, descendants of Gullah slaves. (Photo by Bayard Wooten, North Carolina Collection, University of North Carolina at Chapel Hill.)

As author George C. Rogers stated in his history of the Pinckney family, it boiled down to "Old World culinary arts with New World staples." At the turn of the twentieth century, observers said that one could best sample the distinctive cookery of the Lowcountry's affluent past in private homes, and at turtle suppers, catfish stews, oyster roasts, and barbecues. Fond memories of the feasts served at the great plantations told of wedding cakes that were sometimes four feet high, "and the feasting lasted for several days."

Even plantation breakfasts could be quite sumptuous, causing Englishmen to write home that breakfasts back in Britain were "but a meager repast" in comparison. Mrs. Basil Hall described an 1800s Combahee River plantation breakfast at which the guests were served "such admirably boiled rice, such hashed turkey, broiled quails and Indian corn flour…made into cakes of every description, each one more delicious than the other."

> ### THE PLANTATION KITCHEN
> *Plantations were not merely houses, but little planetary systems around which a whole set of people and buildings orbited…Usually a short distance from the manor, the kitchen was full of the cook's wares: pots, kettles, waffle irons, swinging cranes, bake ovens, scales, iron firedogs holding rotating spits. This was the spot in which Southern cooking had its inspiration and consummation…*
>
> *The plantation became a kind of matriarchy; the real focus was not the planter but his wife…She kept the keys and the recipes.*
>
> —MARSHALL FISHWICK
> THE AMERICAN HERITAGE COOKBOOK, 1954

The same could have been said for the sumptuous foodways practiced at plantations centered around Savannah as well as those situated in the Georgia interior and along the barrier Sea Islands such as St. Simons and Sapelo.

Unfortunately, the gluttonous lifestyle of the "rich and famous" wreaked a terrible price for many of the Lowcountry gentry of the 1800s. Many died before they reached age sixty.

Europeans exploring the New World—led by the Spanish in the 1400s and followed by the French, English, Germans, and other Europeans—reveled at the "vast marine gumbo" of shellfish and fish generally that they found on the South Atlantic coast, especially the two-hundred-mile strip of land that would come to be called the Lowcountry.

The seafood bonanza soon became the foundation for a Lowcountry cuisine embracing such classic dishes as she-crab soup, crab cakes, seafood gumbos, and shrimp and grits, to name a few.

The other big element was the emergence of Carolina Gold rice, which spawned such dishes as pilaus, hoppin' john, and red rice (see Carolina Gold details in chapter 1). All of it on the backs of Africans, of course, who were brought in chains from West Africa's Windward Coast, plus others from sugarcane plantations in the British West Indies.

The Africans—well experienced in working rice fields in West Africa's rice wetlands—proved to be the key to the emerging Lowcountry economy. And, at the same time, the black women cooks became the Lowcountry's amazingly creative kitchen artists. Not to be forgotten was the fact that the slave ships brought many of the initial seeds that led to much of their cooking success: okra, black-eyed peas, peanuts, and the celebrated benne seeds, which grew to six feet high, and each of which yielded hundreds of nutty seeds that flavored dozens of Lowcountry dishes.

What quickly emerged in the Lowcountry, John Martin Taylor noted in *The New Encyclopedia of Southern Culture*, "was a Creole culture, most evident in the kitchen."

Joe Gray Taylor and John T. Edge drew a similar conclusion in the same encyclopedia, declaring that enslaved Africans "reinterpreted European cookery" in dishes ranging from hog's head cheese to collard greens and chess pie, "slipping in a pepper pod here, an okra pod there." The black newcomers were also influential in the increasing use of deep oil cooking as practiced in Africa and in the British West Indies.

Another element in the evolvement of Lowcountry cooking came with the 1670 arrival in Charleston of a shipload of French Huguenots, most of whom had been living in London after fleeing France.

According to Patricia B. Mitchell in her *French Cooking in Early America*, the French and English food lines grew from the same root "since the English royal line was French as far back as the thirteenth and fourteenth centuries."

Looking still earlier, Mitchell said William the Conquerer's Norman conquest of England in 1066 was said by some as the time "when English and French cooking became forever intertwined." Even many English food-related words derive from the French tongue, such as casserole, beef, pork, dinner, venison, veal, mutton, and menu.

And of course, don't forget that fertile lands along the coastal plain proved ideal for growing vegetables. The Lowcountry soon became one of the region's major breadbaskets, producing abundant peas, beans, collards, okra, onions, peanuts, squash, asparagus, lettuce, sweet potatoes, and Irish potatoes, among others. Plus corn, of course, the bedrock of the ultimate comfort food: corn bread.

Charleston

Today's Charleston is filled with dozens of outstanding restaurants, many of them offering traditional Lowcountry dishes with innovative twists. A key player is Hominy Grill, owned and operated for more than a decade by Robert Stehling, winner of the prestigious James Beard 2008 Medal as the Southeast's top chef. When naming his restaurant, Stehling sought a tie to the loca-

Charleston Chef Robert Stehling owns and operates the popular Hominy Grill in Charleston's historic district. (Photo by Ford Walpole.)

tion. In Charleston speech, hominy refers to finely ground corn, which in old Lowcountry terminology becomes hominy (i.e., grits) when cooked. One of Stehling's highly rated specialties—like many other top-rated Charleston restaurants—is shrimp and grits.

While he was a student at the University of North Carolina in Chapel Hill, Stehling spent a lengthy period under the tutelage of the late, great Bill Neal at Crook's Corner, a classic Southern eatery. "It was a great place to work," he told Charleston writer Ford Walpole. "It was European bistro-oriented and Southern. We were doing French and Italian, and the techniques were carried over to Southern dishes."

Stehling told writers Matt Lee and Ted Lee that between the paella and the purloo he remembered an important detour to the Creole rice dish jambalaya.

"It gave me a lot of confidence to see how all three food traditions were connected underneath," he said. From jambalaya he borrowed an ingredient, eggplant, that, while scarce in Lowcountry, became one of his key purloo ingredients in that it helped retain moisture and would melt in the pan, turning almost creamy.

"Simple is best," Stehling laughs. "We don't sell food as much as The Hominy Experience. It's pretty simple food, but a lot of care is taken in it."

Another outstanding Charleston restaurant is FIG ("Food Is Good") on Meeting Street. Chef Mike Lata won the 2009 James Beard Award for Best Chef in the Southeast the year after Stehling won it. Lata is famed for, among other dishes, his Jumbo Carolina Flounder with Littleneck Clams.

Other top Charleston restaurants include McCrady's, where Chef Sean Brock is known for his Caw Caw Creek milk-fed porkers; Slightly North of Broad, where Chef Frank Lee's Pan-fried Quail Breasts over Cheese Grits is a standout; Robert Barber's Bowens Seafood Restaurant near Folly Beach, long noted for its oysters and profiled in the seafood chapter; The Peninsula Grill, where Executive Chef Robert Carter draws praise for his Benne-crusted Rack of Lamb with Wild Mushroom Potatoes; and Hank's Seafood Restaurant, where Chef Frank McMahon is celebrated for his Stone Crab Claws.

Shad Roe & Grits

MAKES 4 SERVINGS

- 3 slices bacon, chopped
- Peanut oil, optional
- 2 sets shad roe (approximately 1 pound)
- 2 tablespoons flour
- 1 1/4 cups sliced mushrooms
- 1 large clove garlic
- 1/2 teaspoon Tabasco sauce
- 2 teaspoons lemon juice
- 1/4 cup thinly sliced green onions

Cook the bacon in a medium skillet over low heat, stirring occasionally, until crisp. Drain the bacon on paper towels, reserving the bacon fat in the skillet. Add peanut oil if needed to give you approximately 1 1/2 tablespoons of fat in the skillet.

Season the shad roe with salt and pepper. Lightly coat the shad roe with the flour, removing any excess flour. Brown the shad roe over medium heat in the same skillet until they are medium rare.

Turn up the heat to medium high and toss in the mushrooms and bacon. Cook for about 1 more minute. Press the garlic clove through a garlic press and toss in with the shad roe mixture. Do not let the garlic brown.

Finish with the Tabasco, lemon juice, and green onions, and take off the heat. Plate quickly so the roe does not overcook.

"It Would Make You Weep, It Tasted So Good"

Ben Moise (pronounce that Mo-Ease), a South Carolina state game warden in his earlier life, is considered one of Charleston's grand pooh-bahs when it comes to everything authentically Lowcountry, particularly in the areas of food, wild game, shellfish, finfish, or whatever's edible along South Carolina's coastal plain.

Nowhere are his considerable skills put to better use than in organizing highly popular oyster roasts. Moise steams bushels of oysters and spreads them out on tables for his hungry fans across the country. Along with the oysters, he often puts out a grand serving of shrimp-based Frogmore Stew (see page 132 in the seafood chapter).

Ben is also quite an expert on cooking purloo, or if you prefer pilau, one of the Lowcountry's favorite rice dishes based for centuries on Carolina Gold long grain rice. Ben has fond memories of great Lowcountry pilaus. He even has his own special spelling for the dish: pileau. A Huguenot spelling, perhaps?

The timeworn notion of "pileau," according to Ben, is poultry (chicken, turkey, doves, duck, etc.) and rice, "although I've enjoyed the above along with loose fried ground pork sausage cooked in with it and also with just the sausage alone. I've even seen pileaus made of pieces parts, such as chicken livers and/or gizzards and cured pork backbone."

The classic pileau that he grew up with, "that momma and grandmother made," was simply chicken and rice. "The chicken was boiled whole in a pot of water," Ben recalled, "usually with some coarsely chopped celery and onions (maybe a garlic clove or two) and generously seasoned with black pepper and as much salt as you could stand (being of the Old South)."

View of Moise Island Cabin. (Photo courtesy of Ben Moise.)

When the meat was falling off the bone, Ben noted, the chicken was carefully lifted from the pot and the meat separated from the skin and bones and then shredded. "The broth was strained and measured: two cups of strained broth to one cup of raw [uncooked] rice. The measured strained broth was then poured back into the pot and brought to a boil." Finely chopped onions and celery were added and cooked on the boil for a few minutes. Then the shredded chicken meat was added.

"When the pot was at the boil again," Ben continued, "the rice was added and stirred in. As the boil again arose, the heat was turned down to low and the pot covered. Twenty minutes later, you had a basic pileau that would make you weep it tasted so good."

Summer Eating on Charleston's Johns Island

Another take on Lowcountry foodways was described to me by an old friend, Charles "Trap" Seabrook, nicknamed for an ancestor, Trapier Seabrook, who grew up on Johns Island, now part of the City of Charleston. We conducted the interview after lunch at Atlanta's Watershed Restaurant, where the kitchen is run by prize-winning executive chef Scott Peacock, another James Beard award-winner.

Photo of Ben Moise's island located near Charleston, South Carolina. (Photos courtesy of Ben Moise.)

"During summers at Johns Island," Seabrook recalled, "my daddy would go out from our house overlooking the salt marshes and the Stono River and head to our rickety old dock built over a tidal creek. He'd use a drop net to catch shrimp, mullet, blue crabs, 'cootahs' [diamondback terrapins], and other creek denizens. The terrapins, by the way, made a delicious soup."

Meanwhile, Charles and his brothers, Jim, Carl, and Wilson, were also in the marshes almost every day throwing castnets into the tidal creeks for seafood goodies. "And at night we went flounder gigging," he recalled.

The Seabrooks' big summer breakfast treat was the small creek shrimp that Mrs. Seabrook served over grits. "For dinner," Charles recalled, "Mama often served brown shrimp gravy over rice. Still today it remains my favorite

Charles Seabrook grew up on Johns Island, now a part of the City of Charleston, South Carolina. Here he looks over Lowcountry marshes. (Photo courtesy of Charles Seabrook.)

food, and the only way I can get it like Mama used to cook it is to go over to sister-in-law Mildred Seabrook's kitchen, the wife of my brother Carl."

Cooking on a Wood-Burning Stove

Seabrook's late mother did all of her cooking on a wood-burning stove. "One of my chores as a boy was bringing in the wood," Charles Seabrook said.

"She would boil the blue crabs that Daddy brought up from the creek, and then she would spread newspapers on the dining room table and have all of us in there extracting the crab meat. We had to pile the meat in the middle of the table because Mama made outstanding crab cakes—absolutely the best crab cakes I ever ate. Unless Mildred still has it, the recipe for crab cakes died with my mama. I remember she used only a dab of mustard and never bread as a filler. I can remember her taking the crab meat we had picked out and balling it up with her hands to cook the cakes."

The Seabrooks loved to take part in church oyster roasts. "We'd put sheets of tin over the fire," Charles recalled, "and throw on the oysters and cover them with croaker sacks soaked in salt water, and then let the oysters steam. It was great fun for the men to go out on a cool morning in the fall to pick several bushels of oysters for the church roasts [from creek banks]." They used simple claw hammers to "pick open" the bivalves.

Sadly though, before Charles Seabrook left the island to go to college, many of the old oyster beds were closed down by the county health department because of pollution.

Although the fish stalls in the City market are filled with crabs and shrimp brought in fresh daily, the majority of Savannah housekeepers prefer to buy their seafoods from the Negro hucksters who...peddle their wares from door to door—carrying on their heads great baskets of shrimp and crabs and oysters, and filling the morning with their familiar cry: "Crab by'er! Yeh Swimps! Yeh Oshta!"

—Harriet Ross Colquitt
The Savannah Cookbook (1933)

Savannah

Flavorful cuisine elegantly served has been a Savannah trademark over the centuries. New England lawyer Jeremiah Evarts wrote fondly of his delight while dining at Savannah's Dr. Kollock's on March 30, 1822.

"Mrs. Bratton, Dr. Kollock's niece," he wrote, "sets the most elegant table in this city. The dinner was best drum fish, with appropriate dressings, ducks and Southern bacon, oysters cooked in two ways, Irish potatoes in two ways, beets, onions, bread, and boiled rice." He chose oysters and the duck and bacon.

"Then came cherry pie, cranberry pie, quince, orange, and other preserves, with salad, cheese, butter, and cream (beat to a foam with the juice of pineapple)…followed by oranges, plantains, raisins, and walnuts with several sorts of cordials and wine…"

Another such dinner was served Thanksgiving Day at the turn of the century at Captain Joseph Manigault's Pennyworth Island home north of Savannah, as published by *The Savannah News Press* in November 1943. The details were given to the newspaper by a woman who, as a young child, had been a Thanksgiving Day guest of the Manigault's:

Dinner was served at two; probably the gentlemen and a few rather daring ladies had toddies beforehand…It began with a turtle soup for which Grace, the family cook, was famed.

Shrimp pie followed, rice slightly pink with tomato, and filled with big pieces of cauliflower. With this was served turkey stuffed with oysters, and thin slices of well-cured ham.

Vegetables were there but to children these were an added burden, and not the delicacy they have now become. Dessert was always the same, vanilla ice cream, a huge mound of it, and the little crescent and diamond cakes, with jelly between, and thin frosting on top.

"Any food can be improved with the addition of a few peaches."

—*Dori Sanders*
South Carolina, peach farmer and novelist

Savannah Cuisine: Southern Cooking Combined with Seafood

Savannah cuisine is described as "Southern cooking combined with seafood." That's how Martha Giddens Nesbit, one of the Hostess City's leading cooks and a keen arbiter of the region's food scene, described it to me in an interview she gave me while taking me on a tour of historic Savannah. For many years she was food editor at the *Savannah Morning News*. Currently, Martha is a columnist for *Savannah Magazine* and is also director of instruction at Oglethorpe Charter School, which she helped found. On top of this, she does a lot of cooking for Savannah charities.

"Before coming to Savannah in 1974," she said, "I knew all about good Southern country cooking. In my family were so many great cooks, particularly my mother, grandmother, and aunts. They made great turkey and dressing and great corn pudding and great corn bread and great Lane cake and caramel and great sweet potato soufflés."

Author Martha Nesbit, a keen arbiter of the Lowcountry food scene and a Savannah Magazine *columnist, is pictured in front of the legendary Johnny Harris Restaurant in Savannah, Georgia. (Photo by the author.)*

When Martha graduated from Georgia Southern College (now University) in Statesboro, got married, and moved to Savannah, she encountered such a plethora of seafood her cooking horizon quickly took on a new layer of possibilities, adding shrimp, crabs, oysters, and the like to her standard fare, and learning to cook fish in ways other than battered and fried.

Along with the traditional okra and tomato, Martha learned to add shrimp or crab meat to the mix. "And then there were the seafood purlows that consist mainly of broth, rice, and seafood," she said.

The dishes that evolved in Savannah among early settlers, Martha told me, depended on what was available (mostly seafood) and who was doing the cooking. "While the English brought their recipes over," Martha said, "the people doing most of the cooking—the African slave women—were not allowed to read, receiving their oral instructions from their matrons. However, the cooks began putting their spin on various dishes.

"While they would throw in fatback in their pots at home, resulting in flavorful dishes, they soon began to do the same in the big house. Hence the cooking that evolved took on a strong African slant, with cooks relying on ingredients they were familiar with, especially vegetables whose seeds had come to the Lowcountry with the slave trade, i.e., okra, peanuts, benne seeds, yams, and the like. Even watermelons."

Martha's wonderfully informative tour took us through Savannah's historic district, then out to the elegant Isle of Hope residential area that backs up to the Skidaway River, part of the Intracoastal Waterway. It also included the famed Wormsloe State Historic site.

Johnny Harris Restaurant has been a popular Savannah restaurant since the 1930s. Here is a 1936 souvenir menu.

Over the years, from past centuries, wealthy Savannahians would spend their summers at Isle of Hope and at islands such as Tybee. Beginning in the 1800s, they were known to spend "summers at the salts" (marshes) to escape the city's excessive heat and dreaded malaria. While at the islands, they got in a lot of fishing plus gardening, "and they loved to throw everything available into the pot."

On our way out to the Isle of Hope, we stopped off at the famous old Johnny Harris Restaurant on the tree-lined Victory Drive dedicated to American World War II servicemen. The legendary eatery still continues its history of cooking up comfort food at reasonable prices. We opted for seafood, of course: crab cakes for Martha and fried oysters for me. Which, I might add, were fried to perfection.

One of Savannah's most famous traditional foods is red rice. Mrs. Nesbit describes it as a perfect covered dish. African cooks often add cut-up sausage or seafood, both of which give the dish a unique flavor.

Another arbiter of Savannah's food traditions is author, teacher, and historian Damon Lee Fowler. He cited the dominating English culture that came to the Georgia colony with founder James Oglethorpe in 1733 as being the true basis of traditional Savannah cuisine.

He also described the Gullah-Geechee traditions and the basic "Holy Trinity"—onions, sweet bell peppers, and garlic, and, at times, celery—as contributing to the Georgia Lowcountry's outstanding cookery.

Author Martha Nesbit, Savannah Magazine food columnist, is pictured in front of Walls Bar-B-Que in Savannah. (Photo by the author.)

There is one aroma that…rekindles concrete thoughts of my mother in the kitchen. This is the smell of chopped onions, chopped celery, chopped green pepper, and a generous amount of finely minced garlic. This was the basis for…at least half of the hundreds of dishes she prepared, and it is a distinctly southern smell.

—The late Craig Claiborne

Ben Green Cooper's Savannah Food Memories

The late Ben Green Cooper, a Savannah native, wrote lovingly of the "Savannah Kitchen" food lore he absorbed while reporting for Savannah newspapers—"rooted in memories of crab stew, deviled crab, shrimp pilau, oyster roasts and soups, fish cakes, fish fried, broiled, and baked."

Savannah kitchen memories followed him on his subsequent odyssey that took him to the Mobile *Press-Register*, the Rome, Georgia, *News-Tribune,* and the Marietta, Georgia, *Daily Journal.*

Here are some of Ben Green's recollections of the Savannah food scene as captured in his self-published *Savannah's Cookin'*, brought out in 1967 by his sister following his death. The following is in Cooper's own words:

The late Ben Green Cooper in one of his favorite poses in front of his stove. Cooper grew up in Savannah during the early years of the twentieth century. (Photo courtesy of Bill Kinney.)

Mother and Dad dearly loved The Pink House, a tearoom [in the 1930s] in the ancient building erected at Abercorn and Reynolds Streets in 1771 as a home for James Habersham Jr. In 1812 the building was occupied by the Planters Bank. We enjoyed the dishes of the tearoom, a most popular place for luncheon, and especially the breads, always freshly made.

Later, Mother and Dad patronized the Pirates' House on East Broad near Bay Street. It was supposedly the death place of Stevenson's Flint the Pirate, who called, "Fetch aft the rum, Darby," but so far as we could discover, Flint was only an author's dream.

Another of our luncheon haunts in those long-ago days was the cozy corner tavern of Johnny Carrick, at Drayton Street and Bay Lane, where we encountered a wonderful fish chowder.

Memory fondly recalls the Tybee Hotel, where Tybee Whiting was a featured dish, [and] Barbee's Pavilion at Isle of Hope, where terrapin soup was made from terrapins grown in Alex Barbee's nearby terrapin farm…

Much of Savannah's most fabulous cooking was done at the majestic [original] DeSoto Hotel, now gone to the wrecking yard…Of the DeSoto's famous dishes, the one we remember best is Shad Roe and Bacon…The shad roe was particularly sought after by visiting Yankees, who quickly learned that the shad came from the nearby Ogeechee River.

At the old Thunderbolt bridge over the Wilmington River was Frank Paris' seafood place, now gone to fire, where crab stew had a flavor surprise in a touch of lemon…You could eat quarts of it.

Savannah's Classic Okra Soup, and Then Some

One of Savannah's classic dishes over the years is okra soup. Its superiority was confirmed by Eugene Walter, the late, great food writer who visited Savannah in the 1970s and was invited to dinner at the home of Mrs. Henrietta Waring.

The hostess's famed okra soup quickly got Walter's attention. "Gosh, it's good!" Walter volunteered, to which Mrs. Waring replied that it reflected her own twist. Her secret ingredient was V-8 juice, which she used as a substitute for the usual tomato paste and water. This, along with celery and parsley, served to offset the okra's slightly acidic taste.

Then she displayed "a twinkling cut-glass cruet" containing a golden liquid with tiny bird's-eye peppers in the bottom. Savannah cooks of an earlier era would often crush a bird's-eye pepper in each soup bowl, then toss it away before pouring the soup since it had such a strong aroma. In earlier years, Savannah gentlemen loved to carry small silver boxes full of the tiny peppers to add to whatever they were eating.

Mrs. Waring also offered Eugene Walter "pepper sherry" for extra heat—scalded peppers combined with dry sherry left standing for twenty-four hours before serving.

～

While modern-day Savannahians turn to fast-food eateries, many restaurants still serve traditional Lowcountry dishes. Among them are Elizabeth's at 37 Street, whose executive chef, Kelly Yambor, seeks to maintain the high standards set by founder Elizabeth

Terry, and the aforementioned Olde Pink House, facing historic Reynolds Square (the old Habersham House), whose chef is Vincent Burns. Olde Pink House is also noted for its downstairs Planters Tavern, one of the city's most popular night spots. Another very popular Savannah institution is the Wilkes Dining Room (see below).

In one of his on-the-road books, the late Charles Kuralt told about a springtime visit to Savannah. He drove out to Desposito's across the Thunderbolt bridge, where he recalled "a helping of hot, sweet, pink, miraculous shrimp…boiled in their shells and served in a steaming pile."

Other interesting Savannah eateries include Georges of Tybee and Paula Deen's The Lady and Sons. And of course, this list includes the aforementioned family favorite Pirates House Restaurant, where pirate ghosts are said to still haunt the upper floors. (See chapter 4 on Savannah for further details.)

The kitchen is where [Lowcountry] race relations have always been at their best, a place where many of the good things that can be repeated from our past come together like fine flavors.

—*Charleston native Jack Hitt*

The Wilkes' Dining Room: Still Going Strong

I felt fortunate indeed in the spring of 2008 to find myself in the long line waiting to enter Savannah's legendary Wilkes Dining Room for the first time. During the wait, I interviewed some of the hungry folks around me.

"We're from Maryland but we're moving to Savannah," Fran Thompson told me. She and her husband would wait for almost an hour in the line that snaked down oak-lined Jones Street.

"The food is worth the wait," she said, recalling her first visit twenty-eight years earlier, in May of 1980.

"It's difficult for me to list everything that I ate that day," she said, "but I can recall the fried chicken, of course, and the butter beans and the sweet potato soufflé, plus the biscuits and corn bread; they have more than twenty different dishes, you know."

"I liked the yams," said Paul Light of Cumming, Georgia, as he strolled out of the eatery. He was probably speaking of a sweet potato casserole, for which the restaurant's African-American cooks have long been noted.

Although Mrs. Sema Wilkes—"the Julia Child of country cooking"—died at age ninety-five in 2002, her dining room is now ably run by younger generations of her family, along with a dedicated cadre of black cooks such as Laverne Gould. The restaurant is still one of those "must visit" eating places for Savannah newcomers and tourists. One of the Lowcountry's great family institutions, it has won many awards, including most recently the "best fried chicken" citation from *Savannah Magazine* and a lifetime achievement citation from the prestigious James Beard Foundation. It's

The Wilkes dining room in Savannah, Georgia, is now being operated by the late Mrs. Sema Wilkes' great-grandson, Ryon Thompson (left), and her granddaughter, Mrs. Marcia Thompson (right). Standing in the middle is one of the legendary restaurant's outstanding cooks, LaVerne Gould. (Photo by the author.)

a testimony to great country "home cooking" that Mrs. Wilkes took to Savannah when she moved there from Toombs County, in the Georgia interior, in 1943.

Heading the staff today as general manager, keeping Mrs. Wilkes's food traditions alive, is her great-grandson, thirty-three-year-old Ryon Thompson. His mother, Marcia Thompson, Mrs. Wilkes' granddaughter, is the hostess in the two dining rooms, and Ryon's father, Ronnie Thompson, runs the cash register and helps out with the purchasing.

The cooks continue to follow Mrs. Wilkes's strict rule to "go natural" on ingredients and offer only the freshest vegetables in season, coming directly from farms near Savannah. Another rule still in practice is to "never serve food that has not been sampled before leaving the kitchen."

After the long wait in the shade of oak trees festooned with Spanish moss, I was happy to be ushered in and seated with nine other people around a round table near the kitchen. The spread before us gave off a tantalizing aroma as waitresses brought in an array of meats and vegetables. We had three platters of meat, including roast beef and fried chicken, baskets of hot biscuits and corn bread, plus a dozen or so bowls of steaming vegetables: green beans, squash casserole, creamed corn, sweet potato pie, butter beans, creamed Irish potatoes, collard greens, and stewed okra, plus big bowls of banana pudding.

When I was in England at the Cordon Bleu, I would yearn for good Southern food and fantasize about a bowl of pot likker and corn bread. And biscuits—ah, our biscuits— feathery, light, split with butter melting inside, or perhaps topped with cream gravy.
—Nathalie Dupree
Southern Memories

I took plenty of time to savor my helpings and gleefully washed them down with sweet tea before staggering out.

Georgia native John T. Edge, the executive director of the Southern Foodways Alliance, expressed regret for his late recognition of Mrs. Wilkes award-winning cooking.

"How blind was I to history," Edge confessed in his introduction to a book on the Savannah restaurant, "that I had not recognized Mrs. Wilkes' [place] for what it is: perhaps the South's most venerable family restaurant, a modern-day reliquary of old-fashioned country cookery, where the tables groan beneath the weight of a midday repast and history stands still on the plate for all to admire."

Thanksgiving and Christmas Dinners in Atkinson County, Georgia

Tell me what you eat and I will tell you who you are.
—Anthelme Brillat-Savarin
The Physiology of Taste, *1825*

According to my Atlanta friend W.F. (Dub) Taft, there is nothing traditional or routine in the Thanksgiving Day meals at the Wilburn and Doris Taft home in southeast Georgia, part of the Lowcountry interior.

"Displayed alongside the turkey and dressing," he says, "you're likely to find pot roast, a big ham, and a platter of fried fish."

Likewise on Christmas Eve, expect the unusual, says Dub. "There'll be four or five gallons of Mother's Brunswick stew, a dozen grilled chickens, and three or four hams and pork shoulders barbecued and pulled. Then on Christmas morning, I help Mother fry seventy to eighty pork chops while she bakes two big platters of sausage links."

Meanwhile, on the back burner, Doris Taft puts on a two-gallon pot of grits, and one of the daughters comes in later with another gallon or two. "Still other sisters and sisters-in-law arrive with containers filled with about sixteen dozen scrambled eggs and almost as many biscuits," according to Dub.

"After the first crowd has gathered, Daddy prays an extra-special blessing, and the line forms at the counter. We feed them in shifts as they arrive tired and hungry from the morning mayhem of opening gifts with their kids around the Christmas trees. I've tried to count heads before, but I lose track somewhere between the first serving and last. Let's just say there's enough family and friends to clear out all the food. And hardly ever are there any leftovers from Christmas breakfast at the Wilburn and Doris Taft house."

Members of Mrs. Doris Taft's family join her in displaying a few of her great dishes at the Taft home in southeast Georgia. She has a pan of biscuits in her lap while others hold a sweet potato casserole, a potato salad, a mashed potato and cheese platter, and a mixed salad. (Photo courtesy of Dub Taft.)

Cousins Ken and Dub Taft display a pan of Christmas morning pork chops, just one of the many different dishes served to the extended Taft family in Atkinson County, Georgia. (Photo courtesy of Dub Taft.)

~

In the fourteen chapters that follow—ranging from Appetizers to Wild Game—you will find a broad representation Lowcountry cooking, including historic recipes from years ago right up to the modern day. *Enjoy!*

CHAPTER 7

Lowcountry Beverages

The stills will be soon at work to make Whiskey and Peach Brandy…Now will come their Season of Festivity and drunkenness…In this both Presbyterians and Episcopals very charitably agree.

—Rev. Charles Woodmason
Charleston-based Anglican missionary to the
South Carolina backcountry in the 1770s

On June 28, 1778, Charleston's leading ladies threw a sumptuous dinner honoring the Lowcountry's Revolutionary War defenders, particularly Colonel Francis Marion and his Second Regiment.

It came on the second anniversary of the victorious Battle of Fort Moultrie and that very same day, the regiment's officers, to show their appreciation, gave their soldiers three barrels of beer and a hogshead of claret.

Charles Town is very well supplied with porter from England at 9 shillings per dozen bottles, which is commonly drank by most people of property at meals or else weak grog or rum punch, for they always can buy the best Jamaica rum…by the puncheon or hogshead. French claret is also to be drank much cheaper than in England…

—An English Traveler in Charleston *(1774)*

Marion, the St. John Parish Huguenot fighter later to become Eastern South Carolina's elusive "Swamp Fox" hero and a brigadier general, issued a regimental order hoping that "the men will behave with sobriety and decency to those ladies who have been so kind as to give them so genteel a treat."

After all, the rough-and-tough volunteer fighters of that era had a reputation for spirited drinking along with their successful guerilla-type fighting.

Historian Eric Emerson tells of a member of the Charleston Light Dragoons who got so "punch drunk" he was unable to mount his horse. And Captain Lionel Legge said that "the astounding quantities of this [Light Dragoons' Punch] recipe seem to fit well with its hard riding title."

Considered as distinctive Charleston, the dragoons' recipe was consumed in large quantities prior to the Civil War, particularly when Charleston attracted cotton buyers from "Up North" as well as from England and France.

The punch continues to be used as a popular beverage at parties, balls and weddings.

Charleston Light Dragoons' Punch

- 4 quarts California brandy
- 4 quarts black tea
- 1 quart Jamaica rum
- 1 quart carbonated water
- 4 cups granulated sugar
- 1 cup peach brandy
- Juice of 24 lemons
- Peels of 6 lemons, cut in thin slivers

Mix all ingredients except for the carbonated water, which should be added before serving.

The recipe for the immortal drink [punch] came from the Far East, together with tea, root ginger…and other new delights, either by way of the fourteenth-century caravan route or by sea around the Cape of Good Hope.

—The Williamsburg Cookbook

Down the road in James Oglethorpe's fledgling Georgia colony, alcoholic beverage consumption was reportedly just as lively, not only among the militia but among common folk as well. Savannah's colonial rum consumption averaged thirteen gallons of rum a year for every man, woman, and child. The English trustees in London took heed of "the pernicious effects of drinking rum and other spirituous liquors [in the colony] creating disorders amongst the Indians [and] destroying many of the English."

Subsequently, the trustees passed an Act "to prevent the further Importation and Use of Rum and Brandies in the Georgia province, or any kinds of spirits or strong waters whatsoever," suggesting instead that they order beer, a less powerful drink, from breweries in Britain. Most Savannahians ignored the rum ban, continuing to drink rum in great quantities at places like Peter Tondee's Tavern at the corner of Whitaker and Broad Streets.

Typical of the strong drink consumed by the Savannah military in the eighteenth century was the punch created by The Chatham Artillery, said to be the oldest such military organization on record in Georgia. George Washington greeted its officers when he visited Georgia in 1791, but the unit's greatest notoriety came from their powerful punch.

Actually it was the women of the organization who created the original recipe only to allow it to be "upgraded" by artillery officers over the years, ending up with the ingredients listed below. The potent punch received additional nationwide attention in 1819 when President James Monroe visited Savannah to christen the steamship SS *Savannah* as it set off across the Atlantic. The night before, so the story goes, he sipped the "suave and deceitful" concoction during a festive cruise up the Savannah River, without any serious consequences.

Chatham Artillery Punch

- 1 ½ gallons strong tea
- 1 ½ gallons Catawba wine
- ½ gallon St. Croix rum
- 1 ½ quarts rye whiskey
- 1 quart brandy
- 1 quart Gordon gin
- ½ pint Benedictine
- 2 ½ pounds brown sugar
- 1 bottle Maraschino cherries

- Juice from 18 oranges
- Juice from 18 lemons
- Case of Champagne

Bring all ingredients except Champagne together in a large container and allow the mixture to mellow in a cool room 36 to 48 hours before your party. Just prior to serving add the case of champagne. Pour the punch over ice in a large punch bowl.

Early on, Charleston's inns, taverns, and "punch houses" became its most important social institutions, according to Robert Rosen in *A Short History of Charleston*. "Despite the protests of some…Charlestown maintained in excess of one hundred taverns during the colonial era." He cited Dillons on Broad Street, Henry Gignilliat's, and the Sign of the Baccus as three of the city's popular taverns.

Early on, punch was considered the standby drink among Lowcountry planters. It was considered an offshoot of the English version of the Hindustani "pauch" from the early 1600s, which translated to the number five. In other words, five ingredients—spirits, water, sliced lemons or limes, sugar, and spice. Or, as the *Gay Nineties Cookbook* described it, minus the spices:

A little water to make it weak,
A little sugar to make it sweet,
A little lemon to make it sour,
A little whiskey to give it power.

The St. Cecelia Society

In 1767 thirty-seven of Charleston's grandees organized the St. Cecelia Society. For many years, concerts were the society's forte. In 1822, however, the concerts gave way to grand balls. Considered Charleston's most prestigious social events, these balls are still held today every January at Hibernian Hall. Along with the balls came a distinctive punch they named, simply, St. Cecelia Punch.

Since the society's exclusive membership is restricted to the city's bloodline descendants, secrecy has been part and parcel of the organization's code, extending even to the contents of its punch! However, Helen Woodward, who contributed to an updated edition of *200 Years of Charleston Cooking* in 1934, was able to obtain the recipe from one of the society's officers.

"Is it possible," Mrs. Woodward wrote, "that St. Cecelia Punch contributes to the glamour?"

Here is the original recipe as reported by Mrs. Woodward (and later published in *Charleston Receipts*), which will yield eighty to ninety servings.

According to James Villas, the recipe reflects the influences of the English (tea), the French (champagne, cognac), and the West Indies (rum) on Lowcountry culture.

St. Cecelia Punch

- 6 lemons
- 1 quart brandy
- 1 pineapple
- 1 ½ pounds sugar
- 1 quart green tea
- 1 pint heavy rum
- 1 quart peach brandy
- 4 quarts champagne
- 2 quarts carbonated water

Slice lemons thin and cover with brandy. Allow to steep for 24 hours. Several hours before serving, slice the pineapple into the bowl with the lemon slices, then add the sugar, tea, rum, and peach brandy. Stir well. When ready to serve, add the champagne and water.

Portugal's famous Madeira wine found a happy reception throughout the Lowcountry beginning in the colonial era, with planters and merchants boasting entire cellars of the coveted beverage. Collectors in the past century included the late Savannah banker Mills B. Lane, who stored his Madeira in the secure confines of his Citizens and Southern Bank. Lane was a member of Savannah's exclusive Madeira Club (restricted to males). Begun more than sixty years ago, the Madeira Club still exists today.

Another ancient "refreshment" dating from colonial times is variously called "Rum Punch," "Plantation Punch," or a similar version made in the Bahamas, the "Goombay Smash." They all use pretty much the same ingredients. For a party, Charleston's Ben Moise likes to combine these plantation punch ingredients:

- 2 ½ cups orange juice
- 2 ½ cups pineapple juice
- 1 cup white rum
- 1 cup dark rum
- ½ cup coconut rum
- ¼ cup lime juice
- 3 tablespoons Grenadine

Mix ingredients thoroughly and serve over ice.

Ben says this will get any party off to a spirited start.

Muscadine, Scuppernong Wines

Back on the farm, we used to call them bullaces. In some places in the Lowcountry, they're called swamp grapes. They're the purplish wild muscadine grapes seen growing all over the lower South, climbing to the top of pine

SOUTHERN COUNTRY BREWING
PERSIMMON-LOCUST BEER

Making persimmon beer was a regular Dutch Fork [South Carolina] ritual around Thanksgiving, which was said "not to be Thanksgiving at all without a barrel full."

Leland Summer prescribes taking "a small basketful of dried persimmons, mashed, and put in a keg or barrel, on which thoroughly boiled honey locusts were placed. Let stand for four days; best drunk when fresh and used up before the end of the week."

To serve the drink properly, use pewter, tin, or ceramic mugs.

—JUANITA C. KIBLER
DUTCH FORK COOKERY

trees and spreading across fences everywhere.

Nowadays the muscadines and their sweeter, fatter, amber-colored cousins—scuppernongs—are getting more and more attention. According to Matt Lee and Ted Lee in *The Lee Bros. Southern Cookbook*,

the scuppernong flavor is likened to "a burst of nectar with hints of honeysuckle, orange flower, and jasmine, with a spike of acidity and lingering accents of cola and ripe melon." Wow!

Many modern-day Lowcountry farmers are switching from tobacco and cotton to grapes. This has led the Clemson University Extension Service to launch a muscadine demonstration vineyard at the school's Pee Dee Research Center in Darlington County, South Carolina. The objective is to show potential grape farmers how to build, plant, train, and maintain a vineyard.

As part of this effort, Florence County extension agent Jody Martin started the *SC Muscadine Newsletter*. Martin cites the pioneering efforts of Irvin House Vineyards run by Jim and Ann Irvin at Wadmalaw Island near Charleston, the Hyman Farms Vineyards in Horry County, owned by Greg Hyman, and the La Bella Amie Vineyards at Little River, owned by Vicki Weigle and Chuck Bell.

According to Ann Irvin, the forty-eight-acre Irvin House Vineyards, nestled near the majestic live oaks on Wadmalaw and open to tours, is Charleston's only domestic winery. It makes and bottles five varieties of muscadine wine.

"People tell us the taste of muscadines transport them back to their childhood," she said. "We have taken this childhood favorite and given it an adult spin."

To bring the Lowcountry alcoholic beverage scene up to date, Irvin House Winery created a muscadine-flavored vodka called Firefly Vodka. A Charleston recipe for "Pluff Mud Martini" calls for 1 ½ ounces of Firefly muscadine-flavored vodka and ½ ounce of Godiva chocolate liqueur, shaken over ice and strained into a martini glass rimmed with chocolate powder.

In Georgia's Bulloch County, Meinhardt Vineyards and Winery have established a fine reputation with their wines. Since 2004, they've bottled wine using muscadine grapes from their twelve-acre vineyard. (See the following photographs.)

A grape stomp festival occurs every mid-September at the Meinhart Winery near Statesboro, Georgia. Here bare-footed revelers enjoy stomping ripe muscadine and scuppernong grapes to squeeze out the juice as was done in the old days. Top photo shows a section of the Meinhardt vineyards. (Photos courtesy of Meinhardt Winery and Vineyards.)

Meinhardt's wines range from dry to sweet and include an Eagle series honoring Georgia Southern University.

One of the up-and-coming Georgia Lowcountry wineries is Butterducks Winery, located in Effingham County near Savannah. Operated by Bill and Barbara Utter, Butterducks' Sweet Peach walked off with *Georgia Trend* magazine's 2008 runner-up "Wine of Distinction" prize among dessert wines. Their objective is to make fine wines from Georgia fruits: peaches, pears, blackberries, blueberries, and of course, muscadines and scuppernongs. Their newest wines in 2008 were Savannah Red and the aforementioned Sweet Peach.

For another angle on muscadines, check out page 297 for a popular Muscadine Hull pie recipe.

～

Grape vineyards and wine-making activities have been going on in the Southeast since the sixteenth century. In 1565 Captain John Hawkins found a French Huguenot colony near the St. Johns River that had fermented twenty hogsheads of wines, probably from muscadines and/or scuppernongs. But wine expert Thomas Pinney was quoted by Sarah Belk, in her *Around the Southern Table* cookbook, as declaring that it was Spaniard colonists who likely were the first to make wine in America at what is now Parris Island, South Carolina.

The Salzburger Germans who settled in the 1730s on the Savannah River north of Savannah were big into beer. Pastor Johann Martin Bolzius wrote that "the inhabitants [at Ebenezer] have the ability [to] cook a healthy beer for themselves out of syrup, Indian corn, and hops, or the tops of white or water firs…."

In 1860 William Summer of South Carolina's Pomaria Plantation Nurseries came up with a muscadine/scuppernong wine recipe that produced a drier table wine than the sweet wines consumed in the German communities near Dutch Fork, South Carolina. He called it Pomaria Plantation Muscadine Wine. Here is Mr. Summer's recipe in his own words:

Select the grapes from your vineyard and mash and press out the juice. Put the juice in jugs and set in a cool place.

The vessels should be full and kept full by adding some of the juice reserved for that purpose.

All the impurities will work off, and in four or five weeks, the fermentation will be complete. The vessels may then be stoppered and a little air occasionally given, until cold weather, when the fermentation will have subsided. Then bottle, cork, and seal close.

In a dry season, the grape juice is rich in sugar and a superior wine can be made without adding additional sugar at all. If the grapes ripen during a wet season, it will be best to add a little sugar to the juice when first put in the jugs.

Rice Wine

In the Lowcountry, wines made with rice were common almost immediately after rice became a major crop in the early 1700s. Here is a recipe credited to Frederick A. Traut that appears in the classic *Charleston Receipts* cookbook.

Charleston Rice Wine

- 1 box seeded raisins
- 1 orange, sliced
- 1 ½ pounds raw rice

- 1 yeast cake
- 2 ½ pounds sugar
- 1 gallon tepid water

Put all the ingredients in a stone crock and cover 3 weeks to 1 month, depending on temperature. (The colder the temperature, the longer you need to keep it covered.) Stir with a wooden spoon daily for a week, every other day the second week, then not at all. Strain. The next day, filter. Set aside 6 months to a year.

There were stills on most Georgia plantations, and apples and peaches were turned into brandy, which was drunk moderately and thankfully. Everybody drank in those days [1800s] except for very strict Methodists.

—*Rev. George Gillman Smith*
The Story of Georgia & the Georgia People

Ratifia Wine

Ratifia, using peach pits as its base, was a version of wine popular in Charleston in the mid-1700s but has about faded from the Lowcountry scene.

In 1756 the noted Charleston planter Eliza Lucas Pinckney recorded a Ratifia recipe in her diary, calling for seventy-five peach kernels, two cups of brandy and a half cup of sweet wine, a half cup of orange flower water, and a half cup of sugar.

And Eliza's daughter, Harriott Pinckney Horry, in *A Colonial Plantation Cookbook*, brought out more recently by the University of South Carolina Press, records her recipe in her own words as follows:

Ratifia

Six hundred peach Kernels sliced to one Gallon Brandy: I Quart of sweet Wine, one Quart Orange flower water 1 pound and ¼ sugar, infuse all these ingredients in the Sun for Six Weeks, shaking the Jug every Day—then Filter it for Use.

Iced Tea (The Table Wine of the South)

Sassafras (tea) cleans you out. Try to find the root…the bigger the bark the better the tea. The best sassafras is to be found around Savannah, Georgia.

—Vertamae Grosvenor

Vibration Cooking or The Travel Notes of a Geechee Girl

No one seems to know who invented iced tea, but food historian John Egerton has a hunch that the popular drink got its start in New Orleans around 1868, coinciding with the beginning of commercial ice manufacturing in the United States.

Egerton credits Thomas J. Lipton, an immigrant lad from Scotland, who worked first as a teenager in the South Carolina rice fields, as the person who popularized black tea around the world. In 1890, by then a New York millionaire merchant, Lipton stopped off in Ceylon on his way to Australia. There he ran across several tea plantations available for a song. He bought them all and the rest is history.

French botanist Andre Michaux grew the first tea in America in 1895 at the site of what became Charleston's Middleton Plantation. His plants did well, but his work was abandoned following his death.

Charleston today is the home of what is believed to be the only tea farm in existence in the United States. The Charleston Tea Plantation, located on Wadmalaw Island, was started as an experimental project in the 1960s funded by—would you believe?—the Lipton Tea Company. It is owned today by R. C. Bigelow Inc. The plantation is home to plants descended from those planted in the Lowcountry more than a century ago. Its American Classic Tea—grown without the use of insecticides or fungicides and designated as South Carolina's "hospitality beverage"—is said to be the freshest available in the United States.

> ## TO MULL WINE
>
> *To every pint of wine, allow a large cup full of water, sugar, and spice to taste. Boil cloves, grated nutmeg, and cinnamon in the water until the flavor is extracted. Then add the wine and sugar. Bring to a boiling point, to serve.*
>
> *—BRYAN FAMILY COOKBOOK*
> SAVANNAH, GEORGIA, 1885

John Egerton's Iced Tea Formula

Since restaurant tea is so uneven in quality, the best tea can be found in homes. Here's John Egerton's method for preparing iced tea. Folks can adjust the strength and sweetness to their individual taste. His recipe will yield 7 8-ounce glasses.

Bring 3 cups of fresh water to a rolling boil in a saucepan. Put in 3 heaping teaspoons of good quality black tea (or 4 tea bags, each of which contains a level teaspoon). Turn off the heat, cover the pan, and let the tea brew or steep for 5 to 10 minutes. Then strain it into a pitcher and add 4 cups of cold water. Fill the glasses with ice, pour in the tea, and season to taste with sugar, fresh lemon, and tender mint sprig.

Incidentally, Irvin House Winery at South Carolina's Wadmalaw Island also makes a "sweet tea" vodka. It is said to taste much like sweet tea but with a decidedly different effect.

Lemonade

Homemade lemonade hits the spot quickly during sultry Lowcountry summer days, especially when poured over ice. When I was growing up in upstate South Carolina, we would pick up a block of ice in nearby Kershaw and place it in the middle of a tub. Then we would pour in the lemonade. Today all it takes are cubes of refrigerated ice in your serving pitcher.

Lowcountry Lemonade

This lemonade recipe is adapted from one that John Martin Taylor describes as the very best. It will make enough lemonade to please a luncheon or dinner group of eight.

- 6 plump lemons
- 1 ¼ cups sugar
- 6 cups water
- Mint sprigs for garnish

Give the lemons a good cleaning, and roll them briefly; cut them in half, and place them in a 2-quart pitcher that is heat resistant. Stir in the sugar.

Bring the water to a boil and pour over the lemons. Stir the mixture to make sure the sugar is well distributed.

When the lemons are cool (in about a half hour), squeeze the juice out of them into the pitcher. Discard the rinds. Put in refrigerator. A few minutes before serving, add more sugar to taste, then pour the lemonade over the ice cubes in a second pitcher, and then transfer to glasses. As an option, garnish with sprigs of mint.

Watermelon Lemonade

This is a wonderful lemonade derivative, contributed by Jaime Harvey, formerly of Gas South.

- 1 ½ pounds sliced seedless watermelons, rinds removed
- Zest of 1 lemon
- ¾ cup fresh lemon juice
- ½ cup wild honey
- 1 ½ cups cold water
- 1 lemon, thinly sliced for garnish

Place the melon chunks into the bowl of a food processor and process until very smooth. Strain through a coarse sieve set over a bowl, stirring to push through any pulp. Pour the juice into a large pitcher and add the lemon zest.

In a bowl, whisk the lemon juice and the honey until the honey dissolves; stir into the watermelon juice.

Stir in the cold water. Cover and refrigerate until very cold. Serve over ice and garnish with lemon slices.

Blenheim Ginger Ale

I don't want to leave this chapter without mentioning one of my favorite drinks, Blenheim Ginger Ale. A Marlboro County, South Carolina, doctor created Blenheim Ginger Ale in 1903 when he mixed Jamaican ginger with the local mineral waters. If you can find this distinctive carbonated drink, you'll never forget the experience of drinking it.

The Blenheim Ginger Ale plant, once located in the town of its namesake Blenheim, moved some years ago and is now located in the hamlet of Hamer, in an adjacent county (Dillon). The bottler was first sold to the Alan Schafer family, operators of the "South of the Border" I-95 motel complex. I was unable to obtain the identity of the current owners.

CHAPTER 8

Hors d'oeuvres, Nibbles, and Finger Foods Led by the Pate of the South

One reason Southerners have such a wide repertoire of party foods is that we have so many parties! We seem to have built our entire society around events for having fun.
—Terry Thompson
A Taste of the South

Some years ago, Charlestonian Nathalie Dupree, a leading arbiter of Southern and Lowcountry foods, came up with the perfect title for pimento cheese, one of the all-time favorite Southern appetizers. She described it as "the Pate of the South."

Indeed. Many Southern kids grew up loving pimento cheese, composed of cheddar cheese and mayonnaise with chopped boiled sweet pimento peppers (a cousin of red bell peppers) plus a bit of water and salt. In earlier days, high schoolers like Susanne Knight would make a beeline on Saturdays to the kids' favorite hangout—in her case Wannamaker's Drug Store on Main Street in Cheraw, South Carolina—to get a "pimennocheese" sandwich and a Coke. And of course hang out with the other kids.

At Anderson, on the western side of upstate South Carolina, Louis Osteen had similar cravings for the cheesy mixture. It was no wonder that when he became a prize-winning chef, he served his pimento cheese version as a bar specialty at his Louis's Restaurant in Charleston, accompanied by freshly baked flatbread. Ooooweeee, how yummy can you get?

Louis is now based at Lake Rabun Hotel in the Blue Ridge Mountains northeast of Atlanta. He declared pimento cheese "the all-purpose food, good for deaths, weddings, birthday parties, all parties, and even the lunch box."

Many hostesses like to serve pimento cheese with crackers, in dips and balls, alongside celery stalks, or in some cases stuffed in celery stalks. Grocery stores carry pimentos in jars that come from canneries in Georgia and Tennessee.

With my thanks to Louis, this recipe will serve a dozen to sixteen people as an hors d'oeuvre.

Louis's Pimento Cheese

- 1 ½ pound sharp cheddar cheese, grated
- 4 ½ ounces cream cheese, room temperature
- ¾ cup Hellmann's mayonnaise
- 1 tablespoon grated yellow onion
- 1 teaspoon cayenne pepper

Chef Louis Osteen. (Photo by Susanne Dabney.)

- 7 ounces whole peeled pimentos, drained and quartered

In the bowl of an electric mixer, place the cheddar cheese, cream cheese, mayonnaise, onion, and cayenne pepper and beat with the flat beater at medium speed for 1 or 2 minutes. This is to mix the ingredients, not to make them smooth.

Add the pimentos and keep mixing until they are shredded and the mixture is somewhat smooth. Be careful not to overmix and avoid its becoming homogenized.

Pack the cheese in crocks, cover with plastic wrap, and refrigerate overnight. Forty-five minutes before serving, remove from the refrigerator. Pimento cheese will keep in a refrigerator for 4 or 5 days if tightly covered.

Cheese Straws

While on the subject of cheese, what is more appropriate as an appetizer in the Lowcountry than cheese straws? It's another all-time favorite across the South. This recipe is adapted from *Two Hundred Years of Charleston Cooking*, containing recipes collected in the 1930s, and brought out in a quality paperback edition by the University of South Carolina Press.

This particular recipe adaptation makes about sixty straws.

- 1 cup all-purpose flour
- 1 cup sharp cheddar cheese, finely grated
- ½ teaspoon salt
- ¼ teaspoon red pepper
- Cayenne pepper to taste
- ¼ cup butter
- 1 egg, beaten

Preheat the oven to 400°F.

Mix the flour, cheese, salt, and peppers. Cut in the butter as for pastry and add the egg. If more liquid is required, add a few drops of water to make it more pastrylike.

Roll thin, cut in strips, and bake 10 to 12 minutes until lightly browned.

Serve at room temperature.

Note: Cheese straws will keep for 2 days if refrigerated in a sealed container.

Since my earliest childhood, I have had what amounts to a passion for cheese straws, particularly those with a tangy bite that comes not only from the cheese but from a touch or more of cayenne.

—*The late Craig Claiborne*
Craig Claiborne's Southern Cooking

Quick & Easy Cheese Ball

My friend Diane Kennedy, a former Savannahian, submitted this recipe for the Isle of Hope Methodist Church's *Day on the Island Cookbook* when she lived there some years ago. It makes for a delicious and quick appetizer.

- 1 8-ounce package cream cheese, softened
- 1 (6- to 8-ounce) jar pimento cheese
- 1 (6- to 8-ounce) jar soft blue cheese
- Chopped pecans (as needed)

Mix cheeses together and roll into a ball. Roll ball in chopped pecans. Chill and serve.

The hors d'oeuvre hour, a Deep South inheritance from the French as hors d'oeuvres chauds and hors d'oeuvres froids—hot and cold dishes—has been a popular practice down through the centuries from mansions in Colonial Williamsburg southward through Charleston, Beaufort, Savannah, and in Lowcountry plantation kitchens.

Among cold appetizers, fresh tomato sandwiches and thinly sliced Vidalia onion sandwiches are very popular. It's always appropriate at party gatherings to serve crisp garden-fresh vegetables cut into neat bite-size pieces.

Unfortunately, many hostesses, according to Charleston caterer Ben Moise, serve their veggies "too big" in size for partygoers.

"Big is not good," says Ben. "I use blanched asparagus, red bell peppers cut into long strips, and baby carrots. If they are too fat, I cut them in half."

Here's Ben's vegetable dip:

Ben's Dip for Raw Veggies (Crudités)

The dip consists of 1/4 cup sour cream to 1/4 cup Helmann's mayonnaise. Add one tin of thoroughly minced flat anchovies; 2 cloves of mashed and finely minced garlic; 3 finely diced green (spring) onions, just the white part; 1 egg, boiled and finely diced; plus salt and black pepper.

Mix everything together and refrigerate for several hours before serving.

Isle of Hope Bacon Roll-Ups

This recipe came to me from the aforementioned Diane Kennedy of Dunwoody, Georgia, and was published some years ago in Savannah's Isle of Hope Methodist Women's *Day on the Island Cookbook*. At the time, Diane's husband, Ted, was serving as Savannah district manager of the old Southern Bell (remember that company?), while Diane served on the church's cookbook committee.

This recipe, which yields about three dozen roll-ups, freezes well or can be made a day in advance and refrigerated.

- ¼ cup butter
- ½ cup water
- 1 ½ cups Pepperidge Farm Herb stuffing
- ¼ pound hot sausage
- 1 egg, beaten slightly
- ⅔ pound bacon

In a saucepan, melt the butter in the water. Remove from the heat. Stir in the stuffing and then add the sausage and egg. Mix well.

Refrigerate for an hour then roll into pecan-shaped pieces. Cut the bacon slices into thirds. Wrap each piece around the dressing and fasten with a toothpick.

Bake in a shallow pan at 375°F for 30 to 35 minutes or until crisp and brown. Turn twice while baking. Drain on paper towels. Serve hot.

Toasted Pecans

Whether you pronounce them "pe-CAHNS" or "PEA-cans," you can't go wrong serving this appetizer, a perennial favorite across the Lowcountry and indeed the entire South. Pecan groves abound in southwest Georgia around Camilla and Baconton, where the perfect soil helps the state continue its dominance as the nation's leading pecan producer.

The first Spanish explorers were said to have found pecans growing wild in south Georgia in the 1500s. However, Mississippi claims that pecans as we know them originated there and migrated to Georgia, Alabama, and Texas.

This particular recipe comes with my thanks to the *Family Night Supper on Edisto Cookbook*. Caroline Clarkson is listed as the contributor. The pecans should be toasted low and slow.

For the younger readers, oleo is an old-timey description of margarine that was invented in the 1870s as a butter substitute. Described by some as "po-man's butter," many oldsters remember it originally as being white as lard and packaged in a squarish pliable bag with an inside dye pack that one mashed to give the margarine a yellowish color.

First pecan trees grown here about 1840 from pecan nuts found floating at sea by Captain Samuel F. Flood and planted by his wife, Rebecca Grovenstine Flood... The first plantings produced large and heavy-bearing trees as did their nuts and shoots in turn. [They were] taken from St. Mary's to distant points throughout the southeastern states [where] they became famous before the Texas pecan was generally known.

—*State Historical Marker*
St. Mary's, Georgia

Edisto Island Toasted Pecans

- 1 quart shelled pecans
- ¾ stick oleo margarine, melted

Mix the pecans with oleo on baking sheet. Bake at 250°F for 20 to 30 minutes, but do not overcook. Sprinkle with salt and drain on paper towels.

Deviled Eggs

Deviled eggs find a warm welcome at family reunions and covered-dish events. Other than mayonnaise, mustard is the ingredient (and sometimes cayenne pepper) that turns stuffed eggs into deviled eggs. Sweet pickle is another popular addition. This recipe yields six servings.

- 6 hard-boiled eggs
- ¼ cup mayonnaise
- ½ teaspoon salt
- ½ teaspoon Worcestershire sauce
- ¼ teaspoon dry mustard
- 3 tablespoons sweet pickle relish

Cut the eggs in half and remove the yolks. Add the other ingredients to the yolks and mix well.

Stuff the yolk mixture in the egg white halves and garnish with sweet pickle bits.

Vidalia Onion and Olive Fiesta Dip

This is a prize-winning recipe from the 2008 Vidalia Onion contest conducted every year in Vidalia, Georgia, home of the popular Georgia sweet onions. (See chapter 16 for the history of the Vidalias.) This recipe was submitted by Jan Williams of Toombs County, Georgia.

- 2 (8-ounce) blocks cream cheese
- 1 (14.5-ounce) can chopped black olives
- 1 (14.5-ounce) can whole kernel corn, drained
- ½ cup finely chopped Vidalia onions
- 1 small package dry ranch dressing mix

Bring the cream cheese to room temperature and combine all the ingredients.

Serve with Fritos or crackers. (The amount of chopped Vidalia onions can be increased if desired.)

Now, Boiled Soybeans!

"Boiled soybeans, called edamame, taste even better than boiled peanuts," declares Lowcountry caterer Ben Moise. "Of course I'm sure the Lee Brothers down here in Charleston would take exception to that."

Commonly found growing in Japan and China, the green-in-the-pod soybeans can be purchased in package form in your favorite grocery store.

You boil them in the pod in much the same way as you do boiled peanuts. After they've cooled, they can be served hot or cold. You eat them by squeezing the kernels out of the pod with your teeth. (For detailed information on boiled peanuts, check out chapter 13).

Seafood Appetizers

Seafood appetizers are especially favored by Lowcountry partygoers. Here are a few recipes that fill the bill.

Skillet Fried Oysters

Nothing tastes better as a hot appetizer than fried oysters. This recipe is adapted from *Famous Recipes from Mrs. Wilkes' Boarding House in Historic Savannah*, with thanks to Marcia Thompson, granddaughter of the late Mrs. Wilkes. Along with her son, Ryon (the general manager), and her husband, Ronnie, Marcia continues to uphold the cooking traditions of the late Mrs. Wilkes, known as "the Julia Child of Southern Cooking."

- 3 tablespoon butter
- 3 tablespoons shortening
- 2 dozen shucked raw oysters, drained
- 2 eggs, beaten
- 1 cup cracker crumbs
- ¾ to 1 teaspoon salt
- ¼ teaspoon pepper
- snipped parsley or paprika
- Lemon wedges

In a heated skillet, melt the butter and shortening. Roll the oysters in egg and cracker crumbs; sauté in butter until golden brown, turning once and sprinkling with salt and pepper. Sprinkle with snipped parsley or paprika and garnish with lemon wedges.

Pawley's Island Crab Balls

This recipe is adapted from *Faithfully Charleston*, published by St. Michael's Episcopal Church, the Holy City's oldest—and one of its most distinguished—historic churches.

- 1 ¼ cups crab meat
- 1 cup crushed round butter crackers
- 1 egg
- 1 heaping teaspoon dry mustard
- 1 tablespoon Worcestershire sauce or to taste
- 1 heaping teaspoon lemon juice

- 1 teaspoon paprika
- 4 dashes Tabasco sauce

Preheat the oven to 400°F. Thoroughly combine all ingredients and form into balls. Place on a baking sheet, and bake 30 minutes.

Carolina-Style Deviled Crab

Deviled crabs have been served with élan across the Lowcountry over the years. They were a great specialty in olden days on Daufuskie Island, South Carolina. To "devil" a dish means that you give it some pizzazz by adding a spicy ingredient or two such as red pepper flakes, mustard, or Tabasco sauce.

I am indebted to the late Gettings and the late Ora Lou O'Hara Cushman of Aiken, South Carolina, for this recipe, which was featured in their *Treasured Southern Family Recipes*. Diane Kennedy tested this recipe. She liked it very much and suggested that some cooks may wish to add a bit more hot sauce, if desired. This recipe adaptation will serve six nice-sized servings or eight smaller ones.

- 7 tablespoons butter
- 2 tablespoons flour
- 2 tablespoons catsup
- 1 tablespoon mustard
- 2 teaspoons fresh lemon juice
- 1 ½ teaspoons Worcestershire sauce
- ½ teaspoon salt
- Dash Tabasco sauce
- 1 cup milk
- 1 small onion, minced
- 1 small green pepper, minced
- 2 cups crab meat, in small pieces
- 2 hard-cooked eggs, minced
- ½ cup soft bread crumbs

Preheat oven to 400°F.

Melt 4 tablespoons butter in the top half of a double boiler. Stir in the flour and add the next 6 ingredients. Mix in the milk slowly and cook, stirring often, until thickened. Remove double boiler from heat, set aside, and cover.

Melt 1 tablespoon butter in a skillet and sauté the onion and green pepper until slightly tender. Add to the mixture in double boiler. Add the crab meat and eggs and mix well.

Pack the mixture into crab shells or small baking mold. Melt 2 tablespoons butter, roll breadcrumbs in it, and sprinkle over top of each filled shell.

Bake for 10 minutes or until crumbs are browned.

Savannah Deviled Crab Casseroles

Savannah native Ben Green Cooper first published a version of this recipe in his *Savannah's Cookin'*.

Using a large skillet, first make a white sauce by heating a tablespoon of butter and blending in two and a quarter tablespoons of all purpose flour, stirring in small increments of milk as needed to thin. Set aside.

Combine four hard-boiled egg yokes (chopped), salt and pepper to taste, and a touch of cayenne. Add a pound of claw crab meat, stir, and add in a teaspoon of ground nutmeg. Mix thoroughly. Cook until crabmeat is hot, stirring and thinning with milk or white wine as needed.

Spoon the crabmeat and sauce into four small casseroles. Brush tops with beaten egg whites, dust with cracker or bread crumbs, and dot with butter.

Place casseroles in 400°F oven to brown crusts, about 14 to 16 minutes, and serve hot.

Marinated Shrimp

University of Georgia alumnus Sonny Seiler of Savannah is known as the Bulldog Nation's Number 1 Fan. He is the caretaker for Uga, the Georgia team's white English bulldog mascot. Unfortunately, Uga VII, age 4, died an untimely death in 2009, of a heart attack.

Sonny and his wife, Cecilia, are also great seafood devotees. My thanks to the Seilers, along with my friend Loran Smith and his wife, Myrna, for giving me permission to run this recipe, published originally in their collection of Bulldog tailgating recipes *Let the Big Dog Eat.*

Sonny Seiler of Savannah, Georgia, whose marinated shrimp is a tailgate favorite, is caretaker of the University of Georgia's bulldog mascot, Uga. (Photo courtesy of Sonny Seiler and Loran Smith.)

Sonny Seiler's Savannah Marinated Shrimp

- 4 pounds shrimp, peeled and cooked
- 1 cup vegetable oil (such as Wesson)
- 1 cup tarragon vinegar
- 2 medium onions, sliced
- 2 cloves garlic, crushed
- Salt, black pepper, and red pepper, to taste

Mix all the ingredients together and marinate in the refrigerator overnight. Serve with toothpicks and crackers. Travels well in a wide-neck soup thermos and makes 4 to 6 servings.

Savannah Shrimp Paste

This recipe for an old favorite originated in Savannah and can be served hot or cold. It yields twenty-four servings.

- 1 ¾ pounds raw shrimp
- ¾ cup softened butter, plus additional butter for dotting
- 1 ½ teaspoons Worcestershire sauce

- 1 teaspoon salt
- Dash cayenne pepper
- Dash black pepper
- 2 cups toasted breadcrumbs

Preheat oven to 450°F.

Cook, shell, and devein shrimp; run through food chopper and mash to smooth paste. Mix in softened butter, Worcestershire, salt, and peppers, and blend to a butterlike consistency.

Press into small loaf pan, top with breadcrumbs, and dot with butter.

Bake for about 15 minutes.

Chill, slice thin, and serve on crackers.

Captain Woody's Oysters on the Half Shell

This recipe is adapted from one appearing in the Bluffton, South Carolina, cookbook *Great Cooks Rise...with the May River Tide*. My thanks to the publishers, The Women of the Church of the Cross Episcopal Church. Bluffton is the home of South Carolina's last oyster factory, located on the banks of the May River.

- Oysters on half shell (use as many as fill a baking sheet)
- Sharp cheddar cheese, grated
- Mild jalapeno peppers (canned or in jars)
- Sour cream

Place the oysters on the half shell on a baking sheet and top with the jalapeno peppers and cheese.

Bake in the mircowave or oven until the cheese melts and the oysters on the half shell are warm. Top with sour cream and serve while warm.

Dragon Wings (Alligator Ribs)

As a finale, here's an interesting appetizer that came from a good friend residing in the heart of the Lowcountry, Charleston, South Carolina. This recipe will yield 4 servings of 4 ribs per person. Here's how he told it to me:

- 16 alligator ribs, legally processed
- Salt and pepper to taste
- 1 cup peanut oil
- 2 tablespoons crushed cayenne peppers
- ½ cup soy sauce

Thaw, separate, and cut the ribs into individual pieces. Add the salt and pepper and parboil in water, just at the simmer, for around 30 to 45 minutes. Drain and chill.

Put peanut oil in a large skillet and bring to medium heat. Pour in cayenne peppers and stir for around 4 minutes or so. Add ribs and soy sauce.

Turn several times with pincers until thoroughly browned, and serve as an appetizer.

CHAPTER 9

The Lowcountry's Splendorous Seafood

Fi-ish! Fresh Fish! I got de porgy!
Oh, de porgy walk a' the porgy talk
De porgy et with de knife an fork!
Porgy! porgy! Fresh Fish!

—Charleston Receipts

It was in the spring of 2008, and I felt fortunate to be riding with kinfolks Robert and Jenelle Grooms, who were giving me a grand tour of Charleston's booming James Island community. Folly Road was busy with afternoon rush-hour traffic as we neared Folly Beach.

Bob turned westward onto a narrow dirt road. With the windows down, we could smell salty breezes blowing off the marshes just ahead of us. Bob, a Citadel graduate engineer who grew up at Folly Beach and still lives nearby, started telling me about the colorful history of the Bowens Island Seafood Restaurant,

Photo showing the old Bowen Seafood Restaurant, which was destroyed by a fire in 2006. A replacement building is scheduled to reopen in the spring of 2010. (Photo courtesy of Robert Barber.)

which, over a span of six decades, had earned its reputation as one of the Lowcountry's truly great seafood institutions and had been known across the country for its stupendous oyster roasts.

"When they roasted the oysters in the big fireplace in the old days," Grooms recalled, "they would scoop them up in square-nosed shovels and bring them to your table that way, pouring them out right in front of you, along with oyster knives so you could pop them open and consume them then and there, with a little Bowens Island cocktail sauce, of course."

The food was great, "but the atmosphere was even better," Grooms recalled. "It was the place to go. South Carolina's leading politicians wouldn't dare visit Charleston without stopping by the Bowens Island institution to check out the oysters and the crowds of customers."

Jenelle Grooms gobbles down an oyster at the legendary Bowens Island Seafood Restaurant near Folly Beach, South Carolina, while her husband, Robert Grooms, uses a special knife to shuck the freshly steamed oysters to take his turn at eating. (Photos by the author.)

Jimmy and May Bowen started the restaurant in 1946, and along with the great seafood, they started accumulating television sets, displaying them one by one all around the eatery's big room with the fireplace nearby. When Jimmy Bowen died, the TV total topped fifty sets. It was something to see in those early years of television, Grooms recalled. That plus a 1946 Seeburg jukebox that played five 78 rpm records for a quarter (and is still in service today).

Lowcountry folks dearly loved to visit the place and proved it with inscriptions that they scribbled across the walls over the years. But that was in the era before the big fire in 2006 that destroyed the place.

As we rolled up and parked under an ancient oak tree, we saw the gutted remains of the main structure to the left, but to the right in temporary quarters, the eatery was still in business with a rebuilt kitchen and a temporary dining deck extending out to the Folly River.

Robert Barber, owner and operator of the Bowens Island Seafood Restaurant. (Photo by the author.)

Ironically, just before the big fire, Robert Barber, the Bowens' grandson, had accepted a James Beard Foundation award in New York, designating the restaurant an American Classic. Well-known over South Carolina as a lawyer and a former legislator, Barber managed in 2007 to get the place reopened in the temporary facilities.

"I took over the management here when my grandmother passed away in 1990," Barber told me after we took our seats. "I had moved back here [to Charleston] in 1983 to practice law. I'd worked in restaurants most all my early life, and as I got older and since I lived close by, I told them I was ready to help out if they needed me. I've been in charge now for almost eighteen years."

He added, "We're intending in the next few months to start rebuilding the old restaurant in the same spot," hoping to preserve part of the gutted main structure. (At the time of writing, completion of the new structure was scheduled by 2009 year end.)

My friends and I took seats in the screened-in dining deck, and we checked out the restaurant's steamed oysters that arrived at our table by the shovel-full just like in the old days.

"Ours are local oysters," Robert Barber told me during a break in the traffic. "They're inter-tidal oysters, being exposed to the air and the sun part of the day and are covered by the tide the other part of the day."

He maintains state leases that surround Bowens Island and his pickers also go to the public beds. "Most of our oysters come to us from within five hundred yards to a mile from here, so they're quite fresh. Two gentlemen pick oysters for me four days a week. They go out in a small flat-bottomed boat and when they reach what looks like a good oyster bed, they get out of the boat and get down in the mud and pick them off the bank. They use a hammer or a pipe to break up the clusters. They bring back the [bigger] oysters and break off the smaller oysters and dead shell, leaving them behind. When the oysters are spawning, the old shells give the newly born oysters a hard surface to cling to. That helps them get started. And of course, leaving the small ones there enhances next year's harvest."

Later, Barber asked us if the oysters we had just gobbled down proved satisfactory. "Oh, yes, they are the very best," said Jenelle Grooms. "There's no question about the oysters you get here." Bob and I signaled ditto.

"The salinity of our oysters is phenomenal," Barber told me. "Some of the folks [in other restaurants] have to sprinkle salt on theirs that come from the Gulf. Ours have a natural saltiness and when you chew 'em they have a nice texture to 'em."

The Bowens Island restaurant does not confine itself to oysters alone. "We do fried shrimp that I think are as good as you'll find anywhere," he said. "And crab cakes. When we do the crab cakes on the seafood platter, we use claw meat."

We left Bowens Island with our appetites fully sated, bellies satisfied and happy. "Come back when we get the place completely rebuilt," Barber said as we headed out the door. "The oysters, shrimp, and crabs will be the same but the surroundings will be a lot more comfortable."

The Lowcountry's Staggering Seafood Riches

The Lowcountry has been blessed over the centuries with staggering seafood riches. Even before the earliest European settlers witnessed it in the 1600s, the Sewee and Santee Indians left behind huge mounds of oyster and clam shells called "middens" up and down the Carolina and Georgia coasts.

Thus shellfish—shrimp, crabs, clams, crawfish and oysters—led in colonial-era popularity from the beginning. Following close behind were finfish such as flounder, shad, snapper, grouper, winter sea trout, and whiting, plus freshwater panfish, found in big numbers in the Lowcountry's vast network of tidal and freshwater rivers, creeks, and inlets. These range from largemouth bass and bream to catfish and perch-like porgys as well as mullet, which swim up into freshwater streams to spawn. And don't forget the big fish swimming in deeper waters off the coast!

As Lowcountry expert John Martin Taylor wrote, shrimp are the backbone of Lowcountry seafood scene while crab and oysters "are its heart and soul." Folk in the Lowcountry coastal plain are fortunate that they can wade out into creeks and estuaries with cast nets when shrimp are running, and soon return with a net full of the deli-cious rascals. Or go crabbing with old chicken necks and pull in blue crabs aplenty. Oystering in creek banks at low tide is also easy.

Even today, shellfish—while not in the abundance of earlier centuries—are so plenteous that shrimp boils, crab boils and oyster roasts have become highly popular outdoor social activities. So much so that Charlestonians Matt Lee and Ted Lee proclaimed that even winter blasts cold enough to curl camellia leaves can't keep Lowcountry people indoors in the face of such sumptuous outdoor feasts.

YOUNG FISHERMAN

During my boyhood years in McClellanville [South Carolina], I became a commercial fisherman, working alone…at Eagle Hummock, Oyster Bay, Five Fathoms Creek. On good days I might catch one hundred good fish. I had my regular customers and sold a "string" of twelve fish for twenty-five cents.

I loved to sell fish to an old gentleman who weighed about three hundred pounds. He always bought a string for the family and one for himself.

I used to sell shrimp and crabs, so that before I was in my teens, I was learning the value of money and had a little of my own jingling in my pockets. Later I was to read old Sam Johnson's pronouncement, "Making money is the most harmless pleasure in the world."

—THE LATE ARCHIBALD RUTLEDGE
THE WOODS AND WILD THINGS I REMEMBER (1970)

Shrimp, the Seafood King

Without a doubt, shrimp are the most favored shellfish among the fortunate folks popu-lating the Southeastern coastal plain. As Bubba observed in *Forrest Gump*, "Shrimp is the fruit of the sea. You can barbecue it, boil it, broil it, bake it, and fry it."

Bubba could have also mentioned that shrimp can also be steamed, smoked, stewed, sautéed, and pickled. They are perfect for use in such revered dishes as Shrimp Pilau, Shrimp Bog, Shrimp Soup, Shrimp Pie, Shrimp Wheels, Shrimp Gravy, Shrimp and Grits, Shrimp and Rice, Shrimp and Sausage, Lowcountry Boil, or its historical progenitor, Frogmore Stew. And the list goes on. You get the picture.

Nothing quite equals the flavor of shrimp fresh from the net. The best are small shrimp harvested in creeks and inlets. My friend Charles Seabrook waxes nostalgic when remembering his teenage shrimping days on Johns Island near Charleston.

"The tiny creek shrimp were so plentiful then," he recalled, "their sharp tails made swimming unpleasant. Only a few throws of the cast net were enough to get a mess of them for breakfast to be mixed with hot, buttered grits."

Our dog-eared copy of the 1956 edition of the classic *Charleston Receipts*, still published by the Junior League of Charleston and more popular today than ever, starts off its seafood section with this shrimp vendor refrain:

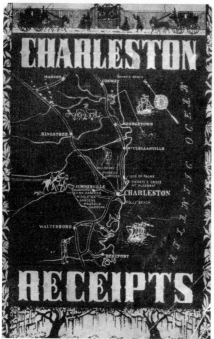

Lady, git yo' dishpan—
Yuh come de swimp-man
Swimpee! Swimpee!
Raw, raw, swi-i-mp

The editors of the renowned Charleston cookbook suggested to their early readers in the 1950s that the tasty small shrimp could best be obtained from black street hucksters. Today, in season, fresh shrimp, as well as crabs and oysters, are available in seafood markets and grocery stores up and down the coastal plain.

While many prefer boiling, the easiest and most popular way to cook the smaller brown creek shrimp is to gently sauté them in butter and serve them hot over grits or rice. Here follows some outstanding recipes for this hearty and scrumptious seafood.

Mills Lane's Creek Shrimp

Savannah native Mills B. Lane Jr., who was the flamboyant president of Savannah's Citizens and Southern National Bank that grew into Bank of America, loved to fix up his own special seafood dishes. In the 1960s he gave this delightful shrimp recipe to the then *Atlanta Journal* food editor Grace Hartley.

"The reason this is such a good and unusual dish," Grace wrote, "is that shrimp make their own gravy." Here's the recipe, with the late Mr. Lane's own humorous wording.

Mills B. Lane Jr. (Photo courtesy of Martha Nesbit.)

Alligator Creek Shrimp

Use small shrimp, if possible, preferably fresh but thawed ones will do. Peel and clean. Use as many as needed to go 'round, based on ½ pound per serving.

Place shrimp in a bowl and sprinkle with soy sauce, which gives them a nice color. Set the bowl in a corner and go have a real cold beer. For a half hour to an hour, give the bowl a stir when you feel like it.

Now take an uncovered frying pan and warm up some cooking oil (peanut oil is best). Put in chopped onion and cook about 5 minutes until you have a sort of oil-onion soup.

Next dump in the shrimp and soy sauce marinade. Give it a good dash of pepper—no salt needed. Gently toss and cook no more than 3 minutes, maybe less.

Now you have really got something! Just have the hominy grits ready and some hot biscuits and you're in business!

> ### MAKING BROWN SHRIMP GRAVY
> *My sister-in-law Mildred Seabrook, who was born and raised on Wadmalaw Island, learned how to make brown shrimp gravy from her mama, and is about the only one who knows how to cook brown shrimp gravy like my own mama made it. No one has ever come even close. Several of the Charleston restaurants can't come close, either. They want to gussy it up too much and put in all kinds of ingredients that never should have been in there in the first place.*
>
> —CHARLES SEABROOK
> ATLANTA, A NATIVE OF JOHNS ISLAND, SC

Chef Louis Osteen. (Photo courtesy of Marlene Osteen.)

Shrimp & Grits, Osteen Style

Some years ago, *Esquire* magazine called Louis Osteen "the premier interpreter of New Southern cuisine." It was Osteen, the prize-winning Beard Foundation chef, who while in Charleston pioneered the elevation of what was then merely a favorite cafe dish loved by dockworkers and Lowcountry craftsmen to the high status it commands today in Charleston's and Savannah's classiest restaurants, as well as eateries along the Carolina-Georgia coastline and beyond.

My thanks to Louis, who now serves as chef at the Lake Rabun Hotel in the Blue Ridge Mountains, northeast of Atlanta. This recipe yields six servings.

Louis's Shrimp & Grits

SHRIMP SAUCE

- 6 slices bacon
- 6 tablespoons butter
- 1 cup onion, chopped fine
- ½ cup green pepper, chopped fine
- ⅓ cup celery, chopped fine
- 2 cloves garlic, minced
- 1 sprig fresh thyme, or ¼ teaspoon dried thyme
- 2 bay leaves
- ⅓ cup white vermouth or dry white wine
- 8 tablespoons all-purpose flour
- 4 cups fish/shrimp stock, or bottled clam juice
- 2 tablespoons tomato paste

- 2 cups heavy cream
- Salt and pepper to taste
- 1 ½ pounds shrimp, more or less, large or small

In a large skillet, set over medium-high heat, cook the bacon until crisp. Remove to paper towels to drain, reserving the fat in the skillet. In the rendered bacon drippings, along with butter, sauté the onions, green pepper, celery, and garlic. Cook for 4 to 5 minutes. Add the thyme and bay leaves and cook for another minute.

Increase the heat to high, add the vermouth, and cook until it evaporates, about 2 to 3 minutes.

Lower the heat to medium and add the flour to the pan, stirring to prevent lumps. Cook the flour for a few minutes to brown it. Be sure to scrape up any of the browned bits that are stuck to the bottom of the pan.

Add the stock and tomato paste and mix quickly with a whisk to avoid lumps. When the mixture starts to bubble, add the cream. Return to a simmer and add salt and pepper to taste.

Sauté the shrimp in butter for around 2 minutes until it is about halfway done. Then blend in the sauce along with the shrimp for another 2 to 3 minutes to complete the cooking.

Serve the shrimp and sauce over hot grits.

GRITS
- 2 cups milk
- 2 cups water
- 1 teaspoon salt
- 1 cup quick grits (not instant)
- 4 teaspoons unsalted butter
- 1 cup heavy cream
- 2 teaspoons freshly ground black pepper

Bring the milk and water to a boil in a heavy-bottomed saucepan over medium heat. Stir in the salt. Slowly add the grits, stirring constantly.

When the grits begin to thicken, turn the heat down to low and simmer for 30 to 40 minutes, stirring occasionally to prevent the grits from scorching. Stir in the butter and cream and simmer for 5 minutes. Stir in the pepper. Keep warm.

Frogmore Stew (a.k.a. Lowcountry Boil)

The shrimp dish Lowcountry Boil was called Frogmore Stew when created in the 1960s (and still so named by many purists). Its namesake is the inventor's old home community on St.

Helena Island near Beaufort, South Carolina. Unfortunately, Frogmore as a place name died with the removal of the community's post office in the 1980s. You can read details of the stew's invention and original recipe [on page 75 in the chapter on Beaufort.]

Actually, the name *Frogmore Stew* is something of a misnomer since, before serving, the mixture is drained of all its liquid. Steamed or boiled, Frogmore consists of a delicious conglomeration of shrimp, sausage, and freshly shucked corn on the cob

Charlestonian Ben Moise shows off a platter of Frogmore Stew that he took to the Pawley Island Red Neck Chowder and Marching Society's annual soiree at Pawley's Island, South Carolina. (Photo courtesy of Ben Moise.)

cut up into cob-ettes. Additional ingredient options include onions and small red potatoes and, on occasion, live blue crabs.

There are many fans of the revered dish. Charleston caterer Ben Moise—one of the Lowcountry's great Frogmore Stew devotees—asserts that after trying out the celebrated dish, "people have been seen spontaneously bowing their heads in a moment of silent prayer." He prefers preparing the dish minus potatoes, as advocated several decades ago by South Carolina State Senator James Waddell of Beaufort. At the time, Ben was serving as a South Carolina state marine game warden. Here is Ben's recipe for Frogmore Stew, along with his recipes for seafood cocktail sauce and coleslaw.

Ben's Frogmore Stew

- 3 cups Old Bay seasoning
- 1 pound Hillshire Farms Kielbasa sausage, cut on the diagonal in ½-inch pieces

- 8 (3-inch) frozen corn "cobettes" (keep frozen until ready to cook)
- 2 pounds (36 to 40) fresh or thawed shrimp (unshelled)

Fill a large pot (one that has a strainer) two-thirds full of water; bring water to a rolling boil and add 2 cups of Old Bay seasoning. Place the strainer in the pot and add the sausage and frozen corn. Bring back to a boil and cook for 10 minutes.

Add the shrimp and cook for 2 to 2 ½ minutes. It is important *not* to overcook the shrimp. Remove strainer and drain.

Sprinkle remaining cup of Old Bay seasoning liberally over the cooked ingredients as you are pouring them from the strainer into the serving bowls. Don't be shy!

This recipe serves 4. If you have a large crowd, you may have to do this in several batches. Do not overcrowd the pot, and remember the water in the pot will expand a little when brought up to the boil.

Serve with coleslaw, seafood cocktail sauce, and squeeze butter (for the corn). Moise prefers using squeeze butter so you can hold your plate while applying it to the corn.

Ben's Seafood Cocktail Sauce

"I like to have my sauce a little loose," Ben Moise says, "so that it will cover the seafood that is dipped into it. Some sauces are so stiff they won't stick to a shrimp or an oyster." Ben uses this sauce for dipping shrimp when he does a Frogmore Stew event or for oysters at an oyster roast. This recipe will serve upwards of fifty people.

- 1 64-ounce bottle Heinz catsup
- 1 small jar ground horseradish (not the creamy prepared sauce)
- ¼ cup "Wooster" (Worcestershire) sauce
- 1 cup Texas Pete hot sauce (or a hotter sauce if desired)
- 2 to 3 cups brown cider vinegar

Mix all ingredients together and serve with shrimp or oysters.

MOISE ISLAND POTATO CRAB CAKES

We were spending a long weekend on our [Moise] island and on Sunday morning discovered that we had a number of baked potatoes and a substantial amount of garden salad left over after a big steak cookout the night before.

We pulled up the crab pot at the end of the dock and found around a dozen good-size blue crabs. We boiled and picked the crabs, which produced around a full soup bowl of crab meat. There probably would have been a little more than that, but a few of the pickers were caught sneaking a bite or two occasionally.

We skinned two of the large potatoes and mashed them thoroughly, adding a little salt and black pepper. We picked out the sliced onion and bell pepper from the salad and diced them, adding them to the mashed potato mix.

Then we sprinkled around a tablespoon of cornstarch over the top of the mix to serve as a binder and stirred in thoroughly. Next we broke an egg over the crab meat and stirred that all together then poured that into the potato mixture and mixed the whole thing together.

I brought up to medium heat a large skillet with a half inch of vegetable oil. Then I took a biscuit-size patty from the mixture, coated it with cornmeal, and put it into the hot skillet. We repeated that until we got a skillet full. I browned them on both sides. I can't remember how many this would serve in terms of 'normal' people, but three of us ate the whole bloomin' thing.

—BEN McC. MOISE,
CHARLESTON, SOUTH CAROLINA

Ben's Coleslaw Dressing

For years, Moise has been using this "receipt" for coleslaw to go along with his Frogmore Stew events.

- 1 (32-ounce) jar Hellmann's mayonnaise
- 1 tablespoon dill weed
- 1 tablespoon garlic powder
- 1 tablespoon black pepper
- 1 teaspoon salt
- 2 tablespoons yellow mustard
- Brown cider vinegar
- Shredded cabbage slaw

Open the mayonnaise and scoop out about 4 tablespoons of mayonnaise from the center of the jar, making a large hole. Into the hole, pour the dill weed, garlic powder, pepper, salt, and mustard. Add enough vinegar to fill the jar to within an inch of the top. Cover the jar, shake well, and refrigerate overnight.

Before serving, shake again, then pour sauce over shredded cabbage slaw in a large bowl, tossing well just before putting it on the table to keep everything crisp.

Harvesting Oysters

Centuries ago, the Indians harvested oysters in small boats. The first white settlers did also, carving dugouts from cypress logs and gathering the oysters by hand. Today, individuals still harvest oysters this way. While it takes three years for an oyster to reach maturity, many oystermen re-seed existing beds each year. Harvesting oysters is usually done in the cooler months from September through January, when the oysters are saltier and more firm in texture.

Oystering at Murrells Inlet, South Carolina
"OUR OYSTERS TASTE REALLY GOOD; YOU DON'T NEED ANY SALT"

I felt privileged to meet oysterman Franklin Smalls in 2008 while making a research visit with the Chandler family at Murrells Inlet, South Carolina. Saltwater marshes facing the Atlantic Ocean surround the six-mile inlet. Local legends have it that Captain Murrell, a pirate, often dropped anchor there before and during the Carolina colonial era.

Sixty-year-old Smalls was born at Brookgreen, South Carolina, one of a family of sixteen children. When he was three, he and his family moved across the King's Highway (U.S. Highway 17) to the Inlet, one of South Carolina's historic oystering areas. There, at age nine, he started picking oysters.

Later in life, after a drinking spree, he picked up the nickname "Snake Man"

With salt marshes in the background, Franklin Smalls and his boss, Bill Chandler, discuss the fine art of oystering at Murrells Inlet, South Carolina. (Photo by the author.)

when he was seen down on all fours one night. He got over that episode in his life, went on the wagon, and became one of the Inlet's most accomplished and respected oystermen. Smalls has been following the trade for more than fifty years.

He currently works for Bill Chandler, an Inlet native who returned home after a distinguished career as a NASA engineer. Currently, Chandler owns a number of oyster leases near his home along the Inlet's marshes. He expressed great pride in his oysters, which he says "are the best oysters that I've ever tasted." He also spoke of great appreciation for his skilled oysterman, Franklin Smalls.

I first asked Smalls about his favorite seafood. He replied quickly that it was winter trout. "Yes sir, speckled trout. The meat is more firmer and courser."

"He fishes at the Inlet more than any other person I know," Chandler said.

"And," added Bill's sister June, "He knows where to get 'em, too."

Here is Smalls' story in his own words, as told to me in the interview.

Franklin "Snake Man" Smalls. (Photo by the author.)

Most of the black folks around here work the marsh lands during the winter months. Then in the summer months they work in the restaurants and hotels at Myrtle Beach and along the Grand Strand. That's true for my brothers and sisters. But I'm an eater and not a cooker. I'm the type of person, I like to be outside. I like to see God's sky over my head. I don't feel too comfortable cooped up in a building.

I been working with Mister Bill Chandler here for fifteen years. Before that I worked for ten years as an oyster picker with his brother, the late Tommy Chandler, right down the road.

The Chandlers, Mister Bill and Miz Anne and their extended family, Miz "Sister" [Genevieve Peterkin] and June Chandler Hora, they don't treat me as a worker, they treat me as a member of the family. Yes sir. When I come to work in the morning, first thing Miz Anne does is fix me a cup of coffee.

In picking oysters out of the mud banks, we use oyster gloves and what we call an oyster knocker, made of iron rebar. That's what you use to knock the little oysters loose from the big ones. You leave the little oysters in the ground [so they can keep growing]. That's what we call 'cultivating.'

Oyster season comes in from September fifteen and goes on through the "r" months. I work the oyster beds in the marshes behind Mister Bill's home, right over on Whale Creek to our left. He has state leases for fifteen acres of oyster beds. [The state calculates the leased acreage as that land situated three feet along the shoreline.]

Going out to pick oysters on the marsh banks, I use that little fourteen-foot-square stern canoe with a small Evinrude engine.

Years ago, when I went into the oyster business, we used to pick twenty, twenty-five bushels of oysters a day. Nowadays, we limit ourselves to harvesting four bushels a day, just so there'll be plenty of oysters left for the years to come. Mr. Bill says that gives us a bigger and better quality oyster down the road. I must say that we harvest quality oysters. Our oysters taste really good; you don't need any salt.

So the boss has me to skip past some oyster beds for three years to let the oysters grow and regenerate there, going north-south and east-west. As a result, we harvest quality oysters. Course Mother Nature has a way of reviving herself.

I also pick clams, but when I'm picking oysters, I concentrate on oysters. When I'm picking clams, I concentrate on clams.

I've been here for fifty-nine years, and I don't know of

OYSTERS FOR SALE IN SAVANNAH IN 1837
OYSTER HALL AT SKIDAWAY FERRY
The subscriber, proprietor of this establishment, would respectfully inform friends and the public, that he continues to put up Pickled Oysters, in superior style, which he warrants to keep in any climate, and that for their better convenience, he has made arrangements to have at all time, during the ensuing season, a full supply on hand in the city. Messrs. Turner, Eastman & Co., will receive any applications for orders, which will be promptly attended to; also, Oysters in the shell put up in barrels, and delivered in two hours after being taken from the water.

—DAILY GEORGIAN
OCTOBER 5, 1837

anyone who's ever got sick from any of our Lowcountry shellfish, on up to North Carolina. That's not the case with shellfish that come from elsewhere.

Oyster Roasts & Recipes

In the 1800s oysters were eaten raw, baked, fried, fricasseed, in soups, pies, and stuffings. According to the *South Carolina Wildlife Magazine*, an 1853 gumbo recipe called for one hundred oysters.

Oyster roasts are still carried out the old-fashioned way in many Lowcountry backyards. As Charles Seabrook says, "With oysters, you toss them on a red-hot sheet of tin, throw a wet croaker sack over them, let them steam a few minutes, and then open them up for eating."

The aforementioned Ben Moise is a master in organizing highly popular oyster roasts. He steams bushels of oysters and spreads them out on tables for his hungry fans east of the Mississippi River. Along with the oysters, Ben often puts out a grand serving of shrimp-based Frogmore Stew as detailed on page 132.

Moise once took his Oyster Roast/Frogmore Stew "movable feast" to Winston Salem, North Carolina. As he and his people dumped several bushels of steamed oysters out on the tables, the ladies "paraded around as if they were looking at animals in a zoo," he recalled,

"Some of 'em thought it was remarkable that the oysters were all closed up like that. They had no idea that there were two sides on the shell. They'd always seen them on the half shell.

A shovel full of steaming oysters is dumped at the table in front of Bob Grooms. The Bowens Island Seafood Restaurant harvests its oysters in nearby oyster fields. (Photo by the author.)

"Who's going to open those things?" several said, and Ben replied, "That would be you."

"After we showed them how to crack them open with oyster knives, they launched forth, [eating] with alacrity, and seemed to enjoy the day's experience, including consuming their share of Frogmore Stew."

Here are some authentic current-day oyster recipes.

Edisto Fried Oysters

Fried oysters are very popular throughout the Lowcountry. On my research tour to Savannah, I enjoyed a scrumptious plate of fried oysters at the historic Johnny Harris Restaurant on Victory Drive.

This recipe is adapted from *Treasured Southern Family Recipes* compiled by the late Geddings de M. Cushman and Ora Lou O'Hara Cushman of Aiken, South Carolina. It's based on a recipe they obtained from friends on South Carolina's Edisto Island south of Charleston. It will yield six servings.

- 1 quart select oysters
- 2 eggs
- 2 tablespoons evaporated milk
- 1 teaspoon salt
- 1 teaspoon pepper
- 1 cup finely crushed saltines

Drain the oysters of all liquid. Beat the eggs well and add the milk and seasonings.

Dip the oysters, one by one, into the egg mixture and roll them in the saltine meal, covering thoroughly.

Drop the oysters one by one into deep fat heated to 375°F so they do not touch and cook about 2 minutes, or until golden brown.

Remove and place on paper towels to absorb excess fat. Serve with lemon wedges, fancy catsup, or tartar sauce.

Note: Some readers may wish to consider using a thin rice flour and cornmeal-based fry dredge sold by Carolina Plantation Rice in Darlington, South Carolina. It can be purchased at carolinaplantationrice.com.

Savannah Angels on Horseback

I can personally testify that eating at The Wilkes Dining Room in Savannah's historic district continues to be an exciting culinary experience, even though the legendary restaurant's namesake, Mrs. Sema Wilkes, passed away some years ago at age ninety-five.

This recipe adaptation is based on Mrs. Wilkes' original recipe book, with my thanks to her granddaughter, Marcia Thompson. It yields six servings.

- 1 pint select chucked oysters
- 12 strips bacon, sliced in half
- ½ teaspoon salt
- ⅛ teaspoon pepper
- ⅛ teaspoon paprika
- 2 tablespoons chopped parsley

Preheat the oven to 450°F. Wash and drain oysters.

Sprinkle the oysters with the salt, pepper, paprika, and parsley. Partially cook the bacon and drain on paper towels. Then roll the bacon slices around each oyster and fasten with a toothpick.

Place in a shallow baking pan on the lower rack and bake for about 10 minutes, or until the bacon is crispy. Remove the toothpicks and serve.

Blue Crabs

It's very easy to "go crabbin" for blue crabs in the Lowcountry's tidal creeks and branches. And thus it's a favorite pastime among people young and old.

All it takes is a lengthy cord and a stinky old chicken neck, which you tie to the end of the cord along with a sinker. Then you throw the

OLD KATE, THE OYSTER WIFE

She's dead! old Kate the oyster wife,
You'll hear her cry no more.
As,"Oyesh-taa! Lady oyesh-taa!" she,
Was wont to cry of yore.
She's dead, old Kate, the oyster wife,
Her oyster days are o'er.
And many a sable fishwife weeps,
Who never wept before.
"Yea, Oyesh-taa! Lady oye-esh-taa!"
And stopt and listened to her notes,
Ere they pass her by.
And stopt again, and listened aft,
As echo backward rung,
"Yea, oyesh-taa! Lady Oyeesh taa!"...
But, now the steps where she sat
The live long winter's night...
So silent and so sad they seem,
So darksome and so drear,
The pany-cake, groundnut girls
No more assemble there.
Her bucket and her calabash,
Have passed to other hands.

—"RALPH RHYME"
CHARLESTON COURIER, 1846

neck and sinker in the water and wrap the other end of the cord around your wrist. Be sure to also carry a long-handled net and a bucket to collect your catch.

Charles Seabrook also used a smelly herring while crabbing there during his younger years, always cautious to keep the crabs from latching on to him with their claws. "We'd snatch up the unwary critter when it gnawed on the meat," he recalled, "and toss it into the net. It took only an hour or so to fill a large bean crate with the clawed creatures."

Stone Crabs

It's a different matter trying to catch stone crabs, which have to be pulled barehanded from their hermit-like holes. As Genevieve "Sis" Chandler Peterkin of Murrells Inlet recalls in her delightful memoir, *Heaven is a Beautiful Place*, her mother, the late Genevieve Willcox Chandler, "was the only white woman around the inlet who would catch stone crabs with just her bare hand."

Looking something like a lobster, the stone crab possesses a claw that will grab you if not carefully caught. And he lives at the bottom of his tunnel, about an arm's length into the oyster rock below the

Genevieve Willcox Chandler pictured at her son Bill Chandler's Murrells Inlet duck blind in 1967. The late Mrs. Chandler was skilled in harvesting stone crabs at low tide. She was also noted for her outstanding 1930s work in interviewing black residents in Eastern South Carolina's Waccamaw River area for the WPA Federal Writer's Project. (Photo courtesy of the Chandler family.)

low tide surface. Mother Chandler would go in after a stone crab at low tide when the mud flats and oyster banks were glistening in the afternoon sun.

"It's the one thing I wouldn't even try," Sis Peterkin recalled. "Mama told me how to do it, but I just wasn't brave enough."

"The stone crab is always facing forward with his giant claw tucked up in front," her mother told Sis. "You feel his smooth back, you crook your fingers over it, and then you snatch him out quick."

If you fail in your mission, the stone crab "can easily break one or more of your fingers," Sis Peterkin says, recounting nightmare stories of people being held down with their arm in the hole until they were drowned by the rising tide.

Sis recalled that her mother got bit by a stone crab one time. "She was lucky because the stone crab caught her in the fleshy part between the thumb and forefinger." Her brother Dick was there and told her to keep still and relax. So she stretched out on the oyster rock with her arm down in the hole for quite a while, "and finally she felt the crab release her," Sis Peterkin recalled.

Deviled Crab Cakes

Some years ago, when the distinguished food writer James Villas and his mother, Martha Pearl, were dining at Pawleys Island, South Carolina, just down the road from Murrell's Inlet, Villas's mother became quite taken with Chef Louis Osteen's crab cakes.

"She not only asked for the recipe," James recalled, "but virtually demanded the chef take her back to the kitchen to show her exactly how he fixed them."

Such is the seasoned skill and deft hand of Louis Osteen, who today is based at Lake Rabun Hotel in northeast Georgia. Therefore it is no wonder that some years ago he was named by the James Beard Foundation as the top chef in the Southeast.

Here is a spicier version of the lump crab cakes that excited Martha Pearl Villas so much, with thanks to Louis and Marlene Osteen for sharing this recipe with me. This yields 10 4-ounce dinner portion crab cakes.

Louis's Deviled Crab Cakes

- 2 cups best quality mayonnaise
- 2 egg whites
- 1 teaspoon Tabasco
- 1 tablespoon plus 1 teaspoon Coleman's dry mustard or spicy dry mustard
- 6 tablespoons minced shallots
- ½ cup minced green onions
- 2 pounds lump crab meat, gently picked over to remove any shell without breaking up the big pieces of crab
- 3 cups dried breadcrumbs made in a food processor from a sliced and dried baguette

- 2 tablespoons unsalted butter, melted and cooled slightly
- 1 cup peanut oil
- 4 tablespoons unsalted butter

Whisk the mayonnaise and the egg whites together in a small bowl until well blended. Whisk in the Tabasco and dry mustard. Add the shallots and green onions and mix well. Carefully fold in the crab meat. Gently fold in 2 cups of the breadcrumbs.

Divide the mixture into 10 equal parts of 4 ounces each and gently pat them into the round shape of crab cakes. Mix the 2 tablespoons of melted butter with the remaining cup of breadcrumbs and gently coat each of the cakes.

Heat the oil and 4 tablespoons of butter in a skillet over medium-high heat. Sauté the crab cakes for 3 minutes on each side, turning once, or until they are nicely browned. Watch the heat; if the fat gets too hot, the cakes will brown on the outside before they are cooked on the inside. When cooked, remove the crab cakes from the pan and drain them briefly on paper towels. Serve immediately or keep warm in a 200°F oven for up to 15 minutes. If the crab cakes stay in the oven longer, they will dry out.

Add more or less seasonings and spices depending on your liking.

Panfish

As I mentioned in my first cookbook, *Smokehouse Ham, Spoon Bread & Scuppernong Wine*, in the Southern Appalachian hill country, the most memorable fish I've ever tasted was skillet-fried mountain trout that my sons and I caught and fried shortly after visiting a trout farm near Hiwassee, Georgia.

Most panfish are small enough so they can be fried whole, typically rubbed with salt and pepper, dredged in cornmeal or egg mix, and fried in deep fat. Fish fillets also can be fried in various ways.

Flounder

Flounder is one of the most popular finfish available in big numbers up and down the Southeastern seacoast. Frying them in butter the French method, *a la meuniere*, is one popular way to cook them.

This recipe, created by my friend, the noted Savannah journalist and cookbook author Martha Giddens Nesbit (*Savannah Entertains*), won plaudits from Chef Bobby Flay when she fried flounder for him at her home in Savannah's beautiful Isle of Hope community.

Savannah Pan-Fried Flounder

Mrs. Nesbit, currently a columnist for *Savannah Magazine*, says her husband Gary loves flounder cooked this way, and occasionally asks, "Why don't you make this more often?" This recipe will serve four.

- 4 flounder fillets
- Salt and pepper to taste
- Flour for dredging fish
- 2 tablespoons vegetable oil
- 3 tablespoons butter, divided
- Juice of 1 lemon
- ½ a 3.75-ounce jar capers

Wash the fillets in cold water and pat dry. Sprinkle with salt and pepper. Dredge fillets in flour.

Place the oil and two tablespoons butter in a flat, heavy-bottomed skillet, and turn heat on medium-high until butter melts.

Keeping the heat at medium-high, cook the fish on one side about 3 minutes (more or less, depending on fillet size) until deep brown and crispy. Turn the fish and cook on the second side, about 3 minutes. Turn the fish only once.

Remove the fish to serving platter.

Turn off the heat. Whisk in the remaining tablespoon of butter into a hot skillet. Add the lemon juice and capers with the liquid in the jar. Whisk all together and pour thin sauce over the fillets. Serve at once.

Fried Catfish

Community fish frys were big doin's during my growing-up years in upstate South Carolina.

Here's a catfish recipe adaptation that comes courtesy of the Catfish Institute. For this version, we're substituting the name benne seeds instead of sesame seeds as listed by the institute. Actually they mean the same thing, but benne seeds have an emotional attachment to the people of the Lowcountry, having been introduced to the United States when first brought to Charleston in the 1600s by slaves coming from West Africa. (See chapter 12 on benne seeds.) This recipe yields four servings.

Fried Catfish with Benne Seeds

FOR THE DIPPING SAUCE

- ¼ cup soy sauce
- 1 tablespoon brown sugar
- 2 teaspoons white wine
- 1 teaspoon crushed garlic
- ½ teaspoon grated fresh ginger

FOR THE CATFISH

- Vegetable oil for pan frying
- 1 pound catfish fillets
- ½ cup all-purpose flour
- 2 egg whites, beaten
- ½ cup benne seeds

Marker showing the site of one of the five locations of The Hot and Hot Fish Club near Pawley's Island, South Carolina. Members included planters in All Saints Parish during the seventeenth century prior to the Civil War.

Fix the dipping sauce first. Mix all the sauce ingredients in a small saucepan. Bring to a boil, reduce heat, and simmer for 1 minute.

Cool and strain.

Heat ½-inch oil in a large skillet over medium heat.

While oil is heating, rinse the fillets and pat dry with paper towels.

Place flour in shallow dish. Place egg whites in another shallow dish. Place benne seeds in another shallow dish. Dredge fillets lightly in flour, adding more flour if necessary. Dip fillets in egg, then coat thoroughly with the benne seeds.

Carefully place catfish in the hot oil, one at a time, and cook for 2 to 3 minutes on each side or until fish flakes easily when tested with a fork. Drain on paper towels. Serve fish with sauce spooned over them or in a bowl on the side.

And Hush Puppies, of Course!

You can't ever hope to have a successful fish fry without plenty of hush puppies, or corn dodgers as they are called by some of the older folks. Here is a scrumptious recipe I've adapted with thanks to Matt Lee and Ted Lee, winners of the prestigious 2007 James Beard Cookbook of the Year award.

Actually, in their *Lee Bros. Southern Cookbook*, Matt and Ted came up with hush puppy recipes styled for each of the Carolinas. Here is my adaptation of their South Carolina version.

Hush Puppies, Palmetto-Style

- 1 ½ cups cornmeal
- 1 cup all-purpose flour
- ½ teaspoon baking soda
- ½ teaspoon baking powder
- 1 ¼ tablespoons sugar
- Salt, to taste
- ½ teaspoon black pepper
- 4 tablespoons minced scallions
- 1 large egg
- ¾ cup buttermilk
- 2 cups canola or peanut oil

Sift the cornmeal and flour into mixing bowl. Add the baking soda, baking powder, sugar, salt, pepper, and scallions and stir with a fork to assure even distribution.

In a small bowl, beat the egg and add it to the dry ingredients. Slowly add ½ cup buttermilk, mixing with a wooden spatula. Add more buttermilk as needed until the batter is flexible and tacky.

In a 9-inch skillet heat the oil until a candy thermometer reaches 375°F. Using a teaspoon, ease 6 teaspoons of the dough into the oil. Fry about 5 minutes, until golden brown. Use spatula to even cooking. Use a slotted spoon to transfer hush puppies to the warming plate.

Repeat, frying in batches of six, until all the batter has been used. Serve warm with various seafood, in particular pan-fried fish.

Now you're ready for the fish fry!

WHY DO YOU WANT TO COME
TO THE LOWCOUNTRY TO EAT
SEAFOOD FROM THAILAND?

> —*Street sign posted at Charleston, South Carolina, in 2008*
> *to urge visitors to buy Lowcountry seafood rather than*
> *the cheaper seafood from Asia (and sometimes from polluted waters).*

CHAPTER 10

Lowcountry Rice: Purloo (Pilau?), Red Rice, and Hoppin' John

I was sixteen years old before I knew that everyone didn't eat rice every day. Us being Geechees, we had rice every day.

—Vertamae Grosvenor
Vibration Cooking, or Travel Notes of a Geechee Girl

We don't say grace on a meal that doesn't have rice in it.

—Ben Moise
Charleston, South Carolina

Charlestonians are often compared to the Chinese in that they eat rice every day, worship their ancestors, speak a foreign dialect, and live behind walls. The same could be said for Savannahians…minus the dialect.

The greatest Lowcountry rice dish of them all is purloo, or quite a few other names for the same dish, which I'll get to shortly. It is without doubt one of the region's authentic signature dishes, so well loved that it stands right up there alongside she-crab soup as one of the Lowcountry's most historically sacred dishes.

No wonder. The Lowcountry, centered around Charleston, became the cradle of rice production beginning in the late 1600s. Rice helped propel the Holy City to its status as North America's wealthiest city, which lasted until the War Between the States, or as some have called it, "the late unpleasantness." Even so, afterward, purloo eventually regained its status as the heart and soul of the Lowcountry rice palate, continuing to the present day.

Of course, after the war's end, with the slaves freed, the region's rice production suffered a disastrous decline accompanied by the shift of rice production to Texas, Louisiana, and Arkansas. Even so, Lowcountry taste buds stuck with rice purloo and still do.

The late Karen Hess, Southern cookery's expert historian, called the dish pilau. She described it as "the most characteristic dish of the Carolina rice kitchen." In her authoritative 1992 book, *Carolina Rice Kitchen: The African Connection*, she devoted forty-eight pages to rice dishes.

It was Mrs. Hess who noted that the dish is popularly pronounced PUHR-loe or pi-LOE. Another opinion had come earlier from the late Harriott Ross Colquitt, author of the 1933 *Savannah Cook Book*. "Many of the old cooks called pilau 'perlew,'" she wrote, "and we are apt to smile indulgently and explain with raised eyebrows that they mean 'pilau.'" But, she added, "We would not feel quite so patronizing about it if we realized their authority. In looking over an old South Carolina cookbook which specialized on rice dishes, I found this spelled 'purlow,' so perhaps our admiring imitators are not so far afield after all."

One observer called it "a dish of amazing variations," and noted food historian John Egerton (*Southern Food*) found sixteen spellings and pronunciations, including *purloo, pilau, pilaf, pilaff, pillaux, pilav, pilaw, pillo, pilloe, pelos, perleau, perlew, perloo, plaw, pullao, purlo,* and *purlow*.

A loud "amen" came from *The Atlanta Journal-Constitution*'s Jim Auchmutey, who proclaimed that the dish is pronounced PER-lo, per-LO, PER-loo, PEE-lo, pee-LO, "and other indecipherable mumbles that begin with 'P.' The rest of America," he wrote, "calls it pilaf." The *Southern Heritage Chicken Cookbook* added its opinion that "the dish is somehow at its most charming when pronounced PERLOO."

Agreement came from author Marjorie Kinnan Rawlings. "We pronounce the word purr-loo," she wrote in *Cross Creek Cookery*. "No [north] Florida church supper, no large rural gathering, is without it," she wrote, "particularly for a large family since the meat goes further [with purloo recipes] than in any other way."

The peripatetic botanist William Bartram found "pillo" to be a popular dish among people he encountered while traveling through north Florida and Georgia in the 1700s. He ate squab "made into a pillo with rice," and another "pillo" featuring raccoon meat.

As to Purloo's ancestry, the word and the dish are said to have originated in ancient Persia (modern-day Iran). In subsequent centuries, the dish's popularity spread in all directions and accumulated many different name tags, such as pilaf in Turkey, pullao in India, and pelau in Provence, France.

Prize-winning Charleston cookbook authors Matt Lee and Ted Lee declare that "pilau, or purloo, as many Southerners call it, may well be the definitive Southern dish," being one-pot cooking in which the rice absorbs the broth of the meat it is cooked with. They added that this method, "whose roots culinary historians trace to thirteenth-century Baghdad… achieves a fullness of flavor that may be the quiet hallmark of Southern cooking."

The exact route this vagabond rice dish took in traveling from Persia to the Carolina and Georgia Lowcountry has eluded historians. However, Mrs. Hess writes that pilau was well known in South Carolina from the early days of rice cultivation, having been introduced by the French Huguenots in the late 1600s.

"Few foods seem to be so at home in South Carolina," Helen Woodward noted in *200 Years of Charleston Cooking* (1931). She added that early traders likely brought the dish from the Middle East when Charleston was a great seaport prior to the Revolutionary War. At the time, Southern cooks "shifted the emphasis from the second to the first syllable, and the ingredients from oil to tomatoes."

Another viewpoint of pilau's odyssey came from Marjorie Kinnan Rawlings, who concluded that the African Moors took the dish to Spain and the Spaniards delivered it to the Lowcountry's near neighbor, Spanish Florida.

Whatever the route in getting to the Lowcountry, and whatever the pronunciation, this rice dish has been a major food mainstay up and down the Southeastern coastal region—and still is. In our home, we call it purlow, and it's one of our all-time favorite dishes.

Meat

Mt. Pleasant Sausage Pilaff

Mrs. E. S. Pegues of the Charleston suburb across the Cooper River from Historic Charleston contributed this recipe to the old *Mt. Pleasantness Famous Recipes* cookbook published some years ago. It will yield 4 servings.

- 1 pound cased sausage
- 2 cups broth from sausage
- 2 cups raw rice

Boil the cased pork sausage in enough water so that at the end of the 1 ½ hours of boiling time, there will be 2 cups of liquid broth.

Add 2 cups of rice to sausage and liquid; put in steamer and steam for about 1 ½ hours. Serve hot.

Charleston Chicken Purlow

Chicken-based purlow (my spelling) has been a staple in Carolina cooking from the early colonial years. The authors of the *Southern Heritage Chicken Cookbook*, from which the following recipe is adapted, suggest that in cooking the dish, cooks are advised that "the rice must remain fluffy, never mushy; the consistency moist, never dry." This recipe will yield 6 servings.

- 4 cups chopped, cooked chicken
- 7 cups chicken broth, divided
- 4 cups uncooked regular rice
- 6 slices bacon, cooked and crumbled
- 4 hard-cooked eggs, chopped
- 1 teaspoon salt
- ½ teaspoon pepper

Combine the chicken and 2 cups chicken broth. Cover and set aside.

In a Dutch oven, combine the remaining broth, rice, bacon, eggs, and seasonings. Bring to a boil. Reduce heat, cover, and simmer 35 minutes until liquid is absorbed.

Drain the chicken and gently stir it into the cooked rice mixture. Cover and let stand 15 minutes or until chicken is thoroughly heated. Spoon into serving dish.

Seafood

Hampton Plantation Shrimp Pilau

Seafood pilaus have been considered one of the Lowcountry's dishes of continuing popularity. The following recipe was associated with the Lowcountry's historic Hampton Plantation. It comes courtesy of the Charleston Junior League's legendary

Charleston Receipts cookbook. The copy my wife, Susanne, and I have has had an honored place on our cookbook shelves since its first printing in 1950.

This adaptation serves 6.

- 5 slices bacon
- 1 cup raw rice
- 3 ½ tablespoons butter
- ½ cup celery, cut small
- 2 tablespoons chopped bell pepper, any color
- 2 cups shrimp, cleaned
- 1 teaspoon Worcestershire sauce
- 1 tablespoon flour
- Salt and pepper to taste

Fry the bacon until crisp. Crumble and save for later use. Add the bacon grease to the water in which you cook the rice. Bring 2 cups of water to a boil. Add the rice, and lower to a simmer for about 20 minutes, or until the rice is cooked.

While the rice is cooking, melt the butter in another pot, and add celery and bell pepper. Cook a few minutes. Sprinkle shrimp with Worcestershire, dredge in flour and add to pot with celery and pepper. Stir and simmer until flour is cooked. Season with salt and pepper. Now add cooked rice and mix until rice is "all buttery" and "shrimpy."

Avoid overcooking the shrimp. Add more butter if you wish. Add the bacon and serve immediately.

(Note: For maximum flavor and to avoid overcooking shrimp, some modern cooks simmer the rice first in shellfish broth, adding the shrimp at the end.)

May River Oyster Purlo

Bluffton, South Carolina, is the site of the state's last oyster-shucking operation—the Bluffton Oyster Company. It's run by Larry, Tina, and Larry Toomer Jr. and is perched on the banks of the scenic May River. Fresh local fish, shrimp, or oysters are available there almost any day of the week in season.

The Bluffton Oyster Company, located on the banks of the May River in Bluffton, is the last oyster-shucking company in South Carolina. (Photo by the author.)

I spent some time in Bluffton in October 2008, and found it to be a lovely and thriving municipality. It's located just off busy Highway 278, connecting Savannah and I-95 to Hilton Head Island.

I obtained this recipe from the beautiful Bluffton cookbook I purchased on my visit there, *Great Cooks Rise...with the May River Tide*. It's published by the Episcopal Church Women of the historic 1854 Church of the Cross and is typical of the current full-color cookbooks you find these days throughout the Lowcountry. It is jammed with beautiful paintings and drawings plus recipes galore.

According to the editor's note on page two of the cookbook, "No claim is made to the originality of these recipes. They have been tried, sometimes altered, adapted, adopted, and enjoyed." This particular recipe adaptation yields 4 servings.

- 6 to 8 slices bacon
- 1 medium onion, chopped fine
- ½ cup finely chopped celery
- ½ cup finely chopped green pepper
- 2 cups fresh oysters
- 2 cups oyster liquid (use chicken stock if needed)
- 1 ¼ cups uncooked rice

In a large skillet, cook the bacon until crisp; crumble and set aside.

Add the onion, celery, and green pepper to the grease and cook until tender.

In a covered saucepan, heat the oysters in their liquid until edges curl. Remove the oysters, reserving 2 cups of the liquid. If necessary, add chicken broth to make 2 cups.

Add the rice, liquid, bacon, and oysters to the vegetable mixture in the skillet. Boil, stirring occasionally. Cover the skillet, lower the heat, and continue to simmer for about 15 minutes until the rice has absorbed the liquid. Serve hot.

Savannah Oyster and Shrimp Purloo

This oyster- and shrimp-based purloo, one of the region's most popular rice dish combinations, was developed by veteran Chef Joe Randall, who runs a busy cooking school in Savannah. He is also the author of a cookbook on new African-American cooking, *A Taste of Heritage*. Here is the recipe, with my thanks to Chef Randall.

- 6 slices slab bacon, cooked and drained
- ½ cup finely diced onion
- ¼ cup finely diced celery
- 2 cloves garlic, minced
- 3 tablespoons butter
- ¼ cup diced green bell pepper
- ½ pound smoked sausage, diced
- 1 pound shrimp, peeled and deveined
- 1 pint oysters, drained (reserve liquid)
- 1 ½ cups long grain rice
- 2 tablespoons tomato paste
- 1 ½ cups shrimp stock (see recipe on next page)
- 2 bay leaves
- 1 teaspoon salt
- 1 teaspoon fresh ground black pepper
- 1 tablespoon chopped fresh parsley

Chef Joe Randall of Savannah, Georgia, pictured here at work in the kitchen, combines shrimp and oysters along with rice in his special purloo recipe. (Photo by the author.)

Fry the bacon in a large sauté pan until crisp. Dice and set aside.

Add the onions, celery, garlic, butter, and green pepper to bacon drippings and sauté until tender. Add the smoked sausage, shrimp, and oysters to the vegetable mixture; sauté until shrimp turn pink and oysters curl at the edges.

Add the rice and tomato paste; stir. Add the shrimp stock, oyster liquid, and bay leaves. Bring to a boil, stirring occasionally. Season with salt and black pepper.

Cover the pan; reduce the heat to low and simmer until the rice is tender and has absorbed liquid (about 20 to 25 minutes). Garnish with diced bacon and chopped parsley.

Shrimp Stock

This recipe, developed by Chef Joe Randall, makes 2 cups.

- ⅛ cup peanut oil
- ¾ pound shrimp shells
- 1 rib celery, coarsely chopped
- 1 small carrot, coarsely chopped
- 1 small onion, coarsely chopped
- 2 cloves garlic, chopped
- 1 quart water
- ⅛ cup dry white wine
- 1 tablespoon tomato paste
- 1 sprig parsley
- 1 sprig thyme
- 2 black peppercorns
- 1 bay leaf

Heat the oil in a stockpot over medium heat. Add the shrimp shells and sauté for 3 to 4 minutes, stirring until the shells look dry.

Add the celery, carrots, onions, and garlic, and continue to sauté for 2 to 3 minutes.

Add the water, wine, tomato paste, parsley, thyme, peppercorns, and bay leaf. Bring the stock to a boil, then reduce the heat and simmer for 1 hour.

Strain the stock through a fine-mesh strainer. Return to the heat and boil until reduced to ½ quart. Will keep 2 to 3 days refrigerated; can be frozen.

Vegetable

Savannah Okra Pilau

THIS RECIPE YIELDS 6 TO 8 SERVINGS.

While meat and rice constitute the primary ingredients in various Lowcountry perlows, vegetable and rice dishes are also well loved, particularly the red rice pilaus.

Okra arrived in the Lowcountry from Africa with the slave trade as early as the late 1600s, and the seeds were called gumbo or gombo. In any okra pilau, use small, fresh okra "no bigger than your little finger" for best results.

This is an okra pilau dish adapted from Lillian Marshall's *Cooking Across the South.* 2 ¼ cups thinly sliced okra

- 4 slices bacon, diced
- ¼ cup chopped onion
- ½ cup chopped green pepper
- 1 cup uncooked long grain rice
- 2 cups chicken broth
- 3 medium tomatoes, peeled and quartered
- 1 teaspoon salt

Sauté the okra and bacon in a large skillet until slightly browned. Add the onion and green pepper and continue cooking until vegetables are tender.

Add the rice, chicken broth, tomatoes, and salt. Bring to a boil; stir well, cover, reduce the heat, and simmer until rice is tender, about 15 minutes.

Use a folk to fluff the rice lightly, and serve.

Note: If fresh tomatoes are unavailable, use a 16-ounce can of tomatoes, drained and chopped.

Red Rice

John Martin "Hoppin' John" Taylor, the articulate chronicler of Lowcountry cuisine, notes a continuing legacy for red rice in family restaurants and cafes across the Lowcountry. Also called Spanish rice or mulatto rice, red rice is one of the region's authentic tomato pilaus, with

THE RICE SPOON
On every proper Charleston dinner table, there's a [rice] spoon that is peculiar to the town. Of massive silver, about fifteen inches long and broad in proportions, it is laid on the cloth with something of the reverential distinction that surrounds the mace in the House of Commons at Westminster...
—SAMUEL GAILLARD STONEY
CHARLESTON, *AZALEAS AND OLD BRICKS* (1937)

a West African heritage. Jessica Harris noted in *Beyond Gumbo* that Charleston's red rice "is but a variant of the red rice that is the national dish of Senegal [West Africa]."

The late Edna Lewis, revered as the grand dame of Southern cooking, was taken by red rice. She experienced her first taste of the tomato pilau during the period when she directed the kitchen at Charleston's Middleton Place Restaurant. It reminded her of a dish she had eaten earlier with friends from Nigeria. In North Africa, the pilau-type dish is referred to as Jolof rice, after the Jolof people of Gambia.

Modern-day cooks combine vine-ripened tomatoes or tomato puree with rice, garden herbs, and sometimes onions and bacon, quite a delicious combination. In many households red rice is still considered a great casserole buffet dish.

Charleston Red Rice

This is an adaptation from Terry Thompson's cookbook, *A Taste of the South*, and will yield 6 to 8 servings.

- 5 bacon slices, diced
- 1 medium green bell pepper, chopped
- 1 large onion, diced
- 4 green onions, chopped
- 2 cups uncooked long grain white rice
- 3 medium tomatoes, peeled and chopped
- 3 ¼ cups poultry stock
- 1 small bay leaf
- ½ teaspoon dried basil
- ¼ teaspoon freshly ground black pepper
- ½ teaspoon dried leaf oregano
- Salt and Tabasco sauce to taste

Cook the bacon in a heavy iron skillet over medium heat until well browned. Remove and reserve bacon, leaving drippings in pan. Add bell pepper, onion, and chopped green onions to drippings. Cook about 5 minutes, until vegetables are slightly wilted and onion is transparent.

Add rice and cook 5 minutes, stirring constantly to prevent sticking. Stir in tomatoes. Simmer about 8 minutes, until tomato liquid has evaporated, stirring often.

Add reserved bacon, stock, bay leaf, basil, black pepper, oregano, salt, and Tabasco sauce. Stir to combine.

Cut heat to medium-low, cover, and cook about 45 minutes until rice is tender and all liquid is absorbed. Discard bay leaf. Serve hot.

Wild Game Pilaus

Dove Pilau

Adapted from James Fitch's authoritative cookbook, *Pass the Pilau, Please*, this recipe calls for "good pork sausage" as a key ingredient. Fitch is executive director of the Rice Museum in Georgetown, South Carolina, in the heart of South Carolina's great Waccamaw-coastal rice plantation country that flourished for two centuries beginning in the mid-1600s. This recipe will yield 5 to 6 servings.

- 10 to 12 doves, dressed
- 1 onion, chopped
- 1 stalk celery, chopped
- Salt and pepper to taste
- 3 ½ links pork sausage, cut into small pieces
- 2 cups rice

In a good-size saucepan, bring water to a boil. Add the dressed doves, onion, celery, salt, and pepper and cook until the doves are tender.

Fry the sausage in a skillet over medium heat until cooked through.

In top of rice steamer, put the rice, 2 cups of dove stock, and 2 or 3 tablespoons of sausage drippings. Pour off the top fat, and use the good brown drippings. Add salt and pepper to taste.

Note: 3 slices of bacon can be used in place of sausage if desired.

Charleston Roast Squab Pilau

Squab pilaus have been a popular fare in the South Carolina and Georgia coastal region since the early English settlements. Stories were told of how black slaves, using torches, would scour the Carolina swamps in the colonial era to harvest wild pigeons by torchlight.

America's premier squab ranch today is located at Sumter, South Carolina, in the Lowcountry interior. The vast Palmetto Pigeon Plant provides squabs for most American restaurants on the U.S. East Coast.

This adaptation of squab pilau is based on a recipe by Mrs. Blanche S. Rhett, one of Charleston's leading hostesses in the early 1900s and wife of Charleston Mayor Goodwyn Rhett. Mrs. Rhett was known to serve squab pilau at formal occasions in her Charleston home. The mustard pickle juice combines well with the pilau stuffing and adds a nice piquancy to the squabs. This recipe yields 4 servings.

- 4 squabs
- 5 slices bacon
- 1 onion, chopped
- ¾ cup chopped celery
- 2 cups rice
- 4 ⅛ cups chicken stock or broth
- 5 eggs
- Salt and pepper
- Mustard pickle juice

Preheat the over to 425°F.

Dress the squabs and use a rice pilau for the stuffing, as follows:

Dice the bacon and cook in a skillet until crisp. Remove the bacon and set aside. Add the onion and celery to the bacon drippings and let them brown.

Cook the rice in the chicken stock in a saucepan until tender and add the bacon and celery mixture.

Beat the eggs and mix in the rice, stirring well so that the rice heat will cook the eggs. Season to taste with salt and pepper.

Stuff the squabs with the mixture and make mounds of the remainder, on which to lay the squabs.

Bake in a 425°F oven for around 25 minutes, basting the squabs frequently with mustard pickle juice.

Hoppin' John!

A New Year's Day Lowcountry Tradition

"Everyone at Mars Bluff [near the Great Pee Dee River in eastern South Carolina] had to eat Hoppin' John and hog jowl on New Year's Day," wrote Mrs. Amelia Wallace Vernon from Florence, South Carolina. Whoever didn't eat both, she added, would have bad luck all year. The recipe she cited was typical, consisting of rice, field peas (cowpeas), and salt pork cooked together. Eating Hoppin' John on New Year's Day also held a positive connotation: that one would experience prosperity during the year ahead.

The editors of the 1954 *South Carolina Cook Book*, published by the state's Extension Home-Makers Council, went a step further, declaring, "On New Year's Day, all will have to have green collards for [midday] dinner, plus Hoppin' John." Tradition dictates that collards will bring green folding money and Hoppin' John "small change the year round."

At Daufuskie Island, South Carolina, Sallie Ann Robinson recalled waking up at midnight on New Year's to shotgun blasts in the neighborhood bringing in the New Year. Afterward the family gathered around the table for a veritable feast following a prayer, including "the most important dish of all, Momma's famous Hoppin' John." Also on the table was a "big bowl of collards, plus a bowl of chitlins, a baked coon, potato salad, and sweet tata pie."

Buttered corn bread is of course another important Hoppin' John accompaniment dish that fans love to have on hand to sop up the tasty collard greens pot likker.

Hoppin' John: An Old Slave Dish

Hoppin' John is one of the Lowcountry's quintessential dishes. Mrs. Hess described it as an African-American dish "that made it to the Big House," as it was a direct descendant of West African cooking. She added that the use of the dish in Sarah Rutledge's 1847 *The Carolina Housewife* reflected the fact that the "old slave dish had been accepted by some of the most aristocratic elements of the Lowcountry."

How Hoppin' John acquired its unusual name is something of a mystery. However, Georgetown, South Carolina, author James A. Fitch, in *Pass the Pilau Please*, noted an

1800s link to Charleston. Miss Josephine Hemphill of the U.S. Department of Agriculture was said to have obtained details of the name's origin. She told of a report she had received from "a Charleston woman" whose grandmother had been born in 1841. As a little girl, the grandmother remembered an aged and crippled Negro named John selling his peas-and-rice dish on Charleston streets.

Each day, so the lady's report went, the old man John—afflicted with one leg shorter than the other—would take his peas-and-rice product in a large tin can out onto Charleston's streets. He doled out the dish to customers with a tin dipper. As he limped through the streets, house to house, according to the report, "he would cry out, 'Here come Hoppin' John.'"

While this account sounds authentic, as mentioned earlier, the rice-peas dish had been popular for centuries in West Africa before reaching our shores.

Many people today practice a New Year's Day tradition by hopping around the table on one foot before sitting down to the peas, rice, and greens.

Here are a couple of authentic Hoppin' John recipes.

> *Now hopping john was F. Jasmine's very favorite food. She had always warned them to wave a plate of rice and peas before her nose when she was in her coffin, to make certain there was no mistake; for if a breath of life was left in her, she would sit up and eat, but if she smelled the hopping-john and did not stir, then they could just nail down the coffin and be certain she was truly dead.*
>
> —Carson McCullers
> A Member of the Wedding

Mr. Dugger's Savannah Hoppin' John

This recipe was passed on to me by Savannah native Sally Bond Tonsmeire, a good friend who lives today in Cartersville, Georgia.

Mr. Dugger, who created the recipe, was the head butcher at Savannah's old Smith Bros. Grocery. His recipe was published in the *Savannah Morning News* more than five decades ago. This adaptation will yield 4 servings.

- 1 cup chopped celery
- 1 ½ cups dried cowpeas (field peas), soaked overnight
- 2 onions, chopped

- 1 bell pepper, chopped
- 1 cup water
- ¾ pound hog jowl, finely chopped
- 2 cups rice
- 1 cup chicken broth

Combine all ingredients except for the rice and chicken broth in a saucepan and turn the heat to medium for 15 minutes. Then reduce to low and cook approximately 1 hour, or until done.

Add the raw rice and chicken broth and cook entire mixture over medium heat for 15 minutes or until done. Serve immediately with corn bread and collard greens.

Note: See page 241 for noted Charleston chef Robert Carter's recipe for braised collards.

Charleston Hoppin' John

This is a recipe used in the South Carolina Lowcountry for many years, adapted with a little updating. Rather than the usual ham hock, this version combines chopped ham with field peas and rice.

- 1 cup diced onions
- 1 cup diced cooked ham
- 2 tablespoons canola oil
- 2 tablespoons chicken stock or broth
- 1 sweet red pepper, diced
- 2 cups field peas
- ½ teaspoon hot pepper sauce
- 3 cups cooked long grain rice
- Salt and pepper, to taste

Combine the onion, ham, oil, chicken stock, and diced pepper in a large skillet, and cook over medium heat for 5 minutes or until the diced pepper is tender.

Add to the mixture the field peas and hot pepper sauce. Combine thoroughly and simmer for an additional 2 minutes. Top with the cooked rice (pre-warmed), add salt and pepper to taste, and serve with corn bread.

CHAPTER 11

Soups, Stews, and Gumbos

CRABS, CRABS...MENS 'N SHE-CRABS...GIT YO CRABS!
—*Black street vender singing out his wares on*
Charleston's Rutledge Avenue in the 1930s

Soup is the ultimate comfort food. When the days are steamy, a bowl of chilled
tomato, red pepper and cucumber soup is like a plunge in the ocean. Cold, blustery
winter nights lose their chilling effect when you've been warmed by hot black-eyed
pea soup.

—*Elizabeth Terry*
Savannah Seasons

What could be finer than to be in Carolina savoring a brimming bowl of sherry-infused she-crab soup?

It's the region's world-renowned soup: classic, creamy, smooth, delicious, and quintessentially Lowcountry.

"In most of America," states *Crazy for Crabs* author Fred Thompson, "the gold standard of crab soups is [the Charleston] she-crab soup." He cites the soup's richness and hints of sherry that make it, in the eyes of some, "the New England clam chowder of the South."

Just about the best authority on the soup's history is *200 Years of Charleston Cooking*, published originally in the 1930s. It states that the soup belonged especially to Mayor Goodwyn Rhett's Charleston household and had been served by Mrs. Rhett to "presidents and princes."

Charlestonian William Deas is considered to be the originator of the world-famous she-crab soup featuring she-crab roe. (Photo courtesy of Everett Presson Jr.)

William Deas, the Rhetts' courtly butler, is generally considered the soup's creator. One story has it that when the city's first lady, Blanche Rhett, was preparing a dinner honoring President Taft (1857–1930), she implored Deas to gussy up his crab bisque a bit. He was said to have added the she-crab roe, which gave it the desired kick.

Described as "one of the great cooks of the world," Deas's basic recipe featured she-crab, and fresh orange crab roe along with a dollop of sherry. What made the she-crab meat so much tastier than that of their male counterparts was the orange roe (fish eggs) produced by the females, mostly during summers. That, plus the addition of sherry and other ingredients, makes for a sublime tasting experience.

The soup's public debut is thought to have occurred at the popular Everett's Restaurant on Charleston's Cannon Street, hard by the Ashley River off Savannah Road. Deas worked there after leaving the Rhetts. Owned and operated by Everett Presson Sr., the restaurateur was delighted when Deas' soup became an instant hit.

One of the soup's great devotees, Charleston's colorful congressman Mendel Rivers often bragged about the signature dish to his fellow congressmen, inviting them to travel with him from

HOW TO TELL A SHE-CRAB FROM A HE-CRAB
In the Lowcountry, crabs come two ways—shes and jimmies. They can be identified very simply using the landmarks of Washington, D.C. Each crab has a distinctive shell on its back. The she-crab shell looks like the U.S. Capitol building, and the jimmie (male) shell looks like the Washington Monument.
—FULL MOON HIGH TIDE:
TASTES AND TRADITIONS OF THE LOWCOUNTRY,
BEAUFORT ACADEMY, SOUTH CAROLINA

Washington to Charleston where they could get the pleasure of personally tasting the celebrated dish in the ambiance of the romantic Lowcountry.

Several decades after Deas's discovery, the legendary queen of Southern chefs—Edna Lewis—found she-crab soup quite extraordinary. That was during the period she was running the kitchen at Charleston's Middleton Place Restaurant.

Here's a modern-day she-crab soup recipe passed to me by one of Charleston's leading current-day connoisseurs. He declares the recipe will serve "four to twelve people depending on their appetites and the generosity of the cook!"

Charleston She-Crab Soup

- 1 small onion, minced
- 1 stalk of celery, stringed (remove the strings from the celery rib) and minced
- 4 tablespoons sweet butter
- 1 tablespoon flour
- 7 cups milk
- 1 pint half-and-half
- 1 pound regular or lump picked crabs
- 4 to 5 tablespoons dry sherry
- ½ teaspoon mace
- Pinch salt
- Pinch ground white pepper
- Several dollops Worcestershire sauce
- 4 ounces orange crab roe
- Parsley, for garnish (optional)
- Paprika, for garnish (optional)

Sauté the onion and celery in pan of melted butter until translucent. Then sprinkle flour over them and stir. (This light coating helps the vegetables float in the soup instead of staying on the bottom of the bowl.)

Meanwhile, begin warming the milk and half-and-half in the top of a double boiler over low heat. Add the crab meat (not the roe) to the pan of sautéed vegetables. Then stir in the sherry, mace, salt, pepper, and Worcestershire sauce.

When the mixture is warm, add it to the milk and cream in the double boiler and cook over an extremely low heat for just under an hour.

If you like, you may add more sherry to the individual servings as the hard roe is crumbled into the bottom of the soup bowl. Garnish each serving with chopped parsley or a light dusting of paprika.

Note: crab roe or eggs are available only in season but may be purchased frozen off-season at most coastal seafood stores.

In some she-crab soup recipes, rice is used as a thickening agent rather than flour. Chef Louis Osteen and John Martin Taylor have favored this method.

In his superb book *Hoppin' John's Charleston, Beaufort, and Savannah,* Taylor says the role of rice as the she-crab soup thickener came from an older recipe based on a precursor from Scotland, partan bree.

Okra Soup

Okra is another one of those classic Lowcountry dishes with an interesting history. The seed first came over on the slave ships in the late seventeenth century. It soon became one of the region's great dishes in the hands of skilled black cooks.

In her delightful 1933 *Savannah Cook Book*, Harriet Ross Colquitt describes okra soup prepared by Savannah cooks as "a real meal and a very popular one in the okra and watermelon season." Translated into the modern-day vernacular, it's a summertime dish to die for.

She told of the "bird's-eye pepper ritual" carried out as the huge tureen of steaming soup reached the table, ready for doling out into individual bowls. The hostess would ask each guest if he or she would like one or two of the tiny (very hot) bird's-eye peppers crushed into the bottom of his or her soup bowl. If she crushed one in a bowl, she would immediately dispose of the pod and its extremely strong aroma.

Savannah Okra Soup

Here's my adaptation of Mrs. Colquitt's okra soup recipe, which she said was quite delicious when accompanied by corn bread and rice.

Okra, of course, with its sticky ooze, provides a wonderful soup thickener; thus it's used also in gumbos and pilaus. Mrs. Colquitt suggested that corn bread, rice, and butter beans be passed around the table, along with the bowls of soup.

- 1 soup bone
- 2 ⅛ quarts okra, sliced
- 1 ¼ pint tomatoes, peeled and diced
- Salt to taste

Put soup bone in large saucepan or pot with enough water to cover. Boil for 1 hour.

Add okra and tomatoes to the pot. Set stove to medium heat (just under boiling) and cook for 3 hours, or until the soup is well blended and thick. Add salt to taste before serving.

The Soups of Dutch Fork

By the 1820s, according to the late food historian Mrs. Juanita Kibler, the hausfrau of South Carolina's Dutch Fork and Saxe Gotha already had more and better varieties of soups than any other nationalities in the United States. Most of the dishes had direct links to the ancient cooking of the Lower Rhine area of southern Germany.

One of these is ribble soup. Distinctive and hearty, it's called Ribbel Suppe in Germany. The name comes from the crumbs of dough put into the soup, called by their German names ribbles, reebles, rivels, and sometimes riblets and ribleys.

This is the recipe for the dish Mrs. Kibler used in 1943 when she married into the Kibler family. The recipe had been passed down from the Bowerses (Bauers) and Kiblers (Kublers) of Upper Dutch Fork to Mrs. Kibler's mother-in-law, who considered ribble soup one of her favorites.

Ribble Soup

- 1 quart beef stock
- 2 cups fresh raw corn
- Salt and pepper
- 1 egg yolk
- 1 cup all-purpose flour

Bring the broth to a boil. Add the corn, salt, and pepper to and continue to boil 5 to 10 minutes.

Combine the egg yolk and flour. Rub between the palms of your hands until you have small, crumbly ribbles.

Add the ribbles to the boiling broth and corn, stirring as you add them. Cook a few more minutes.

When done, the ribbles will look like large boiled rice grains. Serve hot with a sprig or two of fresh parsley.

Cooter Soup

Charleston Receipts carries a cooter soup recipe that starts off, "Kill cooter by chopping off head." These are similar to the opening words used in the Edisto Island recipe that follows.

Cooters (terrapins, or small-size freshwater turtles) are common along Lowcountry cypress swamps and creeks. The word derives from the West African word *kuta*, which translates into softshell and hardshell (diamondback) terrapins. They have been served in Lowcountry soups for generations in concoctions worthy of the culinary artist.

In past eras, Charlestonians were known to keep backyard wire-covered "cooter ponds." These include the native yellow-bellied terrapin.

The following soup is adapted from the *Family Night Supper on Edisto*, a cookbook put out some years ago by the island's Trinity Episcopal Church.

Church member Adelaide Pope noted, "This recipe was a combination of what Carolina Lafayette Hopkinson used and what my mother, Adelaide Hopkinson Seabrook, evolved!" She also noted that Cassina Plantation had its own fish pond and that terrapins were common fare there, along with the fish.

Edisto Island Terrapin Soup

- 1 large terrapin
- 1 large onion, chopped
- 2 large potatoes, diced
- 1 (14.5-ounce) can cream of mushroom soup
- Flour
- 2 hard-boiled eggs, chopped
- Salt and pepper to taste
- Sherry wine to taste

Kill the terrapin by cutting off its head. Hang the body up by its tail so blood will drain into a pan for quick disposition.

Rinse the cooter thoroughly in cold water. Cook in pot of hot water until meat can be separated from the shell. Discard the digestive tract.

Return the meat to the pot of water in which terrapin was cooked. Reduce liquid to about 4 cups. Add the onion, and cook until done. Add the cream of mushroom soup, diluted with 1 can water. Thicken with paste of flour and water to the desired consistency. Add chopped hard-boiled eggs.

Add salt and pepper to taste. Just before serving add the sherry to the soup.

Note: Potatoes may be added as needed to augment the soup.

Oyster Soup

John and Rebecca Maxwell Couper met shortly after the Revolutionary War, married in 1793, and the following year moved from Liberty County, Georgia, down to beautiful St. Simons Island. John, a graduate of Yale and of Scottish ancestry, became one of the antebellum South's leading scientifically trained planters and businessmen, running several rice, cotton, and sugar plantations on the Georgia coast and along the Altamaha River.

The Coupers were fortunate to have in their home the leading master chef of the Georgia coast, French-trained Sans Foix. According to James Bagwell in his book, *Rice Gold*, Mrs. Couper (also a Scot), working closely with Foix, ran their Cannon Point mansion "as graciously as a queen dispensing favors."

The Coupers were famous for their dinner parties, according to *The Christ Church*

Frederica Cookbook, published by the historic St. Simons Island church. Christ Church Frederica is one of Georgia's outstanding historic treasures. Charles and John Wesley conducted services for early St. Simons Island settlers dating back to 1736, three years after the initial Georgia settlement at Savannah.

After her 1846 death, Rebecca Couper left behind a handwritten copy of several recipes, including the following, which comes with my thanks to the editors of the Christ Church cookbook. Here follows the recipe in Rebecca Couper's words:

St. Simons Oyster Soup

6 qts. of oysters, yolks of 18 hard-boiled eggs, 1 teacup of cream, small lump of butter, 1 onion stuck with cloves and a little mace, small bundle of herbs.

Stew your oysters gently for a few moments, then rinse them out into a clean pan, let the liquor settle from it gently off into the pan with the oysters, being careful not to include the sediment.

Return the oysters and the liquor, together with the onion and the herbs, into the liquid now cleaned from the sediment. Let the whole stew gently until the oysters are [unreadable in handwritten recipe]. Strain the oysters from the liquor, which again sat in the boiler. Break the yolks of the eggs, together with the cream and butter on a marble mortar, and mix gradually with the liquor to thicken your soup. Take great care not to burn the oysters to the bottom of your boiler. Salt and pepper as fancy or taste is added.

Chef Louis Osteen (right) poses here with author Joe Dabney. (Photo by Susanne Dabney.)

Stews

Oyster Stew

For this traditional Lowcountry stew, I am indebted to the aforementioned prize-winning Chef Louis Osteen of Charleston, Pawleys Island, and Captiva Island, Florida fame (and now at Lake Rabun Hotel northeast of Atlanta). He says this is one of his most popular winter soups.

"It's a very old recipe, coming from an antebellum rice plantation in South Carolina's Georgetown County," Louis says. "And of course, the benne plant, more commonly known as sesame seed, was brought into the Lowcountry from Africa and was thought to be a lucky plant."

The number of oysters in the stew, Louis says, can vary due to size and the cook's taste. They may be big singles or little ones from clusters, in which case add as many more as you like. This recipe will yield 4 servings.

Louis's Brown Oyster Stew with Benne Seeds

- 4 tablespoons benne seeds
- 2 tablespoons peanut oil
- 2 tablespoons finely diced Benton's Bacon (about 1 ounce)
- 2 tablespoons very finely minced yellow onion
- 2 tablespoons all-purpose flour
- 1 ½ cups heavy whipping cream
- 24 oysters, shucked, with liquor strained and reserved
- 1 ¼ cups fish stock or bottled clam juice
- 1 teaspoon chopped fresh thyme leaves
- 1 tablespoon fresh lemon juice
- 1 teaspoon sesame oil
- 2 tablespoons chopped fresh chervil or Italian parsley
- Salt and freshly ground black pepper to taste

Place the benne seeds in a small, heavy-bottomed sauté pan over medium heat and dry roast them by cooking them for about 9 minutes or until they become dark and fragrant. Remove from the stove. Roughly crush half the benne seeds with a spoon and reserve.

Heat the oil in a heavy-bottomed saucepan over low heat. Sauté the bacon for about 5 minutes, or until crisp and lightly browned. Remove the bacon with a slotted spoon and place on paper towels to drain. Leave the oil and any fat from the bacon in the saucepan.

Add the onion and crushed benne seeds to the saucepan and sauté them for about 3 minutes, stirring frequently to ensure that they brown but don't burn. When the onions are lightly browned, add the flour, stir well to combine, and cook for 2 minutes. Meanwhile, heat the cream in a separate pan to just below a simmer.

Add the reserved oyster liquor, fish stock, and thyme leaves and simmer for 2 minutes, stirring with a whisk until the mixture simmers happily and without lumps. Add the warm cream and simmer for 5 minutes. Add the oysters, the remaining 2 tablespoons of benne seeds, the lemon juice, sesame oil, and chervil or parsley. Leave the oyster stew on the heat until the oysters just begin to curl. Quickly remove the saucepan from the heat and add a pinch of salt and a grind of black pepper, or to taste.

To serve, divide the stew into four warmed soup bowls. Garnish with the reserved chopped bacon and serve immediately. Accompany with oyster crackers or buttered toast fingers. At the table, the stew should be hot and steamy and the oysters plump and juicy.

Brunswick Stew

Despite claims from Brunswick County, Virginia, to the contrary, Brunswick, Georgia, claims to be the birthplace of Brunswick stew. The Georgia town holds a festival every year to promote its claim. Town officials say the stew was invented at an 1828 Brunswick political rally and have even erected a downtown monument of a huge Brunswick stew pot.

Whoever is correct, Brunswick stew, according to an unknown Georgia connoisseur "a highly seasoned rich conglomeration of meats, vegetables, and sauces simmered many hours in a big iron pot over outdoor fires," continues to hold an honored place among Southerners who love it as a side dish to barbecue.

In pioneer days, Brunswick stew featured a foundation of frontier meats, particularly squirrels. However, today the stew is usually made with poultry as the primary meat.

The following recipe is adapted from *The New South Carolina Cookbook*. The stew will serve 20 and freezes well.

South Carolina Brunswick Stew

- 1 6 to 7-pound chicken, cut up
- 5 quarts tomatoes, peeled and sliced
- 2 quarts butter beans
- 2 quarts fresh cut corn

- 1 quart diced potatoes
- 2 medium onions, chopped
- ¼ teaspoon ground red pepper
- Salt and pepper to taste

Put the chicken in a heavy pot and cover with water. Cook until the meat falls away from bone. Add more water if necessary. Add vegetables and seasonings.

Simmer slowly until tender and mixture is thick and well blended. Serve hot.

Pine Bark Stew

In 1909 William Howard Taft, the rotund, well-fed President of the United States, was served a bowl of pine bark stew while visiting Florence, South Carolina, and was said to have "pronounced it good."

The stew—a sharp-tasting, dark brown fish muddle which, by the way, contains no pine barks—is said to have originated in the 1700s in the Pee Dee River area east of Florence.

One of the many stories relating to its unusual name concerns Francis Marion, the Revolutionary War guerilla hero known as the "Swamp Fox." General Marion and his militia were said to have eaten the stew on pine bark plates when they could get a break from harassing King George's Redcoats.

The *Pee Dee Pepper Pot*, a cookbook published by the Women of the Darlington, South Carolina, United Methodist Church, has another theory: "Since seasonings were unobtainable during Revolutionary War days," the cookbook states, "the tender small roots of the pine tree (found by digging about twenty feet from the tree's trunk) were

COOKING BRUNSWICK STEW FOR THE CONVICTS

While I was growing up in Tattnall County, Georgia, my dad served as a county convict guard, working out of a camp near Cobbtown. In those days the convicts would build bridges, clean rights-of-way, and build and maintain the county's dirt roads.

Dad told the county warden that he would like to provide a meal for the convicts when they completed work on a road used by our school bus. So on the day the convicts finished the road work, Dad served the crowd—the convicts and county personnel and friends—a big dinner of Brunswick stew and all the trimmings, including corn bread. He used a sixty-gallon boiler that we also used for washing clothes, making syrup, and making soap. Everyone left happy and thankful.

—REV. JAMES E. RICH
BRUNSWICK, GEORGIA

used for flavoring." Using homemade catsup as a base, the only other seasoning was red pepper.

No matter how the stew got its name, the creators came up with a unique conglomeration of fish and vegetables. Its popularity has carried down to this day.

This recipe, adapted from *Pee Dee Pepper Pot*, is credited to Mrs. B. W. Johnson. It yields 8 servings.

Pee Dee Pine Bark Stew

- 1 pound fatback
- 3 pounds chopped onions
- 3 (14.5-ounce) cans tomato soup
- 1 (14.5-ounce) bottle tomato catsup
- 4 cups water
- 1 tablespoon salt
- 1 tablespoon black pepper
- ½ tablespoon red pepper
- 1 tablespoon Worcestershire sauce
- 6 pounds small, whole, firm panfish (before dressed), cut into pieces
- 2 pounds rice, cooked separately

Using a 10-quart pot, cook the fatback (cut into small pieces) until well done as if the fat is cooked out.

Remove the fatback; add the chopped onions to the fat and cook thoroughly. Then add the tomato soup, catsup, water, and seasonings.

Bring to a roiling boil and taste for seasoning. Drop the fish into mixture and allow to simmer on slow boil for 30 minutes.

Do not stir after adding fish, but the pot may be lifted and whirled gently to keep the stew from sticking to the bottom or scorching. Remove and allow to cool slightly. Serve prepared rice on each deep dish plate, with soup poured on.

If whole fish are used, allow 1 fish with bread for each serving.

Conch Stew

Sallie Ann Robinson, who grew up on Daufuskie Island, South Carolina, describes conchs as "large seagoing snails." She and her family would hunt for conchs on Daufuskie's south end beach. Once or twice a year, they would light a bonfire on the beach and roast them in their shells, eating the meat with forks.

Here is a recipe published originally in 1982 by the Women of Trinity Episcopal Church, Edisto Island, South Carolina, in their cookbook, *Edisto Island Favorite Recipes*. This recipe is credited to Mikel Glen, who says the easiest way to remove conch meat from the shell is to first freeze it. Then you can remove the meat with a fork. Cut off inedible pieces and then run the meat through a meat grinder. Conch stew is best served with hot French bread or saltines and a salad.

Edisto Island Conch Stew

THIS RECIPE WILL YIELD 6 TO 8 SERVINGS

- 2 small onions, chopped
- ½ pound smoked pork butts
- 2 tablespoons flour
- 1 ½ gallons water
- Ground meat of 12 large conch
- 6 medium potatoes, peeled and diced
- Salt and pepper to taste

Using a large kettle, sauté the chopped onions and sliced smoked butts. Add the flour to the mix and brown.

Add the water and the conch meat, along with the potatoes. Add salt and pepper to taste and let cook over low heat for about 2 hours.

Catfish Stew with Boiled Eggs

Here's an interesting catfish stew that is adapted from the original *South Carolina Cook Book* published in the 1950s. It was contributed by Butch Johnston of Dorchester County and serves 6 to 8 people.

- 1 pound dressed catfish
- 1 ½ pounds chopped onions
- 1 ½ pounds smoked bacon
- 6 boiled eggs, chopped
- 1 tablespoon butter
- 1 cup evaporated milk
- Salt and pepper to taste

Boil the catfish in a large pot along with onions until fish leaves the bones, adding water as needed to cover the fish.

Cook the bacon down, pouring off all grease, and add to the fish mixture.

Boil about 1 ½ hours, then add the chopped eggs and butter and boil 10 minutes. Remove from the heat and add the milk, stirring as you pour.

Return to the heat and let simmer until hot, add salt and pepper to taste, then serve.

Gumbo

Some people describe gumbo as a North American rendering of French bouillabaisse. It makes for a splendid Lowcountry dinner during the first cool nights of fall, when crab and shrimp are still plentiful. It's a great dish to serve a large crowd as well as for tailgating.

The word *gumbo* derives from the Bantu word *ngombo*, which means okra. As noted earlier, African slaves brought okra seed to Charleston and Savannah. It quickly became a fixture in Lowcountry recipes, including gumbo, which can be cooked with seafood, poultry, or sausage.

Gumbo Roux

Cooking up a gumbo is not difficult, and you are free to improvise. But as Ben Moise cautions, the prelude to a proper gumbo requires that one make a roux (pronounced roo) as practiced in Louisiana. Here is a general recipe for a gumbo roux.

- ¾ cup vegetable oil
- 4 tablespoons all-purpose flour

- 1 large chopped onion
- 2 to 3 cups water or shrimp stock

Pour oil into a heavy cast-iron pot. (Don't use butter here, as it burns too easily.) Then add flour. Cook on medium heat, stirring almost constantly with a long-handled wooden spoon, until the roux achieves a dark golden brown color.

Be careful not to burn the roux. If you do, throw it all out and start over, because the burnt taste will ruin the gumbo. When the color is right, add chopped onions (also chopped bell peppers and celery if desired). Stir frequently until these vegetables come to a softened translucent state. Then add water or shrimp stock. (Some cooks also add 2 cups of chicken stock at this point.)

Shrimp Gumbo

I've adapted this gumbo recipe from *The Day of the Island Cookbook*, published some years ago by the Women of Savannah's Isle of Hope United Methodist Church. This recipe, which will yield 10 servings, was contributed by Delene (Mrs. D. L.) Browning. In this recipe, making the roux comes second. Some Lowcountry cooks like to add chicken to the shrimp, making it "Carolina Gumbo." Other optional ingredients are smoked sausage, crab meat, or oysters, "all together or in different combinations."

One precaution: Don't overcook the shrimp; otherwise, the meat can get rubbery.

Isle of Hope Shrimp Gumbo

- 1 pound okra, sliced
- 8 tablespoons cooking oil (for roux)
- 4 tablespoons flour (for roux)
- 1 cup cubed ham (pre-fried)
- 1 large onion, chopped
- Garlic to taste, minced
- Salt to taste
- 1 (14.5-ounce) can diced tomatoes
- 2 pounds shrimp (or more if desired)
- Hot sauce to taste

- Parsley if desired
- Precooked rice

Fry the sliced okra for 15 minutes or longer on medium heat. Don't brown but cook until done. Set aside.

Heat the cooking oil in a large saucepan and add the flour. Make the roux, cooking slowly, and stir until it is well browned.

Add the okra and 2 cups water. Add the ham, onion, garlic, salt, and tomatoes and cook for a few minutes. If the gumbo becomes too thick, add more water.

Add the shrimp and continue simmering until shrimp are done (when they turn pink). Add hot sauce and parsley if desired.

Serve over rice with hot garlic bread.

CHAPTER 12

Benne Seeds, a Lowcountry Legacy

Few Lowcountry parties are complete without a plate of benne biscuits either split and buttered while warm, or cooled, halved, and sandwiched together with shavings of Smithfield ham.

—Jean Anderson
A Love Affair with Southern Cooking

In *A Thousand and One Nights*, the hero Ali Baba used an unusual metaphor as the code word to open the door to the "Den of the Forty Thieves."

"OPEN SESAME!" he yelled, the metaphor being the six-foot-tall sesame plants, whose buds, when ripe, have been known to pop open at the slightest touch, exploding seeds in all directions. With his sesame code word, Ali Baba received instant entry into the thieves' den.

In the Lowcountry, they're called benne seeds (pronounce them bennie). They have become one of the great legacy plants of the Carolina-Georgia coastal plain, having come over with the slaves from Africa during the colonial era. *Bene* means *sesame* in Gambia and Senegal. They have long been rated as a Lowcountry food icon, nearing the status of the legendary she-crab soup.

With its humidity and fertile soil, the Lowcountry proved perfect for the planting of the oil-filled, nutty-flavored benne seeds, almost equaling Egypt's Nile Valley, where the drought-tolerant plants were grown long before the time of Moses.

The honey-colored benne seeds flourished magnificently from the first plantings on Lowcountry slave plots, at the end of crop rows, and near servant doorsteps where the

Africans sprinkled the seeds to give them good luck and to shield their families from the feared "Haints."

The slave cooks also were the first to reveal to their plantation mistresses the benne seeds' enormous cuisine possibilities. In time, they became a great base for candies and cakes, eventually finding their way into cookies, wafers, brittles, breads, green salads, and seafood dishes such as oyster stew and benne seed-encrusted shrimp (and chicken).

When toasted, the seeds are a savory appetizer on their own, delighting party hostesses who love to serve them with drinks.

Bakeries in Charleston and Savannah, such as Savannah's Byrd Cookie Company, count benne seed wafers and toasted "Benne Bits" among their bestsellers.

But perhaps the best benne seed creations are baked in hundreds of Lowcountry households. Benne cookies in particular are made with great care and skill.

> South Carolina legend has it that when Africans were seized to serve as slaves on Lowcountry rice plantations, some put benne seeds in their ears and later planted them in the Carolina soil as a reminder of their homeland.
>
> —James Villas
> The Glory of Southern Cooking

One of the most spirited and productive benne wafer aficionados is ninety-five-year-old Charleston native Clementa "Ment" Florio, a second-generation Italian who has been making benne cookies for more than a half century. I spoke with Mrs. Florio in a phone call to her Wadmalaw Island home, arranged by her daughter, Donna Florio, a senior writer at *Southern Living* magazine.

I asked Mrs. Florio about the secret to her longevity. "I guess it's just that the Lord has let me live this long," she said. "God's been good to me. I do what I want, when I want. I get up at 4:00 a.m. every morning, take a nap during the day, and watch Lawrence Welk every night. I go to bed at 11:00. And I sleep well."

As to Ment's kitchen skills, her daughter Donna waxes enthusiastic.

"Her benne cookies are absolutely irresistible," Donna declares. "You can easily eat a dozen or more at a sitting."

Ment Florio usually makes several batches during the Christmas season, maybe five hundred altogether, giving them as gifts to family and friends.

She graciously shared her recipe with me, and I also thank *Southern Living* for permitting me to use this copyrighted version that they tested and published in 2005.

This recipe yields about 10 dozen cookies. *Southern Living* suggests purchasing sesame (benne) seeds at health food stores where they are more reasonably priced.

In our interview, Mrs. Florio gave me two tips: she uses an old-fashioned "iron frying pan" when "parching" the benne seeds, and she shapes her teaspoon-sized dough balls with floured fingertips.

It is said that the Italians are the only immigrants whose cooking has not influenced the traditional cuisine of the South. That may be true, but they have had a remarkable effect on this century, well beyond the obvious popularity of pasta, sun-dried tomatoes, and tiramisu. Clementa Annunciata Iamundo Florio was born in Charleston in 1913. Her recipe for the traditional Lowcountry benne (sesame) cookie yields the lightest, most delicate ones I've ever tasted...

—*John Martin Taylor*
The New Southern Cook

Clementa Florio. (Photo courtesy of Donna Florio.)

Ment Florio's Benne Seed Cookies

- ½ cup benne (sesame) seeds
- ½ cup butter, softened
- 1 cup sugar
- 1 large egg
- ½ teaspoon vanilla extract
- 1 ¾ cups all-purpose flour
- 2 teaspoons baking powder
- ½ teaspoon baking soda
- ½ teaspoon salt

Cook the sesame seeds in a heavy skillet over medium heat, stirring often, 5 minutes or until toasted.

Beat the butter at medium speed with an electric mixer until creamy; gradually add the sugar, beating well. Stir in the sesame seeds, egg, and vanilla.

In a separate bowl, combine the flour, baking powder, baking soda, and salt; stir into the butter mixture. Cover the dough, and chill at least 1 hour.

Preheat oven to 325°F.

Shape the dough into ½-inch balls; place on a lightly greased baking sheet. Flatten to a ¹⁄₁₆-inch thickness with floured fingertips or a flat-bottomed glass.

Bake for 8 to 10 minutes or until lightly browned. Transfer to wire racks to cool.

Benne Seed Biscuits

One of the outstanding ways to utilize benne seeds is in baking biscuits. Here's a standard recipe that takes the small biscuits to an interesting new level of flavor and texture.

- 1 cup benne seeds
- 3 ¼ cups all-purpose flour
- 1 ½ teaspoon baking powder
- 1 teaspoon salt
- ⅔ cup shortening
- 1 cup milk

Preheat the oven to 425°F. Place benne seeds in oven using a shallow pan.

After about 5 minutes, check on the seeds' color. If they haven't reached the desired golden color and toasted smell, remove pan, shake up the seeds, and return pan to oven for an additional 1 or 2 minutes, being careful not to overcook.

Using a large bowl, sift the flour, baking powder, and salt. Add the shortening and use your fingertips or a pastry mixer to work the dough to the consistency of cornmeal.

Add the milk and benne seeds to the dough and mix well.

Place the dough on floured surface and knead for a few minutes. Roll the dough to about ⅛-inch thickness.

Use a small biscuit cutter to cut the dough and transfer to an ungreased baking sheet.

Place in the oven and bake at 400°F for around 12 to 13 minutes until lightly brown. Serve immediately or store cooled biscuits in an airtight container for later serving by reheating.

Sally's Benne Seed Salad

Savannah native Sally Bond Tonsmeire has been preparing and serving benne seed salads for many years. She has found that the benne seeds provide a tasty balance and aroma to her green salads, making them perfect for church suppers.

- ¼ cup benne seeds (toasted)
- 2 heads romaine lettuce
- ½ cup Romano cheese (grated)
- A good Italian dressing, dressed to taste

Toast the benne seeds in a skillet over medium-high heat for about 8 minutes until they are toasted a light golden brown. Be cautious not to overcook.

Tear the lettuce leaves into bite-size pieces and place in bowl. Add the benne seeds, grated cheese, and salad dressing. Toss and mix thoroughly.

Lowcountry Benne Bits

Benne bit nuggets can be purchased in tins in supermarkets, having been baked with flour to perfection. Toasting the seeds brings out the flavor, but you must be careful not to burn them. The "bits" are easily cooked at home. Here is a standard recipe that will yield about 40 bits.

- ¼ cup benne seeds
- 1 cup all-purpose flour
- ¼ teaspoon salt
- Black pepper to taste
- ½ stick chilled butter, cut in pieces
- 1 tablespoon milk
- 1 tablespoon water

Preheat the oven to 350°F. Sprinkle the benne seeds evenly on baking sheet and toast in the oven about 10 minutes or until golden brown, stirring constantly. Allow to cool.

Combine the flour, salt, and pepper in a mixing bowl. Work in the butter with your fingertips. Add the benne seeds, milk, and water and knead with your hands until the dough is smooth.

On a floured surface, roll out the dough to about a ¼-inch thick, and cut into 1-inch rounds. Use spatula to place rounds on an ungreased baking sheet and bake about 11 to 12 minutes, until golden.

Serve immediately, or allow to cool and store in a tightly closed container for up to 2 weeks.

CHAPTER 13

Pinders! Goobers!

Let me fetch you a plate of boil [sic] peanuts, which I just set off de fire. You lak 'em? Most white folks love 'em dat way, 'stead of parched.
—Miemy Johnson
an African American interviewed by the WPA in the 1930s

Peas, peas, peas, peas, eating goober peas,
Goodness how delicious, eating goober peas
—Traditional verse attributed to "A. Pindar"

My friend Mike McDougald, a Rome, Georgia, telecommunications tycoon and a native of deep southeast Georgia, is one of the few former country-born Southerners I've met who know that the real name for peanuts across the "country South" is *pinders*.

I learned the term on the upstate South Carolina farm where I grew up. Mike picked it up during his young years in Bulloch County, Georgia. It was only in recent years, while researching this book, that I learned that the term derived from the Angola word *mpinda*. Another more frequently used term, *goobers*, also comes from the Central African word *nguba* or *ginguba*.

"Pinders, I love 'em!" Mike McDougald told me. "The first money I ever made was from pinders that we grew in the field. My older brothers and I rode in the back of Daddy's Ford pickup truck, the one with the spare tire on the side, and we loaded it up with peanut vines that we'd just pulled from the ground."

They shook off the dirt and then poured buckets of water on the green nuts to get them clean. "Then," Mike continued, "our mother supervised boiling them in a big old black pot in the backyard, with plenty—I mean plenty—of salt."

They packed them in small brown bags, put them in several straw-type baskets, and headed off the five miles to Statesboro, where they walked around hawking their wares.

"The street pavement was so hot on a summer day, it burned our bare feet," he recalled. "Even so we would yell, 'Fresh Hot-Boiled PEA—nuts…Five cents a bag!' They sold quickly…in the courthouse, in the underground barber shop, and in drugstores. We sold a lot of our peanuts to folks who stopped their cars at the red light on Main Street.

"At the end of the day," Mike said, "the little McDougald boys would go home with sometimes two dollars apiece in their overall pockets, and in those depression times, that was a lot of money for a kid."

In the old days, Southern boys dropped roasted and salted nuts into a bottle of Coca-Cola or an RC Cola just dug out of an ice-filled drink box, such as the one found in my dad's country store seven miles out of Kershaw, South Carolina.

Mike McDougald, at the age of twelve, was a masterful boiled peanut salesman in Statesboro, Georgia. (Photo courtesy of Mike McDougald.)

My favorite radio talk show host, Ludlow Porch, insists that for the ultimate enjoyment of salted roasted peanuts one should confine oneself to an old-fashioned six-ounce bottle of "Co-Cola."

"Once you've opened the Co-Cola," he says in *The Fat White Guy's Cookbook*, "you must look around the store until you find the penny peanut machine, the one with the glass globe filled with those red salted Spanish peanuts." (Most of these are difficult to find.)

Before you put the nuts in the bottle for a mid-afternoon treat, Ludlow says you should "take a big drink; this will allow room for the peanuts!"

Peanuts are thought to have originated in the Andes region of South America. They were eaten in Peru as early as 750 B.C. Spanish conquistadors greedily ate the nuts during their brutal sixteenth-century Peruvian conquest. In subsequent years, peanuts made their way from South America to Europe.

From Portugal, slave traders transported the nuts to Africa, according to Jessica Harris in *Beyond Gumbo*, where they became very popular. In the 1600s, the nutritious pinders made their way from Africa to the Carolina Lowcountry via the ubiquitous slave ships.

Most such ships coming to the New World were provisioned with peanuts, says Andrew F. Smith in *Peanuts: The Illustrious History of the Goober Pea*. Smith quoted Philadelphian James Mesa as saying in 1804 that peanuts "were called pinda by the negroes, by whom they are chiefly cultivated." He also reported that starting in the colonial years, slaves planted peanuts in small patches southwest of Charleston, "for market."

When freed slave Denmark Vesey masterminded an attempted Charleston slave uprising in 1822, his coconspirator, Gullah Jack, asked their followers to eat only dry food such as groundnuts and parched corn. The nutritious groundnuts were easily carried in one's pockets just as parched corn was carried by Indians and pioneers taking a lengthy trek.

One of the earliest Lowcountry cookbook listings of peanuts is in Sarah Rutledge's pioneering 1847 *Carolina Housewife*. Her recipes include "Ground-nut soup," "Ground-nut Cake," and "Ground-nut Cheese Cake." Her peanut soup recipe called for the nuts to be "well beaten up" with flour and blended with a pint of oysters!

Dr. Francis Porcher was said to be the first American physician to proclaim peanuts as "rich and nutritious," saying they could be substituted for meat dishes. He reported extensive use of peanuts on Lowcountry plantations. And botanist William Bartram noticed during his Southeastern odyssey in the 1700s that ground-up peanuts combined with ground-up sassafras roots produced a nice substitute for chocolate.

But it was in the 1920s that acclaimed African-American genius George Washington Carver of Tuskegee, Alabama, expanded the peanut horizon by developing an amazing multitude of peanut products

PLANT SOME PEANUTS IN YOUR GARDEN

No Lowcountry garden should be without a row or two of peanuts. They add nitrogen to the soil and protein to the diet, according to Sallie Ann Robinson, who said peanuts flourished on Daufuskie Island where she grew up. She and her family boiled them when they were green and roasted them in the oven.

such as peanut-flavored cakes, candies, ice cream, soft drinks, and even peanut skin creams. In time, his peanut inventions exceeded three hundred, one of which was peanut milk.

In recent centuries, South Georgia has become one of the nation's major producers of peanuts. When Jimmy Carter became our nation's thirty-ninth President, Plains-produced peanuts took media attention center stage. Today, Georgia continues as one of the nation's top peanut-producing states, with several festivals held annually to honor the goober pea.

Boiled Peanuts

In South Carolina, the State Legislature made the boiled peanut the state's official snack food. In the town of Pelion, where farmers have been producing peanuts for more than a century, the town's Ruritan Club throws a huge peanut boil party every year, cooking up more than a hundred and thirty bushels of peanuts in huge pots.

The taste of properly boiled peanuts is something to behold. I love to buy a bag or two from a roadside stand, and I experience a half hour of snacking pleasure, sucking each morsel for a moment, hull and all, and savoring its supreme saltiness before opening it up to get the goody inside.

While boiled peanuts can't be classified as hors d'oeuvres per se, Charleston restaurants such as The Wreck and Hyman's provide customers a nice serving of boiled goobers before taking their orders.

If you want to boil your own peanuts, the key is to make sure you achieve a near perfect salt-to-water ratio. And they taste even better a day or so later, after being refrigerated. During that time, they absorb more of the salt from the hulls.

Here's how to boil peanuts on the stove top, according to prize-winning cookbook authors Matt Lee and Ted Lee of Charleston, who have built a boiled peanut empire mostly through mail-order sales. Started years ago, that business catapulted them into writing lengthy features, mostly on food, for *The New York Times Sunday Magazine* and also led them to write their prize-winning 2006 *Lee Bros. Southern Cookbook*.

Here's a recipe adaptation. This will make enough for twelve people to snack on (four pounds).

> ### "YOU LIKE BOILED PINDERS?"
>
> *I heard that old man Butler at Orange Lake Station had fifteen acres of pinders and wanted to fatten hogs on shares. My shoats had outgrown the table scraps…The old man came to the gate with outstretched hand…*
>
> *"You like boiled pinders?"*
>
> *I confessed I had a passion for them.*
>
> *"Then we'll go pull you some pinders to carry home to boil, and I want you to come back…and tell me they was the best you ever sucked outen the hull…"*
>
> —MARJORIE KINNAN RAWLINGS
>
> CROSS CREEK

Matt and Jed's Boiled Peanuts

- 1 ½ cups salt, plus more to taste
- 2 pounds raw peanuts in shell
- 4 gallons water, plus more as needed

Using a 3-gallon stockpot, dissolve ½ cup of the salt into 2 gallons of water. Soak the peanuts overnight (8 hours) in the salty water. Use a dinner plate to subdue peanuts that wish to float.

The next day, discard the water and fill the pot with 2 gallons of fresh water and the remaining cup of salt. Cover the pot, turn the heat to a boil, then reduce to medium-low and cook at a low boil for 4 to 8 hours. Add water in 2-cup increments to maintain the same level until peanuts are soft.

After 3 hours of boiling, pull out a peanut to sample its saltiness and softness. After it cools, open up the hull and take out the kernels. If they're too salty, ladle out some of the brine, replacing it with an equal amount of fresh

Matt Lee (right) and Ted Lee stir up a batch of boiled peanuts in their kitchen. (Photo courtesy Matt Lee and Ted Lee.)

water. If not salty enough, add salt in ¼-cup increments. Turn off heat for a while to allow peanuts to absorb salt. Afterward, continue the low boiling for another 2 to 4 hours, taking hourly samples to make sure peanuts are getting as soft and as salty as you wish. If you seek extreme softness, 12 hours of boiling may be required.

Cut off heat when the peanuts have cooked to your satisfaction. Allow an hour of cooling, then drain and serve immediately, or refrigerate for as long as 7 days. Peanuts will keep for several months in the freezer.

Sugary Boiled Peanuts
This is another twist to the peanut story—sweet and sugary boiled peanuts.

Dee Dee's Sugarcoated Peanuts

This recipe comes from a delightful cookbook—*Great Cooks Rise…with the May River Tide*. It is put out by the Episcopal Church Women of the historic 1854 Church of the Cross in beautiful Bluffton, South Carolina.

- 1 cup sugar
- ½ cup water
- 2 cups raw shelled Virginia type peanuts, skins on

Preheat the oven to 300°F.

Dissolve the sugar in water over medium heat. Add the peanuts and continue to cook over medium heat, stirring frequently. Continue to boil until the peanuts are completely covered with sugar.

In the preheated 300°F oven, pour the nuts on ungreased cookie sheet and separate the peanuts with a fork. Bake for approximately 30 minutes, stirring every 10 minutes.

Slow Cooker Boiled Peanuts

For an easy-to-prepare version of boiled peanuts, try cooking them in a slow cooker. This recipe will yield 4 servings (1 pound).

- 1 pound raw peanuts, shelled
- Water, as necessary
- 4 ½ tablespoons salt

Place the peanuts in a 3-quart slow cooker, and fill with water. Let soak overnight (about 8 hours). Due to water absorption, add water again until filled.

Add the salt and cook on medium low for 8 hours, then on high for 1 ½ hours.

Toward end of cooking time, taste a few peanuts. If they are not salty enough, add more salt and continue to cook.

Peanut Soup

Colonial America's original peanut soup was likely based on African stews that contained the ground nut, according to cooking school teacher and author Terry Thompson. She found that most modern-day peanut soup recipes contain similar ingredients such as celery, flour, and peanuts, of course. Some cooks like to add tomatoes as an option. This recipe is adapted from Ms. Thompson's *Taste of the South* cookbook, and yields 4 to 6 servings.

Georgia Peanut Soup

- 5 ounces salt pork, rind removed and diced
- 1 medium onion, chopped
- 2 celery stalks, chopped
- 1 large garlic clove, minced
- 3 tablespoons all-purpose flour
- 3 ½ cups poultry stock or chicken broth
- 2 large tomatoes, peeled and chopped
- ¼ teaspoon freshly ground black pepper
- Salt to taste
- ¼ teaspoon ginger
- ¼ teaspoon paprika
- Dash freshly grated nutmeg
- 1 cup whipping cream
- ½ cup finely ground roasted peanuts

Cook the salt pork in heavy 4-quart saucepan over medium heat for about 20 minutes until all fat is rendered. Leave remaining crisp bits of cracklins in pan. Add the onion, celery, and garlic. Cook 12 to 15 minutes, stirring often, until the onion is wilted and slightly browned.

Add the flour and stir to blend. Cook, stirring, 3 to 4 minutes. Slowly stir in the stock, bring to a boil, and boil until slightly thickened.

Reduce heat and add the tomatoes, pepper, salt, ginger, paprika, and nutmeg. Cover and simmer 15 minutes longer. Add the cream and peanuts; stir well and simmer 15 minutes longer. Serve hot.

Savannah-Style Peanut Soup

According to noted Savannah chef Joe Randall, who runs a cooking school in the Hostess City, peanuts in Africa provided the basis for "a silky brew called groundnut stew."

Chef Joe Randall of Savannah takes a break from his stove. (Photo by the author)

The tradition continued with the arrival of slaves in the Lowcountry in the 1600s and for two centuries afterward.

Here is Chef Randall's refinement of the stew, as carried in his authoritative cookbook, *A Taste of Heritage: The New African-American Cuisine*, with my thanks to Joe for giving me permission to run this recipe, which yields 10 to 12 servings.

Cream of Boiled Peanut Soup

- 3 pounds raw, unshelled peanuts
- 1 cup salt
- 1 large sprig fresh thyme
- ½ stick butter
- 1 small onion, finely diced
- 1 rib celery, finely diced
- 3 tablespoons all-purpose flour
- 4 cups chicken stock
- 2 cups light cream
- ½ teaspoon ground white pepper
- Salt to taste

Place the peanuts, salt, and thyme in a saucepan, and add enough water to cover.

Bring to a boil, then reduce the heat and simmer about 30 minutes, until peanuts are tender. Allow to cool in the cooking water.

Drain the peanuts and remove the shells and skin. Set aside ½ cup of peanuts and chop for garnish. Place enough of the remaining nuts in a blender and puree to yield 1 cup.

Using a soup pot, heat the butter over medium-high heat and sauté the onions and celery about 3 to 4 minutes until tender, but not brown. Stir in the flour and cook for 1 minute. Stir in the chicken stock. When evenly blended, stir in the cream. Simmer 10 to 15 minutes until the soup thickens.

Strain the soup through a fine strainer into another pot and discard the solids. Bring the strained soup to a boil, then reduce heat to a simmer. Whisk in the pureed peanuts until smooth. Season with salt and pepper.

Ladle into warm soup plates and sprinkle with chopped boiled peanuts.

Peanut Candies

Peanut brittle-type candies have been favorites across the Lowcountry and, indeed, the Deep South from the 1800s.

Southern Cooking, Mrs. S. R Dull's grand cookbook first published in 1928, included a recipe for peanut brittle that called for a cup of toasted peanuts, a cup of sugar, and ½ teaspoon of vanilla extract.

Later recipes added light corn syrup such as the very popular Karo brand.

Here are three flavorful recipes, representing Charleston, Savannah, and Plains, Georgia, that capture the flavor and texture of what became a Southern favorite early at the turn of the twentieth century.

Charleston Groundnut Candy

This peanut-based candy comes from Sarah Rutledge's pioneering 1847 cookbook, *The Carolina Housewife*.

- 1 quart molasses
- ½ pint brown sugar

- ¼ pound butter
- 1 quart peanuts, parched and shelled

Heat the molasses, brown sugar, and butter over a slow fire; boil for half an hour. Add in the peanuts; boil for a quarter of an hour, and then pour mixture into a shallow tin pan to harden.

Savannah Stovetop Peanut Brittle

You can make this brittle and store it for later consumption. This recipe will make 8 servings.

- 1 cup light corn syrup
- 2 cups granulated sugar
- ½ cup water
- ½ teaspoon salt
- 3 cups raw shelled Spanish peanuts
- 2 tablespoons butter
- 1 teaspoon vanilla extract
- 2 teaspoons baking soda

Heat the syrup, sugar, water, and salt to a rolling boil in a heavy 2-quart saucepan.

Add the peanuts, reduce heat to medium, and stir constantly. Cook to hard crack stage (293°F).

Add the butter and vanilla, then baking soda. Keep in mind that mixture will quickly increase in volume and could spill over saucepan sides. Beat rapidly and pour onto a lightly greased baking sheet, spreading to ¼-inch thickness.

When cool, break into pieces and store in an airtight container.

Jimmy Carter's Favorite Peanut Brittle

In her book, *Miss Lillian and Friends*, the former president's mother declared this President Carter's favorite peanut brittle. It features the aforementioned Karo syrup, favored by many across the South since the early 1900s.

- 3 cups sugar
- 1 ½ cups water
- 1 cup white Karo syrup
- 3 cups raw peanuts
- 1 tablespoon baking soda
- ½ stick butter
- 1 teaspoon vanilla

Boil the sugar, water, and Karo syrup until it spins a thread; add the peanuts.

Stir constantly until syrup turns golden brown. Remove from heat and add the remaining ingredients. Stir until the butter melts.

Pour out quickly onto two cookie sheets with sides. As the mixture begins to harden around edges, pull until thin.

At Plains, Harvesting Peanuts a Tough Job

The busiest of the year…was when we were gathering peanuts and cotton…"Shaking" peanuts was especially difficult, because of the heat, dirt, and the constant stooping all the way to the ground. We had to erect pine-sapling stackpoles, nail on cross-strips to keep the crop a foot off the ground, plow up the peanuts, shake each plant to remove the clinging dirt, and place the root and nuts adjacent to the pole.

We put bunches of grass on top of the stack to help shed the rain…while the vines and nuts slowly dried. If stacked properly, the peanuts could wait even into late fall or early winter to be threshed and taken to market…

—Jimmy Carter
An Hour Before Daylight

CHAPTER 14

Pig Pickins in the Lowcountry

Hot and sweet and red and greasy,
I could eat a gallon, easy
Barbecue Sauce!
Lay it on, hoss.

—*Roy Blount Jr.*

What is it about pork and barbecue that draws such passionate devotion among people across the South, including the Lowcountry?

It's pretty obvious…we native Southerners were born into a pork culture. Until a few short decades ago, hog killing was a supreme Southern ritual, almost as important as Thanksgiving or Christmas. I know for a fact because hog-killing day at our farm in upstate South Carolina was something to behold. The whole community, it seemed, blacks and whites, joined in the festivities, taking part in the work and sharing in the gastronomic bounty.

As John T. Edge reported in *Mrs. Wilkes' Boardinghouse Cookbook*, the Wilkes family—before forced to vacate their Toombs County farm in South Georgia to make way for an air base—looked forward to late November's chilly hog-killing weather.

"Not long after the first frost," Edge quotes a family member, "Mr. Wilkes would gather together with family and friends to kill and quarter a hog." Daughter Marjorie remembered it as a time of celebration:

"They would make all kinds of delicacies from the hog. My father would make souse meat and liver pudding, things you couldn't buy but everyone just loved. And of course we salted our own bacon and hung up our hams…It's kind of hard to explain, but those were festive times."

According to the original *South Carolina Cook Book*, published in the 1950s by the well-loved Extension Service home demonstration agents, "Pork is perhaps South Carolina's most popular meat. Cured hams, shoulder roasts, spare ribs, bacon, sausage, liver pudding, hog's head cheese, and the traditional hog jowl for New Year's Day all play an important part in South Carolina meals. And rightly so, for who can deny that a pork roast with sweet potatoes, turnip greens, artichoke relish, and corn bread is not good eating?"

Here follow some interesting pork dishes that Lowcountry people have favored over the years:

Hog's Head Cheese

In past centuries, hog's head cheese was an honored dish in Christmas celebrations across the Lowcountry. My mother made the dish when I was in my early teens. We called it Souse Meat. It's a delicious dish, although a rarity today.

The following recipe came from the *South Carolina Cook Book*. This recipe was credited to Mrs. J. W. Almeida of Charleston County and yields 6 servings.

In the South, it's a compliment to say someone lives "high on the hog."
—*Bethany Ewald Bultman*

Charleston Hog's Head Cheese

- 1 hog's head
- 2 quarts water
- 2 medium-size onions
- 1 tablespoon vinegar
- Salt and pepper to taste

Wash and clean the hog's head thoroughly. Place in pot with the water. Bring to a boil and simmer until meat drops from bones.

Pick out the meat and grind coarsely or cut into very small bits.

Chop the onions and cook 5 minutes. Combine all the ingredients, using the water left in the pot also.

Pour into a loaf pan and cool until set. Slice and serve with greens and rice.

Liver Pudding

Popular over the years among Scotch-Irish, French Huguenot, and English descendants in the Lowcountry, as well as others who love traditional Lowcountry cooking, this is a different type of breakfast or supper dish. The pudding can be served in cold slices or heated to a near mush along with hot, buttered grits and toast or toasted split biscuits dotted with jelly.

This adaptation comes from the *Treasured Southern Family Recipes* by the late Geddings de M. Cushman and Ora Lou O'Hara Cushman of Aiken, South Carolina. This recipe will yield 8 to 10 servings.

Lowcountry Liver Pudding

- 2 pounds pork jowl
- 1 ¼ pounds lean pork
- 1 pound pork liver
- 1 pig's foot (optional)
- 2 medium onions
- Salt and pepper

In a covered saucepan with water, boil jowl, pork, liver, and pig's foot (if using) around 2 ½ to 4 hours until very tender. The pig's foot should be so well cooked that the meat falls from the bones at the slightest touch. Pour off the broth and reserve it. Allow the meat to cool. Remove meat from pig's foot.

Chop the onion fine, but do not cook it. Combine the onion with the meat and sprinkle with salt and pepper. Put the meat mixture through a meat grinder.

Using your hands, blend the mixture, adding some of the broth as you blend, to moisten. Limit the broth to avoid making the mixture soupy.

Pack the mixture in a pan or a loaf dish and put in the refrigerator.

When the mixture sets, turn out the dish and serve as previously mentioned in cold slices or as a warmed mush.

Liver and Onions

MAKES 4 SERVINGS.

This recipe is adapted with my thanks to the National Council of Negro Women from their book *The Historical Cook Book of the American Negro*. The editors describe this as a nonfat version of the perennially popular liver and onions dish.

- 1½ tablespoons mustard
- 1 cup hot water
- ½ pound sliced liver
- 1 onion, chopped fine
- 1 green pepper, sliced into thin rings

In a frying pan, add the mustard to the hot water and bring to a boil. In the same pan, fry the slices of liver until tender, cooking on both sides. Remove the liver slices from the pan while tender, and place on a plate.

Add the chopped onions to sauce and cook until tender. Pour over the slices of liver and lay on thin pepper rings.

Dutch Fork Backbone Pie

Backbone pie is a rare old German dish popular in South Carolina's Dutch Fork community beginning around 1849, according to the late Juanita C. Kibler, author of the delightful *Dutch Fork Cookery* cookbook. In later years, the succulent dish, cooked with thin "Schneider"-type dumplings, was revered throughout German communities near Dutch Fork. The Schneiders were said to symbolically resemble the snips of cloth that piled up under a tailor's working board. The dish was often served with deviled eggs.

Backbone Pie with Schneiders

- 3 pounds pork backbones
- 1 cup all-purpose flour
- 1 egg

- 1 tablespoon water
- 2 cups stock
- Salt and pepper

Cook the backbones in water and debone to make 2 cups of backbone meat.

Combine flour, egg, and water to form a dough stiff enough to roll. Roll out the dough very thin on a floured surface, and let set for an hour or so. Cut into squares and triangles about 2 or 3 inches per side. These are the "Schneiders." Add these to the boiling stock a few at a time and cook 10 minutes.

Preheat oven to 350°F.

Roll out pie pastry and line a baking dish. Alternate meat, salt, pepper, and Schneiders in two layers. Pour the broth over all. Cover with a top crust such as for a chicken pie and bake until brown.

Boiled Pigs Feet! Oh So Scrumptious

My longtime friend, Martha Durham Hoke, who resides on Lady's Island in Beaufort, South Carolina, has a great love for boiled pig's feet. "I grew up at Sand Mountain, Alabama," Martha said, "and we enjoyed eating pig's feet during hog-killing time. They are delicious if you fix them right, and I still love to cook them."

"I buy the raw, pre-split kind of pig's feet," Martha told me, "and the way I cook them, the flavorful meat juices are sucked up into the batter during cooking. It's not fatty, it's just delicious."

She first boils the pig's feet for a few minutes, "and then I take them out of the pot and let them cool down. In the meantime, I mix a plain pancake batter using buttermilk.

"Next I dip the pig's feet into the batter until they are well coated. You need to get as much batter attached to the pig's feet as possible so they will absorb the meat flavors from the jelly around the pig's feet."

Following this, she fries them in a small amount of oil for about 5 minutes on moderate heat until all the battered pig's feet are golden brown.

"Then comes the eating," she said. "It's just heaven in the mouth. Sooooo scrumptious!"

And Then There's Barbecue!

I like the lyrics of this ditty sung by Robert Earl Keen of Texas:

Barbecue makes one feel young,
Barbecue makes everybody someone.
If you're feelin' puny and you don't know what to do,
Treat yourself to some meat—eat some barbecue...

Or this song, written by North Carolina musician Tommy Edwards, lead singer and guitarist with the Bluegrass Experiment, for my friends John Shelton and Dale Volberg Reed's book on North Carolina barbecue, *Holy Smoke: The Big Book of North Carolina Barbecue*:

Holy Smoke! What smells so good? Is someone burnin' hickory wood?
What's that cookin' on those coals? Why it's a pig, Lord bless my soul,
We're gonna have some barbecue, boiled potatoes, Brunswick stew,
Slaw that's white or maybe red, hush puppies or fried corn bread,
And sauce from an old recipe, known only to the family.
A great big glass of sweet ice tea.
Holy smoke! That's heav'n to me
　　　—"Holy Smoke" by Tommy Edwards ©2007, Hidden Gem Publishing

Whole Hog Barbecue on a Grill, South Carolina Style

Larry Dickerson is the longtime chef at popular Donzelle's Restaurant in Conway, near the South Carolina coast. Jennings Chestnut, an accomplished musician and fisherman, introduced me to Larry. I soon learned that Larry is a master when it comes to cooking whole hogs, as well as chicken bogs (see page 229 in chapter 15 for

Grill-style whole hog barbecue is demonstrated by Larry Dickerson of Conway, South Carolina. (Photo courtesy of Jennings Chestnut.)

his bog style). Here, in his own words, is how Larry cooks a whole hog on a grill for a barbecue feast:

As to barbecue, I cook a lot of hogs, whole hogs, yes sir. It's time consuming, but you have gas grills now so you don't have to keep shoveling your coals in all night.

I get up a lot of mornings at three o'clock and put a 150-pound hog on, and get the grill up to 325 to 350 degrees with the skin up. That way, when the hog cooks, all the drippings fall in your catch basin. That keeps all your moisture in.

After I get him hot, I cut him back down to 225 degrees and then I cook him for a good ten hours. After that, I flip him, take the ribs and all the bones out, clean him up real good, put him back on simmer. But never put any sauce on it though, not until I'm through cooking him.

I like to chop the barbecue up and put it in the skin, so that when folks go down the line, they can get their serving right off the skin, like an old bread bowl. It makes a good centerpiece.

I do salt him down with iodized salt twenty-four hours prior to cooking.

As to sauce, we use an old-time vinegar-based recipe that came from Williamsburg County. I picked it up from my neighbor, an elderly gentleman originally from Kingstree. But my sauce is better than his. I use a gallon of brown vinegar, a cup of butter, a cup of sugar, a half cup fresh red pepper, a quarter cup of Worcestershire sauce, and eight ounces of Texas Pete. I bring that to a boil. Sometimes I put it on the hog, but most of the time I just put it out in a container on the table.

How to Cook a Pig: Lowcountry-Style Pit Barbecue

Bennett Brown III, owner and operator of Lowcountry Barbecue, a full-service catering and restaurant company in Atlanta, tells here in his own words how you should go about cooking a pig in the traditional Lowcountry style:

This method was taught to me by my father, the late Bennett Brown Jr., formerly chairman and CEO of the old Citizens & Southern National Bank in Atlanta that later evolved to

Bank of America. Many of the methods and sauce ingredients come from Mose, an old Gullah native who lived near our family's ancestral home outside Kingstree in Williamsburg County, South Carolina.

The first point to consider is the pig itself. The ideal pig should have a dressed (gutted, no head or feet) weight of 110 to 130 pounds, and be USDA approved. This size pig feeds approximately one hundred persons.

The pig should be split down the breastbone (butterflied), and then sawn partially down the inside part of the backbone enough so the pig can be laid completely flat on the grill. When splitting the backbone, be sure not to cut through the skin. Trim away any excess fat in the pig's inner cavity, and liberally salt the entire cavity. This will help to control bacteria and add flavor.

Lowcountry Pit Barbecue style with a whole hog is demonstrated by Bennett Brown III, owner of Lowcountry Barbecue in Atlanta. (Photo courtesy of Bennett Brown III.)

An easy and inexpensive pit to build is one made of cinder blocks. You will need thirty-nine blocks in order to construct a pit approximately five feet long by four feet wide and two feet (two blocks) high. Be sure to build the pit so as to have an opening at one end large enough to shovel charcoal inside when stoking the pig. Make two cooking racks out of expanded metal. You will need the second rack when it is time to flip your pig. You will also need a large piece of corrugated tin or heavy-duty cardboard to cover the pig while cooking.

About one third of a cord of seasoned hardwood such as hickory, pecan, or oak will be needed to build a fire, which will produce the coals for stoking the pit. Build your fire a couple of hours in advance so it will produce a good bank of coals, which you will use to "prime your pit" fifteen minutes before you put the pig on. This is similar to preheating an oven, and it will also kill any bacteria present on the grill.

Place the pig on the cooking rack rib side down. When shoveling coals into the pit, be sure to arrange them in the four corners of the pit in the outer edges of the shoulders and hams.

It is very important that you maintain a constant average temperature of between 250 and 300 degrees, which generally means stoking the pit every thirty to forty-five minutes. Keep a flashlight handy so you can lean down and look at the underside to make sure you are not burning the meat.

The pig should be ready to turn after ten to twelve hours. Use your second rack to sandwich the hog when flipping over to the back side. After turning, the pig needs constant attention during the rendering and saucing stage of the final four hours.

From this point forward, be aware that the heat from the coals will cause the back fat to liquefy. This grease will "puddle up" in the rib cage cavity, and you will want to use a large spoon or ladle to spoon it out and discard. This grease is very flammable so be careful not to let any drip down onto the live coals inside the pit.

During this final four hours of the cooking process, sauce down the hams and shoulders with a thin Lowcountry-style vinegar-based sauce. This style of sauce will help keep the hog meat moist and full of flavor.

Bennett Brown Jr. (Photo courtesy of Bennett Brown III)

Once the internal temperature of the meat reaches 190 degrees, then it should be easy to pull from the bone and produce a wonderful barbecue for all to enjoy.

Using a Gum Tree Bowl to Display a Whole Hog

One of the eastern South Carolina Pee Dee area traditions is serving a whole split barbecued hog in a large carved wooden bowl. They're usually made from a tupelo gum tree stump.

"They are treasured items and some are quite ancient," says Ben Moise. In the nearby photo, Ben displays his own such bowl that measures two feet by four feet. Quinton Hughes, a Hemingway, South Carolina, barber, carved the bowl from solid gum.

Moise uses it—along with a four-foot-long strip boat—to display his famous Frogmore Stew at big food events.

This bowl, carved from a tupelo gum tree, will hold a barbecued hog, according to Charlestonian Ben Moise (pictured), who uses it often in his catering business. (Photo courtesy of Ben Moise.)

Coca-Cola Barbecues in Swainsboro, Georgia

Charles Hutchins Jr.'s favorite recollection from growing up in Wadley, Georgia, is going to the barbecues held by the Coca-Cola bottler from which his mother purchased bottled drinks for her "Ruth's Country Store."

All of the merchants handling Coca-Cola were invited once a year along with their families. The event always took place just before sundown at the Coca-Cola plant at Swainsboro, Georgia.

"I remember the menu," Hutchins said. "It was barbecue pork, potato salad, white bread, and Coca-Colas. Note that I haven't mentioned Cokes. In those days they were Coca-Colas or as some would say, 'dopes.' To this day, I've never tasted a Coke as good as those Coca-Colas back then. I don't know why; maybe it was the water, the pure sugar sweetener, or the size of that six-ounce bottle. The bottler filled washtubs with ice, and there has never been a better way to cool a drink than in ice."

As to the barbecue, Charles recalled that the men cooked a whole hog, one carrying a lot of fat. "The cooking began the night before, so the meat would be ready the following day," he said. "The sauce, as I recall, was simply vinegar, red pepper, black pepper, and salt.

"That's the way I remember those days," Hutchins says, "and unless someone can correct me, I'm sticking to my memories."

Charles Hutchins, Jr. (Photo by David Hutchins.)

The Great Vandy's Barbecue: Fifty-plus Years and Still Going Strong

Michael McDougald grew up near Statesboro, Georgia, north of Savannah, and went on to fame in the radio world. He first worked as a morning talk show host on Clear Channel WSB Radio broadcasting from Atlanta's historic old Biltmore Hotel. Later, he owned radio stations in Georgia and Alabama. Currently he serves as vice chairman of the Georgia Telecommunications Commission. Here Mike recalls in his own words fond memories of the acclaimed Vandy's Barbecue:

Mike McDougald has been a Vandy's Barbecue fan since his growing-up years in Statesboro, Georgia. While attending Emory University, he hosted a nighttime radio show on Atlanta's WSB Radio. (Photo courtesy of Mike McDougald.)

It would be well into the 1970s and 1980s before the late columnist Lewis Grizzard told us—the folks who had grown up on Vandy's Barbecue—that it was absolutely, without question, officially the Number One source of great and renowned barbecue in the entire state of Georgia. Vandy's had been grinding out barbecue for a very long time, and all Statesborites and Bulloch Countians and many out-of-state visitors well knew that a stop at Vandy's was a stop in that special heaven where pigs go when they involuntarily give up the ghost.

Nobody could perform a treatment on a hungry appetite quite like Vandy could in the simplest possible surroundings with his very special art of just how to treat a cut of meat. Slooowww and eeeeeaaasssyyy all-night cooking,

Vandy's Barbecue in Statesboro, Georgia is noted for its outstanding history. Here the manager, Robert Smith, takes a phone order while pork butts are being cooked out back. (Photos by the author.)

serving it up with "light" bread that came from Savannah's Holsum Flavor Rangers bakery, being trucked in just-baked-fresh before the restaurant opened. The barbecue man kept dozens of these loaves handy just by the chopping block and broke the paper in the middle and pulled out two oh-so-soft slices to go on your plate. You could make your own "sandwich," you could sop with it, or you could put bread in one hand and barbecue in the other and aim it at your mouth—stopping just long enough to savor a spoonful of Brunswick stew.

Nothing fancy, mind you. Walk in to find one very small room, with maybe just three or four tables and a combined ordering and delivery window in the back on the right.

As you stood there, you got to see the master chopper slamming that sharp blade to make it slashed, sliced, pulled, or how you would have it. And as you watched, he'd pile up a whopping serving and slam it into a paper plate held in the other hand. Shake, shake, shake and some sauce gave it all that was necessary to make a feast for a kingly person.

Vandy's was from the very beginning "an eating place" and pretty much invented "fast food." You walk in, they slice or chop as you watch, and fill your plate, sometimes in less than a minute. And their Brunswick stew was to die for. Still is…same recipe…maybe fifty years later.

After a very successful operation for years, Vandy Boyd moved from his Court House Square location to just one block off South Main, in the "Blue Front" store on Vine Street.

Vandy Boyd's first location was just a door or two east of the provincially named Buggy and Wagon Company hardware. Today, in addition to the Blue Front, there is a location in the Statesboro Mall. And then there is Boyd's Barbecue up on the Savannah bypass, run by one of the Boyd children who differed in business ideas from the rest of the family. It's all good—but nothing beats the Blue Front Vandy's very special squeezed-in-tight atmosphere and watch-me-make-your-barbecue-plate-in-a-hurry.

Unless there was a line, you walked right in, ordered your plate, and sat right down to eat. No muss, no fuss, no bother, and a Coca-Cola or R. C. Cola, Dr Pepper or Nehi Orange in their familiar bottle was only a nickel from an icy tub filled to the brim.

PLANTATION HOG-KILLING

When hog-killing time comes in the winter [the plantation foreman] attends to getting everything ready. He has the hogs killed on a growing moon so the meat will not dry up in the cooking, attends to having the meat properly cleaned and cut up, the hams carefully trimmed and packed in a mixture of red pepper, sugar, and salt for curing.

Trying out the lard, making sausages and liver pudding, is left to women who are skilled in the art of seasoning, but his watchful eyes allow no pans or buckets to be stealthily filled before he gives each worker what he considers a proper present of fresh meat.

—JULIA PETERKIN
ROLL, JORDAN, ROLL (1933)

Wherever you took it, you knew you had the best. You might pass someone on the street with the aroma smelling so strong that they likely said, "Vandy's? I'm heading there right now!"

The Georgia Wild Hog Supper

Every January, the informal launching of the Georgia General Assembly's annual session takes place at a Sunday night Wild Hog Supper at Atlanta's historic old Freight Depot near the State Capitol. The commanding general for the pig-pickin' feast over the years has been the state's longtime agriculture commissioner, Tommy Irwin, who told me how the tradition got started with wild pigs from South Georgia's Ocmulgee River swamp:

It was more than four decades ago that we staged our first Wild Hog Supper for the State Legislature, after having been proposed by several of our farm leaders who called themselves "The Friends of Agriculture."

The first wild hogs were delivered to us (well-cooked) by the late Bob Addison, later the sheriff of Wilcox County. His people trapped the hogs in the Ocmulgee swamps, fed them corn for several days to get rid of the wild taste, then barbecued them for our first Sunday evening pig-pickin'.

For several years before that, we had put on a covered dish supper for the legislators on the fourteenth floor of the old Henry Grady Hotel, but the attendance got so huge we had to move it down to the Henry Grady mezzanine.

That's actually where we put on the first Wild Hog Supper. But again, the popularity of the event forced us to move to other areas near the State Capitol until we settled on Atlanta's historic old 1869 freight depot.

When the National Democratic Party held its 1988 convention in Atlanta, the state put on a similar pig-pickin' event for three thousand guests. Afterward, I received a letter from a lady in New Jersey who said she couldn't believe that we had that big of a crowd of folks who had to eat with their fingers.

Tommy Irwin. (Photo courtesy of Georgia Department of Agriculture.)

I replied that, "I'm a country boy, ma'am, and you're very sophisticated, but I'm sure you've heard of finger food."

Of course we have tongs for people to use to pull the pork onto their plate, but at times I'll see a piece of backbone tenderloin that I will pull out onto my plate and eat it with my fingers. Now of course I eat with my fork, too! But when you have a plastic fork and a plastic knife, it's easier to eat with your fingers (with plenty of napkins to clean off the grease).

These days, the hogs are captured and barbecued for us by Bob Addison Jr. from Abbeville, son of Bob Addison Sr. and a former state patrolman. He and his people use a large metal "rabbit trap" type device to capture the hogs. This year, Bob and his sons catered the event, trapping and cooking nineteen 120-pound hogs for us. They also provided forty gallons of Brunswick stew prepared by Lanier King, along with his special mustard-based sauce.

Bob Addison, from Wilcox County, Georgia, captures wild hogs from the Ocmulgee River swamps and cooks them for the Georgia General Assembly's annual Wild Hog Supper. Here he checks over the meat with his son Jason. (Photo by the author.)

Pulled pork barbecue is enjoyed by an attendee at the Georgia General Assembly's 2008 Wild Hog Supper opening event. (Photo by the author.)

South Carolina: Home to Four Barbecue Sauces

The key to great-tasting barbecue is the basting sauce. If you want to experience all four U.S. styles, go to South Carolina, according to Lake Erie High Jr., president of the South Carolina Barbeque Association.

The oldest and simplest of the four is vinegar and pepper, High said, found mostly on the coastal plains of the Carolinas "and to a slight degree in Virginia and Georgia." The most prominent practitioners of vinegar and pepper sauce were the Scottish families, he said, who settled mostly in Williamsburg County northeast of Charleston. He cited the Brown family, the McKenzie, Scott, and McCabe families, "and others who have remained true to their heritage."

The second "in historic evolution," according to High, is South Carolina–style mustard sauce, which he says "can be clearly traced to the German settlers who came here during three decades beginning in the 1730s."

"Britain's Carolina colony encouraged, recruited, and even paid the ocean passage for thousands of German families so they could take up residence in South Carolina," High said. He cited these families who got into the barbecue business: Bessinger, Shealy, Hite, Sweatman, Sikes, Price, Lever, Meyer, Kiser, and Zeigler. The mustard-based sauce "is still in abundant evidence in the German settled areas of the state."

Beginning around 1900 a "light tomato sauce" appeared as the third type of basting sauce to come on the scene in the Palmetto State. "It is found today in the middle part of South Carolina as well as in the Pee Dee upper coastal plain," High said. The sauce is vinegar and pepper, plus tomato ketchup, which adds a little sweetness and other flavors to the mix. This is the sauce most popular today around Lexington, North Carolina.

Author's note: Every May for more than seventeen years, Wilcox County, Georgia, stages an "Ocmulgee Wild Hog Festival" at Abbeville, the county seat. People interested in signing up to go on a controlled wild hog hunt in the Ocmulgee swamps should contact Addison Wild Boar Hunting at (229) 467-2455.

Heavy tomato sauce is the fourth one in South Carolina today, according to Lake High, as well as in the rest of the nation, having evolved in the last sixty or so years and popularized by Kraft Foods nationwide.

Hush Puppies

Where would we be at a barbecue event without hush puppies? Or as some of our older citizens like to call them, "corn dodgers" or just "dodgers."

Matt Lee and Ted Lee, authors of *The Lee Bros. Southern Cookbook*, have come up with separate hush puppy recipes for North Carolina and for South Carolina.

With thanks to Matt and Ted, here is how I adapted their Sandlapper version, which is a little denser and crustier than the Tar Heel one. This recipe yields 30 hush puppies.

Palmetto-Style Hush Puppies

- 1 ½ cups cornmeal
- ½ cup all-purpose flour
- ½ teaspoon baking soda
- ½ teaspoon baking powder
- 1 ½ tablespoons sugar
- ½ teaspoon salt
- ½ teaspoon black pepper
- 3 tablespoons plus 2 teaspoons minced scallions
- 1 large egg
- ½ cup plus 2 tablespoons buttermilk
- 2 cups canola oil or peanut oil

Preheat the oven to 225°F. Place a large ovenproof plate lined with paper towels on the middle rack.

Sift the cornmeal and flour into mixing bowl. Add the baking soda, baking powder, sugar, salt, pepper, and scallions and stir with a fork. Beat the egg in small bowl and add to the dry ingredients. Slowly mix in ½ cup buttermilk. Add more buttermilk until the batter is tacky.

Heat the oil to 375°F (use a candy thermometer to check) in a 9-inch skillet.

One by one, ease 6 tablespoonsful of dough into the oil with back of a second spoon and fry about 5 minutes, or until golden brown. Adjust the oil temperature between 350°F and 375°F as necessary. Using a slotted spoon, shift the hush puppies from the oil to the warming plate. Repeat in batches of 6 until all the batter is used.

Popular Barbecue Hash, South Carolina Style

In lieu of Brunswick stew served in adjoining states, South Carolinians love to eat hash with their pork barbecue, served on warm rice or white bread. Some call it "barbecue hash"—and more than a few Sandlappers over the years have affixed "Got Hash?" stickers onto their cars and trucks.

Saddler Taylor, curator of folklife and research at the University of South Carolina's McKissick Museum in Columbia, stated that in the past, a common Lowcountry hash typically consisted of several deboned hog's heads, supplemented with organ meats like pork liver. "It would be cooked in a stock that favored tomatoes and ketchup," Taylor said, "plus optional use of onions, corn, and potatoes."

SAVANNAH PORK CAKE

One pound of raw pork chopped very fine; add half a pint of boiling water, 1 pound of seeded raisins, ½ pound of shredded citron, 2 cups sugar, 1 cup molasses, 1 teaspoon soda dissolved in a water.

Mix these ingredients; add 1 tablespoon cloves, 1 tablespoon cinnamon, and 1 tablespoon nutmeg.

Stir in 3 cups sifted flour to reach the consistency of common cake mixture. Bake at approximately 300 degrees for 1 hour and 40 minutes.

—MRS. RIGDEN
SWEET AND MEAT AND OTHER GOOD THINGS TO EAT,
PUBLISHED IN 1917 BY THE LADIES SOCIETY OF SAVANNAH'S
GRACE METHODIST EPISCOPAL CHURCH.

But today, few contemporary hash makers continue the use of hog heads and organ meat. "What began as a dish of necessity and improvisation," Taylor said, "has long become a comfort food wrapped in years of nostalgia."

Nowadays, he added, most Palmetto State cooks use more "mainstream" cuts of meat like Boston butts, hams, and shoulders. "Of course, chicken bog and purlow are king in the Pee Dee region," he said, "and you won't find much hash in those parts."

Regional in nature, hash recipes vary widely, including mustard-based hash in the South Carolina Midlands and beef hash in the Piedmont. Among Lowcountry purveyors of pork is Mr. B's Barbecue on Johns Island.

"One thing's for sure," Taylor concluded, "all hash aficionados agree there's no finer accompaniment to a heaping plate of pork barbecue and ribs, all washed down with a glass of sweet tea."

Mr. Limestone's Famed Pork Sausage

My friend Charles Seabrook has fond teenage memories of John Limestone's big country general store on Johns Island near Charleston, South Carolina. "It was redolent of bananas, smoked herring in a barrel, and cookies kept in big jars on the counter."

"Mr. Limehouse was also known far and wide for his pork sausage," Seabrook told me. "Charlestonians would drive out to his store to buy the sausage."

John Limestone prepared the sausage in a building across the road from his store. "On a cold winter morning," Charles recalled, "you could hear the pigs squealing across the salt marsh as Mr. Limehouse first shot them with a .22 rifle, and then dipped them into scalding water to remove their bristles."

Seabrook helped salt down some of the hog meat, which people also bought for barbecues.

And Don't Forget Chitterlings

Chitterlings, more commonly known as chitlins, have had a devoted following in past years, particularly among Lowcountry African Americans, as well as Southerners, white and black, interested in ultimate pork possibilities.

In his book, *The Glory of Southern Cooking*, James Villas notes that, "Whether slowly simmered or boiled, battered and fried, chitlins can be an acquired taste for some, but when they're prepared carefully and served with the right condiments (some style of vinegar, chopped onions, mustard, corn relish, etc.), it's easy to understand why they have been prized for centuries as a major component of soul food."

While the practice of cooking chitlins is something of a limited art in the Lowcountry today, the little town of Salley, South Carolina, continues an annual "Chit'lin Strut" celebration on the first Saturday after Thanksgiving Day, during which some twenty thousand visitors are said to consume five tons of the fried morsels, along with slaw and a slice or two of Wonder Bread.

My friend Harry Chakides, the owner of the famous old Harry's Restaurant on Bay Street in Beaufort, South Carolina (now closed), said that one day an elderly couple came in. They were about to be seated when suddenly they whirled around and left. Harry went over to the waiter and said, "What happened?" The waiter replied that when the pair learned that the restaurant had no chitlins on the menu, "they just upped and walked out!"

In *Vibration Cooking: Travel Notes of a Geechee Girl*, Vertamae Grosvenor, a native of Allendale County, South Carolina, recalled a visit with friends to an upscale restaurant in Paris:

"So these people order for me and they are just on pins and needles, dying, really dying, for me to taste this rare dish. Well thank you Jesus the food arrives, and it ain't nothing but *chitterlings* in the form of a sausage! They call it andouilette."

Many aficionados consider such sausages a delicacy, served across Europe and in fine restaurants in the United States.

Daufuskie Island native Sallie Ann Robinson told me about helping her mother clean chitlins as part of a great feast served early on New Year's Day. It was a laborious task requiring a lot of water poured back and forth, she said, "but when Mama cooked the chitlins by boiling, they were soooo good. She put them in stews and soups."

The extensive cleaning of chitlins is confirmed by Lowcountry expert John Martin Taylor: "The black folks I know who cook them currently still wash them within an inch of their lives."

CHAPTER 15

The Glories of Chicken

Whether we [African Americans] stewed it in an aromatic broth, baked it to succulent goodness, smothered it in a creamy gravy of natural juices, barbecued it to feed a crowd, or fried it for Sunday supper, chicken has been served gloriously at every meal of the day [in black homes across America].

—Savannah chef Joe Randall
A Taste of Heritage

Country Captain

As the legend goes, sometime in the 1800s a tall sailing ship docked in Savannah. Its English captain came ashore on Bay Street and, smelling of strong Indian spices, brought to our shores a new and intoxicatingly delicious way to fix chicken. The captain traded his curry-based recipe for a night's lodging, resulting in a chicken dish called "Country Captain"—bolstered with rich coriander and turmeric-based curry sauce plus onions, garlic, raisins, peppers, currants, and tomatoes.

Whether the story is true or not, Country Captain did indeed come into existence in the nineteenth century, and the recipe spread like English ivy up and down the East Coast and across the South.

Yet the saga is not confined to Savannah alone; other Atlantic seaboard cities claimed the "Country Captain" connection. Savannah food historian Damon Lee Fowler notes in

The Encyclopedia of Southern Culture that one of the earliest Country Captain recipes was published in 1857 in *Miss [Eliza] Leslie's New Cookery Book*. A Philadelphian, Miss Eliza credited British sea captains running East and West Indies trading routes as the recipe's source. Another version credited a Britisher who brought the dish from Bengal, India, to friends in Savannah.

To add a curious link to this story, a 1760 John Greenwood painting titled *Captains in Surinam*, owned by the St. Louis Art Museum, carries the additional notation that the painting "imaginatively depicts the life of the spice trader." Are you now thoroughly confused?

However it came about, the recipe, described as "a slow-simmered, savory stew," won tremendous traction after then-President Franklin D. Roosevelt and General George S. Patton were served a Country Captain casserole at Warm Springs, Georgia, to much adulation.

All right, enough historical conjecturing. How about a taste test…

Country Captain with Chicken and Shrimp

Here is a wonderful recipe that I've adapted from Elizabeth Terry's *Savannah Seasons* cookbook published in 1996, with my thanks to Mrs. Terry. Moving from Atlanta with her family in 1980, Terry and her husband, Michael, turned one of Savannah's beautiful turn-of-the-century Greek Revival mansions into an elegant restaurant: Elizabeth on 37th Street. She soon received high critical acclaim for her innovative cuisine and in 1995 was elected by the prestigious James Beard Foundation as the region's top chef. She and her lawyer husband now live in retirement on the west coast. The restaurant continues to operate as one of Savannah's finest under the ownership and direction of former members of her staff, Gary and Gregg Butch. Talented chef Kelly Yambor runs the kitchen. For more on Elizabeth's at 37th Street, check out chapter 6. This recipe will yield 6 servings.

- ½ cup apple juice
- 2 teaspoons curry powder
- 2 ½ tablespoons currants
- 4 boneless, skinless chicken breasts, diced into ½-inch cubes
- ½ cup minced Vidalia onion

- ½ cup minced green bell pepper
- ½ cup slivered almonds
- 1 cup Granny Smith apple, peeled, seeded, and diced
- 1 14-ounce can diced, pureed tomatoes in juice
- 1 teaspoon salt
- 1 teaspoon hot chili sauce
- 1 recipe Curried Rice (see below)
- ½ cup chicken broth
- 1 pound large raw shrimp, peeled and deveined

Using a medium sauté pan, bring the apple juice, curry powder, and currants to medium warm. Add the diced chicken and set aside to marinate.

Preheat the oven to 350°F. In a large, lidded casserole dish, place the chicken breasts and marinade, then layer in the onion, bell pepper, almonds, and apples, followed by the tomato puree, salt, and chili sauce. Do not stir.

Place the casserole over medium heat and bring to a boil. Add the cooked curried rice, cover, and bake in the oven for 20 minutes, until liquid is absorbed and chicken is cooked.

Remove from oven, stir in the chicken broth, and place the shrimp on top of the rice, chicken, and vegetables. Return to oven, covered, for 5 minutes, until the shrimp turn pink.

The dish can be served with a tossed green salad.

Curried Rice

This is to be prepared in advance for Elizabeth Terry's Country Captain recipe (above).

- 2 tablespoons butter
- 2 teaspoons hot curry powder
- 1 teaspoon minced fresh ginger
- 1 teaspoon grated orange zest
- ½ teaspoon salt
- 1 ¼ cups raw white basmati rice
- 2 ½ cups water

Melt the butter at medium heat in a lidded saucepan. Stir in the curry, ginger, orange zest, and salt, and simmer for 1 minute. Stir in the rice and simmer, stirring, for 1 minute.

Add the water, raise heat, and bring to a boil. Lower the heat, cover, and simmer gently for 15 minutes. Leave lid on. Remove from the heat and place in pan of warm water for at least 10 minutes. This is to finish cooking the rice and to keep it warm prior to serving. Use according to the recipe above.

CHASING DOWN A CHICKEN

Back during the 1930s when we went visiting, we kids had the task of running down one or two chickens. The "woman of the house" would point out the one she wanted us to catch for the midday dinner. Off we would go, all through the yard, 'round the barns, under the house, and everywhere, going after that chicken. It was a contest who would give out first. Sad to say, the chicken always lost.

It was absolutely amazing how the women of those days were able to take one or two chickens and feed a large crowd. I suppose the Lord gave them the gift of "making a little go a long way."

The chicken was sometime fried, usually with a lot of gravy to be eaten with biscuits. And never have I since eaten dumplings as good as I remember from those days.

But to this day, chicken is my least favorite meat. I don't know why. Maybe it's because as a child, we had to run down those chickens for dinner.

—CHARLES HUTCHINS JR.
ATLANTA, A NATIVE OF WADLEY, GEORGIA

Fried Chicken

Most Southerners grew up with fried chicken. The ultimate comfort food, its popularity continues unabated.

My own late mother's sumptuous Sunday dinners—led off with fried chicken and gravy cooked in a big iron skillet on a wood-burning stove—will remain in my memory forever, along with her superb biscuits and scrumptious side dishes.

A recent visit to the Wilkes Dining Room in Savannah came closest to replicating that fried chicken I remember so well at my mother's table. With the blessing of the late Mrs. Wilkes's granddaughter, Marcia Thompson, and Mrs. Wilkes's great-grandson, Ryon Thompson, the general manager, I am happy to include this recipe that I've adapted only slightly. This recipe will yield 4 to 6 servings. In a straw poll conducted by *Savannah* magazine, Savannahians voted the fried chicken at Mrs. Wilkes Dining Room as the best in the city.

Mrs. Wilkes' Savannah Fried Chicken

- 2 ½ pound fryer, cut up and sprinkled with salt and pepper
- 2 ¼ tablespoons evaporated milk
- 2 tablespoons water
- All-purpose flour, enough to "flour" the chicken pieces before frying
- Vegetable oil, enough to cover the chicken pieces when frying

In a bowl, marinate the chicken pieces in milk and water for about 10 minutes.

Dip the chicken pieces in bowl of flour and shake off excess.

Using a deep fry pan, heat the oil to 320°F to 330°F and fry the chicken, making sure the chicken is covered with oil at all times. Fry until golden brown on both sides.

Note: Some cooks like to marinate their chicken in buttermilk beforehand, sometimes for more than an hour, and in some cases overnight. This produces a spectacularly juicy bird.

Asked how to reach Mrs. Wilkes' Savannah restaurant, a driver was told to "Walk along West Jones Street until you smell the fried chicken!"

Chicken Gravy, John Egerton Style

As my friend John Egerton wrote in his monumental *Southern Food*, "There may be no better gravy in the Western world than that made in a black skillet recently vacated by crisp pieces of fried chicken…Like a good roux, it begins with fat and flour, a little water and some salt and pepper to taste, and suddenly a miracle is born."

Such is the way that many Southern cooks have done it down through the centuries, by using the leftover fat and small browned bits left in the bottom of the skillet.

Then, over very low heat, Egerton's method is to "slowly sprinkle in 2 or 3 tablespoons of flour, stirring constantly until the mixture achieves a deep shade of brown."

Continuing to stir to avoid a lumpy product, slowly pour in a cup of lukewarm water and bring the mix to a "simmering bubble." Keep stirring while you cook the gravy for another minute or so, until it thickens.

As a final step, you should season to taste with salt and pepper, and serve warm in a separate bowl.

Note: Cooks at the Wilkes Dining Room also add a touch of Kitchen Bouquet (a bottled condiments sauce) for extra flavor and color to their chicken gravy.

Tomato Gravy and Rice

Many discerning chefs like to serve tomato gravy with fried chicken, among them Atlanta's famed chef Scott Peacock of Watershed Restaurant, winner of the 2007 James Beard medal for the top chef in the Southeast.

Here's a wonderful tomato gravy and rice recipe used for years by Doris Taft of Atkinson County, Georgia, one of Southeast Georgia's truly outstanding cooks. (You will find several more of her great recipes throughout this book, including her scrumptious chicken and dumplings on page 226).

According to Mrs. Taft's son, Wilbur (Dub), to get the full flavor of the original dish, use home-canned tomatoes. The next best alternative would be to stew a pot of vine-ripened, peeled, and cored tomatoes an hour or two until they completely liquefy and the pulp is reduced to small bits in the juices.

"This base," Dub Taft says, "can be used immediately in the recipe or cooled, bagged, and frozen for later use." He notes that store-bought canned stewed tomatoes can be used if that's your only option. He also suggests that cooks should serve biscuits to sop up the excess juice. "It's mighty good and oh so comforting," he says.

> *There's the story told about a man who had developed a breed of three-legged chickens. A couple of years later, a friend asked him how the breeding project was going and whether they tasted good.*
>
> *"Darned if I know," he replied, "I've never been able to catch one!"*
>
> —*Ben Moise*
> *Charleston, South Carolina*

Doris Taft's Tomato Gravy and Rice

- 3 to 6 strips of bacon or pork of choice
- 4 cups jar canned, stewed tomatoes
- A bowl of your favorite white rice, pre-prepared

First fry up the meat in a deep skillet. (In South Georgia, "meat" always means pork—bacon, fatback, streak-o-lean, pork chops or loin, or a few slices of country ham.)

Leave the drippings and wee bits in your pan, but pour off some of the grease if you have anything more than 2 or 3 tablespoons.

Add the tomatoes and bring to a boil. Simmer for 5 minutes. Season with salt, if needed, and pepper (always needed). Ladle the gravy over a plate of your favorite white rice.

You can cook the tomatoes longer than 5 minutes if you wish to have less liquid, "but don't try to thicken it," Mrs. Taft says. "Keep it thin like redeye gravy. Sample the juice while cooking, and if the tomatoes are too tart, add a pinch or two of sugar."

Mrs. Taft says her husband, Wilburn, loves to add generous sprinklings of pepper to the tomato gravy and rice.

Carolina-Style Fried Chicken Livers

This is a splendid dish. For the best results, buy fresh chicken livers from your butcher rather than frozen packaged livers. This recipe will yield 4 servings.

- ½ cup all-purpose flour
- ½ cup whole milk
- Salt and pepper to taste
- Salad oil
- 2 ½ pounds chicken livers (4 to 5 livers per serving)
- Flour for dredging

Mix the flour, milk, salt, and pepper into a batter.

Fill a deep fat fryer half full with salad oil and set the heat for 400°F.

Wash the livers thoroughly and drain on paper towels. Dredge the livers individually in plain flour, then dip into the batter and roll until well covered. Drop the livers one at a time into the hot fat, and cook only 4 to 6 livers at a time. It's important to put a cover on the fryer since livers are known to pop during first minute of cooking.

Cook for 2 to 3 minutes until golden brown. Do not overcook, which will result in dry, tough livers.

Serve while they are hot, with hot buttered toast and French fried potatoes along with plenty of catsup for dipping.

Chicken and Dumplings

Doris's Chicken and Dumplings

Here's another great one, readers, developed and fine-tuned by Doris Taft. If you use a big hen, Mrs. Taft suggests that after the cooking is completed, you set aside some of the meat for another use, rather than putting it all in the dumpling pot.

- 1 hen, cut into parts
- 4 chicken bouillon cubes
- Salt and pepper to taste
- 1 recipe Dumplings (see below)

Place the chicken pieces in large pot and almost cover with water.

Boil until tender. Lift out the chicken, cool, debone, and set aside.

Add the bouillon cubes and 1 to 2 cups water to the broth in the pot and bring to a boil. Layer a handful of dumplings into the pot and sprinkle with pepper.

Once the pot returns to a boil, add another batch of dumplings and pepper.

Continue this process until your pot is adequately full. When the last layer of dumplings comes to a boil, put in the deboned chicken, stir, cover, and cut off your heat. Due to the bouillon cubes, you may not need much salt, adding only for taste.

Dumplings

Make these ahead of time, to use with Doris' Chicken and Dumplings recipe.

- 1 ½ cups water
- 2 to 3 cups all-purpose flour
- 2 eggs

Bring the water to boil. Pour into a bowl and add enough flour until it's almost stiff. Add the eggs and mix until you have a stiff dough, adding more flour if you need to.

Knead the dough then pinch off a handful to place on floured wax paper. Roll the dough into a thin layer and cut into small, serving-size strips. Set aside and repeat the process until you've made all the dumplings.

Mrs. Taft notes that boiling water makes the dumplings tender so no grease is needed for the batter.

"I like to make the dumplings up ahead of time and freeze them. After cutting them, I just leave them on wax paper and place them in a Tupperware container. I keep adding layers of dumplings on wax paper until the container is full. They can keep for months in the freezer."

Doris adds that when you put the dumplings in the boiling broth, just dump them in by the handful. "I used to take my time and lay one dumpling at a time into the pot. I have found that to be totally unnecessary."

> ## ICE-SKATING CHICKENS
>
> *My grandmother Taft always kept a bunch of chickens, but most of them were for layin' not eatin'. A couple dozen hens would give the family plenty of eggs for breakfast and extra eggs for cakes and pies (especially her "egg pies," which we call custard pies today).*
>
> *At night, all the chickens would naturally go to the coop to roost. But on the coldest nights, Daddy remembers they would crouch together in a tight spot underneath the house to stay out of the cold wind.*
>
> *One winter when Daddy was a teenager, he remembered waking up to discover that freezing rain during the night had coated the ground with ice. It was too cold for him to take care of his morning chores, so he threw the chicken corn out the back door. He had a big laugh watching the hens come dashing out from underneath the house—slipping, sliding, and skating across that sheet of ice while trying to pick up the corn.*
>
> *That probably was in 1934 or 1935, when winters brought ice and snow to the Deep South.*
>
> —W. F. (DUB) TAFT
> A NATIVE OF ATKINSON COUNTY, GEORGIA

Chicken Bogs

Pee Dee Area Chicken Bog

Chicken bog—using generous amounts of rice—is very popular to the Pee Dee River area of eastern South Carolina. The late distinguished food historian Karen Hess said the bog may have descended from "an ancient festival dish" from Provence, France, which originally called for mutton, cured pork, onions, aromatics, saffron, and rice.

She surmised that with the deletion of saffron and substitution of chicken for mutton, the new dish emerged. Amelia Wallace Vernon of Florence County, South Carolina, wrote that the chicken bog was made outdoors in washtubs to serve large crowds. Actually, the bog was cooked in large pots, and then collected in washtubs for serving.

Some credit the strange name to the fact that rice is grown in bogs; others say that the chicken is "bogged down" in the rice. However it got its name, chicken bog is so popular that the town of Loris, South Carolina, stages an annual "Chicken Bog-Off" festival every year.

Margaret King Lee

My friend in Dunwoody, Georgia, Margaret King Lee, who was Miss Loris in 1952 and the high school's homecoming queen that year, offered the following Eastern Carolina chicken bog recipe developed in Loris in recent years.

Loris Chicken Bog

- 1 3-pound whole fryer
- 1 cup chopped onion
- 1 ½ pounds smoked sausage
- 1 teaspoon black pepper
- 2 tablespoons Italian-style seasoning
- ½ tablespoon salt
- 2 cups long grain white rice

Boil the chicken and onion in 5 cups of water until tender. Drain the fat off the broth with a grease skimmer. (If broth doesn't measure 5 cups, add necessary water.)

Debone the chicken. Slice the sausage across in ¼-inch pieces. Add the sausage, pepper, Italian seasoning, salt, and rice to the chicken and broth. Simmer 20 to 30 minutes until all broth is absorbed and rice is cooked. Serve hot.

I've seen bogs where chickens, pieces parts and all (without the feathers and feet),
were boiled in water along with chopped celery and onions, and at some point when

the chicken meat had boiled off the bones and was rolling around, rice in some quantity, a whole bag or so, was added to the chicken meat, bones, etc., and simply cooked until most of the liquid was absorbed.

—Ben Moise, Charleston, South Carolina

Horry County Chicken Bog

I interviewed chef Larry Dickinson, a thirty-six-year veteran cook at Donzelle's Restaurant in Conway, South Carolina, named for his mother, the eatery's founder. Here is how Larry makes the famous bog:

I've been in the restaurant business so long I can visualize chicken bog in my sleep. In 1962 I learned how to cook the bog from this African-American lady [in the kitchen], just watching her cook.

The key to cooking chicken bog is the taste. To make sure, you must obtain the right ingredients. I like a good smoked sausage, like Hillshire.

First of all, I cook the chicken, debone it, and put it in the pot; then I throw my sausage in. I get it to boiling good, then I add some Lipton Onion Soup, salt, and pepper.

When I go to add the rice, no matter how big the pot is, I let the rice come to a mound right in the middle of the pot. When the mound gets up to about five inches high, you know you've got enough rice. You stir it down and bring it back to a boil.

When it gets to about a half dried out, you don't stir it at this point, because it'll get gummy. What I do, I stick my spoon in and I pick the rice up from the bottom, going around the pot. Then when it gets three-quarters dried out, I place it in the oven at 400°F for an hour. It bakes around the whole pot and you don't have to clean out the pot afterward. I've got a pot big enough to feed a hundred.

To feed eight people in the family, you buy one chicken, a fryer, debone, sausage it with a pound of smoked sausage, and the Lipton Onion Soup. When you get it three-quarters dried out, stick it in the oven. Keep tasting it to make sure you get the taste right.

Georgia Chicken Barbecue: "It's the Fire in the Sauce"

The following narrative comes from a friend, Phil Whitney, an author from Pine Mountain Valley, Georgia, who has had a lot of experience as a grill master:

My dad would turn over in his grave if he knew I now use a gas grill instead of firing up a bed of charcoal when making chicken barbecue, so I'll start by giving you the basics of that method.

First, start your charcoal with lighter fuel; let it completely burn all the fuel, even turning the coals occasionally to make sure.

Next, for the basting sauce, prepare a mixture of ½ pint of vinegar and ½ stick of margarine. Put them in a saucepan right on the grill, after the flames die down, of course.

A chicken bog master, chef Larry Dickerson of Conway, South Carolina, drops a broiler in the pot (top photo) and later stirs the rice-chicken-sausage mixture (lower photo). (Photos courtesy of Jennings Chestnut.)

When the coals have a layer of white ash over them and the heat is at maximum is the time to put on the chicken. Begin by placing the chicken halves, presentation side down, for 5 to 10 minutes to make "grill" marks for appearance. Now turn the halves over (cut side down), close to the coals. This aids in getting it hot all the way through and also helps seal the outside to prevent it from drying out.

Baste frequently with the margarine and vinegar mixture. Dad said this is the real secret to perfect, moist chicken. The vinegar penetrates and moistens the meat, while the margarine cooks onto the outside, sealing it. This also allows you to remove the skin from the chicken beforehand and still have moist, tender meat when it's done all the way through.

Watch your fire closely when everything starts really cooking because fat drippings flame up fast during this time. (We always kept a spray bottle of water handy to put out the flames.) After fifteen or twenty minutes at this level, depending on the temperature of the coals, raise the rack (or reduce the heat, if using a gas grill) and turn the chicken halves over. Remember to baste with the vinegar/margarine mixture. If your grill has a lid or cover, it further helps to retain moisture and makes the cooking process more uniform.

I know you're wondering, "When do I slop on the barbecue sauce?" Be patient, it'll be worth it!

About this time, you may need to add a little charcoal to the bed of coals, and turn the chicken once more, cut side down. After about an hour of cooking the meat will begin separating from the bone, a good indication that it's almost ready.

GROWING FREE-RANGE CHICKENS FROM THE "SETTIN HENS" TO THE FRYING PAN

In the "olden days," said Mrs. Jessie Hart Conner, eighty-eight, of Reidsville, Georgia, some farmers would order chicks by mail from distant hatcheries. But her parents hatched their own broilers and fryers, using "settin hens."

Shortly after the chicks came off the nest, she said, they scrounged for worms and the like as free-range chicks. "As a child, I remember chicks fighting over worms that the mother hen would scratch up from the dirt," she recalled. "They'd get hold of a worm on each end and stretch it until it would break in two. That was so amusing to us kids."

But when the chicks got bigger, Mrs. Conner recalled, "the hot sun would blister some of them and they would lose their feathers.

"We had one little old rooster about five or six inches high and he looked pitiful. I made him a little jacket to keep him from getting blistered."

Seven to eight weeks after the chicks hatched, the pullets were big enough to fry or broil or bake, she recalled. The most popular method was frying them in lard.

"Mother had a big old frying pan in which she would place the entire cut-up chicken in that one pan, including the pully bone that she had cut out separately. When each piece turned brown, she'd turn it over until it got brown on that side. And tender? It was sooo tender, and mighty delicious. Because you see it was steamed under that big lid."

For chicken and dumplings, she recalled that many women in her community would put in boiled eggs with their dumplings. "But Mother never did," she said.

Another sure sign of doneness is when the juices run clear when pricked with a fork. Don't do this too frequently or you'll waste all the juices you saved. The best (and safest) method is to use a meat thermometer. Poultry must be heated to 185°F for health purposes. Now put on your "secret" barbecue sauce for the last ten minutes or so, just long enough to glaze the chicken thoroughly, and you are ready to impress your family and friends with some of the best barbecued chicken they have ever tasted.

Phil Whitney. (Photo courtesy of Phil Whitney.)

THE PULLY BONE (WISHBONE) CONTEST

There's a certain way that you cut the chicken to get the pully bone out. Mama would always cut that pully bone out and cut the chicken up and start to fry it, including the pully bone, or as some called it, the wishbone.

Then at the dinner table, there were six of us kids and we'd all fight over the pully bone, to pull the bone. The one that got the biggest piece of the bone, of course, would be able to make a wish.

We kids loved the drumstick, but I was the oldest one and I always ended up with the neck or the back. Daddy always got the breast.

—WILLI CHESTNUT
CONWAY, SOUTH CAROLINA

Willi Chestnut. (Photo by the author.)

Pulling the wishbone in the old-fashioned way are John and Katie Revenel Rudolf. (Photo courtesy of Ben Moise.)

CHAPTER 16

A Cornucopia of Lowcountry Vegetables

String beans are good and ripe tomatoes
And collard greens and sweet potatoes
Sweet corn, field peas, and squash and beets
But when a man rears back and eats,
He wants okra...

—*"One Fell Soup," Roy Blount Jr.*

Okra

With the possible exception of rice and sesame," *Beyond Gombo* author Jessica Harris writes, "no food from Africa has been as widely embraced as okra." Okra was one of the first African plants to be adapted and adopted in the New World and was originally known by its West African term, *ukru ma*. *Gombo* is another familiar West Africa term for the plant that originated there.

Naturalist William Bartram told of seeing large patches of okra growing along the Georgia coast in 1773. The earliest published recipes came in Mary Randolph's pioneering 1824 cookbook, *Virginia House-wife*.

In her delightful book *Cross Creek*, the late Marjorie Kinnan Rawlings called okra "a Cinderella among vegetables," adding that only small, tender young pods should be used to bring the lowly plant "to its glamorous fulfillment." To stew them, she suggested first boiling the pods in salted water, leaving the stems on. Then, once cooled, dip the pods into Hollandaise sauce. Voila!

While I grew up loving fried okra, I must have passed the age of sixty-five before I came to appreciate stewed okra. I gave my friend, retired Kennesaw State University professor J. B. Tate of Cartersville, Georgia, several bags of okra from my Euharlee garden, and he taught me how to stew okra, using the small pods, with stems off. Wow, what a pleasant surprise! And they were delectable with only the addition of butter and salt!

Harriet Ross Colquitt's authentic *Savannah Cook Book*, first published in 1933, has a great passage about stewed okra:

> *Take young tender okra pods, cut off ends, and boil in salted water about twenty minutes. Drain, add pepper and salt and butter, and let simmer on stove a few minutes before serving.*

Check the soups chapter on page 169 for a tantalizing okra soup recipe.

Of course frying is the most popular way to cook okra as a side dish or appetizer. James Villas waxes enthusiastic when speaking of fried okra. "Lord, there's nothing more delicious or addictive than a basket of batter-fried okra," he writes in his latest cookbook, *The Glory of Southern Food*.

This recipe adaptation—which serves 4—comes from *The New Southern Basics* by Martha Phelps Stamps. She agrees that cooks, as suggested earlier, should use only small, tender okra.

Batter-Fried Okra, Southern Style

- 1¼ cup cornmeal
- ¼ teaspoon black pepper
- ¼ teaspoon cayenne pepper
- ½ teaspoon garlic powder
- 1 cup buttermilk
- 1 pound okra, cleaned and cut in ½-inch slices
- ½ cup peanut oil
- ½ teaspoon salt

Mix the dry ingredients in a bowl. Pour the buttermilk into another bowl.

Place the okra in the buttermilk.

Using a slotted spoon, lift the okra from the buttermilk and roll in the meal mixture. When the pieces are well covered, place them on a plate and put in the refrigerator for 15 minutes to set the coating.

Using a skillet, heat the oil to 325°F or just below smoking. Add the okra to the hot oil and cook for 5 to 7 minutes, browning on all sides.

Drain on paper towels, sprinkle with salt, and serve hot.

The vegetable garden has been a great tradition across the Lowcountry, especially on big plantations where slaves had their own special plots. In the 1800s, a Georgia Sea Islands planter listed a wide variety of plants found on the slaves' "small patch." Included were "long collards," groundnuts (peanuts), arrowroot, benne seeds, gourds, and watermelons. All, he said, were grown "in commingled luxuriance."

Plantation mistresses sometimes personally oversaw garden plot work and kept detailed records, according to Charles Reagan in the *New Encyclopedia of Southern Culture*. He cited Eliza Mitchell's 1834 diary, which revealed she was growing corn, snap beans, cabbages, strawberries, raspberries, cymblings (squash), and sugar beets.

Thomas Jefferson considered vegetables his primary dishes, with meats serving as mere condiments. Flourishing vegetable gardens kept his Monticello kitchen well supplied with fresh produce throughout the summer and fall.

"CANNING" VEGETABLES: A JOHNS ISLAND TRADITION

Along with fresh vegetable traditions have come preserving vegetable traditions.

"One thing that stands out in my mind is my mama spending almost the entire summer in the kitchen working over the hot wood stove canning vegetables," Johns Island native Charles Seabrook told me in an interview. *"She canned hundreds of jars of tomatoes, okra, butter beans, snap beans, cowpeas, and other vegetables from our garden.*

"I remember that on summer nights Mama had all of us listening for that little 'pop' that told you the seal on the jars of canned vegetables was good and the stuff could be stored safely for months and probably years. Of course, we would eat in the fall and winter a lot of what Mama had canned, but she would can so much we would have much more than we could eat. So, Mama gave away a lot of her canned stuff and people were very happy to get some of 'Mis 'Net's' (as they called my mama) garden bounty."

So it has been with Southerners through the years. "In my younger days," recalled the late Grace Hartley, "it was quite the usual thing to have from six to twelve vegetables on the table at a single meal." One of Grace's secrets for cooking—also favored by my late mother—was light pinches of sugar in soups and vegetables such as collard greens and turnip greens.

Southerners have been accused of overcooking vegetables, but many early cookbooks have cautioned against just that. Georgia's famed Annabella P. Hill, for instance, urged cooks in her 1872 cookbook to use vegetables fresh out of the garden and to pay close attention to the length of cooking. Otherwise, if cooked too long, "they lose their good appearance and flavor."

Tomatoes

Is there anything more satisfying than enjoying a "bait" of fresh homegrown tomatoes on their first summertime arrival on your table? Farms in south Georgia and the Barrier

Islands as well as South Carolina's Johns Island, St. Helena Island, Wadmalaw Island, and Edisto Island have produced juicy "eating tomatoes" over the years, a far cry from the hard-as-a-rock tomato offerings you often get at your chain grocer.

"There's something about the soil over there," according to my friend Charles "Trap" Seabrook, who grew up on Johns Island near Charleston. "The fertile Sea Island loam enables farmers to grow the

Summertime pleasures include fresh tomatoes and cucumbers fresh out of the garden and displayed here by Doris Taft and her son, "Dub" Taft. (Photo courtesy of Dub Taft.)

juiciest tomatoes and tastiest okra and peppers for gumbo, then and now a prized dish on the island."

While he was growing up, the Seabrook family, including Charles's cousins, raised several hundred acres of tomatoes each year. "You go down toward Kiawah and Seabrook—just before you get to the turnoff one way to Kiawah and one road to Seabrook," Seabrook told me, "and that's where my cousins in the late spring and early summer had that place covered with tomatoes. They produced so many tomatoes they had to hire Mexicans to help pick the crop. Of course we raised a lot of tomatoes up on our end of the island, too."

He added that at one time there was an effort to brand Johns Island tomatoes similar to how Vidalia onions are branded and labeled. But it never worked out.

Charleston's Harriott Pinckney Horry, in her 1770 *Colonial Plantation Cookbook*, first told in cookbook form about the many possibilities of

> ### TOMATO HISTORY
> *At one point in early colonial history, tomatoes were considered a member of the nightshade family. It was throught they should be avoided. But thankfully, by the mid-1700s, restraints were loosened in Britain and the United States, and the rest is history. The first early reference to tomatoes in America came in 1710, when William Salmon, an herbalist, reported observing them in the South Carolina Lowcountry.*

the tomato. In one passage, she explains how to keep "tomatoos" for winter by peeling and stewing them with "a great quantity of Pepper and Salt" and then putting up the tomatoes into "pint Potts" and sealing them with melted butter an inch thick.

Squash

There is no tastier vegetable than squash. Nathalie Dupree says that one of the best ways to a man's heart is to cook him a squash dish, a casserole perhaps.

Aunt Fanny's Baked Squash

Many thanks go to my friend, Savannah native Sally Bond Tonsmeire, for this recipe. However, with this one I'm going a bit astray from the Lowcountry, to the famous old Aunt Fanny's Cabin on the northern fringes of Atlanta. Long since a victim of the bulldozers of progress, the

Sally Tonsmeire. (Photo by the author.)

restaurant at Smyrna, Georgia, was famous for authentic, mouthwatering Deep South plantation foods. It was also famous for "rosin potatoes," Irish potatoes boiled in turpentine in a large cast-iron wash pot. When done, the spuds would float to the top ready for the eating, awaiting generous spreads of butter and sour cream.

Mrs. Tonsmeire, wife of a north Georgia Episcopal rector, considers this one of her all-time favorite dishes. It will yield 4 servings.

- 3 pounds yellow squash
- 2 eggs
- ½ cup chopped onion
- 1 tablespoon sugar
- ½ teaspoon black pepper
- 1 teaspoon salt
- 1 stick butter, melted
- ½ cup cracker meal or breadcrumbs

Cut up the squash and boil until tender. Drain and mash. Add all ingredients except the butter and cracker meal or crumbs.

Pour the mixture into baking dish, then spread the melted butter over top and sprinkle with cracker meal or crumbs. Bake in 375°F oven for 1 hour or until it browns on top.

Sautéed Summer Squash, Zucchini, and Tomatoes

Here's a triple threat summer squash dish from Pressly Coker of Hartsville, located in South Carolina's fertile inland coastal plain. I asked Pressly about the number of servings this recipe would yield. His reply was "four servings for adults or five to six for a family with young children, but I guess it all depends on how much you like vegetables. I cook this up for my wife and myself when we eat dinners alone."

- 7 tablespoons extra-virgin olive oil
- 1 large clove garlic, smashed and chopped
- 1 pound zucchini, sliced and cut into halves
- 1 pound yellow squash, sliced and cut into halves

- 1 cup peeled and diced tomatoes
- 10 mint leaves, cut into thin strips
- Kosher or sea salt and pepper

Heat the olive oil in a large skillet and sauté the garlic until golden brown. Increase the heat and add the zucchini and squash. Sauté until tender, approximately 5 to 6 minutes.

Add the tomatoes and mint when the zucchini and squash are done. Season the zucchini, squash, and tomatoes with salt and pepper to taste.

Beans and Peas

In 1783 German traveler Johann David Schoepf had this to say about his visit to the Carolinas:

"In North Carolina and South Carolina, besides corn, a small kind of peas, called Indian peas, is very much raised. They yield heavily and in good years produce forty to fifty for one. They plant them the end of April or the first of May and gather in October."

Field Peas

Across the Lowcountry and the South, field peas (sometimes called black-eyed peas) have been a constant over the years, mostly cooked with fatback or hog jowls. And they are still as nutritious today, with more sophisticated cooking and less fat. The late Craig Claiborne called such peas a regional treasure, adding that some people think them to be the finest of all staples. And of course they are the prime component in the much-loved Hoppin' John dish. (See page 161 for Hoppin' John recipes.)

The peas that you pick in the early morning and shell before the noon meal are the most tasty. On our Upcountry South Carolina farm, we preferred Crowder peas, particularly served with tomatoes.

The best way to fix peas is to cook them in their natural juices, according to Dub Taft. "They'll have enough moisture that you won't need to add water," he says, "and the juice from the snaps gives them a particularly pleasing pea flavor."

In this recipe, handed down from Taft's mother, Doris, the shelled peas should be washed in cold water right before you put them in the pot. If you have peas beyond their early freshness, you may need to add 3 or 4 tablespoons of water while cooking if they dry out before done.

"But you don't need to drown peas in water like some people do," Dub Taft says. "You'll just cook the flavor right out."

South Georgia Fresh Field Peas

- 4 cups peas, fresh or frozen
- 2 to 3 tablespoons bacon drippings
- Salt

Stir peas and drippings in a pot on high heat. Add a little salt and stir constantly until all the peas are heated through and the snaps are wilted. Then turn the heat down to low and cover the pot.

Stir every 10 minutes until the peas are done.

Savannah-Style Butter Beans

Fresh butter beans are a favored summertime eating treat on many Lowcountry tables. Here is a recipe from Savannah-born Sally Bond Tonsmiere that came from her Aunt Dorothy Pierpont, also of Savannah.

Aunt Dot's Curried Butter Beans

- 1 (1-pound) package frozen butter beans
- 9 slices bacon
- 1 chopped onion
- 1 teaspoon curry powder
- 2 tablespoons dry white wine
- 1 (14.5-ounce) can mushroom soup

Cook the butter beans in advance according to package directions.

Preheat the oven to 325°F.

Lightly fry the bacon and brown the onion and curry powder in the bacon grease.

Mix the butter beans along with the other ingredients except for the bacon, and bake 10 to 15 minutes until hot. Place the bacon on top and serve.

Greens

"Hardly a workday passes that I don't eat at least a spoonful of collards," Chef Bill Smith writes in his lively *Seasoned in the South* cookbook. The executive chef of the famed Crooks Corner restaurant in Chapel Hill, North Carolina, favors cooking greens in a pot with a ham bone. Bill also loves to pour what he calls the broth (and what I call pot likker) over rice (if enough is left).

Many Southerners have improved collard greens cooking by using less pork fat and less cooking time. Cookbook author Jeanne Voltz says this will help preserve the greens' fresh flavor, vitamins, and minerals. Cooking teacher Edwina Shaw of Raleigh, North Carolina, also suggests putting freshly bought greens in the freezer in their market bag for a quarter hour before washing. This will eliminate bitterness and make the greens as mild as after a frost.

Braised Collard Greens, Robert Carter Style

Here's a wonderful collards recipe from Chef Robert Carter of Charleston's famous four-star Peninsula Grill. Robert explains, "Having grown up all my life eating collards cooked the traditional way with fatback, bacon, or ham hocks for a long time until the collards become kinda slimy, I now cut my collards into ribbon-like chiffonade to speed up the process of breaking down for tenderness."

Charleston chef Robert Carter. (Photo courtesy of Mr. Carter.)

He also makes a ham hock stock (see below) to cut down on the fat content, "and I love to incorporate cream into the final process, allowing the collard flavor to meld together and make the dish decadent!"

Here is his recipe, which serves 6.

- 1 pound collard greens, cleaned and stemmed
- 2 tablespoons olive oil
- ¼ cup (about ¾ ounce) thin strips country ham

- 2 tablespoons minced shallot
- ⅓ cup aged sherry vinegar, or more to taste
- ⅓ cup tupelo honey, or more to taste
- ⅓ cup Smoked Pork Stock (recipe follows)
- Salt and freshly ground black pepper to taste
- ¼ cup butter

Cut the greens into chiffonade about ½ inch wide and blanch in salted boiling water for 10 seconds. Drain, refresh in ice water, and squeeze dry.

Heat the oil in a large sauté pan over medium heat. Sauté the ham and shallot. Deglaze the pan with the vinegar and stir in the honey. Add the stock and bring to a simmer.

Add the greens and cook at a healthy simmer until tender—10 to 15 minutes. Remove the greens to a bowl using a slotted spoon. Heat the cooking liquid and boil until it is reduced to about ¼ cup. Taste and adjust seasonings. (You may want to add a little more honey or vinegar). Add the butter, stirring constantly until it melts. Return the greens to pan and toss to coat.

Smoked Pork Stock

MAKES ABOUT 9 CUPS

- 2 pounds ham hocks

Rinse the ham hocks and put them in a large stockpot. Add 2 gallons water. Cook, covered, at a full simmer for at least 2 hours. Strain and discard the meat (or use the meat to flavor soups or beans or to make ham salad).

Cool the stock completely and skim off all the fat. The stock may be refrigerated for up to a week or frozen for 6 months.

Savannah Peanut Collard Greens

Brimming bowls of collard greens infused with peanut butter are one of the most popular side dishes served at Andrew and Eileen Trice's Angel's Barbecue located on West Oglethorpe Lane in Savannah's historic district. Andrew picked up the idea from a friend who had visited West Africa and witnessed firsthand how it was done there. On occasion,

Andrew adds hot chili peppers, following another West African practice.

On the rainy late October day that I visited their small restaurant tucked in a lane behind the Independent Presbyterian Church, Andrew and Eileen had sold out of the unusual dish. So unfortunately I did not get to try it firsthand. But they still shared the recipe with me!

Andrew Trice takes an order for his "peanut collard greens" at his restaurant in historic Savannah, Georgia. (Photo by the author.)

Andrew's Peanut Collard Greens

- ¼ cup unsalted butter
- 1 cup diced sweet onion
- ½ cup diced green bell pepper
- ½ cup diced celery
- 6 gloves garlic, chopped
- 1 16-ounce bag fresh or frozen collard greens
- 3 cups chicken stock (from leftover smoked chicken bones)
- Sea salt, to taste
- ½ teaspoon Worcestershire sauce
- ½ teaspoon soy sauce
- Freshly ground black pepper, to taste
- Tabasco sauce, to taste
- 1 cup peanut butter, crunchy or smooth

Melt the butter in a 4-quart saucepan set over medium heat, and sauté the onion, bell pepper, celery, and garlic until translucent. Add the collards (thaw first if frozen), and chicken stock, and season lightly with salt. Add the Worcestershire and soy sauces.

Cook until the greens are tender and lose their bright emerald-green color, about an hour. Taste pot likker (broth) and adjust for salt. Season to taste with black pepper and Tabasco sauce. Remove from the heat and add peanut butter. Serve with pork or chicken dishes.

Ben's Collards au Gratin

The late Ben Green Cooper, a Savannah native, offered this recipe as a tasty way to prepare collard greens, in his *Savannah's Cookin'* cookbook.

Chop 1 pound cooked collard greens and put into a flat (pie pan) ovenware dish and add 2 teaspoons arrowroot starch blended with half cup water.

Add 1 cup white wine, salt and black pepper to taste. Cover with 1 cup bread crumbs and ½ lb. grated cheese. Top with 1 cup crushed saltines and dot with butter.

Place into 375°F oven about 35 minutes, or until crust browns.

Another View of Collards

"I used to hate collards," Mary Nichols told me when I visited Bellville, Georgia, on a research tour in the spring of 2008.

"I hated collards, that is, until an old man gave me the secret to good-tasting collards: He told me to cook them with some smoked sausage.

"That's the only way to cook collards," she added. "You put your sliced smoked sausage into the water and let it boil awhile. That gets the sausage taste into it. Then you put in your collards and boil them for 30 minutes or more. They are wonderful cooked that way. Of course they smell awful during the cooking," Mrs. Nichols added, "but don't worry about that."

Sweet Potatoes

In Colonial times, according to author Jean Anderson (*A Love Affair with Southern Cooking*), physicians believed sweet potatoes could prevent childhood maladies such as whooping cough, mumps, and measles. They went so far as to prescribe baked and boiled potatoes. Those doctors were way ahead of their times. As we have come to know, sweet potatoes are loaded with all sorts of mineral goodies, including carotene.

Besides, they make for tasty dishes, from pies to casseroles to pones, and even as a great supplement in cooking biscuits.

Thanks to sandy soil and warm, moist climates, the Southeastern states—especially the Lowcountry—are well suited to growing sweet potatoes.

Sweet Potato Pone

Mother Dear's Sweet Potato Poona

You will find several sweet potato pie recipes in the dessert section, but here is a special recipe I've adapted with my thanks to Vertamae Grosvenor. It comes from her cookbook, *Vertamae Cooks in the Americas Family Kitchen*. Vertamae says this recipe is based on the Poona version baked by her paternal grandmother, Estella Smart, whom she called "Mother Dear." This is my adaptation.

- 4 medium sweet potatoes
- 1 ¼ cups sugar
- ½ cup evaporated milk
- ¼ cup melted butter
- ½ teaspoon ground cinnamon
- ½ teaspoon ground cloves
- ½ teaspoon ground nutmeg
- ½ teaspoon ground allspice
- Dash of salt
- 1 teaspoon vanilla extract

Preheat the oven to 350°F.

Grease a 9 x 5-inch loaf pan with butter.

Peel the sweet potatoes and finely grate them into a large bowl. You should have about 2 ½ cups.

Add the sugar, evaporated milk, and butter to the grated sweet potato and mix well. Then stir in the cinnamon, cloves, nutmeg, allspice, and salt until evenly distributed. Mix in the vanilla extract.

Place the sweet potato mixture into the greased loaf pan, leveling off the top. Bake 50 to 60 minutes until the poona is firm and golden. Serve hot.

Marvin's Sweet Potato Fries

Chef Marvin Woods. (Photo by the author.)

As celebrated Southern chef Marvin Woods notes, this a change of pace from the usual French fries. Marvin serves these with pork chops and steaks but says they would be a great stand-alone appetizer. This is adapted with my thanks to Marvin from his cookbook *The New Low-Country Cooking*. This recipe will yield 6 to 8 servings.

- ½ teaspoon chili powder
- ½ teaspoon ground nutmeg
- ½ teaspoon celery salt
- ½ teaspoon ground coriander
- ¼ teaspoon cayenne pepper
- ¼ teaspoon ground cumin
- Vegetable oil for deep frying
- 6 sweet potatoes cut into julienne strips

In a small bowl, mix together the chili powder, nutmeg, celery salt, coriander, cayenne, and cumin. Set aside.

Place the oil in a deep fat fryer and heat to 375°F on a deep fat thermometer.

Add the sweet potato strips and cook for 5 to 7 minutes until they are golden and crispy. Transfer the fries with a slotted spoon to several layers of paper towels. Sprinkle with the spice mixture and serve immediately.

Corn

My father had a separate corn patch near our garden where he planted a row of sweet corn every two weeks beginning in mid-April. Thus he had fresh corn coming in through the summer and into the fall. The fresher the corn, the sweeter the taste.

Carolina Creamed Corn

If you are a corn lover, here's a recipe that should tickle your taste buds. I adapted it from *Treasured Southern Family Recipes*. The authors, the late Geddings and Ora Lou O'Hara Cushman of Aiken, South Carolina, declare that the corn you select "should be so young it spurts milk when kernels are pressed." This recipe will yield 6 servings.

- 7 large ears fresh corn
- 2 tablespoons bacon drippings
- ¼ cup water
- Salt and pepper
- 1 tablespoon butter or margarine
- ½ cup half-and-half

Select fresh, tender young corn. Keep unhusked in refrigerator and do not husk until just prior to cooking.

Remove all silk, and rinse the ears thoroughly under cold water.

Using a sharp knife and holding the ears upright, cut down ears all around, cutting tips off kernels. Then using the back of a table knife, scrape down the ears, "milking" the kernels thoroughly.

Heat the bacon drippings in a skillet and add the corn. Sauté for about 5 minutes. Add the water and salt and pepper to taste.

Cover and cook slowly for 25 to 30 minutes at low temperature, stirring often. Add the butter. Let the corn cook until slightly thickened but not dry. Just before serving, add a little half-and-half, stir, and reheat. Serve at once.

Note: If fresh corn is unavailable, use frozen cream style corn and add 1 tablespoon sugar.

Sweet corn is one of the world's four greatest treasures. That and the love of learning, the one you thought of first, and the joy of following in the Lord's will.

—*Garrison Keillor*
Prairie Home Companion

Corn on the Cob

You can't beat the lush, buttery taste of corn on the cob. And it's easy to prepare. First you shuck your fresh corn, removing all the silk that you can.

Using a large pot, put in enough water to cover the corn, bring water to rolling boil, then reduce to simmer. Drop the corn into the water and cook for 10 to 11 minutes. Once cool enough, serve immediately. Most like to add butter and salt to taste.

Slaw

Owen's Twenty-Four-Hour Slaw

Southerners love sweet slaw. Here's a good recipe from my friend Owen Riley of Pine Mountain Valley, Georgia. Owen says the slaw will keep for a week. This recipe will serve 4.

- 1 large head cabbage, shredded
- 2 onions, chopped fine
- Salt and pepper to taste
- 1 ½ cups vinegar
- ¾ cup sugar
- 1 teaspoon celery seed
- 1 teaspoon prepared mustard
- 1 cup salad oil

Mix the cabbage and onions together. Sprinkle the salt and pepper generously over the mixture and let set awhile.

Bring the vinegar, sugar, celery seed, and mustard to a boil and boil for 1 minute. Take off the heat and add the salad oil. Pour the mixture over the cabbage and onion mix.

Put into covered container and refrigerate 24 hours.

Vidalia Onions!

South Georgia farmer Mose Coleman started it all back in the early years of the Great Depression, in 1931. He experienced something of an epiphany when he dug up some of the onions on his Toombs County farm and discovered to his amazement that instead of bringing tears to his eyes, his onions tasted almost as sweet as Coca-Cola!

He lost no time in convincing his local grocery store—some say it was the Piggly Wiggly—to buy several fifty-pound bags of the onions for $3.50 a bag, a princely price at the time.

As the saying goes, the rest is history. Today, Vidalias are the best known sweet onions in the world, with their own brand trademark. And twenty counties in the southeast Georgia area around Vidalia have found themselves the beneficiaries of a $150 million farm gate value boost to the area's economy. It's based on a perfect combination of mild climate, a sandy, low-sulfur soil, and the availability of exclusive seed varieties from the beginning. It's no wonder that in 1990 the Vidalia onion was named Georgia's Official State Vegetable.

Today, around a hundred registered growers in the area plant upwards of twelve thousand acres of the celebrated sweet onions every year. Thanks to controlled atmosphere storage technology pioneered by the apple industry, producers can store twenty million pounds of onions for up to six months, which carries them into the big Christmas marketing season.

There's no end to the creativity of folks using Vidalias. They bake, grill, fry, and microwave the sweet onions, and many simply eat them raw. Imaginative cooks turn the sweet onions into soups, casseroles, pies, pizzas, tarts, onion rings, relish, quiche, salads, dumplings, and dips. Then there are "Vidalia Blossoms," in which a single onion is deep fat fried after being cut into eight or sixteen slices.

Some "blossom" recipes are very elaborate, but I like a simple "octo-onion" version. Place an eight-slice onion into a cereal bowl, spraying it thoroughly with an oil cooking spray. Microwave for three or four minutes, depending on power setting. Then comes the eating, requiring only a little salt to taste.

Vidalia Onion Cabbage Casserole

Every April, when the Vidalia onion harvest gets under way, the town of Vidalia stages a festival including contests for the top recipes. Here is the 2008 "main dish" winning recipe, courtesy of the Vidalia Onion Committee. The recipe was entered by Ron O'Neal of Toombs County.

- 1 medium cabbage, cut up
- 1 large Vidalia onion, sliced
- Salt and pepper to taste
- 1 tablespoon hot sauce
- 2 tablespoons Worcestershire sauce
- Louisiana Cajun seasoning to taste
- 3 to 4 russet potatoes, peeled and sliced
- 2 pounds sausage, browned and drained
- 2 (16-ounce) cans cheddar cheese soup
- 2 cups shredded cheddar cheese

Preheat the oven to 400°F.

Place the cabbage in a deep 13 x 9-inch baking dish. Next, place the sliced onion on top of the cabbage. Sprinkle with salt, black pepper, hot sauce, Worcestershire sauce, and Louisiana Cajun seasoning.

Add a layer of sliced potatoes. Place the sausage meat on top of the potatoes and then spread the cheddar cheese soup on top of the sausage.

Cover and bake for 35 minutes. Remove the casserole from the oven, uncover, and sprinkle top with shredded cheddar cheese.

Return the casserole to the oven and bake 5 to 8 minutes until the cheese is completely melted.

Vidalia Onion and Tomato Pie

This is another first-place Vidalia Onion winner, in the Side Dish category. It was submitted by Toombs County resident Charlene Darley. See the appetizers chapter for another Vidalia Onion price recipe.

- 4 tomatoes, peeled and sliced
- 10 fresh basil leaves, chopped
- 2 Vidalia onions, sliced
- Salt and pepper
- 1 cup grated mozzarella cheese
- 1 cup grated cheddar cheese

- 1 cup mayonnaise
- 1 9-inch prebaked deep pie shell

Preheat the oven to 350°F.

Place the tomatoes in a colander in the sink in one layer. Sprinkle with salt. Allow to drain for 10 minutes.

Layer the tomato slices, basil, and sliced onions in pie shell. Season with salt and pepper.

Combine the grated cheeses and mayonnaise. Spread the mixture on top of the tomato/onion layers. Bake for 30 minutes or until lightly browned.

Cut into slices and serve warm.

Sweet Onions, Wadmalaw Style

While on the subject of sweet onions, I'd like to pay homage to the famous Wadmalaw Sweets, described by many as "the sweetest onions you'll ever eat." For many decades, these onions came from the island by the same name, which has served as Charleston chefs' "backdoor garden" over the years.

Unfortunately, more than a decade ago, the Hanckel family—the prime producers of the famed onion—decided to quit farming, and the Wadmalaw Sweets brand went out of existence. Soon after, Sunny, the family patriarch, passed away.

In memory of the Wadmalaw Sweets and Sunny Hanckel, here is a recipe that comes courtesy of our friend Chef Louis Osteen, who developed the recipe some years ago when he was operating Louis's Restaurant in downtown Charleston. You will have to substitute another sweet onion, of course, for the famed Wadmalaw Sweets listed here.

Wadmalaw Sweets Baked with Rice

- 2 cups vegetable or chicken stock
- 2 pounds Wadmalaw Sweets onions, thinly sliced
- 1 cup long grain rice
- 3 tablespoons butter
- 1 small bay leaf
- 1 large pinch thyme leaves
- Salt and pepper

Preheat the oven to 350°F.

In a heavy, ovenproof saucepan, bring the stock to a boil and cover. Simmer gently, covered, for 5 minutes.

Add the onions, rice, butter, bay leaf, thyme, salt, and pepper. Return to a simmer, cover, and simmer for 10 minutes. Transfer to oven and bake for 15 to 20 minutes.

Fluff with a fork and transfer to a warmed serving bowl.

Fried Onion Rings

Author Philip S. Schulz (*Celebrating America*) says that fried onion rings can be made with any yellow onion, but using one of the sweet varieties "turns a good dish into a delectable one."

Onion rings cooked in an unusual way is a specialty of the two Thomas Bessingers, Senior and Junior, longtime operators of the popular Bessinger's barbecue restaurant on Charleston's Savannah Highway. They use an old-fashioned doughnut machine as their frying vehicle. Their rings—a bestseller since they were introduced in 1950—come out "fat, sweet, and golden."

Beer-Based Onion Rings

Although the Bessingers wouldn't share their secret recipe with me, here's one that I adapted from Schulz's book, with thanks to the author. It features beer as the key liquid ingredient rather than buttermilk. It's similar to a recipe favored by the Lowcountry's John Martin Taylor, who insists that a beer batter covers the sweet onion flesh more effectively, preventing overcooking. This recipe provides 6 to 8 servings.

- 1 cup all-purpose flour
- 1 tablespoon dry mustard
- 1 teaspoon freshly grated nutmeg
- ½ teaspoon salt
- 4 eggs, separated
- 1 cup beer
- 2 pounds sweet onions
- Peanut oil, enough for 2 inches of oil, which will depend on size of saucepan

Combine the flour with the mustard, nutmeg, and salt in a medium-size bowl.

In a second bowl, combine the egg yolks with the beer and whisk until smooth. Combine this with the flour mixture to form the batter, and whisk once again until smooth.

Slice the onions to ¼-inch thickness. Place the sliced onions into a large bowl, cover with ice water, and let stand for 15 minutes.

Beat the egg whites until stiff and fold them into the batter.

Drain the onions, divide the slices into rings, and lightly pat dry with paper towels.

In a large saucepan, heat 2 inches of oil until hot but not smoking. Dip the onion rings into the batter, shaking off excess batter. Fry the rings in hot oil until golden brown.

CHAPTER 17

Luscious Corn Bread & Delectable Spoon Bread

When de Co'n Pone's Hot

When you set down at de table, kin' o'weary lak & sad,
An' youse jes'a little tiahed an' perhaps a little mad;
How yo gloom tu'ns into gladness, how yo' joy drives out de doubt
When de oven do' is opened, an' de smell comes po'in out;
When de 'lectric light o'heaven seems to settle on the spot
When yo'mammy says de blessin' an' de co'n pone's hot

—*Paul Laurence Dunbar*
noted African-American poet and novelist (1812–1906)

Corn bread is part of the soul of the South.

—*Chef Louis Osteen*

Corn bread is something of a religion in the South. Tracing the evolution of corn bread from Indian suppone to elegant spoon bread "is as revealing and wondrous an exercise as exploring history through the study of fossils." Indeed. This according to my friend, John Egerton of Nashville, in his delightful book on Southern cookery and culture, *Side Orders*. His comment relates, of course, to the social and cultural movement of Southern history through Southerners' voracious consumption of corn bread.

Even in the earliest decades of the Charleston colony, Southerners depended on corn bread. Thomas Ashe wrote in his 1682 book, *Carolina, or a Description of the Present State of that Country*: "In short, it's a Grain of General Use to Man and Beast."

Thomas Jefferson, one of our nation's most progressive "gentleman farmers," never lost his love of corn bread. Sent to Paris to serve four years as our first ambassador to France in 1785, Jefferson got turned on to French cuisine. Even so, he grew corn in his residence garden on the Champs-Elysées to assure plenty of grist so his cooks could continue making corn bread.

Likewise, Benjamin Franklin wrote his wife from London in 1766 to ship him some cornmeal so he could have his favorite corn bread to eat.

I'm Southern and self respecting and I put sugar in my corn bread.
—Reader writing in to express his opinion to the
Atlanta Journal-Constitution's "Vent" column

Southern Corn Bread

According to Glenn Roberts of South Carolina's Anson Mills, black skillet corn bread gets much of its tastiness from the meal's natural sweetness—not from sugar in the batter. Such corn bread, he adds, "has an open crumb and a deep, crackling finish."

While many cooks object to the addition of wheat flour, Roberts suggests that a good combination is a half cup of cornmeal with an equal amount of all-purpose flour.

The late Eugene Walter liked to sprinkle benne seeds onto thin batches of corn bread (not included in this recipe).

Doris's Plain Good Skillet Corn Bread

Dub Taft displays a pan of corn bread cooked by his mother. (Photo courtesy of Dub Taft.)

For this first recipe, I turned to Dub Taft for another one of his mother's wonderful recipes.

Dub points out that one of the keys to his mother's corn bread success is her adroit use of bacon drippings, "which form a ring around the perimeter when you pour in the batter."

He suggests that you take a spoon and work some of this oil very lightly over the top, making the crust thicker and tastier. Also, he says, adding flour gives the corn bread more bulk, a great texture, and a nice flavor that goes with any food you're serving.

Back home in Atlanta, Dub sometimes varies this recipe by adding an egg or using milk instead of water to get a richer, moist texture. "But in my opinion," he says, "it doesn't taste as good. What is good is adding cracklins to the batter to make cracklin' corn bread." Cracklins, of course, which can be purchased separately in grocery stores, are the bits of tasty pork morsels left over from the rendering of lard in a hog-killing. (See sidebar on how you can make your own cracklins.)

"Shut your eyes and open your mouth and I'll give you a surprise," she said. It was not often that she made crackling bread; she said she never had time...she knew I loved crackling bread.

—Harper Lee
To Kill a Mockingbird

- 2 tablespoons bacon drippings or oil
- ¾ cup self-rising cornmeal
- ¾ cup self-rising flour

Preheat the oven to 450°F. Coat the inside of cast-iron skillet with drippings or oil and preheat.

Mix the cornmeal and flour with enough water to make a smooth batter. Pour the batter into hot skillet and cook in oven 30 to 40 minutes or until the corn bread is golden brown.

How to Make Your Own Cracklins

I am indebted to Jean Anderson for this recipe, included in her cookbook, A Love Affair with Southern Cooking. *This will yield a cup of cracklins for later use in baking your corn bread.*

The first step, Jean says, is to get your friendly butcher to put aside for you some of his store's fat trimmings. Dice the pork fat into quarter-inch lengths using a very sharp knife.

Preheat your oven to 275°F. Spread the fat pieces over the bottom of a heavy Dutch oven. Add 1 1/2 cups of water, stir well, then cover the Dutch oven, place it on lowest oven shelf and bake for 1 hour.

Remove the lid, stir the pork fat well, and spread it again over the pot's bottom. Bake uncovered for an additional 2 to 2 1/2 hours, stirring every half hour. This leaves behind your cracklins, crisp brown bits.

Drain the bits on paper towels. When cool, store in an airtight plastic container until ready to use in your corn bread.

Corn Bread–Oyster Dressing

No Lowcountry Thanksgiving dinner would be complete without a corn bread or corn bread/oyster dressing to go along with the roast turkey.

The following recipes come courtesy of my friend Grace Riley of Pine Mountain Valley, Georgia. To make this basic corn bread dressing into oyster dressing, you merely add 1 cup of chopped oysters to the mixture.

Glenn Roberts says that oysters "impart frank sensuality to the dressing's texture and a haunting suggestion of wine to its taste."

Grace Riley's Dressing

- 3 cups crumbled corn bread
- 2 ½ cups crumbled day-old bread or biscuits
- 3 eggs, whisked
- ½ cup melted butter
- 1 onion, chopped fine
- ½ teaspoon pepper
- ¼ cup finely chopped celery heart
- ½ teaspoon salt
- ½ teaspoon poultry seasoning
- 4 to 5 cups turkey broth (can make it with bouillon)

Preheat the oven to 425°F.

Combine the breads and all other ingredients. Mix well and be sure it is "soupy" enough (about the consistency of cake batter).

Pour into a greased 12 x 9 ½-inch baking dish and bake for 40 minutes or until lightly browned and turning loose from sides of pan. Don't overcook!

Grace Riley's Corn Bread

Use this recipe to make the corn bread for Grace's dressing.

- ½ cup vegetable oil, such as Wesson
- 2 cups self-rising cornmeal
- 1 egg
- 1 ½ cups buttermilk

Preheat the oven to 450°F.

Mix all ingredients and put into a skillet. Bake for 30 minutes or until the corn bread is firm and lightly browned.

In the North, man may not be able to live by bread alone; but in the South, and particularly in Charleston, he comes mighty near to it, provided the bread is hot.
—200 Years of Charleston Cooking
Blanche S. Rhett and Lettie Gay

Spoon Bread

Spoon bread is something of a corn bread soufflé-mush custard. It sits atop the corn bread food pyramid as the richest and most delectable result of the corn bread art.

Eaten with a spoon, the dish proved extremely popular in Lowcountry and Tidewater plantations during the eighteenth and nineteenth centuries. Sarah Rutledge included the first spoon bread recipe in her 1847 *The Carolina Housewife* cookbook.

Thomas Jefferson served it to his Monticello guests in the morning, noon, and evening. He also had a personal recipe that called for scalding a quart of milk and a fourth of a teaspoon of salt. His cooks then sprinkled in a cup of cornmeal and cooked the batter in a double-boiler for an hour. Finally, they stirred in three teaspoons of butter and three eggs.

Spoon bread continues to have a considerable following today, as a wonderful accompaniment to soups, stews, gumbos, chicken, ham, and gravy, as well as to wild game dishes.

The best modern-day spoon bread, comprised of grits and cornmeal, is lushly rich and impossibly light at the same time, representing the height of corn flavor in casserole form.

"During sweet corn season," says Glenn Roberts, "Charleston cooks add raw kernels to the batter, creating a triumvirate of cascading corn flavor and texture." He adds that the marriage of corn and dairy creates a dizzyingly rich texture and flavor to begin with and, in the recipe below, is enhanced further with a shiny patent-leather glaze of straight heavy cream.

There are no statistics on this, but cornmeal must account for at least ten percent of the weight of your average natural-born Southerner. The only living creatures that eat more corn surely must have hooves.

—*Jim Auchmutey*
Atlanta Journal-Constitution

Awendaw Spoon Bread

This spoon bread recipe, courtesy of Glenn Roberts, is named for an ancient See Wee Indian village along the Atlantic seacoast northeast of Charleston. Native American and Gullah traditions still survive at Awendaw today, and many people stop by the shops on Highway 17 to purchase Awendaw breads, sweetgrass baskets, and mats made by the remaining black natives.

Spoon bread made with this recipe tastes equally sublime with white or yellow grits and cornmeal, but Roberts says it looks slightly more beautiful in yellow.

You will need a heavy-bottomed 2 ½-quart saucepan; a fine tea strainer; a mixing bowl; a balloon whisk; a wooden spoon; a well-seasoned 9-inch cast-iron skillet, a heavy 9-inch cake pan, or a 1 ½-quart casserole dish; and a rubber spatula.

This recipe will yield 6 to 8 servings as a side dish.

- 3 large eggs, lightly beaten
- ½ cup quick grits
- 2 cups spring or filtered water
- 2 tablespoons unsalted butter plus more to grease skillet
- 1 ¼ teaspoons fine sea salt
- ½ teaspoon freshly ground black pepper

- 2 cups whole milk
- 1 cup fine cornmeal
- 1 ½ teaspoons baking powder
- ¼ cup heavy cream

Adjust the oven rack to the upper-middle position and preheat the oven to 450°F. Grease a 9-inch cast-iron skillet or a 1 ½-quart casserole dish with butter and set aside.

Crack eggs into a mixing bowl, whisk them lightly, and set the bowl aside.

Place the grits in a heavy-bottomed 2 ½-quart saucepan and cover with water. Stir once. Allow the grits to settle a full minute, tilt the pan, and skim off and discard the chaff and hulls with a fine tea strainer.

Set the pan over medium-high heat and bring to a simmer, stirring constantly with a wooden spoon, for 5 to 8 minutes. Reduce the heat to low and cook, stirring frequently, until the grits are just tender and hold their shape on a spoon, about 25 minutes. Beat in the remaining butter and the salt and pepper. Whisk in the milk in three additions.

Bring the grits slurry to a simmer, covered, over medium-high heat, whisking frequently, quickly lifting and replacing the lid. Whisk in the cornmeal and remove the pan from the heat. Ladle about a cup of hot grits mixture into the beaten eggs and whisk them to warm. Pour the egg mixture back into the grits. Stir in the baking powder. Scrape the batter into the prepared pan and smooth the top. Spoon the cream over the top. Place the pan in the oven and bake 10 minutes. Lower the heat to 375°F and bake until the spoon bread is nicely risen and golden brown, 15 to 20 minutes more.

Remove from the oven and serve without delay.

Supper's ready. Now bow your head,
Say a quick "A-men," then pass the Cornbread

—*Poet Robert Michie*
Cooking on the Dixie Range (1981)

A Simpler, Older Spoon Bread

During my 2008 research tour of South Carolina's coastal region, I was fortunate to meet Genevieve (Sis) Chandler Peterkin at her beautiful ancestral home overlooking the scenic marshes of Murrell's Inlet, just south of Myrtle Beach. While on my visit, I

learned that Mrs. Peterkin, the author of several books, including *Heaven Is a Beautiful Place*, was a 1950 classmate of my wife, Susanne Knight, at Coker College in Hartsville, South Carolina. Small world.

Sis told me that her grandmother—whose maiden name was Mary Anna Ashe Moore of Bennettsville, South Carolina—cooked up a wonderful spoon bread. Later, I located a copy of the recipe in *NeNa's Garden*, published by Kathy Boyd and her Faith Publishing. With thanks to Cathy and Sis Peterkin, here is the recipe.

Genevieve Chandler Peterkin remembers her grandmother's spoon bread. (Photo by the author.)

Grandma Mary Anna's Spoon Bread

- 4 cups milk
- 1 cup cornmeal
- 1 teaspoon salt
- 1 tablespoon shortening
- 3 eggs, separated

Preheat the oven to 350°F.

In a medium saucepan, heat the milk to boiling point. Stir in the cornmeal and salt. Add the shortening. Stir constantly 5 minutes but do not boil.

Cool the mixture. Add the well-beaten egg yolks. Beat the egg whites until they make a thick froth, and fold into the mixture.

Pour the batter into a greased 2-quart casserole. Bake for 40 minutes. Serve immediately.

CHAPTER 18

Grits Galore

———◆———

Grits are the national dish of the South…a poor man's polenta.

—*John Shelton Reed*
1001 Things Everyone Should Know About the South

Did you hear the story of the South Carolinian years ago who was acquitted of murdering his wife with the defense that "her grits were too loose"?

Such is the strong attachment of Southerners to grits. I'll confess right off: I love grits. I grew up eating grits with gusto…grits and butter, grits and eggs, grits and sausage, grits and chicken gravy, grits and redeye gravy. As Georgia humorist Roy Blount said, "Grits fits in with anything." Or as the late, great Bill Neal of Chapel Hill wrote in his *Good Old Grits Cookbook*, without grits, "the sun wouldn't come up, the crops wouldn't grow, and most of us would lose our drawl."

Back when I was a youngster in the '40s, South Carolina had something of an imaginary rice-grits dividing line running along the Fall Line about eighty miles inland—the ancient seacoast now defined by a twenty-mile-wide strip of rolling sand hills from Augusta northeastward.

In other words, north of that imaginary line, folks were huge grits eaters, whereas to the south, the people were into rice, so much so that the Lowcountry mantra was, "Not a day passes that we don't serve rice in our home." Plus, of course, grits for breakfast. And grits with shrimp.

Grits have been around for a long time. Famed botanist William Bartram got his first taste of a corn-based dish such as grits when he supped with an Indian chief in 1776. He recalled it as "a refreshing repast" and "a pleasant cooling liquor made of homony well boiled, mixed up with milk, and served up in a large bowl with a very large ladle to sup it with."

Today, fine restaurants across the Lowcountry have elevated grits-based dishes such as shrimp and grits to the level of cutting-edge cuisine. In the Lowcountry, the dish almost reaches the level of the high-class grits Europeans call polenta. Chronicling the grits evolution, Charleston's Nathalie Dupree came up with a marvelous book a few years back devoted entirely to shrimp and grits, aptly named *Nathalie Dupree's Shrimp & Grits.*

Southerners who grew up eating grits love to tell stories about their devotion to the lowly dish.

"In my early childhood, a day didn't go by when grits weren't on the table," Dub Taft says. "Sometimes grits appeared at all three meals. They were especially flavorful with fried fish, fried pork chops, fried sausage, fried steak, and, well, fried anything."

Like many Southerners, Dub expressed his highest adoration for grits at breakfast time, particularly when accompanied by biscuits, eggs, red gravy, cream gravy, and blackberry jelly. Plus a cup of coffee, of course.

"We loved grits so dearly," Taft recalled, "the three-gallon pot that Mother cooked and served them from was just like having another family member sitting around the table."

Grits Cooking: The Basics

Before we get into recipes, you should learn the basics that will help you cook up perfect creamy grits. Prize-winning chef Scott Peacock of Atlanta's Watershed Restaurant gives us these fundamentals to follow:

First, start with good grits—that would be stone-ground. There are plenty of instant grits and quick grits out there, but stone-ground are the best. You can order them from various stone-ground gristmills in the South, including the Nora Mill Granary at Helen, Georgia, and Hoppin' John Taylor's culinary website, www.HoppinJohns.com.

Number two, boil your grits in water with the addition of milk and/or broths.

Number three, be prepared to cook your grits a long time, even going so far as to double the length of simmering time as called for in the directions. The longer you cook, the creamier they become. Some chefs suggest that you could put your grits in a slow cooker all night, which is practiced by Southern foodie John T. Edge.

Following these rules should help you cook up some really nice creamy grits. If you have leftovers, you can put them in the refrigerator and reconstitute them later with milk, or fry them with a little flour dusting.

As a further note, some Lowcountry restaurants cook their grits in "beach water" collected from coastal tributaries or from the faucets of those living on the beach front. In her *Shrimp & Grits* book, Nathalie writes, "Beach water has a mineral taste as well as a saltiness, and if pluff mud is there, the water will taste of it, too."

"Hominy Grits" are what you'll see when you look at a package of grits at the grocery store. Hominy means that the grains of husked corn have been dried and the hulls removed in a water-lye solution. After that they are ground into grits, packaged, and marketed. Sometimes stone-ground grits carry a "speckled heart" label. These germ hearts can be seen as dark flecks in the ground grits.

True grits, more grits, fish grits and collards,
Life is good where grits are swallered.

—*Roy Blount Jr.*
One Fell Soup

Simple Grits

Grits are fairly easy to cook. Just boil them in salted water and then add salt and pepper to taste. But grits are also very adaptable. You can add butter, eggs, cheese, or even your favorite hot pepper. And you can bake them or fry them.

Quick grits can be cooked in ten minutes, but as I mentioned earlier, the preference is for stone-ground grits, grits that are ground between two stones, which assures their old-fashioned nutty flavor. But you must be prepared to extend the cooking time much longer. Definitely do not buy instant grits.

Simple Southern Grits

- 4 cups water
- ¾ teaspoon salt
- 1 cup grits
- 1 tablespoon butter
- Pepper to taste

Bring the salted water to a boil in a saucepan and stir in the grits. Reduce the heat to medium and cook for about 20 minutes. Serve hot with plenty of butter plus a little pepper.

Boiled hominy and butter for breakfast as an accompaniment to shrimp, or sausages or bacon, according to the season, and a plate piled high with white fluffy rice for dinner, is as regular a thing in this part of the world as is wine with your meals in France.

—*Harriet Ross Colquitt*
Savannah Cookbook *(1933)*

Creamy Grits

To find out how to accomplish creamy grits, listen closely to prize-winning chef Louis Osteen. While running Louis's Grill in the Omni Hotel at Charleston Place some years ago, Osteen pioneered the shrimp and grits trend among the Holy City's fine restaurants, giving the dish its due. He favors the use of quick grits along with milk and heavy cream.

Louis's Creamy Grits

Here's Louis's recipe that I have adapted with my appreciation to him. It will yield 6 servings.

- 2 cups whole milk
- 2 cups water
- 1 teaspoon salt
- 1 cup uncooked quick grits (not instant)
- 4 ½ cups unsalted butter
- 1 cup heavy cream
- 2 teaspoons freshly ground black pepper

Bring the milk and water to a boil in a heavy saucepan over medium heat. Stir in the salt. Mix in the grits slowly, stirring constantly. As the grits begin thickening, turn the heat to low and simmer for 30 to 40 minutes, stirring occasionally to prevent the grits from scorching.

Add the butter and cream, stirring thoroughly, and let simmer for 5 minutes. Stir in the pepper and serve the grits immediately.

Note: If the grits are too thick, stir in more cream or milk. Also note that the grits tend to get thicker when put on the plates.

Cheese Grits

Cheese grits are probably the most favored of the grits family. The late, great Sema Wilkes, founder and operator of Mrs. Wilkes' Boardinghouse Restaurant in Savannah's historic district, developed the following recipe, and I am indebted to her granddaughter, Marcia Thompson, for allowing me to adapt it. This recipe will yield 6 to 8 servings.

Mrs. Wilkes's Cheese Grits

- 1 cup grits
- 1 6-ounce package garlic cheese (Note: Sharp cheese can be substituted for the garlic cheese.)
- ½ cup butter
- 4 cups water
- 1 teaspoon salt
- 2 eggs yolks, beaten well

- 2 egg whites, beaten stiff
- Cracker crumbs

Preheat the oven to 350°F.

Using a saucepan, combine the grits, cheese, and butter. Bring the mixture to a full boil, then reduce the heat and cook over medium heat for approximately 30 minutes, or until well done.

Add the egg yolks and fold in the egg whites.

Place the mixture in a greased casserole and sprinkle top with crumbs.

Bake at 350°F for 45 minutes.

Fried Grits

Fried Grits

As I mentioned earlier, fried grits can be made intentionally, or with leftovers. This recipe is adapted from the late Craig Claiborne's book on Southern cooking and will yield 8 servings.

- 2 cups water
- 2 cups plus 2 tablespoons milk
- Salt to taste
- 1 cup regular grits
- 3 eggs
- 1 cup fine fresh breadcrumbs
- 3 tablespoons butter

Preheat the oven to 350°F.

In a saucepan, combine the water and 2 cups milk with salt, and gradually add in the grits, stirring often. Cook until done, according to package directions.

Remove from the heat. Lightly beat 2 eggs, then beat them into the grits mixture. Pour into an 8-inch-square pan. Chill until firm.

Cut the mixture into 1 ½-inch squares.

Beat the remaining egg and dip each square into it. Coat with the breadcrumbs.

Heat the butter in a skillet and cook the grits squares until golden brown on both sides, turning once.

In the 1960s when I lived in Manhattan's Lower East Side, one of my favorite places to eat was a small joint that served grits and just about anything you can name—grits 'n salmon croquettes, grits 'n eggs, grits 'n stewed shrimp, grits 'n gravy, grits 'n sausage, grits 'n grillades. Grits are wonderfully versatile because they are bland and take on the flavor of whatever is served with them.

—Vertamae Grosvenor
Vertamae Cooks in Americas' Family Kitchens

Funeral Grits Casserole

Carolina Funeral Grits

Popular across the South, these casseroles are sometimes called funeral grits because they are the near perfect dish to take to a family following a death, or to a family reunion. This recipe will yield 8 servings.

- 4 cups whole milk
- ½ cup plus ⅓ cup butter
- 1 cup regular grits
- 1 teaspoon salt
- ½ teaspoon freshly ground pepper
- 1 cup chopped sharp cheddar cheese
- ½ cup grated Parmesan cheese

Preheat the oven to 350°F.

In a heatproof casserole on the stove top, bring the milk just to boil and add ½ cup butter. Add the grits to the casserole, stirring and continuing to cook until it has the consistency of cereal.

Remove the casserole from the stove and, using an electric beater, add the remaining butter and salt and pepper. Return to stove top to medium heat.

Stir in the cheddar cheese until it melts. Sprinkle Parmesan on top. Bake 1 hour, until crusty on top.

Shrimp and Grits

Of course shrimp and grits have risen Cinderella-like from humble circumstances of earlier years to an honored place on the most distinguished restaurants from Murrells Inlet and Pawley's Island on the South Carolina coast down to St. Mary's, Georgia, and beyond.

Johns Island Shrimp and Grits

My friend Charles Seabrook describes Mildred Seabrook as "the best cook in the Lowcountry, without peer." He should know. The Johns Island native (now residing in Atlanta) visits Carl and Mildred Seabrook as often as possible and often heads straight to Mildred's table.

Here is Mildred's recipe for making shrimp and grits and shrimp and rice that will yield four servings. She doesn't use a written recipe, only recalling how her mother did it.

She assumes that you know how to fix grits or rice in advance and have them on the stove ready for the shrimp.

Her first rule to assure success is to insist on using small creek shrimp that can be found in Lowcountry tidal waterways.

"During the year," she says, "my husband, Carl, goes out in his john boat with a net and brings in the creek shrimp, which we freeze in plastic one-pound butter or margarine containers."

After thawing the container, she peels the shrimp and puts them to the side. (They would have been beheaded before they were put in the freezer).

Mildred then uses an iron skillet to fry 3 slices of bacon good and crisp, draining the grease except for 3 or 4 drops for use with frying the shrimp. She uses paper towels to pat the bacon good and dry and reserves it for later use.

"You should sauté the shrimp at a medium temperature for only a few minutes," Mildred says, "until they are a deep pink, or until all the moisture of the shrimp has totally disappeared."

She then takes 3 or 4 tablespoons of flour and sifts the flour onto the shrimp "the way my mom did."

GRITS, "A RARE NOUN"

In 2002 Georgia's State Legislature named grits the state's "official prepared food." The bill's cosponsors, Republican Rep. Doug Everett of Albany and Democratic Rep. Dorothy Pelote of Savannah, included one interesting detail in the bill, declaring that "grammatically, the word 'grits' enjoys the notable distinction of being a rare noun which is always plural but which may properly be used as either singular or plural in writing and speaking."

At this point Mildred stirs the flour and shrimp until the flour turns slightly brown. "Then you start pouring in a small amount of water at the time into the skillet," she says, "until the mixture turns a golden brown."

At this point Mildred crumbles the bacon and sprinkles the pieces on top. When the mixture is added to the hot grits or rice, you have, voila, a traditional Lowcountry meal of distinction, good enough for a king or a queen, or for a hungry brother-in-law who wanders in.

JOHN EGERTON'S ODE TO GRITS

Grits…stand for hard times and happy times, for poverty and populism, for the blessings and curses of a righteous God. They stand for custom and tradition, for health and humor, for high-spirited hospitality…

They belong to the South almost exclusively; no one else in this country pays much attention to them.

—JOHN EGERTON
SIDE ORDERS: SMALL HELPINGS OF SOUTHERN COOKERY & CULTURE

CHAPTER 19

Wild Game in the Lowcountry

The roebuck or deer are numerous on this island...the tiger, wolf, and bear hold yet some possession, as also raccoons, foxes, hares, squirrels...Opossums are here in abundance, as also polecats, wildcats, rattlesnakes, glass snake, coach-whip snake, and a variety of other serpents.

Here are also a great variety of birds, the grey eagle, the bald eagle, the fishing hawk, the ground doves. They are remarkably beautiful, about the size of a sparrow, and their soft and plaintive cooing perfectly enchanting...

—William Bartram
reporting on his 1773 visit to a barrier island near Savannah

Some years ago, when the grand dame of Southern cuisine, the late Edna Lewis, ran the kitchen at Charleston's Middleton Place Restaurant, poet Nikki Giovanni made a special trip from Virginia to Charleston to meet and visit with her idol at the well-known restaurant on Ashley River Road.

As reported in the food section of the *Atlanta Journal Constitution*, the two hit it off from the start and soon were into a lively discussion about food. Miss Lewis asked the poet to tell her something about her favorite dish. Ms. Giovanni replied that it was fried quail and she began detailing how she went about cooking the bobwhites.

"I noticed she got a funny look on her face as I was talking," the poet recalled. It was only later when Ms. Giovanni got back home and was going through Miss Lewis's highly praised cookbook, *In Pursuit of Flavor*, that she realized she had been cooking the quail recipe from that very cookbook. "I had been cooking Miss Lewis's recipe for so long," the poet declared, "I thought it was mine."

Jimmy Hagood's Bacon-Wrapped Quail

This is an outstanding recipe for quail by Charleston's celebrated barbecue chef and caterer, Jimmy Hagood, and his company, Food for the Southern Soul. This recipe will serve four as an appetizer or two as an entree.

- 4 quail
- 2 cups BlackJack Marinade Sauce (available at www.foodforthesouthernsoul.com)
- 1 teaspoon thyme
- 1 teaspoon rosemary
- 1 teaspoon basil
- 1 small onion, quartered
- 4 strips bacon
- 4 toothpicks
- Black pepper and salt

In a nonreactive pan, marinate the quail overnight in refrigerator with the BlackJack Marinade Sauce or a tomato-based substitute.

Start a charcoal fire.

Remove the birds and set aside the marinade. Sprinkle the herbs evenly over the quail. Place one-quarter onion in cavity of each bird, wrap with bacon, and secure with toothpicks. Add salt and pepper.

Arrange charcoal on two sides of the grill and place a drip pan between charcoal mounds. Place the birds on grill, over the drip pan, and grill for 18 to 20 minutes, turning several times.

Baste with BlackJack Marinade Sauce. Arrange the quail directly over coals for 5 to 8 minutes, turning several times. Remove from the grill and serve.

Geese, turkeys, quail and ducks were favored on dinner tables, but nonpareils, cardinals and bluebirds often ended up in decorative cages. in 1750, Peter Manigault wrote from London to his mother in Carolina, "Mrs. Brailsford…brought the Red birds you were so kind to send me as far as Dover, but coming to London, the Poor creatures died in the Post Chaise…"

The first day of Thanksgiving week signals the start of the Lowcountry's quail-hunting season. At Lowcountry plantation quail reserves, swarms of hunters arrive on foot, horse-drawn wagons, and jeeps. Carrying shotguns locked and loaded, they're accompanied, of course, by eager pointer dogs. The quail hunting season lasts until March 1 in most states.

This continues a great bird hunting tradition that began in the colonial era. As chef Marvin Woods notes in *New Low-Country Cooking*, the Lowcountry's forests and wetlands were filled in the early 1700s "with quail, snipes, pheasant, woodcocks, duck, partridge, and turkey." Those, together with the availability of exotic spices in port cities like Charleston and Savannah, "created signature poultry dishes."

The South Carolina WPA Guide, written and published during the Great Depression

THE WILD SOUTH CAROLINA COASTLINE

When I was growing up, I had for my hunting ground that wild and beautiful stretch of coast lying between Georgetown and Charleston, South Carolina, and thence southward toward the Georgia Line.

There, in this famous old rice-growing country, countless myriads of wild ducks came, attracted by the garnerings of grain. Out of the lush pinelands trooped great flocks of wild turkeys. Quail came, and doves. I doubt if there is a crop that birds of nearly every kind love so much as they do rice, and while it was standing and in a soft condition as "in the milk," thousands of reedbirds fed on it. In the old days of rice growing, "bird-minding" was one of the regular expenses of the crop.

~

Friends and neighbors will meet on Christmas mornings at one of the great plantations…some on horseback, and behind the latter will be trailing their deer hounds in the order of their enthusiasm. On such an occasion all the packs of the countryside hunt together. I have known as many as eighty hounds to be used on such a hunt…About such a holiday company there is a spirit of wholesome irresponsibility, of genial laxity, that Southern hunters, who usually take their sport with gravity, almost as if it were a religious rite, do not usually manifest…

—ARCHIBALD RUTLEDGE
THE WOODS AND WILD THINGS I REMEMBER

(1940), notes, "From the days when beaters in the rice fields kept the big plantation house supplied with rice birds, these little creatures have been a delicacy."

Indeed. Bobwhite quail is South Carolina and Georgia's official game bird. You can hear it whistling at a high pitch in the evening: "Bob, Bob White, Bob, Bob White."

Quail are often served in the Lowcountry as a tasty breakfast dish. This is especially true during the hunting season. At other times of the year, frozen birds are available from Manchester Farms, the nation's largest quail farm. Located at Dalzell, near Sumter, South Carolina, Manchester ships 110,000 birds daily through food service and retail distributors nationwide.

Offering succulent white meat, quail often top the menu at swank weekend brunches and dinners in Charleston, Beaufort, and Savannah as well as in other cities and towns along the coastal region. And wild doves and squabs (pigeons) are generally cooked in the same manner as quail.

Quail and Doves

Mourning doves are less readily available than quail. Federal government regulations prohibit selling doves, as doves are migratory birds. So to get to taste the dove delicacy, you need to go on a dove shoot yourself or receive several from a generous friend. The dove season generally begins the Saturday before Labor Day and extends to the middle of January.

BOBWHITE QUAIL POPULATION DECLINING
Georgia was once considered the bobwhite quail capital of the world. However, according to the Georgia Department of National Resources, the state's quail population has declined by more than 70 percent since the early 1960s, mainly due to loss of quality early successional habitat. To address this concern, the state is conducting a Bobwhite Quail Initiative (BQI), which is funded through the sale of vehicle license plates. The objective is to provide private landowners with technical assistance and financial incentives for habitat improvement not only for quail but also for songbird species.

Darlington County Quail and Doves over Rice

This recipe by S. Pressly Coker III, from Hartsville, South Carolina, comes from *Candlelight and Camellias*, a cookbook published in Hartsville, home of the great Coker Pedigreed Seed Company. In this recipe, you can use both quail and doves. I have set an arbitrary number of 6 and 6. This recipe yields 4 to 6 servings.

- 6 quail and 6 doves, dressed
- Salt and pepper
- 5 to 6 tablespoons bacon grease
- Flour (roll and dust quail and doves to coat them thoroughly)
- 1 medium onion, diced
- 2 stalks celery, diced
- 1 green bell pepper, diced
- 2 teaspoons chopped garlic
- ½ cup red wine
- 1 (10.5-ounce) can cream of mushroom soup
- 1 (10.5-ounce) can French onion soup
- Cubes of Kitchen Bouquet
- 1 16 0z. can beef broth
- 3 cups cooked rice

Season the birds with a little salt and a lot of pepper. Place them in a bowl and let them sit for 20 minutes or so.

In a large cast-iron skillet, heat the bacon grease (or olive oil if you prefer). Cover the birds with flour and brown them in the oil.

Remove the birds when they are browned and add the onion, celery, bell pepper, and garlic, and cook until tender. Deglaze the pan with the red wine.

Add the cream of mushroom soup and the French onion soup. Adjust the color by using cubes of Kitchen Bouquet. (I like my gravy to be dark tan in color and not brown. One or two cubes should be adequate.)

Place the birds back into the skillet with the gravy, cover, and simmer on the stove or in a 350°F oven for 1 to 1 ½ hours. If the gravy is too thick, use the beef broth to thin down. Serve over the precooked rice and enjoy.

Ducks

According to *South Carolina Wildlife* magazine, the wood duck—the only migratory waterfowl that nests regularly across the southeast—accounts for half of all waterfowl bagged in the region. The magazine adds that landowners can encourage the bird to nest on their land by constructing nesting boxes on special pond locations.

How to Cook Marinated Duck Breasts (According to Ben Moise)

Here are directions for cooking duck breasts as described by my good friend, retired South Carolina State Game Warden Ben McC. Moise of Charleston, South Carolina:

Breast out and skin any kind of duck breasts. Slip them into a heavy Ziplock bag and gently pound with the edge of a cutting board or kitchen mallet until they are fairly flattened. Carefully remove them from the bag and place in a bowl and cover with buttermilk and refrigerate for three or four hours. Dry the flattened fillets and dredge in a mixture of flour, salt, and pepper.

You can add a little touch of garlic powder or cayenne pepper or both to the flour mix if you like. Fry in a pan with a little olive oil and butter at medium heat until the breasts are just browned. Set aside.

Mince a couple of cloves of garlic and finely chop one small onion. Sauté these in a pan with a little butter and olive oil and add around a cup of chopped shiitake mushrooms and stir for a bit. Then add a can of chicken broth and a little white wine, probably around a half a cup or so. Using a stout fork, mash about one quarter stick of cool butter, which has been cut into thin slices, with around two tablespoons of flour until it forms a paste. Roll into a cylindrical shape and chill. This is called in the trade a French roux. Reduce the cooking liquid down to just below half of what you started with and add the French roux about a half an inch at the time, stirring well.

Meanwhile, when all is thickened, stir in a small container of sour cream. Put in the duck breasts and bring up the heat for around four or five minutes, turning once. Carefully

> ### Plucking a Duck
>
> *One of the biggest questions raised by those who'd like to cook duck soup is: "How do you pluck a duck?" That's one of the easiest to answer: Buy your duck frozen. That way, the fowl can't get fresh and, like the silly goose, you won't have to hang it.*
>
> *Actually, making duck soup is as easy as falling off a log. And the only bump is the one given your taste buds when the steaming aroma of hot duck soup hits them.*
>
> —Ben Green Cooper
> Savannah's Cookin

remove the duck breasts and put them on a plate upon a bed of rice and pour the remaining sauce over them. This is a lot easier than it sounds and is a pleasant departure from the usual fare of grilled or roasted duck.

Venison

Bill Green is a Charleston-area native and descendant of Gullah slaves. For many years, he has been a deer driver at Charleston's Middleton Hunt Club and is the elusive "fox" for the Middleton Place Hounds' drag hunts. The following is based on an interview I conducted with Mr. Green in 2008. Here he describes his techniques in training the club's horses and dogs. For a glance into another part of Bill Green's life, turn to page 15 in the West Africa Connection chapter.

Deer driver William (Bill) Green Jr., pictured atop his horse Mike on the Pinckney Trail at Charleston's Millbank Plantation. (Photo courtesy of Henry Lowndes.)

As a young man, I went out to Colorado on a Jobs Corps program, and for a while I worked there at a dude ranch. It was there I started learning to work with horses, breaking horses and riding horses. But I learned real quick that you'd get beat up if you didn't use the right equipment, particularly the right saddles. Just putting a bridle on a horse and riding bareback could get you bruised up real fast.

I got to where I loved riding horses there at the ranch. We used to sneak out and ride the horses on weekends, horses that belonged to people who had gone back to their homes. Sometimes we'd ride those horses half a day. That's where I learned a lot about horses.

I came back to Charleston in 1970 and went to work at the Middleton Place. The Middleton deer hunts were going on then, and I met up with the deer drivers since I was working back and forth from the kitchen to the gardens to the woods. I met people there at the Middleton Hunt Club like Oscar Leach, the head deer driver, and Edward Lowndes, the hunt master. One day I mentioned that I could help 'em with their horses.

Mr. Leach said, "Bill, I didn't know you could ride a horse," and I said, "Yeah, I can!" So the next year coming, he called me and I started working with them and I been doing it ever since. Been a deer driver now almost forty years. These days I'm training young men, including my two sons, to be deer drivers in the future.

I learned at an early age to have respect for every living thing. And in the woods, you learn a great deal about animals and how to deal with them. I've learned a lot about horses and hounds at the Middleton Hunt Club.

The most important thing in training a horse that will work with you is to show lovin' kindness and respect toward him. The animals love to be treated nice, just like humans. That's all your horse asks. Give him a pat on the back after a long deer drive and tell him, "You did good, boy!"

Once you get your horse where you and the horse are a team, that's going to make you a top deer driver. The same holds true with your hounds. We Gullah drivers help raise the hounds and train the hounds, mostly English hounds. A lot of 'em are crossbreeds.

When the puppies are three days old, before they open their eyes, you go in there and hold them and stroke them from the head to the tail. Then we start working with them when they're five to six weeks old, young pups. Over a period of time, after they're culled out, they grow and get better and better and they become members of a team. You get six to seven years of good hunting out of them.

The hounds develop their own leader, and you stay with them so much they become almost like humans. Over the years, the hounds get to know the driver and respond instantly to a call. They'll come straight to you when you pop the whip or blow the horn.

At certain times of the year, we only go after the buck deer, and other times of the year, we hunt the doe deer. And how the horses and dogs can distinguish that is a mystery. But it's part of the training they get. They're up against some smart deer; a deer's got a keen ear;

they can hear you from a half mile away. That's just one of the aspects of training your dogs and horses.

My work as a deer driver at the Middleton Hunt Club and at fox "drag hunts" with the Middleton Place Houses have been wonderful experiences and I hope to continue for years to come.

The forty-member Middleton Hunt Club is located at the Middleton Gardens complex near the banks of the Ashley River north of Charleston. The club uses nine thousand acres of land owned by Middleton and Millbrook plantations and is one of the oldest such clubs in America. During the deer hunting season, starting August 15 and lasting until January 1, the club conducts around thirty hunts, usually on Saturdays and holidays.

The late Edward Lowndes was the club's hunt master for six years and deer driver for twenty-two years, starting in the 1970s. His brother, Henry Lowndes, continued the family tradition in the role of hunt master for twenty-four years until he retired in 2007; he is now a deer driver with the club.

Middleton has a separate fox hunting club—the Middleton Place Hounds—but there are no foxes involved. "Bill Green is the fox," Henry Lowndes says with a smile. "He goes out front and drags the scented dragon on a long rope behind his horse. We give him a few minutes' head start then loose our hounds on his trail. It's a lot of fun, with the horses and the dogs and the camaraderie of members."

Members atop their horses wear white and buff britches on a hunt, along with scarlet and black coats, including the noted "pink" coat named for the British tailor-designer. After the hunt, the rider participants join together at a breakfast in front of the eighteenth-century Middleton Place House, partially rebuilt after the Civil War.

Bill Green's Take on Venison

"I love venison," Bill Green told me during our interview at St. Helena Island. "It's just about all the meat I eat, except for wild hogs on occasion. It's one of the best meats you can eat."

"I especially like the hams and shoulders, which are lean and nutritious, mostly muscle. They've got to be cooked just right, though, baked or roasted in the oven. And you have to use something like canola oil when you're cooking the meat, and a lot of it.

"You bake a venison ham at 300 to 350 degrees three and a half hours. Afterward, uncover it and when it cools off, you got to baste it with a lot of seasoning. Then you have some good eating."

Brunswick Roast Leg of Venison

Attributed to Mrs. L. L. Bright of Brunswick, Georgia, this recipe appeared in Grace Hartley's *Southern Cook Book* published in 1988. Her recipe calls for the use of lard in preparing the meat for roasting, but present-day cooks may want to substitute a shortening such as Crisco.

The tester of this recipe, Joe Anderson of Statesboro, Georgia, tried it using lard and found it to be very good. He tried it again adding bay leaves and muscadine wine with bell peppers, celery, carrots, and onions and found the roast venison to be greatly improved.

This recipe adaptation yields 4 to 6 servings.

- 1 4-pound venison leg
- 6 thin slices salt pork
- ⅛ teaspoon thyme
- 2 bay leaves
- Salt
- 2 cups dry white wine
- 2 carrots, scraped and sliced
- 6 peppercorns
- 2 onions, peeled and sliced
- ¼ cup light cream

Trim the excess fat from the venison leg. Slash gashes in the meat and rub in the lard with salt pork slivers. Place in a deep dish and add the seasonings, wine, and vegetables. Let stand in the refrigerator 1 to 2 days, turning the meat several times.

Preheat the oven to 300°F. Remove the meat from the marinade, drain, and dry. Place the meat in open roasting pan. Strain the marinade and reserve.

Roast the meat uncovered for 1 hour; raise temperature to 450°F and bake 15 minutes longer. Remove the meat to heated platter; keep hot. Strain the pan juices into marinade, skimming any fat. Pat the vegetables dry and place them around the roast.

Simmer the marinade until about three quarters of liquid remains. Add the cream, season to taste, and reheat, but do not boil. Serve the sauce hot with the meat.

Pan-Fried Venison

Pee Dee Pan-fried Venison

Here is another outstanding recipe from S. Pressly Coker III of Hartsville, South Carolina, who hunts deer in the Pee Dee River area of Eastern South Carolina. This recipe was used also on moose in Canada.

- 2 pounds venison
- 2 cups celery, diced
- Seasoned flour (see directions)
- 1 1/2 cups lard or vegetable oil substitute
- 3 medium onions, sliced or diced
- Garlic to taste
- 1 tablespoon Worcestershire sauce
- Dash Tabasco sauce
- 2 cups diced tomatoes
- 1 red sweet pepper, diced
- Salt and pepper, to taste
- 2 cups beef broth

Preheat oven to 325°F.

Cut and trim venison; cover with slightly salted water and soak overnight in the refrigerator to remove blood. Change the water frequently until clear. Dry pieces on

HUNTING DEER ON JOHNS ISLAND

Charles Seabrook of Atlanta, a native of Johns Island, South Carolina, describes his experiences hunting deer as a young man on Johns Island near Charleston:

We had a community way of hunting deer at Johns Island when I was growing up there in the 1950s. We'd go out on some of those hammock islands, they called them. We'd post people on the perimeter around the hammocks and somebody would go in the interior there and run the deer out.

That was just our community's doing—not a hunting club. 'Course during the '50s and '60s, we did not have all the deer we have now. At that time, deer were pretty scarce. Mainly because of the screwworms. They were eventually eradicated by irradiating the screwworm flies, making them sterile and releasing the sterile flies from airplanes over infested areas.

Now Johns Island is flooded with deer. Not too long ago my brother set out hundreds of dollars worth of photina red tip plants, for a hedge. The next day, they were all gone; the deer had eaten every last one of 'em.

a paper towel. Mix sufficient seasoned flour to your own taste (salt, pepper, paprika, and your favorite herbs). Depending on my mood, I use a pinch of dry thyme and a little crushed chili pepper or rosemary. Coat the pieces well.

Heat the canola oil or bacon fat in large frying pan over medium-high heat and brown both sides of the venison. Remove from the pan and deglaze the pan with the onions, garlic to taste, celery, Worcestershire, a touch of Tabasco, tomatoes, and red pepper. Season with salt and pepper to taste.

Layer the browned venison in a buttered casserole dish and cover with the fried onion mixture. Add the beef broth to cover. Bake for 1 ½ hours or until tender.

Serve on pasta, rice, or mashed potatoes. Serve with veggies of your choice and have your favorite wine on hand.

Small Game

Hunting Possums and 'Coons in Tattnall County

Here, in his own words, eighty-five-year-old Rev. James E. Rich of Brunswick, Georgia, describes a small game hunt during his youth in Southeast Georgia:

I'll never forget going on a winter hunting trip in the Yoemans section of Tattnall County, Georgia, in the 1930s. I was right young, around twelve years old, and it was my first such hunt. My brothers and the others were reluctant at first to allow me to accompany them. But after much pleading, and with a promise that I would carry all the game caught, they said ok.

So off we went into the dark Ohoopee Swamp. The sun was going down. I'd never seen so many vines, stumps, and bogs, plus mud holes and little branches to cross. I had a time just trying to keep up with the crowd.

About first dark, the dogs treed, and right off we caught two big 'possums. Into my croaker sack they went.

About midnight, getting very cold and tired, we set fire to a choice fat stump, lay down, and went to sleep. I used the 'possums and sack for a heading. Every few minutes, I would turn from side to side to keep warm. Sometime later, we all got up and started out again.

At daybreak, our little female blue tick dog treed a coon up in a hollowed-out tree on the riverbank. The fellows goosed the coon out of the hollow and he locked jaws with our blue dog. They fought it out until both wound up in the river. The other dogs chimed in on the river battle, but the coon almost drowned the dogs and the coon headed for the riverbank. A bulldog was waiting there that knew how to kill coons. He was turned loose. In a few minutes the coon was dead. Into my bag went the dead coon.

> ### CAPTURING A POSSUM
> *Old Blue treed, I went to see.*
> *There sat the 'possum on a 'simmon tree.*
> *He grinned at me, I looked at him.*
> *I shook him out, Blue took him in.*
> *I took him home and baked him brown.*
> *Placed them taters all around.*
> —FOLKLORIST A. P. HUDSON

We all walked home tired, hungry, and sleepy, and I was even more tired, having to carry those two live 'possums and the dead coon in my croaker sack.

But several days later, after penning up one of the 'possums and feeding him corn to get him cleaned out, our family got to enjoy a delicious 'possum supper. Of course we first parboiled him, following which we roasted him over fireplace coals, along with a bunch of sweet potatoes. That was mighty fine eatin'. We gave the coon meat and the other 'possums to friends, who also enjoyed some real home cooking.

Roast Gopher: "Tastier than Chicken"

Rev. Rich gave me another small-game account—a gopher hunt—also in Tattnall County, Georgia, northwest of Savannah:

Hunting gophers was part of our family's survival ritual (and fun) in the 1930s. During those Depression years, rabbits, squirrels, birds, fish, and gophers were choice morsels that helped keep us alive. In particular we loved to eat gopher meat; it was outstanding. In fact, back then, I favored gopher meat cooked in rice more than chicken.

Rev. James E. Rich (Photo courtesy of Rev. Rich.)

We often took a sack or the wagon out to the "Sand Hill" near the Ohoopee River to bring back a bunch of the critters that would end up later on our eating table.

We could catch gophers in many ways. The easiest was to grab them when we saw them crawling in the woods or crossing a road. The second was to use a hook mounted on a long pole to snag them as they were going into their hole and then drag them out.

If he was a big one, we often used a shovel to dig him out of his crooked tunnel. We also fixed traps at the mouth of their holes, burying a large can that we covered over with twigs. Thus when the gopher started to crawl into his hole, he would fall into the bucket and couldn't climb out. Into our sack he would go.

But gopher hunting could be very dangerous. Their holes were often used by rattlesnakes in the winter to raise their young.

Coon Stewed in Red Wine

Here's how Ben Moise turns coon meat into a delicacy:

I used this recipe numerous times for the annual wild game supper we used to have at Charleston's Variety Store Restaurant. It always happened before the fall hunting season began to give everybody a reason to clean out their freezers.

Since I never was a very good shot, I never had much surplus to draw from, so I had to go searching. There were always enough fat coons behind Bushy Peak's restaurant over near Folly Beach.

I cooked this stew in a large black iron pot, called a potjie, which I had brought back from one of my South African safaris. One year I used the meat from one beaver and one coon. The crowd loved it and they were mopping the bottom of the pot with their corn bread.

Here are the directions for cooking raccoons:

Fry out ½ pound of bacon in a large frying pan until browned, then remove the bacon from the grease and drain.

Bone out all the meat from two good-size coons and cut into roughly 1-inch pieces. Bring the bacon fat up to a good heat (moving but not smoking). Brown the coon meat in the fat a little at a time and drain. Be sure to turn the meat to brown on all sides.

Pour all the bacon grease out of the pan and bring back up to medium heat and then pour in around half a bottle of a good red wine, bring up to heat, and scrape up any of the browned bits stuck to the bottom of the pan. Whisk into this one good tablespoon of tomato paste. Cook for around 4 minutes and then pour into a large pot.

Crush the fried bacon into small bits and add to the pot along with the coon meat. Add around 3 cans of beef bouillon, a two-finger pinch of ground thyme, 1 tablespoon of sugar, 4 cloves of finely minced garlic, 3 bay leaves, ½ teaspoon of black pepper, and ½ teaspoon kosher salt. Cook just at the bubble with the lid on and stirring often for around 3 hours.

Using a stout fork, mash together a half stick of butter cut into ½-inch pieces with ½ a cup of flour until it

> ## BARTRAM FOUND THE LOWCOUNTRY A WILDLIFE TREASURE TROVE
>
> Indians called William Bartram Pug-Puggy, or "flower hunter." Benjamin Franklin fondly referred to him as "my dear son." George Washington, John Adams, and Thomas Jefferson subscribed to his pioneer book describing his travels in the Carolinas, Georgia, and other areas of the South…
>
> John Fothergill of London learned of the American's work. A wealthy physician who cultivated exotic plants on his estate at Upton in Essex, Fothergill was eager for rare specimens from America. So he agreed to pay Bartram's expenses. [Bartram] left Philadelphia for Carolina early in 1772, aboard the ship Charleston-Packet. During four years in southeastern North America, Bartram…sent a stream of seeds, specimens, and drawings to England.… Both of the Carolinas, said Bartram, were awesome and sublime.…
>
> As a result of Bartram's passion, today we can view the flora and fauna of Carolina [and Georgia] as they appeared more than 200 years ago.
>
> —WEBB GARRISON
> CAROLINA TALES

forms a paste and roll into a cylinder and chill. Drain off several cups of the stew broth in a bowl and cut small pieces of the butter-flour paste into it and whisk until it dissolves. Pour back into the stew pot and stir in and cook for around one half an hour longer. Add to the stew 2 cans of drained button mushrooms and 2 cans of drained pearl onions and cook for around 10 minutes longer. If during the cooking process the stew broth gets a little low, stir some more bouillon into the pot. Taste for salt and serve over a plate of rice.

A Lowcountry Wild Hog Hunt

The following is condensed from a feature written by my friend, South Carolina's Dan Huntley. It is used by permission of the author:

In the grainy half-light of dawn, Craig Sasser paddled his duck boat silently up a winding tidal creek deep in South Carolina's Lowcountry.

A wildlife biologist and Lowcountry native, Sasser was leading nine people on a wild hog hunt. Each year, he kills a wild hog to use in a barbecue event at his island hunting cabin fifteen miles northeast of Georgetown, South Carolina.

We approached Sasser's Island, which is surrounded by a swamp grove of knobby-kneed cypress and tupelo gum trees. The Sasser family owns about six hundred surrounding acres—mostly wetlands with about one hundred acres of uplands. The land was part of a 1730 land grant from the King of England. It was later at the heart of the rice-growing aristocracy that flourished in this region before the Civil War. Remnants of the old rice dikes still exist here.

"The Vanderbilts imported Russian wild boars in the early 1900s for their hunting preserve," he said. "During Hurricane Hugo in 1989, I think a good many were washed down the river. We started seeing them among the old rice fields."…On the island [tiptoeing along a narrow boardwalk] Sasser moved with the stealth of an assassin. The wild hogs continued rooting up the black earth and snorting, but they remained partially hidden in the bush. Sasser braced himself against an oak, waiting for one to step out for a clean kill shot.

After more than a minute with his finger on the trigger [of his .280 caliber rifle], Sasser squeezed off the shot. In front of us what had been a snarling wild hog lay still on the ground. Other hogs continued to mill about, rooting in the damp earth and clicking their ivory tusks like pairs of dice. They were oblivious to the downed 185-pound sow or even the approaching hunter. Amazingly quick and thick-shouldered, the hogs finally trotted to the swamp out of sight into the waist-high, wheat-colored grass.

"Whooooo! That's about as easy as it gets out here," Sasser said as he leaned his rifle up against a tree and examined the hog. Steam began to rise from the hog's black-bristled back.

"We could just as easily been out here in the mud all day and not seen them. We're lucky… Let's get this hog ready for the pit."

Wild Boar: "Free-Range Organic Pork"

The Coxe family in Darlington County, South Carolina, has a heritage of hunting, going back at least five generations.

"Our family owns a lot of land here on the Pee Dee River," Campbell Coxe told me when I visited with him in 2008.

"It was mostly farmland, much of which was converted to timber in the 1800s. We now run a commercial hunting lodge. It's almost a year-round venture, now that we have turkey seasons.

"We bring in sportsmen from the entire United States, deer hunting, turkey hunting, and wild boar hunting. We put our guests up at our lodge and serve them food grown here on the farm, including a lot of rice, chicken bogs and the like, fish stews, and venison.

"And wild boars. We call that 'free-range organic pork.' Actually, wild boar meat is good. Like anything else that you eat, it's the handling and preparation of the meat and the sauce [that is necessary]. That doesn't hurt."

Campbell told me that wild boar meat is "real lean. No fat. The trick is to cook the whole hog in the pit slow and low. You have to cook it that way since they have almost no fat in the skin. Usually you have to cook it eight to ten hours. Cooking it outdoors makes it different from cooking it inside. And with the whole hog, you get so many good parts."

The Joys of Fishing

Jennings Chestnut's Big Fish Fry

On my 2008 research trip into the South Carolina Lowcountry, I visited with Jennings Chestnut, a great five-string banjo player who also builds beautiful mandolins and operates a music store on Main Street in Conway, South Carolina. Jennings, I soon learned, is also one of the state's freshwater fishermen supreme. He fishes all the river systems in the Pee Dee area of eastern South Carolina, embracing the Little Pee Dee River, the Waccamaw River, the Black River, and

Jennings Chestnut is one of eastern South Carolina's top freshwater fishermen, with largemouth bass being his specialty. (Photo by the author.)

of course the Great Pee Dee. He favors fishing for largemouth bass, which are tasty and plentiful.

Every summer, Jennings stages a well-attended Blue Grass Music Festival underneath Conway's Waccamaw River Bridge and on the Sunday afterward, he puts on a Sunday fish fry for festival volunteers at his home out in the country.

"That first time, I knew I could get out some of my largemouth bass fillets from the freezer," Chestnut said. "Then I called my friend Gary Payne down at Johns Island. He's also a five-string banjo player like I am. Gary shrimps during the short shrimping season from September through December. So Gary said he would be happy to bring the shrimp and fix us up a Frogmore Stew. So every year, along with his shrimp, Gary brings along his big pot and strainer and we have us quite a feast."

Jennings sets up an eight-foot-long table in his yard and covers it with a bed sheet. Then, in addition to the bass fillets, he and Gary spread out the Frogmore Stew—shrimp and onions, sausage and corn cobbettes— right on the bed sheet.

"We string that on both sides of the table along with the bass," Jennings said, "and people go there with tongs and pick out what they want to put on their plates."

Chestnut and his wife, Willi, also like to fry fish right at the

Fried fish is Wilburn Taft's favorite dish. Here he holds up some freshly fried catfish from the family fish pond in Atkinson County, Georgia, while his wife, Doris, looks on with a smile. (Photo courtesy of Dub Taft.)

river right after a nice catch. "It's best to fry your fish as soon as possible after you catch them," Jennings says, "and you won't find a finer or tastier fish than a largemouth bass."

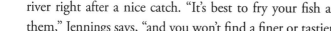

Alligators lived in the Okefenokee Swamp and basked along the Altamaha River long before any humans had seen the area, let alone named the region Georgia. America's largest reptiles inhabited the coastal marshes and inland waterways as they do today, tracking the fresh waters through the ages…in response to rising or falling sea levels.

—The Spirit of Southeast Georgia

Fishing Choctahatchee Creek

By Jimmy Carter

As a boy growing up in Archery, Georgia, I worked fields that drained into Choctahatchee (or as we called it, Chock-li-hatchet) Creek. Choctahatchee Creek joins Kinehafoonee Creek, which merges with Muckalee Creek and then flows into the Flint River just above Albany.

The Choctahatchee was where I fished [as a young man]. It was where I learned about the out-of-doors, where I learned to explore and where I learned how not to get lost.

It's where my playmates and I, and occasionally my father, had many hours and days together. We had an immersion in the natural world that has marked my whole existence. The Choctahatchee drainage is really the origin of my life. I still feel more at home and more in a natural element and closer to God when I'm out in the woods by myself, or just with Rosalyn, than at any other time.

Anyone who wants to experience the way Georgia was when God made it or the way it was when it was first settled by white people can go to the upper parts of the Flint River and see how beautiful it is. It is breathtaking…And the wildlife that exists in that river corridor— otter, fox, muskrat, beaver, bobcat—you cannot describe it. It is a treasure that is appreciated by an increasing number of people as the generations pass…You hope and pray that it will be there a thousand years in the future, still just as beautiful and undisturbed.

—From the preface to *The Flint River*,
A Recreational Guidebook to the Flint River & Environs.
Used with permission from Fred Brown & Sherri M.O. Smith,
publishers of CI Publishing, Atlanta.

The Fish That Got Away

I had fun interviewing oysterman Franklin "Snake Man" Smalls at Murrells Inlet, South Carolina. Here's an interesting fishing story Snake Man told me:

When was it, Wednesday morning? Yeah, Wednesday morning. I went to my boss man's house [Bill Chandler at Murrells Inlet] and had my cup of coffee Miz Anne fixes for me every mornin'. So I went outside and worked for a while on Mister Bill's truck bed.

Later on the tide was coming in and the boss said, "Snake, you can go fishin' for a couple of hours till the tide falls." That made me mighty happy. I'd wanted to go fishin' so bad that day, my hands wuz tremblin'.

As I went down to the dock, I jumped in my little canoe and fixed my bait on my [plastic] grubs. I've got a special place [to fish] in the saltwater inlet, so going through this little slue, I was twistin' my little rod, to swish my grubs.

Franklin "Snake Man" Smalls loves to tell stories about his fishing exploits in the marshes near Murrells Inlet, South Carolina. (Photo by the author.)

I looked back and the rod tippled and then doubled back. I said, "Oh God, this is an old spot tail." I decided I had to pull him in and clean him off. I just knew he was a spot tail bass. But this fish stayed down a long time and I kept fightin' him, tryin' to pull him in.

When I got where I could see that fish, it was a winter trout! So help me God. He was the biggest winter trout I've seen in that inlet in five years. I knew he would make Mister Bill's [earlier catch] look like a baby [fish].

Well, when I almost got that trout in, he ran into the tip of the propeller, fightin' so hard. Then he popped my line and my cabin line and everything and disappeared.

He was a big one, must'a been twenty-five inches [long]. That's the honest God-in-heaven truth.

Walkin' back, I went up the hill to Mister Bill's house with my rod in my hand and all I kept sayin' was, "Oh Lord—Ooooh Lord. The big fish always get away."

I've spent many a good hour on this [Ogeechee] river; there's nothing better a man can do. And I'll tell you one thing: The fish out of the Ogeechee River are the best eating fish anywhere because the water is pure enough to drink. You can cook up fish from another river, and I'll pick out the ones from the Ogeechee every time; they just taste better.

—*George Altman*
The Ogeechee

CHAPTER 20

Favorite Lowcountry Desserts

The Southerner's sweet tooth reached its apotheosis in Charleston and Savannah in the seventeenth and eighteenth centuries. Not only did the residents have access to abundant sugar but they were exposed to exotic fruits like bananas and coconuts.

—*Chef Marvin Woods*
The New Low-Country Cooking

Even in the days of the Depression, our family always had pies, pies, pies. Our mother baked them daily—fruit pies when fruit was in season or dried fruit pies or sweet potato custards and pies from the giant potato banks in winter."

Thus wrote Juanita C. Kibler in *Dutch Fork Cookery*, her touching culinary history of the Dutch Fork area northwest of Charleston. The area was settled in the early years of the nineteenth century by hundreds of immigrants from southern Germany.

"When fruit and sweet potatoes were out," Mrs. Kibler wrote, "then rice puddings, bread puddings, and egg custards would come in to take their place." Cooking schedules in that era linked closely to the calendar, "as surely as the temperature changes or the color of the countryside."

In Dutch Fork homes, as in many similar dwellings across the Lowcountry, "some form of desserts was present at every dinner and supper," she wrote. "Even the family of humble means had its cakes and pies at each meal."

Pies

Muscadine Hull Pie: Passing of the Torch

Liz Hood shows off muscadine hull pie, now a Pryor Family Reunion tradition. (Photo by the author.)

Muscadine hull pie is a great traditional dessert in middle and south Georgia, where the dark and delicious muscadine grapes and their fatter, sweeter cousins, the scuppernongs, flourish on thousands of farm arbors or wild in the woods. I fondly remember the muscadine grape arbor at our South Carolina hill country farm, where we grabbed clusters of the grapes, gobbling down each grape and spitting out the tough skin.

The muscadine hull pie tradition continues at the Pryor Family Reunion on the first Sunday in October. It began October 4, 1903, to celebrate Penelope Tyson and Shepherd "Shep" Green Pryor's golden wedding anniversary. Except for a few war years, the reunion has been held ever since—and is one of the country's longest-running family reunions.

In recent decades, Ruth Young Pryor's muscadine hull pie was a much anticipated reunion dessert favorite. "After her death," stated Mrs. Liz Hood, a Pryor descendant on her mother's side, "her daughters, granddaughters, my sister, and I congregated to make a batch of muscadine hull pies using Aunt Ruth's traditional recipe. We took them to the 2008 reunion in Leslie, Georgia. All turned out edible, and not a slice was left uneaten.

"The fact that this task was moving on to another generation was not lost on any of us," said Mrs. Hood, a Statesboro, Georgia, native who currently resides in Cartersville, Georgia. "And now we consider it to be an ongoing family tradition that will continue, we hope, for many decades to come."

Here follows the recipe that came from the kitchen of the late Ruth Young Pryor.

Pryor Family Muscadine Hull Pie

- 3 cups muscadine grapes
- 2 tablespoons lemon juice or juice of ½ lemon
- ½ teaspoon grated lemon rind
- ¾ cup granulated sugar
- 2 tablespoons cornstarch
- ¼ teaspoon salt

Preheat the oven to 400°F.

Slip the hulls from the grapes. Put the hulls and pulp in separate pots and bring to a boil. Press the pulp through a sieve to remove the seeds. Add the pulp to the hulls with lemon juice and rind.

Using a saucepan, cook the mixture on low heat until the hulls are tender, about 30 minutes, stirring often. Add hot water if mixture gets too thick.

Mix together the sugar, cornstarch, and salt. Stir into pulp/rind mixture, place the pie mixture into the 9-inch lower pie crust, and cover with latticework or a solid crust. Cut slits if top is solid, to keep the filling from boiling over in the oven. In the preheated 400°F oven, bake the pie fifteen minutes, and then at 375°F for 45 minutes, until the crust becomes light brown. Serve while hot.

Note: For instructions on making pie crust, please check Hoppin John's Grape Pie recipe on pages 300–301.

Southern Pecan Pie

Another traditional pie well loved across the Lowcountry and the South is loaded with the South's ever-lovin' pecans.

For instance, every Thanksgiving and Christmas, pecan pie is the dessert for Ben and Anne Moise in their Charleston, South Carolina, home.

This recipe, named for Anne's grandmother, Margaret Pierce Miller, "is the only way to cook pecan pie," Anne says, "because it's just delicious, not gooey or teeth fuzzing." She recalled that when Grandmother Miller visited them in the Holy City, "she always liked to get in the kitchen and cook something special. I loved it when she let me help—which she always did."

Grandma Miller's Pecan Pie

- 1 ⅔ cups sugar
- 1 cup hot water
- 1 tablespoon brown vinegar
- ½ cup butter
- 4 eggs, beaten
- 1 heaping cup chopped pecans
- Additional whole pecans for the top of the pie

Combine the sugar, water, and vinegar and bring to a boil while stirring constantly. This will take some time. Stir until the mixture is thick and sticky enough to form a thread.

Keep stirring and remove from the heat. Add the butter. Keep stirring. Slowly pour the beaten eggs into the mixture while constantly stirring. Then mix in the pecans and pour into a thin pie crust and bake until done. Use whole pecans on top as an extra delicious bonus.

PIES WITH "KIVERS" AND PIES WITHOUT

My longtime Atlanta neighbor Arnold Sego recalled that when he was around ten years old, he got a kick out of lunchtime visits with his grandfather, James Asbury Sego, during which the elder Sego would recite this ditty:

There's pies with kivers,
And pies without kivers,
Just reach and take 'taters;
There's 'maters over there.

Grandpa Sego died in the mid-30s, but Arnold has kept the verse alive, having taught it to his grandson, who likes to recite it at Christmas get-togethers. Arnold plans to copyright the verse but gave me a one-time permission to use it here.

Sweet Potato Pie

As Southern food historian John Egerton pointed out, sweet potatoes and yams had an interesting traveling history before they reached these shores. From Central and South America to Europe, they returned to the Americas in the 1600s with the Spaniards. In his pioneering cookbook, *Southern Food*, John ventured to say that it's possible the sweet potato pie was a delicacy in England even before that.

Today, sweet potato pies, custards, soufflés, and the like have long become essential

Southern mainstays, particularly at Christmas and Thanksgiving. Some cooks add pecans to give the traditional pie an even greater pizzazz.

The following adapted recipe comes from *The New South Carolina Cookbook*, brought out in a splendid edition by the University of South Carolina Press. The original 1953 *South Carolina Cookbook* is a prized part of my wife' and my cookbook collection, a pioneering publication of the South Carolina Council of Farm Women. Actually, the book contains three separate sweet potato pie recipes, but I chose the following to adapt.

South Carolina Sweet Potato Pie

The tester of this recipe, Linda Waugh, was thrilled with it: The pie "turned out perfect in texture, creamy smooth pumpkin color with the specks of spices throughout…I will place it in my album of 'Choice Recipes.'"

- 2 ¼ cups mashed sweet potatoes
- ½ cup margarine or butter
- 1 ½ cups sugar
- 1 tablespoon all-purpose flour
- ½ teaspoon salt
- ½ teaspoon ground ginger
- ½ teaspoon cinnamon
- ½ teaspoon ground nutmeg
- ¼ teaspoon ground cloves
- 2 eggs, beaten
- 2 5-ounce cans evaporated milk
- ⅔ cup whole milk
- 2 9-inch unbaked pie shells

Preheat the oven to 425°F.

In large mixing bowl, combine the sweet potatoes and margarine or butter. Mix until blended. Add the sugar, flour, salt, and spices to the batter. Beat until well blended. Add the eggs and milks. Beat until the mixture is smooth.

Divide the mixture evenly between pie shells. Bake for 10 minutes. Reduce heat to 300°F and bake for about 50 minutes more or until filling is firm. Cool before slicing.

Grape Pie

This is a Lowcountry classic, although something of an unknown dessert, according to my friend and noted author John Martin "Hoppin' John" Taylor, who calls this his favorite pie.

Vitas rotundifolia, or native American muscadines (the purple kind that climb trees and trellises all across the Deep South), and the scuppernong, a muscadine subspecies that boasts fatter, plum-size, amber-colored, sweeter grapes, are perfect candidates for this pie. I gather gallons of muscadines on my arbor at Euharlee every fall, plus additional gallons from my scuppernong vine that crawls down my property fence line. So this recipe is right down my alley!

I'm grateful to John Martin for giving me his blessing to adapt this recipe, which comes from his book, *Hoppin John's Low Country Cooking*. He favors a pie crust made with lard and urges that cooks avoid touching the pie dough with their hands, which he says will give the dough a tougher consistency.

Here is John Martin's website, hoppinjohns.com, where he lists his cookbooks, and has stone-ground corn products available.

Hoppin John's Grape Pie

CRUST INGREDIENTS

- 4 cups unbleached all-purpose flour
- 1 tablespoon sugar
- Pinch salt
- ½ cup water, plus ice cubes
- ⅔ cup chilled lard or any combination chilled lard, shortening, and butter

FILLING INGREDIENTS

- 4 ½ cups muscadine, scuppernong, or Concord grapes
- ¾ cup sugar
- ½ tablespoon rice flour

- Reserved pastry dough and filling
- Whole milk or half-and-half
- Sugar

Sift the flour with the sugar and salt in a large mixing bowl. Add a few ice cubes to the measured water and set aside. Cut the lard into the flour with a large fork or two knives until the mixture resembles small peas. Avoid hand-touching of the dough, and make sure the bowl remains stable to avoid its shifting around.

Using a large, metal slotted spoon, deftly scoop up large spoonfuls of the mixture from the bottom of the bowl, while sprinkling cold water into the mixture in small increments. Halt the water sprinkling quickly if you feel the dough will hold together without more water. At this point, seize the entire mass of dough in your hands into a ball. If the pie filling is ready, wrap the dough in plastic and put it in the freezer for 10 minutes. If the pie filling is not finished, put the wrapped dough into the refrigerator to chill while you prepare the fruit.

For the filling, pulp the grapes by squeezing them over a nonreactive pot. Reserve the skins. Cook the pulp at medium heat for 5 minutes, to loosen the seeds. Press the pulp through a colander to remove the seeds. Combine the pulp with the skins, sugar, and rice flour. Sweet grapes such as Concords may require flavoring with a small amount of citrus peel and juice. Scuppernong skins have a tartness on their own.

Preheat the oven to 450°F. Remove the pastry dough from the freezer or refrigerator and place on a lightly floured surface. Avoid touching it with your hands. Roll it out to a 1/8-inch thickness.

Place a 9-inch pie plate on top of the dough, and with a blunt knife, cut around the dough so that a plate-size area is marked off as one piece. Remove the pie plate. Take a rolling pin and from one edge of the large piece of dough, gently roll it up off the surface onto the pin. Take the dough on the pin and gently allow it to roll off the pin onto the pie plate, all the while avoiding touching it with your hands. Press it lightly on the plate, allowing any excess dough to hang over the sides. Fill with the fruit.

Cut the remaining dough into long strips and gently form a lattice top on the pie. Run a sharp knife blade around the ie, trimming off excess dough. Brush the pie crust top lightly with milk or half-and-half, then crimp the pie crust edge with a large fork. Sprinkle the pie lightly with a small amount of sugar.

Place the pie in the middle of the oven and bake for 10 minutes or until the crust has a rich golden brown color all over, certainly enough to avoid a soggy crust. The pie should be allowed to reach a lukewarm temperature before serving, Avoid using any cream since it would overshadow the distinctive grape flavor.

Cobblers

Mrs. Juanita Kibler's descriptions of cobblers from South Carolina's German community kitchens in earlier years make for scrumptious reading, in particular her narratives about blackberry, peach, and apple cobblers.

"I can see one now coming from the [giant outdoor] oven oozing dark, rich blackberry juice," she wrote. "Strawberry pies in the late spring. Peach and huckleberry pies in the late summer."

Peach Cobbler

Georgia and South Carolina are known for their outstanding peaches, and nowhere are fresh peaches put to better use than in peach cobblers.

Even though in past years Georgia has been called the "Peach State," South Carolina's Piedmont and Midlands areas have moved ahead to become the South's primary peach producer, indeed second only to California in the United States.

This particular cobbler recipe is adapted from one of my friend Nathalie Dupree's earlier cookbooks, *New Southern Cooking*, and, as she claims, "This is the best peach dessert to be found."

This recipe's tester, Brenda Jarman of Atlanta, shared the cobbler with her co-workers and received rave reviews. This recipe serves 6 to 8.

Charleston Peach Cobbler

- ½ cup butter
- 1 cup all-purpose flour (soft wheat)
- 1 ½ teaspoons baking powder
- ½ teaspoon salt
- 1 cup sugar
- 1 cup whole milk
- 2 ½ cups peaches, peeled and sliced, with juices reserved

Preheat the oven to 350°F.

Place the butter in a 9 x 13-inch serving dish and put in the oven to melt. Mix together the flour, baking powder, and salt in a bowl and stir in the sugar and milk for the batter.

Remove the hot dish with the melted butter from the oven and pour in the batter.

Spoon the peaches and the juices evenly over the batter.

Place the dish back in the oven and bake until the batter has turned brown and has risen up and around the fruit, about 30 minutes.

Serve warm with cream or ice cream.

Fig Cobbler

Bountiful fig trees adorn practically all the older farm home spreads across the Deep South and Lowcountry. At my country place at Euharlee in Bartow County, Georgia, I'm proud of my young Brown Turkey Fig bush, which is just a few steps from my front porch.

I first got turned on to figs when I tasted fig preserves made by my late sisters-in-law, Jeanette Taylor Dabney of Rock Hill, South Carolina, and Lib Jones Dabney of Jackson, South Carolina. As the old saying goes, "When I took that first taste, I thought I had died and gone to heaven!"

Carol's Fig Cobbler

When I received this recipe for fig cobbler, it gave me goose bumps just imagining a hot fig cobbler on our dining room table topped with a scoop of vanilla ice cream. Carol Cliatt Moore, of Leslie, Georgia, developed the original recipe. "The Celeste fig tree was always one of Mama's greatest treasures," Carol said, "and it was an honor to be invited to pick the fat figs from her tree. She cherished picking, cooking, eating, and sharing the figs."

- 35 fresh Celeste figs, peeled
- ½ cup granulated sugar
- ⅓ stick margarine, cut in small pieces
- 3 teaspoons lemon juice
- ¼ teaspoon cinnamon
- ¼ teaspoon mace
- Lemon zest to taste

Preheat the oven to 300°F.

Place the peeled figs in casserole dish sprayed with cooking oil spray. Mix the remaining ingredients and sprinkle on top of the figs.

Place the strips of pastry over the mixture to form a lattice work. Bake 35 to 45 minutes until the pastry is brown, but begin checking after 25 minutes. Serve warm with vanilla ice cream.

Mrs. Joyce Hosford's fig preserves are so good that her grandson, Charleston chef Robert Carter, uses her recipe in his four-star Peninsula Grill. (Photo courtesy Robert Carter.)

Fig Preserves

While we're on the subject of figs, how can we go further without a good recipe for fig preserves? Here it is, thanks to one of Charleston's supreme chefs, Robert Carter, executive chef-partner of the four-star Peninsula Grill Restaurant. Carter proudly serves fig preserves from a recipe given to him by his grandmother, Joyce Summers Hosford, of Hosford, Florida.

"Grandmother is a pistol," Carter says, "and a great cook. She is the family matriarch. Every year, she smokes twelve to twenty turkeys for the holidays and still makes *all* desserts for family get-togethers."

Here is Mrs. Hosford's fig preserves recipe in her own words:

Grandmother Hosford's Fig Preserves

- 8 cups figs
- 4 to 6 cups sugar
- 1 lemon, thinly sliced

The canning process is very important so have the proper tools for canning before you start. Select firm, sound fruit, cut off the stems, and do not peel. Clean and wash the figs thoroughly. In layers, sprinkle the sugar over the figs, then let the figs stand overnight in the refrigerator.

The next morning, take out and add water to the figs (not too much water, just enough to aid in the syrup production), then place on low heat until boiling point is reached; add lemon slices.

Continue to boil until the syrup reaches a desired thickness; remember you don't want the syrup too thick.

Once it reaches the desired thickness, I remove most of the lemon slices before packing the figs and syrup into hot jars.

Be sure to use a proper canning process to safely seal your preserves.

For canning the preserves, leave ⅛ inch of head space. Seal the jars, then let stand until the lids pop, signifying the completion of the sealing process. Do not touch until this has happened. Adjust your boiling bath to account for altitude if needed.

Cakes

Then, in the late fall, came the puddings, grape pies, and cakes.

—*Juanita Kibler*

At the turn of the nineteenth century, coconuts and cane sugar were put on rafts at Charleston and floated upriver on the Santee/Congaree Rivers to Granby, where they were purchased by German immigrant farmers coming to market with their produce.

It was no wonder that two decades later the Germans of Saxe Goth and Dutch Fork were reputed to have "more varieties of cakes than any other nationalities in the country." These included "roll cakes" (Fastnacht Kuche), which were opened up and packed with preserves, molasses, or honey.

A similar dessert evolution occurred among housewives in Georgia's Lowcountry interior. Eighty-seven-year-old Doris Taft of Atkinson County in deep Southeast Georgia cooks a pecan cake highly sought after by members of her family and neighbors. During the Korean War, one of the Taft relatives stationed overseas wrote to say he missed pecan cake so badly, would she please ship him one, which she promptly did. Another fan of the pecan cake is her son Dub, who bakes the cake himself for friends in Atlanta, where he lives and works.

Doris Taft's Pecan Cake

"We call this a cake," Dub Taft says, "but it's more like a dessert bread, minus icing. The secret is that Mother uses lots of pecans, and on occasion adds chopped walnuts, which makes it even more delicious."

People who enjoy the recipe after cooking the cake the first time (and who won't?) are advised that there would be no problem should they wish to add more nuts to the mix in subsequent bakes.

- 2 ¾ cups self-rising flour
- 2 to 3 cups chopped pecans
- 1 ½ cups sugar
- 1 ⅓ sticks butter, melted
- 3 eggs
- 1 teaspoon vanilla
- Whole milk or buttermilk (enough for batter consistency)

Preheat the oven to 350°F.

Mix all ingredients together and add enough milk to make the mix the constitution of a cake batter. Pour into a large, greased iron skillet. Bake at 350°F for approximately 45 minutes or until done (when toothpick comes out clear).

Japanese Fruitcake

Every Christmas, our entire family looked forward to my mother's big, nutty Japanese fruitcake creation, a scene doubtless repeated in households across the South.

And while this is not a strictly Lowcountry dessert that's in vogue these days, I'm offering it anyway because of its "Southernness." The cake carries an exotic name. At one time, it was called Oriental Cake, according to the late Bill Neal. But as he and others have pointed out, there's nothing oriental about the cake's ancestry or makeup, and in fact it isn't really a fruitcake, except for raisins and the finely grated zest of oranges and lemons.

The Asiatic name had been something of a mystery over the years, but cooking historian and author Damon Lee Fowler of Savannah discovered that "Japanese Cake," similar to present-day recipes, appeared in the 1895 *Tested Recipe Cook Book* published by the Cotton States & International Exposition held in Atlanta, something of a world's fair of its time.

Dutch Fork Japanese Fruitcake

This particular recipe is adapted from one published by the Juanita C. Kibler. She called Japanese fruitcake probably her favorite dessert. First recorded in the Dutch Fork community in 1890, it has been commonly used since.

Some cookbooks, such as the late Grace Hartley's *Southern Cookbook*, uses buttermilk rather than sweet milk plus a half teaspoon of salt. Grace's recipe also calls for one cup of chopped nutmeats in addition to the pecans. The tester of this recipe added a half cup dried cranberries to Mrs. Kibler's old recipe.

- 4 eggs
- 2 cups sugar
- 1 cup butter, softened
- 3 cups all-purpose flour
- 3 teaspoons baking powder
- 1 cup coarsely chopped pecans
- 1 cup whole milk
- 1 cup raisins
- ½ cup dried cranberries
- 1 teaspoon cinnamon
- 1 teaspoon cloves
- 1 teaspoon allspice

Preheat the oven to 350°F.

Beat the eggs with a whisk. Add the sugar and continue beating. Add the butter. Sift together flour, baking powder, and pecans, and add to batter with milk, alternatively.

Using 9-inch pans, bake two-thirds of the batter in three layers. In the remaining batter, add raisins, cranberries, and spices. Bake in two layers. Bake layers 25 to 30 minutes, or until tops are brown and a toothpick inserted in the center of each layer comes out clean.

Put together alternately, beginning with the white layer. In between each layer, spread filling (recipe follows).

Filling

- 1 fresh coconut, grated fine
- 2 cups sugar
- 1 cup boiling water
- 1 tablespoon cornstarch
- Grated rind and juice of 2 lemons

Boil all ingredients until the mixture begins to thicken. Spread between layers while warm, and stick layers with fork tines or toothpicks to increase the absorption of the filling.

Note: Breaking open a coconut can be difficult, as the tester of this recipe, Cathy Sadler, discovered. Friends from Latin America tell us they use a machete to break open the big nuts, and I recall that my father used a hammer, after draining the milk with an ice pick. For those who don't wish to go to those extremes, pre-shredded coconut is available at most groceries. However, you will lose a bit of taste with pre-shredded nuts.

The Fruitcakes of Claxton, Georgia

If you drive down Main Street in Claxton, Georgia, between Labor Day and mid-December, you'll smell hundreds of fruitcakes baking in huge ovens. The legendary Claxton Bakery, Inc. will be busy turning out thousands of cakes for the Thanksgiving and Christmas season trade. And so will the nearby Georgia Fruit Cake Company.

The story of the Claxton Fruit Cake dynasty began in 1902, when Savino Tos, a seventeen-year-old immigrant from Italy landed in New York City with $40 in his pocket.

The Claxton Fruit Cake Company was started in 1910 in Claxton, Georgia, by Italian immigrant Savino Tos and was later sold to the Parker family. Today it bakes more than six million cakes annually, mostly during the Christmas season. (Photos courtesy Claxton Fruit Cake Company.)

Master baker Ira S. Womble Sr., who began his bakery career in 1917, founded the Georgia Fruit Cake Company in Claxton, Georgia. (Photo courtesy of Georgia Fruit Cake Co.)

After a few years as a dishwasher, Tos opened a small bake shop in Brooklyn but became frustrated with the crowded city life and moved south to Macon, Georgia, where he took a job with an ice cream manufacturer.

Later Savino and his wife, a Savannah native, visited Claxton, where Tos opened a bakery. The Italian's culinary wizardry, ranging from fresh bread to fruitcakes, quickly caught on.

In particular, his fruitcakes—a generous blend of fruits and nuts, flavored with citrus peels—became a runaway bestseller during the Thanksgiving and Christmas holiday seasons. According to the family, 72 percent of the cakes contain "choice fruits and nuts including raisins, walnuts, and almonds from California, pecans from Georgia, cherries from Oregon and Michigan, pineapple from Mexico, and candied lemon and orange peel mix from Florida.

Tos advertised his holiday cake with this tantalizing slogan:

Hold a thin slice to the light and it will resemble a stained-glass church window.

In 1945 Tos sold the bakery to his understudy, Albert Parker, who had worked with the founder since age eleven, sweeping floors, preparing dough, and making ice cream. Parker decided to specialize in fruitcakes. His big break came in 1952, when a visitor from Tampa suggested that his Civitan Club in Florida possibly could sell the cakes as a community project fundraiser. Today the Civitans sell more than one and a half million pounds of the cakes each year nationwide. Other civic clubs followed suit. In addition, the cakes are sold in supermarket chains nationwide and by mail order.

In 1948, on Claxton's nearby Duval Street, the Georgia Fruit Cake Company was started by

MISTER BULWINKLE'S CHRISTMAS CAKE

Back when I was a kid, everybody in Charleston society had to have one of the old-timey Christmas cakes from Mister Bulwinkle's Bakery. And if you didn't get your reservation in by November, you wouldn't be able to get one in time.

The cake consisted of three layers of sponge cake, and in between the layers were jam and jelly and then mounds of homemade whipped cream and topped with cherries. The layers were about an inch thick and the cake measured about ten inches in diameter.

Oh my, those cakes were soooo delicious.

—JENELLE BEACH GROOMS, JAMES ISLAND, CHARLESTON, SOUTH CAROLINA

Ira Womble Sr., who also got his start as a Savino Tos intern. Interestingly, Womble's baked goods caught the attention of Henry Ford, who, for a couple of years, had Womble bake his birthday cakes. The firm also uses fresh Georgia pecans, California walnuts, and cherries imported from France, and its major markets are military bases. They also sell cakes retail and on the internet.

Charlestonian Jenelle Grooms recalls "Mr. Bulwinkle's Christmas Cake" that she enjoyed as a young girl. (Photo by the author.)

Puddings

Beaufort Bread Pudding

The following recipe is adapted from a stunning cookbook published by the Beaufort Academy Parents Association, *Full Moon, High Tide: Tastes and Traditions of the Low Country*. Martha Durham Hoke, a Berry College alumnae and a great friend who lives in Beaufort, passed the cookbook on to me.

Betty Ward's Bread Pudding with Bourbon Sauce

- 4 cups whole milk
- 2 cups bread cubes, crusts removed
- 1 tablespoon butter
- 1 cup sugar
- 2 egg yolks
- 1 egg
- 1 teaspoon vanilla
- ⅛ teaspoon salt

Preheat the oven to 350°F.

Heat the milk in a saucepan; add the bread cubes and butter, then set aside. Combine the sugar, yolks, and egg; add the vanilla and salt, mixing well.

Combine milk mixture and sugar mixture. Pour into prepared 6 x 9 x 2-inch baking dish. Place dish in pan of hot water and bake for 45 minutes or until set. Use the 2 remaining egg whites to make meringue. Spread on bread pudding and brown in a 350°F oven until the batter becomes thick.

BOURBON SAUCE FOR THE PUDDING
- ½ cup butter
- 1 5-ounce can evaporated milk
- 1 cup confectioners' sugar
- 1 egg yolk, beaten
- 3 teaspoons bourbon

Combine the butter, milk, sugar, and egg yolk in double boiler and cook until thickened, stirring frequently.

Remove from the heat and stir in the bourbon. Serve over the warm bread pudding.

Banana Pudding

No Southern cookbook would be complete without a recipe for banana pudding, the region's ultimate comfort food dessert. This is particularly the case in the coastal areas of Georgia and South Carolina, as banana pudding is an excellent follow-up to various seafoods, Lowcountry boils, or barbecue.

Several notable food historians have described banana pudding as a corruption of the classic English trifle. If it is, it's a delectable corruption.

Soperton Banana Pudding

This recipe is adapted from Grace Hartley's *Southern Cookbook*, which touted "Over 40 Years of Recipes from *The Atlanta Journal*," and whose slogan read, "Covers Dixie Like the Dew." Grace was the food editor when I worked on *The Journal* in the 1960s, which had a strong circulation across South Georgia at the time. The recipe tester, my friend Mollie Curlee of Dunwoody, Georgia, received rave reviews for this pudding, and among those adding amens was myself, since she let me sample a slice. Truly scrumptious! The recipe is credited to Mrs. L. L. Phillips of Soperton, Georgia, north of Savannah, and will serve six.

- 1 cup sugar, plus 2 tablespoons
- ½ cup all-purpose flour
- 2 cups boiling water
- 2 eggs, separated
- 1 tablespoon butter
- 1 teaspoon vanilla
- Dash salt
- 1 box vanilla wafers
- 6 bananas, sliced

Preheat the oven to 325°F.

For the sauce, mix 1 cup sugar and flour well. Slowly add the boiling water, stirring constantly. Cook over low heat until the mixture begins to thicken. Stir in the beaten egg yolks. Continue to cook until thick. Add the butter, vanilla, and salt. Let cool.

In a quart-size casserole, place a layer of vanilla wafers. Cover with a layer of bananas, then a layer of sauce. Beat the egg whites until stiff. Add the remaining 2 tablespoons sugar. Spread over the pudding and bake a few minutes until golden brown, keeping an eye on the topping.

Doris's Old South Banana Pudding

Here is another banana pudding recipe from our friend Doris Taft, which calls for the use of milk instead of water. Doris says if you don't have a double boiler, you can cook this pudding in a saucepan on low heat, stirring more often and watching that you don't scorch it.

"This makes a pretty layered dish," Doris says, "but if I'm in a hurry, I don't bother with the layers—I just mix it all together. It's good that way, too!"

- 2 tablespoons all-purpose flour
- 1 cup sugar (more or less depending on taste)
- 1 teaspoon vanilla
- 3 eggs

- 4 cups whole milk
- 5 bananas
- 1 box of vanilla wafers

Mix the flour and sugar. Blend in the vanilla and eggs, then mix in the milk. Pour into a double boiler and cook over medium heat. Stir occasionally. When the batter thickens and forms a custard, set aside. In a pretty dish, put a layer of wafers on the bottom, pour in a layer of pudding, and a layer of bananas. Repeat until you use all the pudding and bananas. Top with wafers. Refrigerate.

Note: Starch can be substituted for flour. If you have difficulty keeping the whites from clumping when using whole eggs, just use the yolks in the custard. The whites can be whipped with a little sugar to form a topping on which you can place wafers.

Trifle, Syllabub, and Ambrosia

Trifle

And now, here is the famed trifle, a sinfully delightful dish that has been a Lowcountry favorite for centuries.

Savannah native Sally Bond Tonsmeire recalls how her mother, Sarah Pierpont Bond, prepared her famous trifle at her Savannah home when her friends would come over to play canasta or bridge.

"Mother would get ladyfingers and she would put seedless raspberry jelly and sherry on each ladyfinger," Mrs. Tonsmeire remembered. "Then she would stand them up in her beautiful crystal dessert bowl. She would put chopped pecans in the bottom, then would pour in the wonderful custard, topped with whipped cream. All of her friends would want seconds."

Sarah Bond's Savannah Trifle

- 3 egg yolks
- ½ cup sugar
- 2 cups scalded milk

- 6 to 8 ladyfingers
- 1 tablespoon raspberry jelly
- ⅛ teaspoon salt
- 1 teaspoon vanilla extract
- 1 tablespoon sherry
- ½ cup finely chopped pecans
- Whipped cream

Beat the eggs slightly with the sugar, and gradually add the hot milk. Add the salt and vanilla extract. Cook in a double boiler until the custard coats a silver spoon. Strain.

Slice the ladyfingers lengthwise, spread with raspberry jelly, and put a little sherry on each finger.

Place in individual dishes and sprinkle chopped pecans in the bottom of each dish. Pour in custard and top with whipped cream.

Aunt Sophie's Irish Potato Candy

I would stay with my granddaddy after my grandmother died and his sister, Aunt Sophie, stayed there with him. She was a sweet little round woman with red hair. Everybody loved Aunt Sophie and she loved us grandchildren. We'd go over to visit and Aunt Sophie would treat us by making some "Irish Potato Candy."

She'd take one Irish potato and she'd boil it. Then she'd put it into a bowl, skin it and mash it up, and then sprinkle powdered sugar on it. At this point she would roll it out like a jelly roll. Then she'd take peanut butter and she'd spread peanut butter on the potato roll. Then she'd cut it up into sections like a jelly roll, sprinkling a bit more powdered sugar on it.

We children just loved it. It entertained us and kept us out of her hair for a while.

—Mary Nichols
Reidsville, Georgia

Syllabub

Syllabub—a rich, wine-infused cream—was a very popular holiday delight from early colonial days, being a traditional English dessert. Actually, it goes back to Sillery, in France's Champagne district, where a "Sille" wine was used along with fresh milk to make the cream.

An old recipe from the eighteenth century noted that one should "Sweeten a quart of cyder with refined sugar and a grating of nutmeg, then milk your cow into your liquor until you have the amount you consider proper, then top it off with about a half a pint of the sweetest, thickest cream."

In South Carolina's Dutch Fork area, there were three Christmas drinks—syllabub, egg nog, and hot rum mull. But syllabub was always a favorite. Lowcountry hosts served the drink up through the mid-twentieth century.

Juanita Kibler's Syllabub

This is Mrs. Kibler's modern-day recipe as published in her 1989 *Dutch Fork Cookery*, offering several options as to alcoholic infusions.

- 1 cup whipping cream
- 3 tablespoons sugar
- 1 teaspoon lemon juice
- 2 to 4 (or more) tablespoons sherry, brandy, or sweet wine
- 2 egg whites, stiffly beaten

In a large bowl, blend cream and sugar (at low speed if you're using a mixer). Add lemon juice, alcohol, and egg whites (last). Continue mixing at low speed for 2 or 3 more minutes. Serve promptly.

Ambrosia

The late Betty Talmadge, wife of Georgia Governor and later U.S. Senator Herman Talmadge, loved to serve ambrosia—"the food of the gods"—at dinner parties she hosted at her Lovejoy, Georgia, plantation home. Set in the rolling hills south of Atlanta, some say Margaret Mitchell used it as her model when writing *Gone with the Wind*.

Here is my adaptation of Mrs. Talmadge's dish that appeared in her cookbook, *How to Cook a Pig and other Back-to-the-Farm Recipes*. This recipe, which will yield a gallon, should be prepared twenty-four hours in advance. It's often served as a traditional Christmas dessert, and some cooks like to add sliced bananas and heavy cream to the mix.

Betty Talmadge's Ambrosia

- 3 to 4 dozen oranges
- 1 ½ pounds grated coconut, fresh or frozen
- 2 cups sugar

Peel the oranges, removing rind and all white membrane. Separate the sections and remove seeds.

Place the orange sections and juice in a large bowl. Add the coconut and sugar; mix thoroughly. Cover tightly and refrigerate until time to serve.

CHAPTER 21

The Lowcountry Interior: Its Food and Folklore

How gently flow thy peaceful floods, O Altamaha. How sublimely rise to view, on thy elevated shores, yon Magnolian groves, from whose tops the surrounding expanse is perfumed by clouds of incense…

—*William Bartram, 1776*

No greater offense can be given in the rural South than to refuse a meal.
—*Marjorie Kinnan Rawlings (1942)*

The Gullah-Geechee Land," the late Ben Green Cooper wrote, "extended all the way from the South Carolina Lowcountry to Brunswick, Georgia, and included the rice and cotton plantations far up into the mighty Altamaha, Savannah, and Ogeechee River valleys."

Cooper, who lived on Jones Street in the city's historic district in his early years and later at the Collinsville suburb, became a "two-finger typing whiz" of a police reporter with the Savannah newspapers in the 1930s. Cooper went on to become an editor and food columnist with other Southern papers.

In his elegant, privately printed cookbook, *Savannah's Cookin'*, Ben asserted that "Gullahs [African Americans] are found over the Carolina Low Country, and they are called Geechees from the Savannah River southward through the Bryan and Liberty [County] Necks in Georgia, having been given this name from the Great Ogeechee River."

When wealthy latecomers to the South Carolina Lowcountry went looking for plantation lands in the eighteenth century, they eyed the new colony Georgia, which had opened up for slavery in 1750, after a seventeen-year prohibition insisted by founder James Oglethorpe. The planters soon began buying up plantation sites hugging the great rivers such as the aforementioned Ogeechee, Savannah, and Altamaha. They also acquired big spreads on the Barrier Islands south of Savannah such as Sapelo, St. Simons, and Butler Island, all of which were ideal for long-staple Sea Island cotton, rice, and sugarcane.

For instance, wealthy Charleston merchant and planter Henry Laurens, who later would serve as president of the U.S. Congress during the American Revolution, owned at least eight plantations in South Carolina and Georgia Lowcountry. His Georgia holdings included a 1763 grant from King George III near the Altamaha River, which later became the admired New Hope Plantation.

In addition to attracting wealthy planters, the interior regions of South Georgia also witnessed waves of Scotch-Irish yeomen, mostly descendants of Lowland Scots, whose ancestors had been planted in Northern Ireland's Ulster province by King James in the 1600s. A century later, those Lowland Scots came by the shiploads to the U.S. port of Philadelphia. From there, thousands of their descendants swarmed south into the Carolinas and Georgia traveling the Great Philadelphia Wagon Road, which ended in Augusta.

In addition to farming, newcomers found rivers overflowing with fish. This was the case up into the twentieth century. *Atlanta Journal* writer William Neal told about how the river "harbors sturgeons weighing 330 pounds or more and carrying up to eighty

The Eye of God: *This painting by an Englishman hung for many years behind the rostrum of the Providence Baptist Church in Toombs County, Georgia. See the sidebar on page 319. (Photo courtesy of Mary Nichols.)*

pounds of excellent caviar." Shrimpers told him that the Savannah delta's streams and tributaries were "jumping with tarpon from June through August." It's no wonder that from the colonial era, Lowcountry interior families developed their own unique cuisine featuring traditional Southern cooking topped with fresh, local seafood.

The Rev. James E. Rich, eighty-six, a native of the Cobbtown area north of Savannah, recalls his family's feasts during the 1930s, despite the Great Depression that wouldn't end until the beginning of World War II.

"During those years there in Tattnall County," he told me, "we fished the Ohoopee River for catfish and bream, we raised our own pork and beef, eggs, milk, and syrup, and Dad took the corn to the mill to grind for cornmeal and grits. We ate three typical meals every day. There was breakfast:

THE SHIPWRECKED ENGLISH ARTIST WHO PAINTED THE EYE OF GOD

This happened before 1850, I understand. This sea-faring Englishman survived a shipwreck on the Altamaha River, and he spent weeks making his way upriver through the river swamps. He told people that he managed to survive on berries, roots, and rats.

When he reached our community in Toombs County, Georgia, the members of Providence Baptist Church took him in, fed him, and housed him. Later on, he became a preacher. He was an artist, also, and some years after his arrival, he created a large painting of a giant eye. It was his way of thanking the church members for their kindness.

Folks said it represented the "Eye of God." It said:

Thou Eyee Sees Me At All Times In All Places

Church members hung it right behind the pulpit. I remember as a little girl looking up at that painting every Sunday at the worship service. It seemed to be looking straight at me no matter where I sat. I don't know whether it was the preacher's sermons that saved our souls, or that eye looking down at us.

Some years ago, they moved our church to a new location, but still near the Altamaha River. At that time, the deacons relocated the painting. It now hangs in the church foyer, where young children don't have to fear its ominous presence during the worship service.

—MARY NICHOLS
REIDSVILLE, GEORGIA

grits, gravy, fried eggs, hot biscuits, meat, syrup, and coffee. We would also drink milk—plain or chocolate. But no cereal or flapjacks [pancakes]."

At the noontime dinner, they relished Lowcountry favorites—rice, corn bread, and vegetables grown on their farm, such as peas, squash, potatoes, tomatoes, and onions.

"I remember Mother made corn pone bread with a crust," he recalled. "Dad would remove the crust and eat the inside for dinner. Then for supper he would put the crust in

Mary Nichols (left) and her mother, Jessie Conner, of Reidsville, Georgia. (Photo by the author.)

the pot likker, the juice left over when Mother cooked leafy vegetables such as turnips or mustard with meat. Oh yes, Dad's crust from the corn pone and pot likker was delicious—mostly for Dad, though."

Supper, the evening meal, consisted primarily of dinner leftovers.

"Mother always cooked in abundance," Rev. Rich recalled. "It was always a big pot of whatever she was cooking. With a total of thirteen to cook for, big pots were more economical. Occasionally, his mother would bake bread, but generally the noontime leftovers were "warmed up for supper and put on the table along with fresh sliced tomatoes in season and raw onions. Iced tea was our favorite drink for the noon and evening meals."

Rich recalled some usual dishes. "Have you ever eaten sweet potatoes fried with a little sugar sprinkled on them?" he asked. "What about candied yams? What about cooking tomatoes with some milk and egg in them? What about skimmed cream on grits for breakfast, and salmon or grits and stewed tomatoes?" He and his siblings ate them all "and the list is a lot longer." Talk about food improvisation!

Rev. Rich told me that he still loves the same old foods and table manners, "and I practiced them in my home when rearing my children. They are still with me and I can't forget them. Really, I don't want to."

When I was growing up, Daddy always told us back then we'd be better off to eat a light supper, a big breakfast, and a big [midday] dinner. Many a night we'd have only bread and sweet potatoes like or milk for supper. That's all.

—*Frank Pressley*
Lakeland, Georgia

Frank Pressley. (Photo by the author.)

Great Country Cooking in the Georgia Interior

Sweet Potato Memories

Sweet potatoes are a Lowcountry cornerstone. My friend Mike McDougald, a native of Bulloch County, Georgia, northwest of Savannah, ate them all the time.

"I had a school buddy named Roscoe Hill and we often ended up in the late afternoon in his mother's big kitchen where a huge old wood-burning stove dominated the room," he said. "Roscoe's father almost always would have a batch of sweet potatoes in the oven that he'd rubbed with bacon grease before several hours of baking. These were for Mrs. Hill's noontime 'dinner' for their field hands.

"When we dropped in, Roscoe would pull out one for each of us. Maybe a bit cold, but they sure tasted good to little hungry mouths late in the afternoon."

Jessie Hart Conner, eighty-eight years old, of nearby Reidsville, Georgia, told me of her love for sweet potato pies, casseroles, and the like. "When I was growing up," she said, "we had plenty of sweet potatoes to eat all through the winter months because we'd bury them after we harvested them in the summertime.

"When we plowed them up, we first collected the little ones that we'd use for the following year's planting. Then we'd dig a big hole to store the fully grown sweet potatoes brought up from the field. We'd put in a layer of pine straw and a layer of sweet potatoes, layer of straw and a layer of potatoes until we built up a good-sized mound that we'd top with a lot of dirt, plus a piece of tin to keep out the water and a heavy rock to keep the tin from blowing off."

She hated having to go out to the sweet potato bank on a cold winter day to dig out a mess of sweet potatoes for the family. "All that dirt and straw," she said. "Finally you'd find enough sweet potatoes for supper. We had plenty of 'em to eat right on until summertime when the new crop came in."

Another example of superb Lowcountry interior country cooking can be found in Atkinson County, Georgia, in the kitchen presided over by eighty-five-year old Doris Leavens Taft. Here follows a loving tribute written by her son, Wilbur F. "Dub" Taft, a longtime friend and a great cook in his own right.

My mother has been cooking old-time country dishes since 1931, the year her mother died. Then eight years old, she cooked her first meal one fall morning when her older sister Eliza Jane accidentally sewed a nettle into her thumb while working on a new frock.

Mother recalled that, "Sister was in too much pain to cook dinner that day so she told me what to do; I put the field peas on top of the heated wood stove, peeled and boiled the Irish potatoes, and then prepared the corn bread dough."

Back then, self-rising meal was not available, which required the addition of baking soda to the mix, creating a very sharp taste. So Mother began adding flour to the mix, which not only took care of the soda problem but also gave the corn bread a thicker and lighter texture plus an enhanced flavor.

The flavor of Mother's fresh peas also improved as she learned to leave out water, forcing the peas to steam in their own juices. And she stewed potatoes so buttery that my brothers loved to slurp up the leftover liquid.

To this day, no one makes better corn bread, field peas, and stewed new potatoes. Not to mention chicken and dumplings, neck bone and rice, turkey dressing, mustard greens, lima beans, fresh creamed corn, fried okra, butter beans, biscuits, blackberry cobbler, pecan pie, and dozens of other Southern dishes perfected during her eighty years in the kitchen.

My parents still live in the same South Georgia farmhouse where they spent their wedding night on April 27, 1941. "We raised chickens, cattle, and hogs," Mother said, "so we always had plenty of meat and lard. We had a good milk cow that gave lots of milk, cream, and butter. We ground our own cornmeal and made our own syrup. So when I went to town,

I only had to buy flour, grits, crackers, spices, sugar, and the fruits and vegetables we couldn't grow ourselves."

In the days before electricity, Mother would prepare for the winter months by drying, pickling, or canning fruits and vegetables. In particular her canned stewed tomatoes served as a wonderful base for sauces, soups, and stews, helping to liven up spirits on

Doris Taft checks out catfish that were caught the day before by her husband, Wilburn. (Photo courtesy of Dub Taft.)

cold, bleak days. A jar of her tomatoes heated with bacon drippings and poured over a plate of white rice, grits, or a couple of hot biscuits would sate one's appetite in a hurry.

Mother still cooks what I call "big food"—lots of choices and large quantities. "You never know who might drop by," she says. Oftentimes she'll call up friends and invite them over. "I've got fresh field peas, okra, lima beans, deer steak, and gravy," she'll say, "plus mashed potatoes, turnips, hoe cake, and banana pudding. Come on and help us eat it."

My parents have been known to invite complete strangers should they happen to be near the house at dinner time. "We were just fixin' to eat," they'll say. "Come in and join us."

The Germans in South Carolina

Germans arrived in big numbers in South Carolina's Lowcountry interior in the eighteenth century, starting in the 1730s and continuing for more than two decades, coming from Southern Germany's Lower Rhine Valley. The South Carolina colony recruited hundreds of German families to settle in what had become Britain's Royal Colony—sometimes even paying their ocean passage.

The former Rhinelanders and their descendants were described by Lake High of Columbia, South Carolina, as "a hardworking, sturdy, and resourceful people" who were given to family farms in contrast to the large slave plantations favored by South Carolina's English and West Indies planters.

The Germans went first to Dorchester County near the Edisto River. Others were given land grants up the Santee, Congaree, Broad, and Saluda Rivers as they arrived in successive waves into the 1750s. Still others settled along the Cooper River in Berkeley County.

The newcomers and their descendants clung for centuries to their German breads, meat and onion pies, sausages, krauts, scrapples, and "liver kniep" dumplings.

One of their specialties, according to the late food historian Juanita C. Kibler, was baked bread, "owing largely to their great brick and stone outdoor bake-ovens" shaped like turtles.

Today, though German descendants bake breads in "less effective modern ovens," they still love to serve the old-fashioned home-baked staple, "mixed breads," rather than the usual Southern corn bread. The old basic recipes called for the use of cooked grits, although some old-timers substitute scalded cornmeal. The traditionalists would save a cup of grits from a breakfast serving for making mixed breads. The following recipe makes one loaf.

Dutch Fork Mixed Bread

- 1 package dry yeast
- 1 cup lukewarm water
- 1 teaspoon shortening
- 1 teaspoon salt
- 1 cup cooked grits, cooled
- 2 cups flour

Dissolve the yeast in lukewarm water. Add the shortening, salt, grits, and enough flour to make a stiff dough. Let rise in a warm place until double in size. Then place in a greased loaf pan or, more authentic, on a greased baking sheet. Brush with butter and let rise. Bake in a preheated oven at 400°F for 50 minutes. Brush lightly with butter.

Serve warm. The finished result should resemble a wasp nest—full of holes!

A Fish Stew Celebration, Black and White

Dr. Dan T. Carter, prize-winning University of South Carolina history professor emeritus and a friend of the author, tells here of an experience growing up in South Carolina's Lowcountry Interior:

The universe in which I lived as a child and a teenager was of course the world of the segregated South. I use the term segregated *with some sense of the irony of the word. It was certainly an oppressive culture in which blacks were relegated to the bottom rung of every economic ladder and barred by law from the schools of my childhood, and by custom from the ballot box of my community. But it was hardly segregated. Some of my earliest playmates were black and beginning the summer I was nine, I worked long days side by side with black men and women in the tobacco fields of Florence County.*

At the end of summer's long 1953 tobacco harvest season, one of the farm owners for whom I had worked arranged a "last cropping" dinner. With the tobacco securely hung in the barns, all of us—black and white—went over to the pump and freshened up and then returned to the shed beside the barn. The meal was fish stew, a spicy mixture of freshwater bream and redbreast cooked in a tomato sauce and poured over rice—all washed down with sweet iced tea and a loaf of soft, sliced bread.

I can still smell the wood fires under the black pots of stew and the pungent sweetness of the tobacco barns, saturated from generations of curing tobacco. As I sat with the other children, teenagers, and womenfolk and finished off the evening with a plate of fresh hand-churned ice cream, I watched several of the men as they drifted away out under the trees and began passing mason jars of corn whiskey, laughing nervously like little boys away from the censoring eyes of womenfolk and respectability.

I saw nothing incongruous about the mixing of black and white or the absurdity of those nuanced cultural conventions which decreed that, since the sky was over-

Dr. Dan Carter. (Photo courtesy of Dr. Carter.)

head, it was permissible to eat side by side in a way that would have triggered a riot in one of the handful of restaurants in nearby Florence. And when I saw the two mason jars of corn whiskey passed around—one for blacks and one for whites—I saw without understanding.

Now as I look back nearly sixty years, I think of that evening around the open wood fire and I like to believe that the human interaction that always surrounds the sharing of a meal softened the worst aspects of a system that divided white and black Southerners from the rich history we have shared together.

Candied Sweet Potatoes and Fresh Peach Ice Cream

Gwen Hodges, ninety-five, offers here what she calls "a few vivid memories" from her childhood in Elloree, South Carolina in the Lowcountry interior. She and her husband Carl (see next vignette) have resided in Atlanta for many decades.

Carl and Gwen Hodges. (Photo by the author.)

First, candied sweet potatoes. They may have been boiled slightly before they were sliced crosswise and doused into a sauce made with water, ridiculous amounts of sugar, lots of butter, a bit of salt, and maybe a little vanilla extract, into a thick syrup. They were then cooked all day on our wood stove, all day in a casserole made to be served once a day at our house.

And there was a white squash, which I don't see these days: It was shaped like a bell or like a jelly fish. This was sliced crosswise and seasoned with salt and pepper, dredged lightly in flour, and fried in a small amount of oil. Oh, so good!

So was the macaroni that my mother made with lots of sharp cheese, fresh eggs, milk, salt, and pepper.

Then there was fresh peach ice cream. This began with fresh egg custard. It was slowly churned until it began to harden. Then the mashed fresh ripe peaches were added and the cream hardened and the churn was packed down with ice and rock salt until supper...

Now we've messed up all those great dishes with some knowledge of nutrition!

At His Mother's Table

Gwen Hodges' husband, ninety-five-year-old Dr. Carl Hodges, a native of Guyton, Georgia, and a veteran Georgia educator, describes a Sunday mealtime at home:

My most vivid food memory of growing up in the early 1900s was the "Sunday dinner" that my mother served right after we returned home from church. The table was covered with fried chicken, rice and gravy, butter beans, beets and perhaps another vegetable, biscuits and butter, iced tea, and finally, my favorite dessert, peach shortcake.

No food I have eaten in the more than eighty years since has compared with my memory. Contributing factors, I'm sure, were these:

The meal was prepared on our wood-burning stove by my mother and eaten along with Mother, Father, my sister, and two brothers. Also contributing perhaps: All the food except rice, tea, and flour had been grown on our farm and I, a boy of fourteen, had helped to plant, tend, and gather most all of it! I even slaughtered the chickens, a gruesome task, but in doing what no other family member wanted to do, I felt I was making a major contribution.

All of these factors doubtless contributed to one of life's most pleasant memories, but there was another factor, perhaps the most significant of all—the food tasted so good!

Fourth of July Ogeechee River Fish Fry Reunion

I interviewed ninety-six-year-old Eleanor Beasley Akins at her home in Statesboro, Georgia, in the spring of 2008, about her grandfather's July Fourth Fish Fry near the Ogeechee River, still carried out every year.

My grandfather, Enoch Beasley, had a wonderful old farm on the Ogeechee River and every Fourth of July he would have all his children and his grandchildren to come home to his fish fry reunion.

Two sons and several sons-in-law would fish for two days ahead of time to have plenty of fish, fresh out of the river. And we fried 'em and had corn dodgers [hush puppies] to go with them and we drank lemonade. Grandpa always said we had to have lemonade.

Eleanor Beasley Akins. (Photo by the author.)

Some of the men that morning would go to Rocky Ford and get a block of ice and buy the lemons and sugar, and come back and squeeze the lemons. It was a job rolling those lemons to make 'em soft so you could squeeze that juice out. It took a lot longer than today but the lemonade tasted a lot better. I think it was because we rolled 'em by hand.

The boys would mix the lemonade in one of Grandpa's empty beer barrels and would serve it from there.

Grandpa kept several barrels of beer at his place year-round—beer that he had fermented himself of corn and syrup. I remember that he always kept a tin cup on his barrel of beer, and if anybody wanted a drink, Grandpa would pour them a can full and let 'em drink all they wanted and then he'd have some.

After Grandpa died, we stopped having the reunions for a while, but we cranked it up again in 1968. By then, people were too busy to take time to fish beforehand so we started buying the fish. So yet today, the Enoch Beasley descendants return to the riverside home place for the July Fourth weekend fish fry. And we always have lemonade to drink, and people bring in covered dishes, including desserts. But we tell 'em to bring no meat 'cause "we're gonna have fish." In the earlier days, we did our frying in three fry pans over a fire. Now some of the boys bring in these cookers, and they just pour the oil in the pan and sit there and turn the fish. They still taste mighty good.

~

THE START OF CHRISTMAS: THE FALLING OF THE PECANS

Christmas began when pecans started falling. The early November rains loosened the nuts from their outer shells and sent them plopping like machine gun bullets on the roof of the veranda. In the night you'd listen and you'd know it would soon be here…

—LILLIAN SMITH
MEMORY OF A LARGE CHRISTMAS

Grandpa Beasley also had a bunch of beehives at his farm, and he invited all his young'uns to come with their kids to watch him carry out the "robbery" of his first beehive. We kids loved it because he gave us, the little fellers, the first honey that he harvested.

We strung honey from our mouths to our elbows and played in the woods there amongst the scrub oaks and wiregrass, and had ourselves a good old time. We'd get so dirty...

What happened to the other hives of honey? That went to the older members of the family for their families. Grandpa split it up amongst them all according to their need.

Grandpa was quite a character. I can remember that when his toenails got long, he would sit down on the front door steps to trim 'em. We young'uns thought that was a sight. We'd set around him and watch him and when he trimmed his big toenail, he would cut a "v" in it.

"Grandpa, what's that for?" we asked him, and he said, "That keeps it from growing together." Back then we didn't know what an ingrown toenail was!

The Altamaha Raft Run

The last of the Altamaha River timber raft runs occurred in the 1930s. Railroad tracks had been built not far away and large trucks were coming into use. By then, Darien, at the mouth of the river, had lost its place as a port, replaced by nearby Savannah. In the following interview I had with Dr. Del Presley, retired professor at Georgia Southern University, he describes the reenactment of an Altamaha raft run similar to those that disappeared nearly a century ago.

It was one of the great moments of my life when I was able to organize the Great Altamaha River Timber Rafting Expedition, a commemorative event. Hundreds of volunteers helped us pull it off.

Professor Del Presley. (Photo by the author.)

We re-created everything just like the pioneer runs, building up a sixty-ton timber raft that we rode a hundred and forty miles down to the port of Darien. There, in the old days, the timber would be transferred to seagoing vessels for shipments around the world. The construction timbers for the Brooklyn Bridge, for instance, came off the Altamaha River, having been cut from Georgia forests upstream…huge longleaf yellow pines, oaks, and cypress.

We assembled the raft out of big timbers—longleaf pines and cypress. Old-time river man Bill Dean, ninety-two, served as our pilot, and we put in at Murdoch McRae's Landing on the Ocmulgee River. Our raft measured eighty-five feet long, thirty feet wide, and sported enormous sweeps. Dean would call out "bow white" (left) and "bow Injun" (right) since the Creek Indian frontier was to the west in the 1800s. Our team re-created everything, right down to the foods that the old-time raft hands ate! We filled a "cook stove" firebox with sand where we brewed coffee, fried fish, eggs, and bacon, using a three-legged spider and a Dutch oven.

We also ate resin-baked potatoes, a South Georgia favorite. Old hand Carlos Crosby dropped the Irish potatoes into the kettle's hot cauldron of turpentine. A half hour later, the resin-coated spuds would float to the surface, ready for the eating. Mouthwatering! We also ate typical raft hand food… catfish stew, grits, eggs, hush puppies, and sawmill gravy, plus coffee to drink.

Captain Bill Dean (left) and his crew prepare to take their river raft down the Altamaha River to Darien, Georgia, in a commemorative run. (Photo courtesy of Prof. Del Presley.)

At night, as we came in to tie up, and as our raft nudged up against the bank, the fish would literally leap up on top of our raft, providing us fresh fish for supper! Catfish, bass, and mullet. It's true, I saw it with my own eyes. Of course, mullet have the run of the Altamaha year-round, anyway.

All told, more than twenty thousand people came to celebrate the history, music, food, and culture of the bygone age of timber rafting at our stops at Lumber City, Baxley, Jesup, and

Darien. The famed Sea Island (Gullah) Singers from St. Simons provided entertainment, along with others. We ended up at Darien just in time for the "blessing of the fleet" and remained there for several days, recalling "the great days of Darien's [seaport] majesty." The folks there treated us royally.

In the old days, the raft hands would walk back home. My great-grandfather, Jesse A. Braswell, a river raft man and farmer, did just that. In the 1890s, after such a run, it took him four days to walk from Darien the hundred and forty miles back home to Turkey Creek in Laurens County.

I didn't realize just how important the river was in the lives of local people until I started visiting the communities along the route, talking about the project. I guess the greatest came when elderly people would come up and earnestly say to me, "Now I'm really proud to be called a River Rat."

Before I die, I hope to write a book about the whole experience.

Pinder Boilins and Syrup Makin' in an Earlier Era

The aforementioned Michael McDougald of Rome, Georgia, here recalls growing up in Bulloch County, in Southeast Georgia:

Nobody seemed to be rich in Bulloch County before and after World War II, nobody put on any "airs," and everybody seemed comfortable with their station in life. You didn't know who was rich and who wasn't. As most folks were into farming, it made sense to have a party along with such seasonal events as "grinding cane and making cane syrup," "bringing in the peanut crop," and having a "pinder boilin' party." It was fun visiting country homes on such occasions, sitting on the expansive porches that surrounded most farm homes.

We had fun looking on at cane grindings with a mule pulling the grinder around in a circle, and checking out the cooking of the syrup in a huge metal vat built into a fire-oven. The "cook" would patiently sweep the "scum" off the top and dismiss it, leaving the warm, sweet cane juice-soon-to-be-syrup bubbling quietly over the hot fire. Always, guests got

to take home a couple of bottles of warm syrup just produced, and patiently wait for breakfast when it could be poured over morning pancakes.

A great country summer dinner that evening capped off the full day and it began with fried chicken and country ham, sweet potato casseroles with browned and toasted marshmallows, silver-queen corn on the cob gobbed with homemade butter, potato salad with lots of pickles embedded, and big old cathead biscuits and a chance to douse them with some of that home-made syrup.

Michael McDougald. (Photo courtesy of Mr. McDougald.)

We always went home with a huge brown bag full of freshly boiled peanuts, plus of course, a jar of that sweet syrup.

Life was good in Bulloch County back then.

Swamp Hollering

Just as darkness settled in, I returned to camp. Then I heard more of that strange music which always startles me—swamp hollering. I was unversed in the unwritten rules of the matter, and I assumed my friends at the upper end of the island were having fun. Expecting to meet them on the way home, I started out toward them. Soon all of us were together again around our campfire.

Gator Joe asked me somewhat impatiently if I had heard them holler, and if so, why I hadn't answered. "When you hear anybody hollerin', you holler back," he said with undisguised sternness. Clearly he was concerned about my getting lost or being harmed.

And so Joe taught me Rule 1 about the art of hollering. Even if I had been aware of what was required, I was then—and am yet—totally incapable of producing a sound at all akin to the marvelous swamp hollering [I heard].

Of course I could have made some loud noise, but it would have been a virtual desecration in an atmosphere that had been reverberating with the exquisite music made by two masters, Gator Joe Saunders and Bryant Lee.

—Francis Harper, 1912

For the Love of Bananas

When I was growing up, I could never get enough banana pudding or banana sandwiches or bananas period.

But I got my fill of bananas at one homecoming "dinner on the ground." Four of the church sisters prepared banana puddings and I got to sample a big helping from each. It left me with a painful bellyache and big banana-breath belches for the rest of the afternoon. That cured me for a week or two.

The same thing happened one holiday season when my father brought home a whole stalk of bananas. As we kids clamored around him, he held the stalk high so we could see what it might look like hanging from the tree. It was one of the most amazing sights to children during those days before television. We all thought Christmas had come early.

All through the holidays that year, it was a thrill for us to pick bananas "off the tree" as they ripened on the stalk.

—Dub Taft

Cleaning the Mullet in Adel

When I was a teenager, I got a job with Wilbur Dickson's Grocery store in my hometown of Adel, Georgia. Mullet was the popular fish around there in those days, and my job was scaling and cleaning the fish.

Independent fishermen from the "armpit of Florida," the Gulf Coast near Crystal River and Panacea, would deliver the fish to us in their pickups. They came in large wooden crates with the fish covered in ice. We would sell the mullet whole, undressed.

Walter Weeks. (Photo by the author.)

Mister Dickson had a little shed on the alley in back of the store which had a kitchen sink. That's where I would do the fish cleaning for customers who had just bought the mullet. Several customers would buy our fish because I was careful to scrape the skin and remove the membrane.

We loved to eat mullet and grits at our home. Mother would usually cook the fish in a deep fat fryer. But first the fish pieces were "mealed" in a paper sack partly filled cornmeal, salt, and pepper. We would shake the bag thoroughly. From there they went into the boiling fat.

Afterward, we would deep fry the hush puppies in the same fat. Mother had a great recipe for hush puppies, making them with cornmeal with onions and spices. They were sooo goood! I'll never forget.

—Walter Weeks, Dunwoody, Georgia,
a native of Cook County, Georgia

Swamp Gravy

This recipe comes from Tarver Inn of Colquitt, Georgia, which promotes Georgia's official Folklife Play, "Swamp Gravy," put on at certain times of the year at Colquitt's Cotton Hall Theater.

Fry some fish golden brown. Pour off the grease but leave some of the drippings. Use the drippings to brown the following:

- 4 to 5 potatoes, finely diced
- 2 to 3 onions, finely diced
- 1 bell pepper, any color, chopped (optional)

When mixture is tender, add a large can of tomatoes, salt, and pepper to taste and 1 teaspoon of Louisiana Hot Sauce.

Pick some of the meat of one or two of the cooked fish and add to the mixture. Simmer for as long as you can resist the wonderful aroma.

CHAPTER 22

Lord, Bless This Food

And you shall eat in plenty, and be satisfied, and praise the name of the Lord your God.

—Joel 2:26

Lowcountry Blessings

At the 11:00 a.m. first seating in the famed Wilkes Dining Room in Savannah, Georgia, Ryon Thompson, the young general manager, or his mother, Mrs. Marcia Thompson, the hostess, asks everyone, cooks and customers all, to pause a moment for the invocation of God's blessing on the food.

It continues a custom begun by the late Sema Wilkes, Ryon's great-grandmother, when she started the boardinghouse dining room in 1943.

The grace handed down by Mrs. Wilkes—continued today—is simple but straight from her strong Christian upbringing in Toombs County, Georgia, north of Savannah:

> **Good Lord, bless this food to us, and us to thy service, Amen...Enjoy your meal, folks!**

Afterward, the "boardinghouse reaches" soon are seen passing chicken and casseroles at the ten-seat round tables, groaning under God's bounty as skillfully prepared by the black cooks: steaming bowls of okra gumbo, scalloped eggplant, corn pudding, numerous casseroles such as squash, sweet potatoes, and Savannah red rice. The list goes on, including platters of three meats, plus peach cobblers and southern sweet tea to wash down the feast fit for a king.

A similar adherence to the role of a before-the-meal "blessing" was emphasized by the late Mrs. Juanita Kibler, of Dutch Fork, South Carolina.

Mrs. Kibler's *Dutch Fork Cookery* contains informative food lore and folklore minutia relating to the close-knit German communities clustered around Dutch Fork. Her son, University of Georgia professor James C. Kibler, who did the artwork for the book, wrote me that he felt sure his mother would have been happy to share the contents of her book for publication here. (Take note of Mrs. Kibler's recipes in the desserts chapter, in particular.)

As to table graces, Mrs. Kibler noted that the traditional Dutch Forker would never fail to invoke God's blessing on a meal. "It is a necessary part of the eating ritual," she wrote, "and sets its tone of reverence, thoughtfulness, and thankfulness."

Besides its obvious purpose, Kibler said a spoken blessing often helps calm children, encourages good behavior and manners, and "slows things down for the proper enjoyment and appreciation of the food itself."

Tattnall County, Georgia, native Rev. James E. Rich recalled how the members of his large family growing up—including himself and ten siblings, six of whom were in school at the same time—ate meals together on a long table with their parents, and kept their hands off the food until properly blessed by their father, "regardless of what the hurry might be."

While mealtime rituals have been practiced among Lowcountry families over the centuries, family meals are becoming less frequent, except for perhaps Christmas and Thanksgiving. In today's whirl and rush, many parents regret that work and school hours discourage group meals during the workweek, to say nothing of the missed opportunity to witness an expression of thankfulness for the Almighty's generous provisioning.

Here follows a sample of table blessings I have collected—including a number of hand-me-downs from ancestors—with thanks to all who contributed their favorites. And thanks go also to the Georgia State Market Bulletin, which ran my appeal for table graces from its readers. Unfortunately, the editors of the equivalent South Carolina bulletin failed to respond to my request for similar space in their publication.

Thank the Lord for supper.

—*Radio talk show host Ludlow Porch,*
quoting "Mr. Jackson," the father of his best school buddy

This first blessing, author unknown, was offered by my friend Bill Balmer, who says it can be sung before a meal to the tune of Edelweiss:

Thank you Lord, Thank you Lord,
For our being together,
For this time, for this place,
For your love all around us.
Fill us Lord, Bless this food,
Bless your church forever.

Typical of many contributions was this one from Amarien Corpening of Ridgeland, South Carolina, as spoken by her father, the late Frank Mackey Corpening:

Accept our thanks, Heav'nly Father, for these and all thy many blessings. Forgive our sins. Save Us. We ask in Christ's name. Amen.

Lynne Hummell of Hilton Head Island, South Carolina, grew up in a staunch Southern Baptist household in Columbia, South Carolina. As kids, Lynne and her two siblings were expected to say their own blessings, "and we weren't able to cop out with the standard, 'God is great, God is good'…" She said her father, Angus Jack Cope, led by example and today, at age ninety, "never wavers from his script." It goes like this:

Lord, make us truly thankful for these gifts we are about to receive and nourish them to our bodies so that we might better serve you. In Jesus' name, we pray. Amen.

Lynne's mother, a native of Cheraw, South Carolina, who grew up on Columbia's Calhoun Street (behind the governor's mansion), has her own blessing variation:

Heavenly Father, we thank you for this food and pray you would nourish it to our bodies and us to your service. In Jesus name, we thank ya'… Amen

I am indebted to African-American sisters Norma Jean and Carole Darden for the following mealtime invocation spoken by "Papa Darden," included in their cookbook, *Spoonbread & Strawberry Wine.*

Heavenly Father, from the abundance of your streams, field, and earth, You have seen fit to bless our table, and we are grateful.

We pray for your constant guidance in all things, and let us never forget to give thanks for the way You have blessed the hands of the cook. Amen.

David Lauderdale, a columnist with the *Hilton Head Island Packet*, sent me the grace spoken before meals by his favorite grandfather, Horace Attaway Burke, who lived with his grandmother, Eugenia Swan Burke, on a farm in Jefferson County, Georgia.

After their retirement from their respective jobs in Atlanta, the Burkes returned to the family farm and worked hard growing cotton, soybeans, and corn, "and raising a herd of Black Angus, with a couple of milk cows names Babe and Beauty." David recalled the story of how his grandparents, on a Christmas Eve in earlier years, after putting their ten children to bed, would sit down and enjoy a bucket of fresh oysters, obtained in a horse and buggy trip to the nearest rail line. David remembers his grandparents heading out to church on a Sunday morning, Mrs. Burke holding some gladiolas for the church sanctuary and his grandfather holding his worn bible and Sunday School quarterly.

Here's Grandpa Burke's table blessing:

Lord, make us thankful for these nourishments we are about to receive. Amen.

God bless the cook and the man who chopped the wood.

—*Anonymous*

This more expansive contribution came to me from Lynita (Stubby) Tate, a former member of the U.S. Army Signal Corps:

Hello, Lord. Thank you for allowing us to come together to eat a wonderful meal, made from loving hands and hearts of the people here today.

Lord, you know some in our family can't boil water and don't know the difference between grilled and burned, but their help has not gone unnoticed. They've run to the store for that "vital missing ingredient" and have kept the little ones out of the kitchen.

Today, we'd like to give you the praise and let you know it's our honor to be called your children. And for me, it's an honor to be a part of this family. Thank you, Amen.

This has been Deborah R. Winkles' favorite blessing for forty-five years:

God bless the sick, the poor, and the hungry. Help the sick to get well, the poor to be happy, and the hungry to be fulfilled.

Elizabeth Jarvis of Moultrie, Georgia, did her student teaching in an elementary school in Vidalia, Georgia's sweet onion capital. "This was back when prayer in schools was acceptable," she said. "My mentor teacher had taught her students the following prayer, which they said daily before lunch."

For the bounties of the earth, and the joys of heaven, We thank thee, our Father. Amen.

One of the most concise invocations was delivered by my friend, the Rev. Denny Spear, former chaplain at Atlanta's Hartsville-Jackson International Airport and former pastor of Dunwoody, Georgia, Baptist Church.

Much obliged, Lord!

Here's a delightful "Table Grace for Old Friends," with thanks to the staff of the *Christ Church Frederica Cookbook* on lovely St. Simons Island, Georgia:

We thank you, Lord, for bringing our friends to our table tonight. We haven't been together for such a long time and there's so much to catch up on. We'll be talking way past midnight.
But, Lord, before we dig into each other's lives, give us Your blessing through this beautiful meal before us. Let us be aware of Your presence here among us and let us feel Your hand in ours as we offer You our prayers and thanksgiving. Amen.

He gave us rain from heaven, and fruitful seasons, filling our hearts with food and gladness.

—*Acts 14:17*

While this is not a blessing per se, it is part of a "Mother's Recipe" and was passed on to me by good friend Diane (Mrs. Ted) Kennedy, formerly of Savannah, but currently residing in Dunwoody, Georgia.

My mom's the finest cook on earth,
And she told me long ago,
That bread's no good unless you add
Some lovin' in the dough.

Diane also mailed me this blessing, which came from the *Dining with Grace Cookbook* of our near neighbor, Dunwoody United Methodist Church:

O Heavenly Father,
We thank thee for food, and remember the hungry,
We thank thee for health, and remember the sick,
We thank thee for friends, and remember the friendless,
We thank thee for freedom, and remember the enslaved,
May these remembrances stir us to service,
That thy gifts to us may be used for others, Amen.

Ben Moise emailed me his invocation for an outdoor meal:

Lord, we thank you for this most amazing day ... for this true-blue dream of sky...
for the leaping greenly spirits of trees...and for everything which is natural, which is
infinite, which is, YES.
We ask your blessings upon this event, for the people assembled here and the bounty
of our table. Amen.

Ben also passed on this grace spoken by his grandfather, South Carolinian James Edmund McCutchen, a staunch Presbyterian:

Lord, make us thankful for the refreshments which we are about to be served, please
pardon our sins. In Christ's name we ask it, Amen.

Every man should eat and drink, and enjoy the good of all his labor; it is the gift
of God.

—Ecclesiastes 3:13

International Blessings

Here are some blessings from around the world. Probably the most famous is one repeated in Christian communities worldwide that came from the pen of famed Scot poet Robert Burns:

Some hae meat, and canna eat,
And some wad eat that want it;
But we hae meat, an we can eat,
And say the Lord be thankit.

This blessing is from Ireland:

Oh thou that blest the loaves and fishes,
Look down up these two poor dishes,
And tho' the murphies are but small,
O make them large enough for all,
For if they do our bellies fill,
I'm sure it is a miracle.

An old Scotch table grace:

Thank you, Lord, for the world so sweet,
Thank you for the food we eat,
Thank you for the birds that sing,
Thank you, God, for everything.

Methodism founder John Wesley's famous blessing:

Be present at our table, Lord,
Be here and everywhere adored,
Thy creatures bless, and grant that we may
Feast in paradise with Thee.

And this last contribution came from Jill Momper, who clipped this from the *Atlanta Journal-Constitution* in the late 1990s. She has kept it pasted on her computer and refers to it often. While it is not a table invocation, it provides a beautiful conclusion to this chapter.

According to Ms. Momper, Jean Shaw's husband, Harry, had died of cancer and Mrs. Shaw found comfort in prayer. During the funeral, at Druid Hills Baptist Church, the pastor recited the following, which he called "an obscure prayer."

Oh Lord,
Support us all the day long
Until the shadows lengthen
And the evening comes
And the busy world is hushed
And the fever of life is over
And our work is done.
Then in thy mercy
Grant us a safe lodging
And a holy rest
And peace at the last.

Bibliography

Anderson, Jean. *A Love Affair with Southern Cooking.* New York: Morrow, 2007.

Bagwell, James E. *Rice Gold: James Hamilton and the Plantation Life on the Georgia Coast.* Macon, Georgia: Mercer University Press, 2000.

Bailey, Cornelia Walker & Christina Bledsoe. *God, Dr. Buzzard and the Bolinto Man.* New York, Random House, 2000.

Bass, Robert D. *Swamp Fox: The Life and Campaigns of General Francis Marion.* New York: Henry Holt, 1949.

Belk, Sarah. *Around the Southern Table.* New York: Simon & Schuster, 1991.

Berendt, John. *Midnight in the Garden of Good and Evil.* New York: Random House, 1994.

Bessonette, Colin. *Back Roads & City Streets.* Atlanta: Peachtree Publishers, 1984.

Boyd, Kathy. *NeNa's Garden: Recipes from the Heart.* Hartsville, South Carolina: Faith Publishing.

Brown, Marion. *Marion Brown's Southern Cook Book.* Chapel Hill: University of North Carolina Press, 1968, 1970.

Burn, Billie. *Stirring the Pots on Daufuskie.* Privately published, 1985.

Burrison, John A. *Roots of Region: Southern Folk Culture.* Jackson: University Press of Mississippi, 2007.

Carney, Judith A. *Black Rice: The African Origins of Rice Cultivation in the Americas.* Cambridge: Harvard University Press, 2001.

Carter, Jimmy. *An Hour Before Daylight.* New York: Simon and Schuster, 2001.

Cashin, Edward J. *A Wilderness Still the Cradle of Nature.* Savannah: Beehive Press, 1994.

Chandler, Genevieve W. *Coming Through: Voices of a South Carolina Gullah Community from WPA Oral Histories.* Columbia: University of South Carolina Press, 2008.

Claiborne, Craig. *A Feast Made for Laughter,* New York: Doubleday, 1982.

———. *Craig Claiborne's Favorites from the New York Times.* New York: Times Books, 1975.

———. *Craig Claiborne's Southern Cooking.* New York: Wings Books, 1987.

Colquitt, Harriett Ross. *The Savannah Cook Book.* Charleston: Walker, Evans & Cogswell, 1933, 1960.

Colwin, Laurie. More Home Cooking. New York: HarperCollins, 1993.

Conroy, Pat. *The Pat Conroy Cookbook.* New York: Nan Talese/Doubleday, 2004.

Cooper, Ben Green. *Savannah's Cookin'.* Mableton, Georgia: Privately printed, 1967.

Cotton, Ann Coopehaven and Gaillard, Henrietta Freeman. *Charleston Entertains.* Greensboro, North Carolina: Legacy Publications.

Cushman, Gettings and Ora Lou O'Hara. *Treasured Southern Family Recipes.* New York: Hastings House, 1966.

DeBolt, Margaret Wayt. *Georgia Entertains.* Nashville: Rutledge Hill Press, 1983.

DeVorsey, Louis, and Marion J. Rice. *The Plantation South.* New Brunswick, NJ Rutgers University Press, 1992.

Doren, Mark Van, *Travels of William Bartram.* New York: Dover, 1928.

Dull, Mrs. S. R. *Southern Cooking.* Marietta, Georgia: Cherokee Publishing, 1987.

Dupree, Nathalie. *Nathalie Dupree's Shrimp & Grits Cookbook.* Charleston: Wyrick & Company, 2006.

———. *Southern Memories.* New York: Clarkson Potter, 1993.

Edgar, Walter. *South Carolina: A History.* Columbia, University of South Carolina Press, 1978.

Egerton, John. *Corn Bread Nation I.* Chapel Hill: UNC Press. 2007.

———. *Side Orders: Small Helpings of Southern Cookery & Culture.* Atlanta: Peachtree Publishers, 1990.

———. *Southern Food.* New York: Knopf, 1987.

Fancher, Betsy. *The Lost Legacy of Georgia's Golden Isles.* New York: Doubleday, 1971.

Federal Writers' Project. *Georgia Guide (WPA).* Athens: The University of Georgia Press, 1996.

Federal Writers' Project. *North Carolina: A Guide to the Old North State, 1939.* Chapel Hill: University of North Carolina Press, 1939.

Federal Writers Project. *South Carolina: The WPA Guide to the Palmetto State. 1941.* Columbia: University of South Carolina Press, 1988.

Fitch, James A. *Pass the Pilau, Please.* Georgetown, SC: Custom Printing, 2001.

Fowler, Damon Lee. *Classical Southern Cooking.* New York: Crown Publishers, 1995.

———. *Savannah Cook Book.* Charleston: Gibbs Smith, 2008.

Fracaros, Dana and Michael Pauls. *Old South.* London: Cadogan Books, 1986.

Fraser, Walter J. Jr. *Charleston! Charleston!* Columbia: University of South Carolina Press, 1985.

———. *Savannah in the Old South.* Athens: University of Georgia Press, 2003.

Garrison, Webb. *A Treasury of Georgia Tales.* Nashville: Rutledge Hill Press, 1987.

Grovesnor, Vertamae. *Vertamae Cooks in The Americas' Family Kitchen.* San Francisco: KQED Books, 1996.

———. *Vibration Cooking or The Travel Notes of a Geechee Girl.* New York: Doubleday, 1970.

Guess, William Francis. *South Carolina: Annals of Pride and Protest.* New York: Harper, 1957, 1960.

Harrigan, Elizabeth Ravenel. *Charleston Recollections and Receipts.* Columbia: University of South Carolina Press, 1983.

Harris, Jessica B. *Beyond Gumbo.* New York, Simon & Schuster, 2003.

Hartley, Grace. *Grace Hartley's Southern Cookbook.* New York: Galahad Books, 1980.

Hess, Karen, *The Carolina Rice Kitchen: The African Connection.* Columbia: University of South Carolina Press, 1992.

Holmgren, Virginia C. *Hilton Head: A Sea Island Chronicle.* Hilton Head Island Publishing Company, 1959.

Isle of Hope Methodist Women. *Day of the Island Cookbook,* 1975.

———. *Moss, Marshes & Memorable Meals.* 2006.

Joyner, Charles. *Down by the Riverside: A South Carolina Slave Community.* Chicago: University of Illinois Press, 1984.

Junior League of Charleston. *Charleston Receipts.* Charleston, South Carolina: 1950.

Kahn, E. J. Jr. *From Rabun Gap to Tybee Light.* Marietta, Georgia: Cherokee, 1978.

Kibler, Juanita C. *Dutch Fork Cookery.* Athens, Georgia: Dutch Fork Press, 1989.

Kuralt, Charles. *Charles Kuralt's America.* New York: Putnam, 1995.

———. *Charles Kuralt's American Moments.* New York: Simon & Schuster, 1998.

Leigh, Jack. *The Ogeechee: A River and its People.* Athens: University of Georgia Press, 1986.

Leighton, Clare. *Southern Harvest.* Athens, Georgia: University of Georgia Press, 1997.

Lewis, Edna and Scott Peacock. *The Gift of Southern Cooking.* New York. Knopf, 2003.

———. *In Pursuit of Flavor.* New York: Knopf, 1988.

———. *The Taste of Country Cooking.* New York: Knopf, 1997.

Lustig, Lillie S. *The Southern Cook Book.* Reading, Pennsylvania: Culinary Arts Press, 1939.

Marshall, Lillian Bertram. *Cooking Across the South.* Birmingham: Oxmore House, Inc. 1980.

McFeely, William S. *Sapelo's People.* New York: Norton, 1994.

Miller, Joni. *True Grits.* New York: Workman, 1990.

Mitchell, Patricia B. *French Cooking in Early America.* Self-published, 1991.

———. *Girth of the Nation.* Self-published, 1994.

Neal, Bill. *Good Old Grits Cookbook.* New York: Workman, 1991.

Nesbit, Martha Giddens. *Savannah Entertains.* Charleston: Wyrick & Co., 1996.

Osteen, Louis. *Louis Osteen's Charleston Cuisine: Recipes from a Lowcountry Chef.* Chapel Hill: Algonquin Books, 1999.

Osteen, Marlene. *Great Chefs of the South.* Nashville: Cumberland House, 1997.

Overton, Ray. *New American Cooking: The South.* San Francisco: Williams-Sonoma, 2000.

Peterkin, Genevieve. *Coming Through: Voices of a South Carolina Gullah community from WPA Oral Histories.* Columbia: University of South Carolina Press, 2008.

———. *Heaven Is a Beautiful Place: A Memoir of the South Carolina Coast.* Columbia: University of South Carolina Press, 2000.

Peterkin, Julia. *A Plantation Christmas.* Boston: Houghton Mifflin, 1934.

———. *Roll, Jordan Road.* New York: Robert O. Ballou, 1933.

———. *Scarlet Sister Mary.* New York: Grossett & Dunlap, 1928.

Pinson, Maxine & Malyssa Pinson. *Lowcountry Delights: Cookbook and Travel Guide.* Savannah: SSD, Inc., 2004.

Prevost, Charlotte K. and Effie L. Wilder. *Pawley's Island, A living Legend.* Columbia: The State Printing Co., 1972.

Randall, Joseph, and Toni Tipon-Martin. *A Taste of Heritage: The New African American Cuisine.* New York: Wiley, 2002.

Rawlings, Marjorie K. *Cross Creek.* New York: Scribner, 1933, 1960.

———. *Cross Creek Cookery.* New York: Simon & Schuster, 1970.

Reed, John Shelton and Dale Volberg. *1001 Things Everyone Should Know About The South.* New York: Doubleday, 1996.

———. *Holy Smoke: The Big Book of North Carolina Barbecue.* Chapel Hill: University of North Carolina Press, 2007.

Rhett, Blanche S. and Lettie Gay. *Two Hundred Years of Charleston Cooking.* Columbia: University of South Carolina Press, 1976, 1990.

Robinson, Sallie Ann. *Gullah Home Cooking the Daufuskie Way.* Chapel Hill: University of North Carolina Press, 2003.

Rogers, George C. Jr. *Charleston in the Age of the Pinckneys*. Columbia: University of South Carolina Press, 1969.

Rosen, Robert N. *A Short History of Charleston*. San Francisco: Lexikos, 1982.

Russell, Preston and Barbara Hines. *Savannah: A History of Her People Since 1733*. Savannah: Frederic C. Bell, 1992.

Rutledge, Archibald. *Home by the River*. Lexington, SC: The Sandlapper Store Inc., 1974, 1976.

———. *The Woods and Wild Things I Remember*. Columbia: R. L. Bryan, 1970.

Rutledge, Sarah. *The Carolina Housewife* (facsimile of 1847 edition). Columbia: University of South Carolina Press, 1979.

Savannah Unit, Georgia Writers Project, WPA. *Drums and Shadows*. Athens: University of Georgia Press, 1940.

Schulz, Phillip Stephen. *Celebrating America: A Cookbook*. New York: Simon & Schuster, 1994.

Schulze, Richard. *Carolina Gold Rice*. Charleston: History Press, 2005.

Sibley, Celestine. *For All Seasons*. Atlanta: Peachtree Publishers, 1984.

———. *Small Blessings*. New York: Doubleday, 1977.

Smith, Andrew F. *Peanuts: The Illustrious History of the Goober Pea*. Chicago: University of Illinois Press, 2002.

Smith, Lillian. *Memory of a Large Christmas*. New York: W.W. Norton, 1962.

Spalding, Phinizy. *Oglethorpe in America*. Chicago: University of Chicago Press, 1977.

Stann, Kap. *Georgia*. Emeryville, California: Moon Handbooks, 2005.

Stoney, Samuel Gaillard. *Charleston: Azaleas and Old Bricks*. Boston: Houghton Mifflin, 1937.

———. *Plantations of the Carolina Low Country*. New York: Dover, 1938 and Charleston: The Carolina Art Association, 1938, 1939, 1964.

Sullivan, Buddy. *Early Days on the Georgia Tidewater*. Darien, Georgia: McIntosh County Commission, 1991.

Taylor, Joe Gray. *Eating, Drinking, and Visiting in the South*. Baton Rouge: LSU Press, 2008.

Taylor, John Martin. *The Fearless Frying Cookbook*. New York: Workman, 1997.

———. *Hoppin' Johns Charleston, Beaufort & Savannah*. New York: Clarkson Potter, 1997.

———. *Hoppin' Johns Lowcountry Cooking*. Boston: Houghton Mifflin, 2000.

Thompson, Fred. *Crazy for Crab*. Boston: The Harvard Common Press, 2004.

Thompson, Terry. *A Taste of the South*. Los Angeles: HP Books, 1988.

Todd, Helen. *Tomochichi.* Atlanta: Cherokee Publishing, 1977.

Villas, James. *The Glory of Southern Cooking.* New York: Wiley, 2007.

———. *My Mother's Southern Kitchen.* New York: Macmillan, 1994.

———. *Stews, Bogs and Burgoos.* New York: Morrow, 1997.

Walter, Eugene. *Hints & Pinches.* Atlanta: Longstreet Press, 1991. *American Cooking, Southern Style.* New York: Time Life Books, 1971.

Wittich, Rich aned Betty Darby. *Insider's Guide to Savannah and Hilton Head.* Guilford, Connecticut: Globe Pequot Press, 2008.

Woods, Marvin. *The New Lowcountry Cooking.* New York: Morrow, 2000.

Permissions

———◆◆◆———

We have made every effort to trace the ownership of all copyrighted material and to secure permission from copyright holders. In the event any question arises as to the use of any material, we will be pleased to make the necessary corrections in future printings.

The author gratefully acknowledges permissions to quote from the following works:.

Back Roads and City Streets, by Colin Bessonette. Reprinted by permission of Colin Bessonette.

Beyond Gumbo, Creole Fusion Food from the Atlantic Rim, by Jessica Harris. Recipe comments reprinted by permission of Ms. Harris.

Carolina Gold Rice: The Ebb and Flow History of a Lowcountry Cash Crop, by Richard Schulze. Reprinted by permission of Dr. Schulze.

Carolina Rice Kitchen: The Africa Connection, by Karen Hess. Reprinted by permission of the University of South Carolina Press.

Charleston Receipts. Reprinted by permission of the Junior League of Charleston, South Carolina.

A Colonial Plantation Cookbook, by Harriott Pinckney Horry, and edited by Richard Hooker. Reprinted by permission of the University of South Carolina Press, Columbia, South Carolina.

Collected Poems of Paul Laurence Dunbar. Reprinted by permission of the University Press of Virginia.

Cooking Across the South, by Lillian Bertram Marshall. Reprinted by permission of Oxmoor House.

Dictionary of Charlestonese by Frank Gilbreth. Reprinted by permission of *The Charleston Post & Courier*.

Day on the Island Cookbook. Recipe adaptations reprinted by permission of the Women of the Isle of Hope Methodist Women, Savannah, Georgia.

Down by the Riverside, by Charles Joyner. Reprinted by permission of the University of Illinois Press.

Dutch Fork Cookery by Juanita C. Kibler. Reprinted by permission of Professor James E. Kibler Jr.

Famous Recipes from Mrs. Wilkes' Boarding House in Historic Savannah. Recipe adaptations reprinted by permission of Mrs. Marcia Thompson, Mrs. Wilkes' granddaughter.

French Cooking in Early America by Patricia B. Mitchell, reprinted by permission of Mrs. Mitchell.

Full Moon, High Tide: Tastes and Traditions of the Lowcountry. A recipe adaptation reprinted by permission of the Beaufort, SC, Academy Cookbook Committee.

The Glory of Southern Cooking, by James Villas, recipe comments reprinted by permission of Mr. Villas.

Good Cooks Rise . . . with the May River Tide. Recipes reprinted by permission of the Episcopal Women of The Church of the Cross, Bluffton, South Carolina.

Georgia Entertains by Margaret Wayt DeBolt. Reprinted by permission of Mrs. DeBolt.

Gullah Home Cooking the Daufuskie Way, by Sallie Ann Robinson. Reprinted by permission of the University of North Carolina Press.

Heaven Is a Beautiful Place by Genevieve Chandler Peterkin. Reprinted by permission of the University of South Carolina Press.

The Historical Cookbook of the American Negro. Reprinted by permission of the National Council of Negro Women.

Home by the River, by Archibald Rutledge. Reprinted by permission of Sandlapper Publishing, Orangeburg, South Carolina.

The Lee Bros. Southern Cookbook, by Matt Lee and Ted Lee. Recipe adaptations reprinted by permission of the authors.

Louis Osteen's Charleston Cuisine, by Louis Osteen. Recipes reprinted by permission of Louis Osteen.

My Mother's Southern Kitchen, by James Villas, recipe comments reprinted by permission of Mr. Villas.

Nathalie Dupree's Southern Memories, by Nathalie Dupree. Recipe adaptation reprinted by permission of Nathalie Dupree.

The *New Encyclopedia of Southern Cooking (Volume 7 Foodways)*, edited by John T. Edge, with permission of the University of North Carolina Press.

The New Low-Country Cooking, by Marvin Woods. Recipe adaptation reprinted by permission of Mr. Woods.

The New South Carolina Cookbook, reprinted by permission of the University of South Carolina Press.

The New Southern Basics, by Martha Phelps Stamps. Reprinted by permission of Ron Pitkin, Cumberland House Publishing.

Pass the Pilau, Please!, by James A. Fitch. Reprinted by permission of Mr. Fitch.

Savannah Seasons, by Elizabeth Terry. Recipe adaptation reprinted by permission of the author.

Savannah Entertains, by Martha Giddens Nesbit. Recipe reprinted by permission of Mrs. Nesbit.

A Short History of Charleston, by Robert Rosen. Reprinted by permission of Mr. Rosen.

South Carolina: A History, by Walter Edgar, reprinted by permission of the University of South Carolina Press.

Treasured Southern Family Recipes, by Geddings de M. Cushman and Ora Lou O'Hara Cushman. Recipe adaptation reprinted by permission of Hastings House.

Two Hundred Years of Charleston Cooking, By Blanche S. Rhett and Lettie Gay. Reprinted by permission of the University of South Carolina Press.

Vertamae Cooks in the Americas' Family Kitchen, by Vertamae Grosvenor. Recipe adaptation reprinted by permission of Ms. Grosvenor.

Vibration Cooking or the Travel Notes of a Geechee Girl, by Vertamae Grosvenor. Reprinted by permission of Ms. Grosvenor.

The Woods and Wild Things I Remember, by Archibald Rutledge. Reprinted by permission of Don Rutledge.

Index

About the Author

Joseph E. Dabney is a retired newspaperman and public relations executive who has studied the Carolina and Georgia Lowcountry, Appalachian, and hill-country food traditions for many years.

His first cultural cookbook, *Smokehouse Ham, Spoon Bread & Scuppernong Wine*, won the James Beard Cookbook of the Year award in 1999, and was a selection of the Book of the Month Club's Good Cooks Division. After fifteen printings, a special tenth anniversary edition is now available.

Dabney is also the author of the highly acclaimed *Mountain Spirits*, which *Time* Magazine described as "a splendid and sometimes hilarious history" of the Southern Appalachian moonshine culture.

Dabney has appeared on NBC's *Today Show*, was elected a "Knight of Mark Twain" by the *Mark Twain Journal*, and was awarded the 2005 Jack Daniel's Lifetime Achievement Award by the Southern Foodways Alliance at the University of Mississippi in Oxford.

A native of South Carolina, Dabney has five grown children and currently lives in Atlanta, Georgia, with his wife Susanne.